A LIST OF EMIGRANTS FROM

ENGLAND TO AMERICA

1718-1759

A LIST OF EMIGRANTS FROM ENGLAND TO AMERICA 1718 - 1759

Transcribed from microfilms of the original records
at the Guildhall, London.

By

JACK and MARION KAMINKOW
by Courtesy of the Corporation of London

A NEW EDITION

containing 46 recently discovered records

GENEALOGICAL PUBLISHING CO., INC.

CONTENTS

	Page
Introduction	ix
Illustration of Form A	xvi
Wording of Form A	xvii
Illustration of Form B	xviii
Wording of Form B	xix
List of Agents with Key to Abbreviations	xxv
Abbreviations Used	xxv
Additions and Corrections	xxvii
The List	1
Appendix. Analysis of the Emigrants' Destinations in the American Colonies	257
Index of Places	259
Additional records	289

INTRODUCTION

A NOTE ON THE HISTORY OF INDENTURED SERVITUDE

Soon after the settling of Jamestown, there was a tremendous demand for labour, skilled and unskilled, in the American colonies. Many ordinary individuals, who for numerous varying reasons wished to emigrate to the colonies, were quite unable to pay for their passage, and so a scheme gradually evolved whereby the emigrant could receive a free passage to the colonies provided that he were willing to be sold into bondage for a few years upon arrival. The agent received an acreage of land for each servant he brought into the colony and the servant, at the end of his time, received a reward in the shape of land, tools, etc.

Like all schemes dealing with humanity, this one suffered many abuses and many of the indentured servants, as they were called, suffered from great hardships. Unscrupulous dealers occasionally kidnapped persons and sold them abroad, while conditions of servitude in the colonies often left much to be desired. It is the opinion of various scholars, however, that without some such scheme, the 17th and 18th century settlement of the American colonies could not have taken place. It has been estimated that one half to two thirds of all white immigrants were indentured servants, redemptioners (a similar scheme) or convicts.

When the prospective servant offered his services, he was issued an indenture, which he carried away with him as proof of his terms, and was supposed to register himself as soon as he arrived in the colony. A copy of the indenture was supposed to be kept in the office where he registered in England but it seems that in the majority of cases this was not done. Very few copies of the hundreds of thousands of indentures issued were kept, and those which are extant are in several different forms. In Bristol an entry book was used. Middlesex kept an actual copy of the agreement. London used a special printed form whereon the details of the indenture were copied. Certain details were copied into a register book also.

GENERAL NOTE ON THE RECORDS

The details transcribed in this volume are taken from the records at the Guildhall in London labelled AGREEMENTS TO SERVE IN

AMERICA. They have been arranged in chronological order by the archivists and carefully numbered. From their location in the Guildhall and the fact that most of them were witnessed by the mayor of London or an Alderman of the City, it is presumed that they were issued at the Guildhall, possibly under a special arrangement of the City of London, for they are mostly copied by the same hand and in the same style and signed by successive mayors, while all the participants are young and unmarried. Why they exist for this period only is not known; perhaps they were kept only during the lifetime of a certain official. From a study of other records at the Guildhall it is clear that the present series are survivals and certainly do not represent the origin of the system.

The printed forms are of two kinds, one intended for persons over 21 and the other intended for persons under 21. In the spaces were written in by hand the date of issue, name of servant, parish and county of origin, agent, destination, but not the name of the ship on which the servant was to sail. The forms were signed or marked by the servant and also by the mayor or alderman, usually on the same date on which the indenture was issued but occasionally several days later. Specimens of the forms are shown at the end of the introduction.

In 1733 Latin was suddenly discarded. "Memorandum" and "Jurat coram me" were crossed out and "be it remembered" and "sworn befor me" written in by hand. Later the forms were printed that way.

Occasionally an indenture was copied twice, probably through an error, but on several occasions the same person crops up again, days, months, or even years later. One can only conjecture the circumstances which delayed his departure the first time.

The old-fashioned handwriting is often difficult to read. The spelling of personal names varies considerably even on the same form, and towns are frequently spelled phonetically. Occasionally there are outright lapses of memory on the part of the scribe, when he has written such things as "vintner" for destination, when he presumably meant Virginia. One wonders how many undetectable lapses occured and whether these lapses are also responsible for some of the untraceable places which the servants are said to have come from.

The register book which accompanies the Agreements to Serve does not tally completely with the separate forms. Many of the forms were not entered in the register and there are a number of entries for which there is no form.

INTRODUCTION

The following notes are arranged under the headings of the various components of each Agreement.

NUMBERING

Each year has been placed in order by the archivist and numbered, starting afresh at No. 1 each year. The numbers are given in this transcription at the end of each entry, so that by means of the number and the year, any original document can be easily located if desired.

DATE

On form A the date appears at the top and again at the bottom, usually the same date, but sometimes several days later. Where there is a discrepancy, the date at the top has always been used. On form B the date appears only at the bottom, often in latin and difficult to decipher.

There appears to be an unbroken run of forms from 1718 to May 1725, after which there are none until Oct. 1725 followed by a great many in November, as though the office had been closed for a period. After this there are several gaps and a number of mutilated forms, indicating that many have lost. From 1739 to 1749 there is a long gap of ten years, after which the copying is not quite so careful. Many are still in the same handwriting but there are frequent appearances of other hands. Form B is used indiscriminately for all ages and there is less attention to detail. Ages are frequently omitted and although the parish is nearly always given, the county is often lacking.

Until 1752 the old type of calendar was used, where the year began on March 25th, so that January, February and March up to the 24th of March, 1735, for instance, immediately preceded March 25th, 1736. They have been numbered, however, as though the year began on Jan 1st.

OCCUPATION.

In many cases, though by no means all, the occupation of the emigrant is given. The occupations are extremely diverse, for besides the main stream of sawyers, coopers, cordwainers, smiths, etc. there are several schoolmasters, apothecaries and a dancing master. There is also a sprinkling of young boys described as "poor lads." Most of the carpenters and sawyers seemed destined for Jamaica. All were single men and women, the girls described as spinsters or widows. There are also several French and Dutch and even a few from America. It has not been thought necessary to index the trades.

AGENT

All the servants were bound to serve a person, whom we shall call an agent, or his assigns, for a certain number of years. Since there were not a great number of agents, they are indicated by key letters, and a list of the agents with their key letters is given following the introduction. Some names, such as John Taylor, William Burge and Neale MacNeale occur numerous times; others may occur but once. Most appear to be London tradesmen, but there are a few sea captains as well as two women victulers and a widow.

AGE

The overwhelming majority of servants are in their teens or early twenties. In a few cases the age is not given, but since these are on form B, one can possibly assume that they were over 21.

SEX

The proportion of male servants to female servants is approximately 2959 males to 163 females.

NAME

Although the names of the servants are not always easy to decipher, the task has been made much easier by the fact that the name appears twice on each form and it has usually been possible to work it out between the scribe's copy and the signature at the bottom. The signature is frequently spelled differently from the scribe's entry and where this is the case, the different spelling has been included in brackets after the first appearance and the alternative name entered in the alphabetical system. Where the difference is only one letter, this has been added in brackets in the appropriate place. In about half the cases the servant could not sign his name but drew his mark below the copy of his name written by the clerk. This consisted sometimes of a simple cross, sometimes of initials, and sometimes of a complicated squiggle of circles and dots. A name that seemed extremely unlikely has occasionally been confirmed from an early local directory.

Sometimes it is apparent that a brother and sister, or two brothers or two friends have registered together. In the case of relatives, this will show up in the alphabetical system, but in the case of friends, this can probably be checked from the place name index and the date.

In some cases a relative was present at the signing and a note is on the form "in presence and with consent of his mother. . ." followed by the name, or sometimes, father or uncle, or in the case of a released apprentice, his master.

PLACE OF ORIGIN.

It must not be assumed because the indentures were entered into in London that the majority of the emigrants were Londoners. They came to London from all over the British Isles, from Inverness in Scotland to Penzance in Cornwall, maybe to find work in London, but decided to emigrate, perhaps because of lack of work.

Until 1749 the parish and county from which the emigrant came was always listed. The place names gave more trouble in deciphering than any other part of the work for a variety of reasons.

The scribe was often unfamiliar with the name of the place and wrote down only what he heard, often phonetically, or according to the dialect in which it was said to him. Such examples are Suddick, which was probably the local pronunciation of Southwick; Darkin, which is how a country person would pronounce Dorking; Byerton, which is probably how Barton was pronounced in Yorkshire. Welsh place names almost defeated him and we often find Cl or H for the familiar LL. Since the emigrant often could not spell his own name, and certainly not his parish, it is not surprising that there are so many curious spellings.

Some parishes have changed their names over the years. An instance is the parish of Green in Sussex, which is now Wisborough Green.

Some county boundaries were changed by the boundary acts of 1832 and accordingly some parishes have changed their county also, making them now untraceable in any work on their original county.

Several counties have even changed their names. The county of Southampton, is now Hampshire; the county of Galloway in Scotland is now Wigtown and Kirkudbright; the county of Teviotdale in Scotland is now Roxburghshire.

A few parishes seem to have disappeared altogether, for although they appear in Camden's and Speed's maps, they no longer appear in Bartholomew's Gazetteer.

For a very few place names there is no explanation that we can find. Neither they nor anything resembling them appears on any map of any period, so they must be very minor localities or outright mistakes.

The system we have followed is always to write down first what appears on the form. If it is merely a matter of a letter or two missing to bring the spelling up to the present-day spelling, we have added these in brackets in the appropriate place, or listed the entire place afterwards in brackets. If there is some doubt about the name of the place intended, we have added the most probable place with a query. If there is absolutely no clue as to what place was intended, we have simply left it as written, with a query. Sometimes the place is quite obvious, although spelled differently, such as "berry" for "bury, " "Edenborough" for Edinborough, and we have left it alone. For counties, the modern spelling or abbreviation is used in all cases. A list of abbreviations will be found on page xxv.

There are a number of cases towards the end, where no county is listed, but many of these places were in what is now London. It should also be remembered that parts of Kent, Surrey, Middlesex, Hertfordshire and Essex have now been swallowed up by London.

The clerk had a habit of putting a final s on the saint's name of every parish, and we have followed this except where the name itself ends in s, such as St. James.

Reference has been made to the following books:
Bartholomew's Gazetteer of the British Isles; Lewis's Topographical Dictionary; Speed's Theatre of the Empire of Great Britain; Camden's Magna Britania; The Place-Name Society's volumes, etc.

TIME OF SERVICE AND DESTINATION

The time of servitude varies from 4 yrs. to 7 yrs. and occasionally 8 yrs. , the younger people frequently having to serve longer than the older ones   Sometimes special terms are mentioned, e. g. "to have 12 pounds per annum, current money of Maryland, " or "clothes to find himself. " Sometimes the stipulation appears "provided he is a workman and understands his trade, " but these have not been transcribed.

Abbreviations have often been used for the destinations and a list of these can be found on page xxv.   An analysis of the destinations and the number of emigrants bound for each of them can be found in the appendix on page 257.

INTRODUCTION

We do not presume to hope that a work of this nature is entirely free from errors; we do hope, however, that they are reasonably few.

Finally, we wish to express our thanks to Mr. P. E. Jones, Deputy Keeper of the Records at the Guildhall in London, for his constructive criticism of this introduction and his assistance in obtaining the necessary permission for us to undertake this work.

London the *2* Day of *January*
One Thousand, Seven Hundred and *34*

2.

Be it remember'd, That *Robert Frankl...*
Vicar of Aston in the County of York
and Baker of [...] London Fleet Street
London [...] did by Indenture bearing like Date herewith
agree to serve *William Burye of London*
Chapman or his Assign *five* Years in
Maryland (his) Majesties
Plantation and did thereby declare h *imself* to be then of the
Age of *Twenty one* Years, a single Person, no Apprentice, nor
Covenant, or Contracted Servant to any other Person or Persons. And
the said Master did thereby Covenant at his own Cost, to send his said
Servant to the said Plantation; and at the like Costs to find h *im*
all necessary Cloaths, Meat, Drink, Washing, and Lodging,
as other Servants in such Cases are usually provided for, and allowed.

Robert Frank[...]

Acknowledged the 2t: Jan[uar]y
1734 before

Rich: Brocas

xvi

The wording of a specimen of Form A
shown on opposite page

London, the 21 day of January, 1734.

Be it remembered that Robert Franks of Tadcaster in the County of York and late of St. Brides, Fleet St., London, Drawer, did by Indenture bearing like Date herewith agree to serve William Burge of London, Chapman, or his Assigns, Five Years in Maryland (his Majesties plantation in America) and did thereby declare himself to be then of the Age of seventeen Years, a single Person, no Apprentice, nor Covenant, or Contracted Servant to any other Person or Persons. And the said Master did thereby Covenant at his own Cost, to send his said Servant to the said Plantation; and at the like Costs to find him all necessary Cloaths, Meat, Drink, Washing and Lodging, as other Servants in such Cases are usually provided for and allowed.

Acknowledged the 21 January 1734 before Richd. Brocas.

London *ss.* **T**Hese are to certify, That *Samuell Harris of the parish of St Faith London Joyner Aged Twenty four years*

came before me one of His Majesty's Justices of Peace, and Voluntarily made Oath, That *this* Deponant *is* not Married, no Apprentice nor Covenant, or Contracted Servant to any Persons, nor listed Soldier, or Sailor in His Majesty's Service, and *is* free and willing to serve *William Burge* or his Assigns *four* Years in *Virginia*

His Majesty's Plantation in *America*, and that *is* not perswaded, or enticed so to do, but that it is *his* own Voluntary Act.

Samuell Harris

Sworn the 18th January 1734 before me

Richd —

The wording of a specimen of Form B
shown on opposite page

London.

        These are to certify, That Samuell Harris of the parish of St. Faiths, London, Joyner, Aged Twenty Four Years, came before me one of His Majesty's Justices of Peace, and Voluntarily made Oath, That he this Deponant is not Married, no Apprentice nor Covenant, or Contracted Servant to any Persons, nor listed Soldier or Sailor in His Majesty's Service, and is free and willing to serve William Burge or his Assigns Four Years in Virginia, His Majesty's Plantation in America, and that he is not perswaded, or enticed so to do, but that it is his own Voluntary Act.

Sworn the 18th January 1734 before Richd. Brocas.

LIST OF AGENTS WITH KEY TO ABBREVIATIONS

SA	Stephen Avis of St. Saviours, Southwark, Surrey. Girdler
AB	Anthony Bacon
J BALL	John Ball of London, vintner
J BANKS	John Banks
HB	Henry Barlow, Stepney, Mddx. Mariner.
J Ba	John Barnes of St. Olaves in Southwark, Gent.
T Ba	Thomas Barrow
RB	Richard Bateman of London, Vintner
J Be	Capt. John Beame of London. Marriner.
W Be	William Beckford
HB	Humphrey Bell of London. Merchant.
JDB	Capt. John Dod Benett of London. Mariner
J Bl	John Blackwood of London. Chapman.
JB	Capt. Joseph Boasley
H Bo	Henry Bosch of London. Baker.
T Bo	Tobias Bowles of London. Merchant.
Jo B	John Otto Boyer of Antigua.
WB	William Bradley of London. Bookkeeper.
J Br	James Bradshaw of London. Merchant.
Ri Br	Capt. Richard Brook of London. Mariner.
R Br	Robert Brown of London. Mariner.
W Brown	Capt. William Brown of London. Mariner.
R Bu	Richard Budding of Philadelphia
TB	Thomas Bundock, St. Botolphs, Aldgate, London. Cordwainer.
W Bu	William Burge of London. Chapman.
JC	John Cann of Md. Merchant.
T Ca	Capt. Thomas Carlett.
SC	Samuel Carne of Charlestown, N. C. Apothecary.
RC	Robert Cary & Co. of London. Merchants.
A Cash.	Alexander Cash of London. Weaver
WC	William Cash of London, Cheese monger. Or plain Wm. Cash
WC2	William Cash of London. Silk thrower.
W Ch	William Champion of Gravesend. Chapman.
NC	Nathaniel Chew of Md. Merchant.
T Cr	Capt. Thomas Christies of Burnt Island. N. Britain

LIST OF AGENTS

AC	Ambrose Cock of St. Pauls, Shadwell, Mddx. Tobacconist.
EC	Edward Comber of London. Baker.
J Co	John Cook of London. Plaisterer. Or plain John Cook.
J Csn	John Cookson of King St. Westminster. Yeoman.
TC	Capt. Thomas Coram of London. Gent.
MC	Capt. Morgan Cornock of London. Mariner.
CC	Capt. Christopher Cowton of Bridlington, Yorks. Mariner.
J Cr	John Crisp of London. Chapman.
HD	Capt. Henry Danbus of London. Mariner.
BD	Capt. Benjamin Davis of Pa. Mariner.
J Den	Capt. John Dennis of London. Mariner.
J De	John Dent of London. Chapman.
WD	William Dick of London. Marriner.
J Di	John Dickenson of the Middle Temple, London. Gent.
AD	Alexander Duck of London. Merchant
JD	John Dykes of London. Victuler
EE	Capt. Edward Edwards of Boston, New England. Marriner.
HE	Henry Edwards of London. Chapman.
JE	Jonathon Ewer of London. Merchant.
WF	Capt. William Finch of London. Marriner.
SF	Stephen Finney (sometimes Finner) of London. Chapman.
BF	Capt. Benjamin Fisher of London. Mariner.
JF	Joseph Freethey, St. Saviours, Southwark. Pinmaker.
EF	Capt. Edward Friend of London. Mariner.
RF	Rowland Frye of London. Merchant.
J Gar	John Gardner of Jamaica.
J Gee	Joshua Gee Jnr. of London. Merchant.
JG	James Gerald or Gerreld of Bishopsgate, London. Vintner.
JoG	John Gerald. St. Martins in the Fields, Mddx. Vintner.
J Gi	John Gibson of London. Merchant.
SG	Samuel Gloynes of London. Chapman.
J Go	James Gordon of London.
BG	Brian Grady of St. James, Westminster. Gent.
J Gr	John Grant of London. Millwright.
J Hal	John Hallhead of Jamaica

LIST OF AGENTS

JH	John Halton
J Ha	Joan Harriett of London. Victuler.
HH	Henry Hicks of Jamaica.
T Hi	Thomas Hill
VH	Van Holland
TH	Thomas Hudson of London. Merchant.
JH	James Hume of London. Mariner.
T Hu	Capt. Thomas Huntar of Whitby.
WH	William Hunter of St. Andrews, Holbourn.
RH	Robert Hutchings of London. Merchant.
WJ	William Jarvis of Antigua.
EJ	Edward Jessup of St. Christophers.
RJ	Capt. Robert Joad, Sandwich, Kent. Mariner.
JJ	John Johanson of London. Joyner.
GJ	Capt. George Johnstone of London. Marriner.
J JONES	Joseph Jones of London. Planter.
GK	George Kennard of Virginia. Sawyer?
CK	Charles Kingsley & James Murray of London. Druggists.
IK	Capt. Isaac Kitson of Rotherhithe, Surrey. Mariner
JL	Capt. John Larkin of Stepney, Mddx. Mariner.
TL	The Honbl. Thomas Lee Esq.
J Le	Capt. John Levett of London. Mariner and master of the ship Nassau.
WL	William Lightfoot of Va.
JL	James Lindsay, St. Martins in the Fields, Mddx.
AL	Arnold Livers of Md. Merchant.
A Lo	Capt. Andrew Lovie of St. Annes, Westminster.
J Lo	Capt. James Lowrey of Pa.
PM	Philip Mackduel of London. Mariner.
NM	Neale Mackneale of London. Chapman.
S Mi	Samuel Miller of London. Book keeper.
SM	Samuel Montague.
CM	Charles Moore of London. Chapman.
JM	Josiah Morgan of St. Martins in the Fields. Vintner.
VM	Valentine Morris of Pearcefield.
WM	William Murray of Md. Marriner.

LIST OF AGENTS

TN	Capt. Thomas Nesbitt of London. Mariner.
JO	John Oslo
J Pa	John Park of London. Chapman. Also citizen and draper.
GP	George Payne of London.
WP	Capt. William Peacock of London. Mariner.
JP	John Penant.
EP	Edward Perry of London. Chapman.
J Pe	John Perrey of London. Chapman.
PP	Philip Pinnook of Jamaica.
RP	Richard Post of London. Merchant.
J Pr	Capt. John Prichard of London. Marriner.
TP	Thomas Pulleine.
CP	Charles Pye.
JR	James Rammags of Jamaica. Merchant.
BR	Brett Randolph of Virginia. Planter.
HR	Henry Read St. Thomas, Southwark Surrey. Gent.
MR	Capt. Martin Read of London. Marriner.
J Ri	Joseph Richardson of London. Marriner.
TR	Thomas Richardson of London. Chapman.
CR	Charles Rogers of London. Merchant.
SS	Samuel Saunders.
IS	Capt. Isaac Scarth of London. Mariner.
R Sc	Robert Scott of London. Merchant.
J Se	John Seton of London. Merchant.
P Si	Peter Simpson of London. Victuler.
JS	John Smith of London. Chapman.
PS	Philip Smith of London. Merchant.
J St	Dockter John Stevenson of Md.
NS	Nicholas Stevenson of London. Marriner.
JS	James Steward of London. Merchant.
FS	Francis Stewarts of London. Merchant.
RS	Robert Stogdon of St. Michaels, Cornhill. Draper.
WS	Dr. Walter Sydsirfe of Antigua.
R Sy	Capt. Richard Sympson.
AT	Ann Taylor of London. Widow.

LIST OF AGENTS

JT	John Taylor of London. Yeoman. Also Chapman.
J Ta	Joseph Taylor of London. Barber.
W Ta	William Taylor of St. Margarets, Westminster. Merchant.
W Th	Capt. William Thompson.
J Ti	Joseph Tireman.
J To	John Tomlinson of Antigua.
ST	Capt. Samuel Towers.
WT	William Trottman of London. Chapman.
RT	Robert Turlington of London. Gentleman.
CV	Christopher Veale of Shoreditch, Mddx. Woolcomber.
TV	Thomas Vickerman of Scarborough.
SV	Samuel Vincent of London. Clerk.
R Wa	Robert Wade of Kingston. Merchant.
MW	Mark Walker. Or Mark Walker and Co. of London. Chapmen.
WW	Capt. William Wallace.
W Wa	William Ward of Whitby.
JW	John Weasenham of Coleman St. London. Barber.
Ro W	Capt. Robert Wheatley of London. Mariner.
J Wh	Joseph Whilton Sr. Lambeth, Surrey. Chapman. Also of London.
R Wh	Richard White of London. Barber Surgeon.
S Wh	Susanna White of London. Victuller.
AW	Capt. Anthony Wick of London.
JoW	Capt. John Wilcocks of London. Mariner.
J Wi	John Williams of Lambeth, Surrey. Tobacconist.
J Wil	John Wilson of London. Chapman.
NW	Nathaniel Wilson of London. Chapman.
R Wi	Hon. Richard Wilson. Chief Judge of St. Christophers.
RW	Richard Worsam.
SW	Samuel Wragg of London. Merchant.
BW	Benjamin Wright & Co. of London. Chapmen.

ABBREVIATIONS USED

ENGLISH COUNTIES		AMERICAN COLONIES	
Beds.	Bedfordshire	Barb.	Barbadoes
Berks.	Berkshire	Ga.	Georgia
Bucks.	Buckinghamshire	Jam.	Jamaica
Cambs.	Cambridgeshire	Md.	Maryland
Glos.	Gloucestershire	N. E.	New England
Hants.	Hampshire	N. Y.	New York
Herts.	Hertfordshire	N. C.	North Carolina
Hunts.	Huntingdonshire	Pa.	Pennsylvania
Lancs.	Lancashire	St. C.	St. Christophers
Leics.	Leicestershire	St. L.	St. Lucia
Lincs.	Lincolnshire	S. C.	South Carolina
Mddx.	Middlesex	Va.	Virginia
Northants.	Northamptonshire	W. I.	West Indies.
Notts.	Nottinghamshire		
Oxon.	Oxfordshire		
Salop.	Shropshire		
Staffs.	Staffordshire		
Warwicks.	Warwickshire		
Wilts.	Wiltshire		
Worcs.	Worcestershire		
Yorks.	Yorkshire		
Mon.	Monmouthshire		

ADDITIONS AND CORRECTIONS

Where no age is given it does not appear on the original.

128	After Whitham add (Witham)
181	After Whitham add (Witham)
192	After Westham add (West Ham)
246	After Esscott add (East Cottingwith?)
512	After Diggit add (Ditcheat?)
539	After Betherton add (Petherton)
648	After Somerset add Coachman.
751	After Norfolk add writer.
851	After Md. add 18. S.
883	After Sneed add Beds.
886	After Empersfield add John.
918	After Ridgley add (Rugeley?)
958	After Hembruff add (Hemingbrough?)
996	After Deebridge add (Douebridge?)
1054	After (Garrot,) add Robert.
1073	After (D) add William.
1087a	GLOVER, Lattimor (Latimore) Nottingham. JD. 5 yrs.
	Md. 19. S. 1 Feb. 1724 38
1127	After Westborough add (?)
1198	After Bucks add (Berks?)
1220	After Kelminston add (Kilmington? Kelweston?)
1502	After Willington add (Wellington)
1578	JONES, Samuel. St. Giles in the Fields, Mddx. JD.
	8 yrs. St. C. or St. L. 14. S. 11 Aug. 1722 86
1595	After Cheshire add Husbandman.
1621	After Watham add (Waltham)
1661	N. E. means New England.
1667	Swansea is in Glamorganshire.
1671	Non-existent.
1680	LAWSON, John. Aldgate, London. JG. 5 yrs. Va.
	18. M. 25 July, 1721 57
1717	After Abergenny add (Abergavenny.)
1772a	MACE, George. Shrewsbury, Salop. Cordwainer. JT.
	4 yrs. Pa. 19. S. 11 July, 1728 31
1784	After Kirkoven add (Kinharvie?)
1848	After SF. add 5 yrs. Jam. Father at Lea.
1887	After Meridith add St. Brides, Fleet St.

ADDITIONS AND CORRECTIONS

1889 After Rayner add (Raynham)
1920 After Notts. add (Northants?)
1956 After Marbeth add (Narberth?)
1958 After Lee add (Leigh on Sea?)
2005 After Kaisher add (Castor?)
2035 After Maddermarket add Weaver.
2038 Whetstone is in Mddx.
2044 After Marsfield add (Makerfield?)
2046 After Swalwin add (Swarland?)
2141 After Denton add (Ditton?)
2188 After Bartonley add (Barton?)
2320 After Mddx. add Gardner.
2325 After Westborough add (Westbury?)
2335 After Hunnington add (Honington)
2365 After Kirkawdey add (Kirkcaldy?)
2468 Non-existent.
2565 After Hollywell add (Holywell)
2573 After Rowell add (Rothwell?)
2616 After Stow add (Stowe or Stow on the Wold?)
2637 After Henry add Salisbury.
2746a THOMPSON (Tomson) William. Barkin(g) Essex. JT.
      4 yrs. Md. 18. S. 30 Jan. 1720   13
2747 After Langer add (Langar)
2766 Non-existent.
2770 After Dunhead add (Donhead)
2776 After Chirrell add (Cherhill)
2909 Non-existent.
2922 After Eden add (Etton?)
2929 After Cureville add (Curry Rivel?)
2963 After Longberry add (Long Bredy?)
2987 After Mddx. add Water Gilder.
3117 After Ridgely add (Rugeley?)
3118 QUANT, Robert. St. Martins in the Fields, Mddx. JT.
      5 yrs. Jam. 15. M. 9 Nov. 1725   148
3119 QUINO, Samuel. Tower Liberty, London. Barber. JG.
      4 yrs. Md. 21. S. 9 Nov. 1724   70
3120 QUINTIN, James. St. Gregorys, Norwich. Barber and perry-
      wig maker. NM. 5 yrs. Va. or Md. 19. S. 28 July, 1735. 59
3121 QUIRRY, Stephen. Aldgate, London. JT. 4 yrs. Jam.
      20. S. 4 Jan. 1722.   12

The details of each immigrant are arranged in the following order: Name; parish and county; occupation; initials of agent (see key on page xx); years of service; colony to which he was bound; age; whether signed or marked (S or M); date of indenture; page number. The occupation is only given in about half of the cases, while ages and counties are occasionally missing.

1   ABBERT, Peter; Christ Church, Spittlefields, (Mddx.) gardiner; N. W.   4 yrs.   Md.   40;   S.   8 Aug. 1739   97

2   ABBITT, Abraham; Chessington, Suffolk (Perhaps Chevington, Suffolk, or Chessington, Surrey.)   Husbandman; J. T. 4 yrs.   Jam.   19   M.   2 April, 1724   42

3   ABBNEY, John.   St. Martins in the Fields, Mddx.   Smith; J. G.   6 yrs.   Md.   24   S.   23 Jan. 1724   22

4   ABBOTT, Peter.   Kirk Hammerton, Yorks.   Hostler;   N. M. 4 yrs. Jam.   24   M.   5 Oct. 1733   87

5   ADAMS, John.   Watford, Herts.   Labourer;   J. D.   4 yrs. Md. and Pa.   20   M.   30 Jan. 1719   20

6   ADAMS, Philip.   St. Paul's Covent Garden.   N. M.   4 yrs. Jam.   21   S.   3 Nov. 1736   122

7   ADAMSON, John.   Largo, Fifeshire, Scotland.   J. G.   5 yrs. Md.   18   S.   2 Aug. 1723   68

8   ADCOCK, John.   St. Mary, White Chappell, Mddx.   N. M. 4 yrs. Pa.   18   S.   24 Sept. 1733   71

9   ADCOCK, John.   St. Vedast, Foster Lane (London)   Barber and perriwigmaker.   S. F.   4 yrs.   Jam.   21   S 15 March, 1737   30

10   ADDAMS, Robert.   Deptford, Kent.   J. D.   6 yrs. Pa.   17 S.   19 Oct. 1725   116

11   ADDERLY, Ralph.   Marabone (Marylebone) Mddx.   J. G.
4 yrs. Md.   16   M.   16 Dec. 1730   217

12   ADDEY, William.   Oundell (Oundle) Northants.   C. V.
4 yrs.   Va.   18   S.   21 July 1720   94

13   ADNEY, George.   Portsmouth, Hants.   P. Si.   4 yrs.   Md.
18   S.   26 Jan. 1733   17

14   AIKENHOAD, Patrick.   Dublin, Ireland.   Book keeper.
J. T.   4 yrs.   Jam.   20   S.   1 Sept. 1731   193

15   AINSLY, Thomas.   Chadbrough (Jedburgh?) Teviotdale
(now Roxburghshire) Scotland.   Carpenter and joyner;   J. Wi.
4 yrs.   Md.   19   S.   30 Aug. 1720   118

16   ALBA, Peter.   Stepney, Mddx.   J. D.   5 yrs.   Md.   18
M.   31 July, 1718   38

17   ALDERTON, William.   St. Giles Criplegate, London.
Mother Elizabeth Alderton.   J. Cooke.   6 yrs.   Md.   16
S.   21 Jan. 1724   14

18   ALDRIDGE, Randall.   St. Mary, Whitechappell, Mddx.
silk throwster;   W. C.   4 yrs.   Pa.   20   S.   20 Oct. 1725
130

19   ALEXANDER, Ambrose.   Fodenbridge (Fordingbridge) Hants.
Labourer;   N. M.   4 yrs.   Jam. or Barb.   22   M.
22 Sept. 1733   68

20   ALEXANDER, Mary.   St Giles in the Fields, Mddx.
spinster;   N. M.   4 yrs.   Jam.   18   S.   12 March 1735   10

21   ALLAM, George.   Elland, Yorks.   J. T.   4 yrs.   Jam.
17   M.   3 Jan. 1723   2

22   ALLAWAY, Stephen.   St. Martins in the Fields, Mddx.
J. G.   4 yrs.   Md.   17   S.   7 Feb. 1723   24

23 ALLBONE, Isaac. St. Margarets Westminster. Coach
maker; N. M. 4 yrs. Jam. 21 S. 3 Jan. 1736 6

24 ALLBURY, John. Loughton, Essex. husbandman; father
and mother dead. M. W. 5 yrs. Antig. 19 S.
4 Nov. 1738 62

25 ALLEN, James. Glasgow, Scotland. W. C. 2. 4 yrs. Pa.
19 S. 8 July, 1728 13

26 ALLEN, James. St. Botolphs, Aldersgate. labourer; S. F.
4 yrs. Jam. 21 S. 7 Dec. 1736 191

27 ALLEN, John. St. Margarets, Westminster, Mddx. carpenter; J. G. 4 yrs. Antigua 25 S. 12 Feb. 1722 35

28 ALLEN, John. St. Botolphs by Billingsgate, London.
labourer; J. T. 4 yrs. Jam. 20 S. 5 Oct. 1730 132

29 ALLEN, Samuel Winchester, Hants. labourer; J. T.
4 yrs. Jam. 17 S. 29 June, 1730 55

30 ALLEN, William. Woodford, Northants. J. D. 8 yrs.
Md. 14 M. 25 Sept. 1719 51

31 ALLEN, William. Brandford (Brentford) Mddx. labourer;
J. G. 4 yrs. St. Christ. 21 S. 1 Jan, 1722 5

32 ALLFORD, Susannah. Portsmouth, Hants. spinster; C. V.
5 yrs. Va. 19 S. 4 April, 1720 60

33 AMBROSE, Thomas. St. James Westminster, Mddx.
coachman. R. B. 4 yrs. Jam. 20 M. 25 Nov. 1725
206

34 AMOS, William. Gurton (Gunton?) Norfolk. C. V. 5 yrs.
New England. 19 M. 11 April, 1724 44

35 AMPHLETT, Benjamin. Worcester. book keeper; J. Cr.
4 yrs. Jam. 20 S. 2 Sept. 1749 9

36 ANDERSON, Francis. Christ Church, London. W. C. 4 yrs.
Pa. 15 S. 9 Oct. 1725   112

37 ANDERSON, John. Glasgow, Scotland. Schollar. C. V.
4 yrs. Va. 19 S. 2 Oct. 1722   138

38 ANDERSON, John. Eling (Ealing) Mddx. husbandman;
J. Co. 4 yrs. Jam. 26 S. 6 March, 1724   77

39 ANDERSON, Thomas. St. Botolphs, Bishopsgate (London)
cordwainer   father dead, mother Mary Burton; N. W. 5 yrs
Pa. 20 M. 8 Jan. 1738   4

40 ANDERSON, William of Island of Orkney in Scotland. J. Wi.
5 yrs. Md. 18 S. 20 Aug. 1718   27

41 ANDERSON, William. St. Martins in the Fields, Mddx.
Taylor; C. V. 4 yrs. Va. 20 S. 22 Sept. 1724   53

42 ANDREWS, John. St. Giles in the Fields, Mddx. I. K.
7 yrs. Md. 15 M. 30 July, 1718   40

43 ANDREWS, John. A native of the East Indies and late of
St. Clement Danes, Mddx. AC. 8 yrs. Md. 17 M.
27 Jan. 1719   18

44 ANDREWS, John. Hampstead, Mddx. Father Joseph
Andrews; master Jacob Rempel; N. S. 7 yrs. Pa. 15
M. 31 July 1739   93

45 ANDREWS, Joseph. Abbotsbury, Dorset. J. D. Va. or Md.
18 S. 31 Jan. 1720   15

46 ANDREWS, Mary. Oler (Aller?) Somerset. spinster; E. C.
5 yrs. Va. 18 M. 4 April, 1720   62

47 ANDREWS, Thomas. Wellington, Herefordshire. husbandman; E. P. 4 yrs. Jam. 20 M. 17 Feb. 1737   19

4

48   ANGIER, John. Braintree, Essex. woolcomber; C. V.
      4 yrs. Md. 21 S. 26 Nov. 1724   78

49   ANGUS, Thomas. Bury St. Edmunds, Suffolk. perriwig-
      maker; N. M. 3 yrs. Carolina or W. I. over 21 S.
      10 Aug. 1736   51

50   ANSELL, Matthew. Lilley, Herts. groom; J. T. 4 yrs.
      Md. 18 M. 24 Oct. 1718   59

51   ANSELL, Thomas. St. Pauls, Covent Garden. cooper;
      M. W. 4 yrs. Jam. 20 S. 11 Dec. 1736   197

52   ANSUP, Henry. Duffield, Derbyshire. S. G. 4 yrs. Jam.
      18 M. 6 Nov. 1725   146

53   ANTRUM, John. Hamilton, Nr. Portsmouth, Hants. J. D.
      8 yrs. Md. 15 M. 30 Nov. 1719   101

54   APPLETON, Jonathan. Hailwood, Childwell (wall), Lancs.
      WC2 4 yrs. Pa. 17 S. 13 Aug 1728   81

55   APPLETREE, Joseph. St. Georges, Southwark. J. G. 6 yrs.
      St. L. or St. C. 15 S. 17 Aug. 1722   99

56   APTEY, Thomas. Milton next Sittingbourne, Kent. J. D.
      4 yrs. Md. 19 S. 19 Aug. 1720   108

57   ARCHER, John. Little Milton, Oxon. labourer; S. G.
      4 yrs. Va. 18 S. 29 Nov. 1727   1

58   ARCHER, Theodorus. Hisson (Histon) Cambs. JT 4 yrs.
      Jam. 18 S. 7 Nov. 1729   14

59   ARDIN, Abraham. St. Martins, Ludgate, London. stay-
      maker. JT 4 yrs. Pa. 19 S. 15 Aug. 1728   83

60   ARDINGTON, Henry. Cowick, Yorks. JD 8 yrs. Md.
      14 M. 23 Nov. 1719   98

61   ARGENT, George.   Sibil Inginham (Sible Hedingham,)
Essex.   JTa   7 yrs.   N. C.   17   M.   5 July, 1736   27

62   ARMSTRONG, Thomas.   Newberry, Berks.   labourer;   JT
4 yrs.   St. C.   20   S.   7 July, 1722   47

63   ARNELL. William.   Ditchett (Ditcheat,) Somerset.   JT
4 yrs.   Jam.   18   M.   1 May, 1725   90

64   ARNOLD, Robert.   St. Margarets Westminster, Mddx.   JG
5 yrs.   Md.   18   S.   30 Dec. 1723   125

65   ARNOLD, Elizabeth.   St. Martins in the Fields.   spinster;
J Ta   4 yrs.   Jam.   20   M.   18 Oct. 1736   95

66   ASH, Robert.   Roddell, Yorks.   JL   6 yrs.   Md.   17   M.
1 Feb. 1719   23

67   ASHERS, John.   Birmingham, Warwicks.   joyner and carpenter;   EP   4 yrs.   Jam.   22   S.   25 May, 1738   44

68   ASLEY, Mary.   London.   J Bl.   3 yrs.   Antigua;   18   S.
29 Oct. 1756   24

69   ASPINALL, Thomas.   St. Clement Danes (London)
blacksmith;   EP   4 yrs.   Md.   35   S   20 Dec. 1737   80

70   ASTWOOD, Abraham.   Atleborough, Norfolk.   baker;   JD
4 yrs.   St. L.   19   S.   30 Oct. 1722   174

71   ATHRON, William.   St. Andrews, Holbourn, London.
sawyer;   JG.   4 yrs.   Jam.   29   S.   24 Dec. 1729   84

72   ATKINS, Abraham.   Wooton (Wotton-Under-Edge?) Glos.
butcher;   W Bu.   4 yrs.   Pa.   22   S.   17 Feb. 1735   6

73   ATKINS, Henry.   St. Clement Danes, Mddx.   taylor;
NM   3 yrs.   S. C. or W. I.   over 21?   S. 10 Aug. 1736   47

74   ATKINS, William.   St. Georges, Southwark (Surrey)   hatter
NM   4 yrs.   Jam.   21   M.   19 Nov. 1736   164

75 ATKINS, William. Worcester. mason; JS. 5 yrs.
    Jam. S. 20 Oct. 1752   9

76 ATKINSON, John. Winnell (Willenhall?) Warwicks. J Bl.
    4 yrs. Jam. S. 7 Aug. 1753   24

77 ATWOOD, John. St. Albans, Herts. husbandman; NM
    4 yrs. Md. 21 S. 8 April, 1735   21

78 AUSTIN, Edward. Clerkenwell, Mddx. sawyer; W Bu.
    4 yrs. Jam. 28 S. 30 April, 1731   115

79 AUSTIN, William. St. Giles in the Fields, Mddx. baker;
    W Bu. 4 yrs. Md. 19 M. 8 Aug. 1735   69

80 AVISSON, Thomas. Waltham Abbey, Essex. JD 4 yrs.
    Md. 18 S. 25 Aug. 1718   44

81 AYERS, John. Yaldin(g) Kent. labourer; NW 4 yrs.
    Jam. 27 S. 31 Oct. 1739   116

82 AYLWARD, Henry. Swanzey (Swansea), Glam. Wales.
    butler and gardner; NM 4 yrs. Jam. 28 S.
    3 Sept. 1734   79

                              B
83 BACKAS, John. Mickhills (St. Michaels?) Lancs. J BALL
    4 yrs. Antigua. 19 M. 10 Dec. 1728   116

84 BADCOCK, John. Falmouth, Cornwall. P. Si. 4 yrs.
    Pa. or N. Y. 19 S. 18 July, 1728   39

85 BADDISON, John. Ipswich, Suffolk. W Bu. 5 yrs. Md.
    19 S. 10 Feb. 1729   24

86 BAGOTT (BAGGOT) Ann. St. Annes, Westminster, Mddx.
    spinster. JT 5 yrs. Md. 20 M. 30 Jan. 1719   22

                              7

BAGGOT. See 86

87 BAGWELL, John. Parkgate, Cheshire. Labourer; NM
4 yrs. Jam. 20 S. 24 Aug. 1736   60

88 BAILEY, Jonathan. St. Ann, Soho. Vintner; father and
mother dead. JT 4 yrs. Jam. 18 S. 21 Nov. 1739
                                                          123

89 BAILY, Richard. St. Giles in the Fields, Mddx. JD. 7 yrs.
Md. 15 S. 27 Aug. 1722   114

90 BAIRD, James. Bamf (Banff) Scotland. J Cr. 4 yrs.
Jam. 18 S. 26 Aug. 1749   5

91 BAKER, Henry. Chillington, Devon. Kitchen gardner;
WM. 5 yrs. Md. 19 M. 14 Feb. 1754   8

92 BAKER, Humph(e)rey. Stowerbridge (Stourbridge,) Worcs.
W Bu. 6 yrs. Md. 18 S. 29 Dec. 1729   86

93 BAKER, John. Ramsbury, Wilts. Husbandman; SV.
(for Maj. John Marshall of Jamaica) 4 yrs. Jam. 17 M.
27 Aug. 1720   116

94 BAKER, John. St. Leonards, Shoreditch, Mddx. Cordwainer; JT 5 yrs. Jam. 19 S. 9 Jan. 1733   11

95 BAKER, Joseph. St. Saviour, Southwark, Surrey. CV.
5 yrs. Md. 16 S. 23 Sept. 1723   94

96 BAKER, Nicholas. St. Anns Westminster. Coachman;
CV 4 yrs. Md. 19 M. 4 Oct. 1722   161

97 BAKER, Sarah. St. Giles in the Fields, Mddx. Spinster;
RJ 4 yrs. S. C. 19 M. 17 June, 1736   24

98 BAKER, Thomas. St. Mary, White Chappell. Upholder;
MW 4 yrs. Jam. 24 S. 27 Nov. 1738   69

99   BAKER, William.   Henvill (now Henfield?) Sussex.   JD
      7 yrs.   Md.   18   M.   17 Feb. 1720   23

100   BAKER, William.   Henvill (now Henfield?) Sussex.   JD
      6 yrs.   Md.   19   M.   17 Jan. 1721   11

101   BAKESON, Margaret.   St. Andrews, Holbourn, London.
      Spinster.   P Si.   4 yrs.   S. C.   18   M.   4 Sept. 1733   48

102   BALBEE, Anthony (Antone Balbi) a native of Italy.   P Si.
      4 yrs.   Jam.   20   S.   30 Aug. 1733   39

      BALBI.   See 102

103   BALDWIN, John.   Aldgate, London.   Uncle John Sheppard.
      T Bo.   6 yrs.   Md.   17   S.   20 July, 1718   10

104   BALDWIN, John.   St. James, Norwich   Weaver;   JG.
      4 yrs.   Barb.   20   M.   13 July, 1721   51

105   BALDWIN, John.   St. James, Westminster, Mddx.   Wheel-
      wright;   JG   4 yrs.   Jam.   19   No S or M.   16 March, 1722
                                                                   44

106   BALL, Sarah.   Chessun (Cheshunt?) Herts.   Spinster;   CV
      6 yrs.   Va. or Md.   17   M.   Last Feb. 1720   25

107   BALL, Thomas.   Astwood, Bucks.   Taylor;   TB.   4 yrs.
      Md.   20   S.   4 Sept. 1722   118

108   BALLARD, Joseph.   Christ Church, Spitlefields, Mddx.
      Bricklayer;   W Bu.   4 yrs.   Jam.   22   S.   3 May, 1731 120

109   BALLDWIN, Thomas.   St. James, Norwich.   Two brothers,
      William and John Baldwin.   JG.   6 yrs.   Barb.   17   M.
      13 July, 1721   52

110   BALLETT, Samuel.   Boston, Lincs.   Carpenter;   EP.   4 yrs.
      Jam.   27   S.   26 Nov. 1737   67

9

111   BALLING, Thomas.   Bristoll.   Upholsterer;   NM.   4 yrs.
       Jam.   25   S.   30 Nov. 1736   181

112   BALLMER, Michael.   St. Giles in the Fields, Mddx.   Taylor;
       W Bu.   4 yrs.   Jam.   23   M.   27 Dec. 1731   295

113   BAMFORD, William.   Northampton.   Hostler;   WC.   4 yrs.
       Jam.   22   S.   14 Oct. 1730   144

114   BAND, Nathaniel.   Coventry, Warwicks.   JT.   5 yrs.
       New England.   20.   M.   14 March, 1721   29

115   BANES, Thomas.   Hereford.   Taylor;   JG.   4 yrs.   Md.
       20   S.   1 Dec. 1721   89

116   BANFIELD, James.   Canterbury, Kent.   Labourer;   JT
       4 yrs.   Jam.   33   S.   20 Nov. 1725   192

117   BANFIELD, William.   Exeter, Devon.   J BALL.   4 yrs.
       Antigua.   18   M.   4 Dec. 1728   112

118   BANKS, Henry.   Marrabone (Marylebone) Mddx.   JD   5 yrs.
       St. C or St. L.   17   S.   9 Aug. 1722   79

119   BANKS, Joseph.   Edenborough in Scotland.   Carpenter;
       JT.   4 yrs.   Jamaica.   20.   S.   16 Jan. 1721   10

120   BANKS, Thomas.   A national of the East Indies, late of
       Chelsea, Mddx.   JG.   4 yrs. Va.   19   M.   20 Feb. 1720
                                                                        25

121   BANKS, William.   Broomsgrove, Worcs.   JD   6 yrs.   Md.
       or Pa.   19   M.   25 Sept. 1719   50

122   BANNESTEN, John.   St. Annes, Soho.   Schoolmaster;
       NW.   4 yrs.   Md.   24   S.   Dec. 19, 1738   77

123   BARBER, John.   York.   Cordwainer;   JT.   4 yrs.   Jam.
       28   S.   14 Sept. 1727   34

124 BARDEN, Samuel (Smallwill Bardon) Suddick (Southwick)
Parish of North Bradley, Wilts. P. Si. 4 yrs. Md. 18
S. 8 Nov. 1727   26

BARDON. See 124

125 BARFOOT, Henry. Town Sutton, Kent. Carpenter; P Si.
4 yrs. Jam. 25 S. 12 Oct. 1730   140

126 BARKER, Benjamin. Brewen (Bruen) Stapleford, Cheshire.
Husbandman; NW. 4 yrs. Jam. 18 S. 27 Sept. 1739
                                                        109

127 BARKER, Daniel. Sheilds in the North of England. JD
8 yrs. Md. 15 M. Last Jan. 1723   13

128 BARKER, Elizabeth. Whitham, Essex. Spinster; JW.
5 yrs. Va. 20 M. 29 July, 1721   60

129 BARKER, Thomas. Ruston, Norfolk. AC 4 yrs. Va.
16 S. 15 Sept. 1720   127

130 BARKER, William. Oxford Footman; RB 4 yrs. Jam.
18 S. 24 Nov. 1725   199

131 BARKER, William. Branford (Brentford) Mddx. Taylor;
NM 4 yrs. Jam. 29 S. 7 Dec. 1736   187

132 BARLOW, John. Hatton, Warwicks. Husbandman; NM
4 yrs. Jam. 24 M. 4 Aug. 1731   179

133 BARNARD, Jeremiah. Byerton (Barton?) Warwicks. Labourer; J Bl. 4 yrs. Jam. 23 S. Jan. 14, 1758   1

134 BARNES, James. White Chappell, Mddx. Mother Sarah
Barnes. P Si. 8 yrs. Md. 14 M. 24 Nov. 1729   29

135 BARNES, Joseph. St. Marys, Leicester. JD 7 yrs. Pa.
17 M. 15 Oct. 1725   114

136 BARNES, Thomas. White Chappell, Mddx. Mother Sarah
Barnes. P Si. 5 yrs. Md. 19 M. 24 Nov. 1729 30

137 BARNES, Thomas. Oxford. J Bl. 7 yrs. Va. 16 S.
16 April, 1751 47

138 BARNES, William. Glos. Book keeper. AT. 4 yrs.
Jam. 18 S. 10 Nov. 1750 41

139 BARNET, John. St. Andrews, Holebourn, London.
Plaisterer W Bu 4 yrs. Jam. 22 S. 27 Feb. 1730 90

140 BARNETT, Isaac. Stepney, Mddx. Weaver; Mother
Martha Barnett. CV. 5 yrs. Md. 19 M. 11 Feb. 1724
68

141 BARNFIELD, Herbert. St. Martins in the Fields, Mddx.
Cook; NM. 4 yrs. Jam. 22 S. 1 June 1734 59

142 BARNFIELD, John. Old Brandford , Eling (Old Brentford,
Ealing) Mddx. Brick and tyle maker; JT. 4 yrs. Jam.
20 S. 6 Aug. 1731 181

143 BARNS, William. St. Giles in the Fields, Mddx. JD
6 yrs. Md. 17 M. 8 Oct. 1724 59

144 BARRET, William. St. Martins in the Fields, Mddx.
Taylor; 4 yrs. Jam. 19 S. 6 Dec. 1729 56

145 BARRET(T), William. St. Giles in the Fields, Mddx.
Carpenter and joiner; J Wh. 4 yrs. Jam. 27 S.
21 March 1738 54

146 BARROW, Robert. Moppus (Malpas?) Cheshire. Labourer;
NM 4 yrs. Md. 20 M. 9 July, 1735 47

147 BARROW, Thomas. Emser (Emsworth?) Hants. JD 5 yrs.
Pa. 20 M. 4 Sept. 1723 86

148 BARRYCIFF (CLIFF), John. (D)Ringhouses, Nr. York. J Co.
4 yrs. Md. 16 M. 1 Feb. 1724 37

149 BARTLE, Richard. Norwich. Weaver; P Si. 4 yrs. Pa.
or N. Y. 20 M. 10 July, 1728 25

150 BARTLET (?) John. Stepney, Mddx. Weaver; Father
Robert Bartlet(?) SF. 6 yrs. Jam. 17 S. 28 Aug. 1736
63

151 BARTLETT, John. Stanway, Glos. JG. 4 yrs. Pa. 19
S. 19 June, 1722 35

152 BARTLETT, John. Wells, Husbandman; NM 4 yrs.
Va. or Md. 20 S. 7 Jan. 1736 21

153 BARTLEY, Thomas. St. Andrews, Holbourn, London. SG.
4 yrs. Jam. 18 S. 2 Nov. 1725 138

154 BARTON, George. St. James, Westminster. Bricklayer
and mason; NW. 4 yrs. Jam. 36 S. 21 May, 1739
72

155 BARWICK (BERWICK), Andrew. Faulkland, Fifeshire,
Scotland. JT 5 yrs. Jam. 16 S. 3 July, 1730 58

156 BASFORD, Mary. St. Leonards. Shoreditch, Mddx.
Spinster; JG. 6 yrs. Va. 18 M. 7 Feb. 1720 20

157 BASQUFIL, Thomas. Marther (Merthyr Tydfil?) Brecknock,
Wales. Tanner; W Bu 4 yrs. Pa. 28 S. Feb. 17,
1735 7

158 BATEMAN (BATTEMAN) John. Kensington, Mddx.
Joyner; W Bu. 4 yrs. Jam. 26 S. 14 Sept. 1731 211

159 BATEMAN, Thomas. Clapham, Yorks. Husbandman; EP
4 yrs. Va. or Md. 22 S. 19 April, 1737 48

160   BATES, Richard.   Crostick (Costock or Cortlingstock?) Notts.
       Taylor; J Cr. 4 yrs. Jam. S. 1 March, 1749   10

161   BATH, Samuel.   Bursleton, Southampton (Hants.) 4 yrs.
       JD Md. 19 M. 24 Oct. 1719   80

162   BATHELL (BETHELL), Peter. St. James, Westminster, Mddx.
       BG 4 yrs. St. L. 17 S. 1 Nov. 1722   178

163   BATT, Robert.   St. James, Bristol. JD 6 yrs. St. L.
       17 S. 6 Oct. 1722   152

164   BATT, Robert.   Dublin, Ireland. RB. 6 yrs. Md. or Pa.
       18 S. 19 Feb. 1723   33

       BATTEMAN.   See 158

165   BATTEY, Thomas.   Leeds, Yorks. Husbandman; NM
       4 yrs. Jam. 30 M. 17 Aug. 1730   71

166   BAUGHT, Stephen.   Rye, Sussex. JD 6 yrs. Md. 16
       S. 5 Jan. 1719   5

167   BAWCOCK, William.   Bishops Stortford, Herts. Labourer;
       JD 5 yrs. Pa. 19 S. 22 May, 1719   12

168   BAXTER, Henry.   Dunmow, Essex. Skinner and glover;
       RB 4 yrs. Jam. 17 S. 24 Nov. 1725   201

169   BAYLISS, John.   Southwark. Cooper; WD 5 yrs. Va.
       19 S. 3 May, 1731   55

170   BAYLY, John.   Abbersand (perhaps Abbatston, alias
       Abberston Nr. Alresford, now lost or changed) Hants.
       Husbandman; J Bl. 5 yrs. Md. M. 21 July, 1753   13

171   BEAGHON, Stephen.   Dublin, Ireland. NM 6 yrs. Md.
       15 S. 19 Dec. 1729   78

14

172   BEALE (BEAL), Edward. Modesfont (Mottisfont) Hants.
Coachman; JT 4 yrs. Jam. 19 S. 25 Nov. 1723   113

173   BEALL, John. Banbury, Oxon. WB. 4 yrs. Va. or Md.
18 S. 13 Nov. 1719   89

174   BEALLE. George. Stillingrave (?) Northants. WC2
7 yrs. Jam. 17 S. 5 Aug. 1730   65

175   BEANS, William. Portsmouth, Hants. J Bl. 5 yrs. Md.
17 S. 26 March, 1750   11

176   BEAUMONT, Richard. Bradford, Wilts. P Si. 4 yrs.
Md. 16 S. 18 Nov. 1727   18

177   BEAVOUR, Benjamin. Stepney, Mddx. NM 7 yrs. Md.
15 S. 1 Dec. 1733   130

178   BEAZLEY, Thomas. St. Martins in the Fields. Carpenter
and joiner; NW 4 yrs. Jam. 25 S. 21 May, 1739 71

179   BECK, Christopher. Foley Hill (?), Worcs. Taylor;
NW 4 yrs. Md. 20 M. 23 Feb. 1738   28

180   BECK, William. Loughborough, Leics. Tailor; mother
and father dead. J. Wh. 6 yrs. Va. 17 S.
2 Dec. 1737   70

181   BECKETT, John. Witham, Essex. Labourer; EP. 4 yrs.
Va. or Md. 23 S. 19 April, 1737   46

182   BECKLEY, Edward. Marlborough, Wilts. Labourer; SF
4 yrs. Jam. 21 S. 7 Feb. 1737   10

183   BECKLEY, William. Sutton, Staffs. WC2. 7 yrs. Pa.
15 M. 6 Aug. 1728   67

184   BEDFORD, George. Droytwich, Worcs. Husbandman; NM
4 yrs. Jam. 38 S. 28 July, 1735.   55

185   BEDFORD, George. St. Marys White Chappell, Mddx.
Smith; JT. 4 yrs. Antigua or Barb. 21 S.
7 Aug. 1735   67

186   BEDMAN, Thomas. Pausher (Pershore?) Worcs. Husbandman. AC 6 yrs. New England. 19 M. 4 March, 1721
27

187   BEDNALL, Thomas. Hins (Hints) Staffs. Brickmaker; JD
St. C. or St. L. 18 M. 9 Aug. 1722   77

188   BEEDING, Henry. St. Andrews, Holbourn, Mddx. Mother
Bridget Beeding and father John Beeding. JT 7 yrs. Md.
12 M. 6 Feb 1719   37

189   BEENE, John. St. Margarets, Westminster, Mddx. Labourer. JT. 4 yrs. Jam. 20 M. 17 Dec. 1730   220

190   BEESTON, John. Bingham, Notts. Briches maker. CV
4 yrs. St. C. 19 S. 11 July, 1722   50

191   BELFELT, (BIELFELD) John Christopher. A native of
Leubeck, Germany. Brazier; J Ta. 4 yrs. N.C. 26
S. 7 July, 1736   28

192   BELHOOKE, Jeremiah. Westham, Essex. JD 6 yrs. Md.
16 M. 19 Oct. 1719   75

193   BELL, David. Woolscome, (Woolcombe) Somerset. JS.
5 yrs. Jam. M. 2 Jan, 1756   3

194   BELL, John. St. Helens, City of Worcester. JD 5 yrs.
Md. 19 S. 17 Aug. 1719   21

195   BELL, John. St. Georges, Hanover Square, Mddx. Labourer. WC2. 4 yrs. Md. 19 S. 31 Dec. 1728   122

196   BELL, Lewis. Burnham, Essex. JD 7 yrs. Md. 15
S. 6 Oct. 1724   57

197 BELL, William. St. James, Westminster, Mddx. Labourer;
WC2 4 yrs. Md. 18 M. 31 Dec. 1728 121

198 BELLFORD, Joseph. Christ Church, Bristol. JT 7 yrs. Pa.
15 S. 21 Sept. 1733 65

199 BENNET, James. Taunton, Somerset. Husbandman;
W Bu. 4 yrs. Jam. 20 M. 5 Dec. 1729 55

200 BENNET, John. Bigglesworth, (Biggleswade) Beds. JT
7 yrs. Pa. 15 M. 10 July, 1728. 30

201 BENNET, Sarah. Newington Buts, Surrey. Spinster;
J Wi. 7 yrs. Va. 15 M. 5 April, 1720 64

202 BENNETT, John. Durham. NM 4 yrs. Jam. 18 S.
17 July, 1736 41

203 BENNETT, John. Cheshire. Servant; J Bl. 4 yrs.
Antigua. S. 26 July, 1755 7

204 BENNETT, Sarah. St. Mary, Newington Butts, Surrey.
Spinster; TH 6 yrs. Pa. 18 M. 18 Feb. 1723 31

205 BENNETT, Thomas. Nottingham. Butcher; NM. 4 yrs.
Va. or Md. 29 S. 6 Jan. 1736 16

206 BENT, Josèph. Sapcote, Leics. Carpenter. Father and
mother Richard and Jane Biddle. JG 4 yrs. Antigua.
19 M. 17 Aug. 1728 90

207 BENTLEY, Benjamin. St. Olave, Southwark, Surrey.
cordwainer; father and mother dead. NW. 4 yrs. Md.
19 S. 12 Nov. 1739 119

208 BENTLEY, George. Manchester, Lancs. Weaver; W Bu
4 yrs. Jam. 30. M. 1 June, 1734 57

209 BERNHOSE, John. St. Lawrence, Jewry. Surgeon; EP.
4 yrs. Jam. 23 S. 14 April, 1738 34

210   BERRIDGE, Joseph. March, Isle of Ely, Cambs. Carpenter
and joyner; CM 4 yrs. Jam. 20 S. 10 April, 1735 24

211   BERRIDGE, Margrett Sophia. St. Anns, Soho. Housekeeper
J Cr. 4 yrs. Jam. S. 3 Jan, 1756 6

212   BERRY, John. Stepney, Mddx. JD 7 yrs. St. C. or L.
15 M. 9 Aug. 1722 80

213   BERRY, John. Aberdeen, Scotland. School master; NM
4 yrs. Md. 24 S. 13 Sept. 1735 81

214   BERRY, Peter. Gadlane, (?) Leics. Husbandman; P Si.
4 yrs. Md. 20 M. 8 Dec. 1729 60

215   BERRY, Thomas. Alton, Hants. EC 5 yrs. Carolina.
17 M. 17 Dec. 1718 1

216   BERTLY, James. Dublin, Ireland. Surgeon; NM 4 yrs.
Jam. 22 Not signed or marked. 9 Dec. 1735 116

BERWICK. See 155

217   BETEILHE, John. St. Anns, Westminster, Mddx. Book-
keeper. NM. 4 yrs. Jam. 30 S. 19 Oct. 1733 94

218   BETELER, Gregory. Clare, Suffolk. Apothecary; JG.
4 yrs. Jam. 18 S. 20 Jan. 1729 8

BETHELL. See 162

219   BETTELEY, Ann. St. Margarets, Westminster, Mddx.
Spinster; JT 4 yrs. Jam. 22 M. 1 Sept. 1733 47

220   BETTERSON, Christopher. St. Oliver (Olave) Silver St.,
London. Joyner; P Si. 4 yrs. Pa. 33 S. 6 July, 1728
9

221   BETTERTON, Thomas. Cricklade, Wilts. R Wh. 5 yrs.
Md. 16 S. 1 Dec. 1729 48

222 BETTS, Joseph. Litchfield. EC 7 yrs. Md. 15 S.
6 Feb. 1720   19

223 BEVERS, John. St. Georges, Southwark. Weaver;
J BALL. 5 yrs. Md. 27 S. 23 Nov.1727   11

224 BICKNELL, John. North Petherton, Somerset. H Bo.
6 yrs. S. C. 16 S. 30 May,1720   82

BIELFELD. See 191

225 BIGG(S) Sarah. Spittlefields, (London)   Mantymaker;
Elizabeth Ham, mother. SF 4 yrs. Pa. 19 M.
31 July, 1739   92

226 BIGGS, John. Burgate (Margate?) Nr. Canterbury, Kent.
JT. 4 yrs. St. L. 18 S. 8 Oct. 1722   156

227 BIGNALL, Grace. Ditton, Surrey. Spinster; HR. 5 yrs.
Va. 17 M. 2 Oct. 1719   62

228 BILLINGHURST, Matthew. St. Martins in the Fields, Mddx.
Cook; NM. 4 yrs. Jam. 26 S. 8 Oct. 1735   113

229 BINGHAM, Charles. Allhallows, London Wall. Clerk or
writer. NM 4 yrs. Jam. 22 S. 11 May, 1734   53

230 BINGHAM, Samuell. St. Giles in the Fields. Taylor;
NM. 4 yrs. Jam. 28 S. 6 Oct. 1736   84

231 BINGLE, Joseph. St. Margaret Patten(s) London. Labourer;
NM. 4 yrs. Jam. 26 S. 31 July, 1736   43

232 BIRD, Hannah. St. Andrews, Holbourn, Mddx. Spinster;
TB 4 yrs. St. C. 20 M. 17 July, 1722   55

233 BIRD, John. Tamworth, Staffs. CM 4 yrs. Md. 20
M. 5 May, 1735   34

234 BIRD, Stephen. Hull, Yorks. Cooper; JT. 4 yrs. Jam.
18 S. 29 Nov.1734.   113

235 BIRD, Thomas. St. Sepulchers, London. Brush Maker;
P Si. 4 yrs. Antigua. 35 S. 26 April, 1734   51

236 BIRKHEAD, George. St. Giles, Colchester, Essex. Weaver. WB 5 yrs. Jam. 18 S. 27 Aprill, 1719   7

237 BIRT, Joseph. Froome (Frome) Somerset. Cloath dresser;
NM 5 yrs. Jam. 17 M. 8 Nov. 1736   140

238 BISHOP, John. Asfordby (Ashfordby,) Leics. Tailor; NM.
4 yrs. Jam. 21 M. 31 Dec. 1736   220

239 BISSEY, Anthony. St. Botolphs, Bishopsgate, London. P Si.
4 yrs. Pa. 18 M. 17 Aug. 1728   89

240 BITHIN, Mary. Torsely (Trosley, spelled Trottiscliffe?) Kent.
Spinster. J Wi. 5 yrs. Va. 18. M. 19 April, 1720.   76

241 BLACK, John. Elverton, (Elvetham?) Hants. Coachman;
JD 4 yrs. Pa. 19 S. 7 Oct. 1725   106

242 BLACKABY, John. Waisley (Waresley?) Hunts. Gardner;
NM 4 yrs. Va. 36 S. 28 Oct. 1731   253

243 BLACKMAN, Robert. Richmond, Surrey. Bricklayer; JT
4 yrs. Jam. 22 S. 11 Sept. 1731   202

244 BLACKWELL, James. St. Andrews, Holbourn. Sawyer;
Mother Ann Blackwell. SF 4 yrs. Jam. 21 M. 6 Jan. 1736 19

245 BLACKWOOD, John. Coventry, Warwicks. Cordwainer;
JT 4 yrs. Jam. 18 S. 12 Sept. 1733   56

246 BLADES, Margret. Esscott. Yorks. Spinster; P Si. 4 yrs.
Pa. 19 S. 19 June, 1731   160

247 BLAKE, John. St. Botolphs, Bishopsgate, London. Labourer. NM 5 yrs. Md. 22 S. 7 March, 1733   31

248 BLAKE, Roger. Wootton Bassett, Wilts. JG. 7 yrs. Jam.
17. M. 23 Sept. 1730   121

249 BLACKERBY William. Lynn, Norfolk. Husbandman;
W Bu. 4 yrs. Jam. 40. S. 29 April, 1731   114

250 BLAKEY, Mabell. St. Olaves, Southwark, Surrey. Widow;
CV. 5 yrs. Md. 32. S. 16 Jan. 1722   20

251 BLEW, Richard. Roadley (Rodley) Glos. J BALL. 7 yrs.
Pa. or Md. 15. M. 13 Aug. 1728   80

252 BLISS, Ann. St. Margarets, Westminster, Mddx. Spinster;
WT. 7 yrs. Jam. 17. M. 7 Jan. 1730   12

253 BLISS, Mary. St. Margarets, Westminster, Mddx. WT.
7 yrs. Jam. 14. M. 7 Jan. 1730   16

254 BLISS, Rachel. St. Margarets, Westminster, Mddx.
Spinster. WT. 7 yrs. Jam. 15. M. 7 Jan. 1730   15

255 BLIZARD, John. Overbury, Glos. JT. 6 yrs. Md. 16.
M. 4 Jan. 1719   4

256 BLOOD, Richard. Roadley, (now Rothley) Leics. P Si.
5 yrs. Pa.or Md. 15. M. 29 July, 1728   57

257 BLUNDEN, Thomas. Bristoll. Tavern drawer; father and
mother dead. JT 4 yrs. Antigua or Jam. 17. S.
28 Dec. 1739   130

258 BLUNT, Charles. Nottingham. Carpenter; W Bu. 4 yrs.
Jam. 28. S. 8 Dec. 1730   199

259 BLUNT, Henry. St. Sepulchers (London) Surgeon. NM.
4 yrs. Jam. 35. S. 3 Nov. 1736   121

260 BLUNT, Richard. Prachin, (?) Northants. Husbandman.
JT. 4 yrs. Jam. 18. S. 16 Nov. 1734   109

261 BOAG, John. Kirkwell (wall) Isle of Orkney, Scotland.
P Si. 4 yrs. Jam. 18. S. 17 July, 1733   25

262 BOARDMAN, James. Ingatestone, Essex. W Bu. 7 yrs.
Md. 18. M. 16 Dec. 1729   73

263 BOIZO, Abraham. Stepney, Mddx. WB. 5 yrs. Md. or
Pa. 17. S. 15 Sept. 1719   37

264 BOLDEN, John. St. Saviours, Lambeth, Surrey. JT. 6 yrs.
Jam. 15. S. 16 Oct. 1730   152

BOLTON. See 283

265 BOND, Francis. St. Aus(t)ell, Cornwall. Labourer. SG.
4 yrs. Jam. 23. S. 16 Nov. 1725   169

266 BOND, John. St. Margarets, Westminster. Carpenter.
CV. 4 yrs. Jam. 30. S. 17 Feb. 1724   71

267 BOND, Richard. St. Saviours, Southwark. Writer. NM
4 yrs. Jam. 21. S. 9 Nov. 1736   144

268 BONNER, Francis. Boston, Lincs. Cordwainer. JD.
4 yrs. Md. 21. S. 14 Dec. 1724   95

269 BONNER, Joseph. New Castle Upon Tine, Northumberland.
Surgeon. NM. 4 yrs. Jam. 26. S. 17 April, 1731
     106

270 BONNETH, John. Monmouth, Wales. JT. 8 yrs. Md.
15. M. 14 Oct. 1719   70

271 BONNETT (BUNNETT) Thomas. St. Andrews, Holbourne,
Mddx. Coachman. JT. 4 yrs. Jam. 23. S.
24 Dec. 1724   108

272 BONWICKE, Benjamin. St. Georges, Hanover Square, Mddx.
School master. NM. 4 yrs. Jam. 42. S. 31 Aug. 1736
     68

273 BOO, George. Earkups (?) North Britain. Weaver. Father and mother dead. RS. 4 yrs. Jam. 20. S. 1 Oct. 1736   80

274 BOOKER, John. South Ockendon, Essex. Schoolmaster. NW. 4 yrs. Md. 31. S. 28 Jan. 1738   10

275 BOOKINGHAM, (BUKINGHAM) William. St. Mary Le Bow in Cheapside, London. AC. 5 yrs. Md. 19. S. 22 Nov. 1721   76

276 BOON, John. Bedford and late of Portsmouth, Hants. NM. 5 yrs. Pa. 16. S. 24 Jan, 1735   1

277 BOORER, John. Alberry (Albury) Surrey. JT. 4 yrs. Jam. 20. S. 11 March, 1724   82

278 BOORN, John. St. Martins in the Fields, Mddx. Mother Mary Green. JG. 5 yrs. Jam. 15. S. 7 Sept. 1733
                                                                                            49

279 BOOTH, Elizabeth. Deptford, Kent. Spinster. CV. 5 yrs. Md. 20. M. 16 Nov. 1722   185

280 BORD, Benjamin. St. Mailes, (Michaels?) Lichfield, Staffs. Husbandman. NM. 4 yrs. Jam. 28. S. 5 Oct. 1736
                                                                                            83

281 BOSWELL, Charles. Newport Pagnell, Bucks. Stone Mason. EP. 4 yrs. Jam. 23. M. 23 May, 1738   41

282 BOUFETT, William. Canterbury, Kent. J Bl. 4 yrs. Jam. M. 15 Dec. 1757   19

283 BOULTON, (BOLTON) Daniel. St. Margarets, Westminster. Cooper. NM. 4 yrs. Jam. 22. S. 14 Dec. 1736 202

284 BOURGIER, Ezekiel. Spitlefields, Stepney. Father, William Bourgier. J BALL. 6 yrs. Md. 18. M. 28 Nov. 1727   3

285 BOURGIN, Barnaby. St. Giles in the Fields. Distiller.
NM. 4 yrs. Jam. 26. S. 10 March, 1736   39

286 BOWERS, Jacob. Shadwell, Mddx. WC2 6 yrs. Va.
16. M. 20 Nov. 1729   25

287 BOWERS, Matthew. Stamford, Lincs. Carpenter. JT.
4 yrs. Jam. 25. S. 6 Nov. 1730   172

288 BOWLEY, Isaac. Mansorell, (Mountsorrel?) Leics.
Labrer. R Sy. 6 yrs. on board ship. 16. M.
24 Jan. 1757   8

289 BOWLEY, Samuell. St. Butolph, Aldgate, London. Apothecary and surgeon. NM. 4 yrs. Jam. 21. S.
8 Oct. 1734   96

290 BOWMAN, Edmund. St. Giles, Criplegate, London.
schollar. JG. 4 yrs. Md. 20. S. 13 Sept. 1720   125

291 BOWMAN, Thomas. St. Augustine, Norwich. WC2.
8 yrs. Md. 18. M. 2 Feb. 1729   21

292 BOX John. Ware, Herts. W Bu. 5 yrs. Pa. 18, S.
30 July, 1728   60

293 BOYD, William. St. James Westminster, Mddx. Barber
and peruke maker. J Co. 4 yrs. Jam. 23. S.
26 Nov. 1725   209

294 BOYER, Mary. St. Andrews, Cambridge. JT. 5 yrs.
Va. or Md. 20. M. 2 Nov. 1719   84

295 BRADBURY, John. St. Giles in the Fields. Shoemaker.
TR. 4 yrs. Md. 19. M. 7 Feb. 1750   5

296 BRADBURY, Thomas. Litchfield, Staffs. SG. 5 yrs.
Jam. 17. M. 2 Nov. 1725   137

297 BRADBURY, Zachary. Brumagim (Birmingham) Book-
keeper. J Wh. 4 yrs. Jam. 24. S. 26 March, 1739
63

298 BRADFORD, Jacob. Langport, Somerset. P Si. 6 yrs.
Md. 18. S. 10 Dec. 1729 64

299 BRADFORD, Richard. St. Andrews, Holbourn. Labourer.
NM. 4 yrs. Jam. 19. S. 3 Nov. 1736 126

300 BRADLEY, James. St. Giles, Criplegate, London. TB.
5 yrs. St. C. or L. 16. S. 15 Aug. 1722 97

301 BRADLEY, Joseph. Birmingham, Warwicks. Cutler. NM.
4 yrs. Md. 25. S. 27 Feb. 1733 29

302 BRADLEY, Richard. Dublin. Cooper. NM. 4 yrs.
Jam. 21. S. 16 Nov. 1736 162

303 BRADLEY, William. St. Georges, Hanover Square (London)
Peruke maker. J Bl. 4 yrs. Jam. S. 7 Aug. 1753 22

304 BRADNER, William. St. Dunstans in the West (London)
Gold beater. Father William Bradner. NM. 5 yrs.
Jam. 17. S. 16 Nov. 1736 161

305 BRADSHAW, Robert. Stepney, Mddx. Weaver. JT.
4 yrs. Jam. 26. S. 7 Jan. 1730 13

306 BRADY, Michael. Whitechappell, Mddx. Carpenter and
joyner. NM. 4 yrs. Jam. 20. S. 10 July, 1735 48

307 BRAISE, James. Hampton, Herefordshire. Husbandman.
JG. 4 yrs. Jam. 20. M. 8 March, 1720 29

308 BRANDISH, (BRUNDISH) Thomas. Mendim, (Mendham)
Suffolk. Taylor. NM. 4 yrs. Md. 22. S.
6 Feb. 1733 25

309 BRANTON, William. Thorney, Isle of Ely, Cambs. Cordwainer. JG. 4 yrs. Md. 20. S. 22 Dec. 1729   82

310 BRASON, Jacob. St. Peters a Mancroft, Norwich. Cordwainer. NM. 5 yrs. Jam. 17. S. 9 Aug. 1731   185

311 BRAUGHAL (EL), Christopher (fer). Kildrocker (Kildrought?) (Co. Kildare) Ireland. Stocking weaver. WT. 4 yrs. Jam. 19. S. 2 Feb. 1730   39

312 BRAY, John. Richmond(d), Surrey. JG. 4 yrs. Va. 18. M. 27 Oct. 1720   164

313 BREEDEN Richard. St. Andrews, Holbourn, Mddx. JT 4 yrs. St. L. 19. S. 2 Oct. 1722   139

314 BRIAN (BRYAN), Lewis. St. Butolphs, Bishopsgate, London. SF. 4 yrs. Jam. 19. S. 16 Dec. 1734   118

315 BRIDGER, Isaac. Brighthelmston (Brighton), Sussex. Husbandman. NM. 4 yrs. Jam. 33. S. 20 Aug. 1730   77

316 BRIDSON, John. Kerkudbright (Kirkudbright) Galloway, Scotland. Labourer. JT. 4 yrs. Jam. 19. S. 4 Feb. 1719   33

317 BRIGHT, Henry. Limington (Lymington), Hants. Barber. JT. 4 yrs. Jam. 19. M. 16 Jan. 1721.   7

318 BRIGHT, Henry. St. Martins in the Fields, Mddx. CP. 2 yrs. Md. 24. S. 26 June, 1733   20

319 BRIGHTON, Thomas. Colchester, Essex. Weaver. R Wh. 4 yrs. Md. 20. M. 19 Nov. 1729   23

320 BRIGHTWELL, Elizabeth. St. Edmunds Bury (Bury St. Edmunds), Suffolk. Spinster. CV. 4 yrs. St. C. 20. S. 17 July, 1722   58

321 BRIGHTWELL, Frances. St. Andrews, Holbourn, London. spinster. Father Benjamin Brightwell. W Bu. 4 yrs. Pa. 17. S. 19 Feb. 1735   8

322 BRITTAIN, Charles. St. Andrew Holbourn, Mddx. Coachman. CV. 4 yrs. Va. 19. M. 4 April, 1720   61

323 BRITTAIN, James. Ringwood, Hants. JD. 6 yrs. Md. 18. M. 26 Sept. 1723   101

324 BROADGATE, Edward. St. Andrews, Holbourn, London. Taylor. J BALL. 4 yrs. Va. 21. S. 21 Nov. 1727   17

325 BROADWAY, Rowland. St. Georges, Hanover Square. Book keeper. J Cr. 4 yrs. Jam. 19. S. 30 Nov. 1750
44

326 BROCK, William. City of Bristol. Labourer. JG. 4 yrs. Va. 17. M. 27 Oct. 1720   163

327 BRODIE, George. Alginay (Elgin?), Moray, Scotland. Sadler. JT. 4 yrs. Jam. 21. S. 28 March, 1734 37

328 BROOKBANKS, John. St. Andrews, Holbourn, London. W Bu. 8 yrs. Md. 16. M. 30 Dec. 1729   88

329 BROOKE, Henry. Nantwich, Cheshire. A poor lad. JD 8 yrs. Pa. 15. M. 23 June, 1720   87

330 BROOKES (BROOKS), John. St. Andrews, Holbourn, Mddx. JD. 6 yrs. Md. or Pa. 17. S. 19 Jan. 1719   14

331 BROOKS (BROOKE), Charles. Chere (Clare?) Market,London. Taylor and staymaker. WD. 5 yrs. Va. 19. S. 3 May, 1751   56

332 BROOKS, George. Wisbitch (Wisbech) Isle of Ely, Cambs. A poor lad. J Wi. 7 yrs. Va. 15. M. 6 April, 1720
66

333   BROOKS, John.   Aveley (Alveley), Salop.   Schoolmaster.
        JS.   4 yrs.   Jam.   S.   31 July, 1754   20

334   BROOKS, Samuel.   Manchester, Lancs.   Cordwainer
        NM.   4 yrs.   Md.   23.   S.   19 Dec. 1729   80

335   BROOM, Mary.   St. Andrews, Holbourn, London.   P Si.
        4 yrs.   Pa.   19.   M.   19 June, 1731   161

336   BROUGHTON, Joseph.   Hacklescourt (Hugglescote?), Leics.
        Husbandman.   Father at Burcherton (Barkestone?), Leics.
        MW.   4 yrs.   Jam.   20.   M.   19 Oct. 1738   56

337   BROUGHTON, Thomas.   Leicester.   Gardner.   Father and
        mother dead.   SF.   4 yrs.   Jam.   16.   S.   21 Dec. 1739
                                                                   128

338   BROWN, Adam.   St. Andrews, Norwich.   JD.   6 yrs.
        St. L.   16.   M.   10 Oct. 1722   159

339   BROWN, Ambrose.   Poplar, Parish of Stepney, Mddx.
        Gardner.   JT.   4 yrs.   St. C. or St. L.   19.   M.
        4 Aug. 1722   71

340   BROWN, Benjamin.   White Ruden (Roding) Essex.   Carpen-
        ter.   WC.   4 yrs.   Pa.   21.   S.   24 July, 1728   48

341   BROWN, Daniel.   Stepney, Mddx.   Gardner.   WC2.   4 yrs.
        Pa.   20.   S.   8 July, 1728   14

342   BROWN, Dennis.   Chelsea, Mddx.   CV.   4 yrs.   St. C. or
        St. L.   18.   M.   14 Aug. 1722   95

343   BROWN, Elizabeth.   Portsmouth, Hants.   Spinster.   BD
        5 yrs.   Pa.   20.   M.   22 Sept. 1720   134

344   BROWN, George.   Offerton (Ollerton), Notts.   JD.   5 yrs.
        Md.   18.   M.   12 Oct. 1719   68

345   BROWN, George. Rippon, Yorks. Barber. W Bu. 4 yrs.
      Md. 21. S. 8 Sept. 1731.   198

346   BROWN, George. Appleby, Leics. Husbandman. NM.
      4 yrs. Jam. 21. S. 13 Dec. 1736   199

347   BROWN, Hishersay. Nottingham. P Si. 4 yrs. Jam.
      18. M. 12 Aug. 1731   187

348   BROWN, James. New Castle Upon Tine, Northumberland.
      Butcher. AW. 4 yrs. Jam. 20. S. 16 Dec. 1724
                                                           100

349   BROWN, James. Dean, Lancs. J Le. 4 yrs. Sherbro
      River on the Coast of Africa. 18. S. 5 July, 1734
                                                            63

350   BROWN, James. Whitechappell, Mddx. Labourer. NM
      4 yrs. Md. 24. S. 23 March, 1735   13

351   BROWN, John. Kirbeen.(Kirkbean) Galloway, N. Britain.
      AC. 7 yrs. Md. 15. M. 13 Aug. 1718   35

352   BROWN, John. Whitechappell, Mddx. JD. 7 yrs. Md.
      17. M. 7 Dec. 1719.   105

353   BROWN, John. New Windsor, Berks. Labourer. JT
      4 yrs. Md. 18. S. 26 March, 1720   51

354   BROWN, Jonathan. St. Stephens, Bristol. Joyner and
      cabinet maker. J BALL. 5 yrs. Md. 23 S. 24 Nov.
      1727   7

355   BROWN, Jonathan. Sudbury, Suffolk. Peruke maker and
      barber. NM. 4 yrs. Jam. 26. S. 23 Dec. 1736   208

356   BROWN, Nathaniel. St. Margarets, Westminster, Mddx.
      Labourer. JG. 4 yrs. Md. 21. M. 24 Sept. 1724. 54

357 BROWN, Richard. Ticknell, Derbyshire. JD. 8 yrs. Md.
15. M. 23 Aug. 1720 112

358 BROWN, Richard. St. Michaels at Coslena (Coslany),
Norwich. Weaver. JG. 5 yrs. Barb. or Va. 19 M.
26 July, 1721 58

359 BROWN, Richard. Maer, Staffs. JD. 6 yrs. St. C. or
St. L. 15. M. 14 Aug. 1722 94

360 BROWN, Robert. St. Anns, Westminster, Mddx. Groom.
JG. 4 yrs. Md. 19. M. 3 Nov. 1731 257

361 BROWN, Robert. Lewton (Luton), Beds. Gardner. NM.
4 yrs. Jam. 28. S. June 1, 1734 60

362 BROWN, Samuel. Ipswich, Suffolk. AC. 6 yrs. Md.
or Pa. 18. S. 5 Feb. 1719 36

363 BROWN, Thomas. Embury (Amesbury?) Wilts. EC. 4 yrs.
Md. 20. M. 25 Sept. 1719 52

364 BROWN, Thomas. St. Andrews, Holbourn, Mddx. JG.
7 yrs. Md. 16. S. 30 Dec. 1719 115

365 BROWN, Thomas. Blandford, Dorset. Husbandman. JT.
4 yrs. Jam. 20. M. 28 July, 1730 63

366 BROWN, Thomas. Wandsworth, Surrey. Husbandman.
NM. 4 yrs. Md. 24. S. 15 Dec. 1730 211

367 BROWN, Thomas. St. Anns, Westminster, Mddx. Bricklayer. JG. 4 yrs. Jam. 19. M. 26 Oct. 1733 101

368 BROWN, Thomas. Bishops Stor(t)ford, Herts. Carpenter
and sawyer. J. Pa. 4 yrs. Va. 17. M. 6 Feb. 1749
7

369 BROWN, William. Rolchester ? Norwich. Weaver. JT
4 yrs. Md. 20. M. 15 Dec. 1722 193

370   BROWN, William. Lambeth, Surrey. Gardner. NM.
4 yrs. Jam. 21. S. 3 Oct. 1735   97

371   BROWN, William. Maryland. Labourer. J Pr. 4 yrs.
Md. 25. M. 10 Dec. 1736   195

372   BROWN, William. Edenburgh. Cooper. JS. 7 yrs.
Va. 18. S. 20 April, 1751   50

373   BROWNING, Elizabeth. Norrill (Northill?) Beds. Spinster.
P Si. 4 yrs. Pa. or N. Y. 18. M. 10 July, 1728 24

374   BROWNING, Elizabeth. Biglesworth (Biggleswade?) Beds.
P Si. 4 yrs. Pa. 20. M. 17 June, 1731   157

375   BROWNING, Mary. Partnal (Pertenhall?) Beds. Spinster.
CV. 7 yrs. Va. or Md. 18. M. 4 March, 1720 28

376   BROWNLOW, Thomas. St. James Westminster, Mddx.
Labourer. WT. 4 yrs. Jam. 22. S. 22 Feb. 1730
                                                  85

377   BRUFF, Mary. St. Giles, Criplegate, London. Spinster.
JD. 4 yrs. Pa. 19. M. 7 Oct. 1725   105

BRUNDISH. See 308

378   BRYAN, Humphrey. St. Dunstans, Stepney, Mddx. TB.
4 yrs. St. C. or St. L. 18. S. 13 Aug. 1722   90

BRYAN (Lewis). See 314

379   BUCK, Robert. Stamford, Lincs. JG. 5 yrs. Jam. 19
M. 4 Nov. 1725   151

380   BUCKENHAM, Edward. Garboldisham, Norfolk. Husbandman. NM. 4 yrs. Jam. 28. S. 13 Dec. 1736 198

381   BUCKLER, Richard. Northampton. NM. 4 yrs. Md.
18. S. 4 Sept. 1735   75

382 BUCKLEY, Robert. New Brandford (Brentford) Mddx. JG
7 yrs. Md. 18. S. 14 Feb. 1732   2

BUKINGHAM. See 275

383 BULL, Edward. St. Peters in Cornhill, London. JT. 4 yrs.
St. C. or L. 18. S. 15 Aug. 1722   98

384 BULL, Miles. Shrewsbury, Salop. JT. 4 yrs. Jam.
20. S. 6 April, 1722   33

385 BULLAN (D), Richard. Maidstone, Kent. JG. 4 yrs.
Jam. 19. S. 18 May. 1725   94

386 BULLEN, Joseph. Allhallows, London Wall. Mother, Mary
Bullen. Barber. NM. 6 yrs. Md. 16. S. 16 Dec.
1730.   218

387 BULLEY, Thomas. Portsmouth, Hants. Blacksmith. NM,
5 yrs. Md. 24. M. 11 Jan. 1737   4

388 BUN, Allen. Allows (Allhallows) the Great, Thames St.
W. Bu. 5 yrs. Md. 16. M. 13 Feb. 1729   28

389 BUN, William. Carl(e)ton, Norfolk. Brickmaker. P Si.
4 yrs. Pa. 17. M. 9 June, 1731   146

390 BUNN, John. Dorc(h)ester, Dorset. Saddler. NW. 4 yrs.
Jam. 24. S. 27 Feb. 1738   36

BUNNETT. See 271

391 BURBIDGE, Thomas. St. George's Southwark, Surrey. JD.
6 yrs. Md. 19. S. 26 Jan. 1724   25

392 BURBIDGE, Timothy. Litchfield, Staffs. Husbandman.
JD. 5 yrs. Md. 20. M. 4 Oct. 1725   100

393 BURCH, Anthony. Rotherhithe, Surrey. Gardner. W Bu
4 yrs. Md. 19. M. 11 Feb. 1729   25

394 BURCH, Thomas. Old Radnor, Co. of Radnor, Wales.
Husbandman. JT. 4 yrs. Md. 19. M. 3 Dec. 1720
171

395 BURCHETT, Thomas. Green (now Wisborough Green),
Sussex. Husbandman. JT. 4 yrs. Jam. 20. M.
15 Sept. 1730 104

396 BURDITT, Thomas. Warnfield (Warmfield) near Wakefield,
Yorks. Stonemason. JD. 4 yrs. St. C. or L. 20. S.
7 Aug. 1722 75

397 BURDOCK, George. Gillingham, Norfolk. Husbandman.
NM. 4 yrs. Jam. 34. M. 25 May, 1731 141

398 BURDON, Samuel. Wanstrow, Somerset. JT. 4 yrs.
Jam. 16. S. 8 May, 1735 36

399 BURDUS, Richard. New Castle Upon Tine, Northumberland.
Book keeper. W Bu. 5 yrs. Md. 20. S. 24 Dec. 1734
120

400 BURGES, James. Highgate, Mddx. Carpenter and joyner.
W Bu. 4 yrs. Jam. 25. S. 5 Feb. 1733 23

401 BURGESS, Francis. St. Andrews, Holbourn, London. Cordwainer JT. 7 yrs. Jam. 16. S. 1 Nov. 1733 105

402 BURK, Edward. Deptford, Kent. Brickmaker. W Bu.
4 yrs. Md. 27. M. 8 Sept. 1731 199

403 BURKETT, George. St. Giles in the Fields, Mddx. Carpenter and joyner. JG. 4 yrs. Jam. 31. S. 3 Feb. 1730.
42

404 BURKETT, Thomas. St. Andrews, Holbourn, Mddx. Shoemaker. WB. 4 yrs. Jam. 19. S. 27 April, 1719 8

405 BURKS, Patrick. Dublin, Ireland. Book keeper. Father
and mother dead. J. Wh. 4 yrs. Jam. 18. S. 30 June,
1739 88

406   BURM (BURN) INGHAM, Henry.   Staines, Mddx.   Smith.
JT.   4 yrs. Jam.   21.   S.   14 Aug. 1734   73

407   BURN, John.   Brimrig (?) Northerland(?)   J Cr.   4 yrs.
Jam.   19.   S.   26 Aug.   1749   6

408   BURNARD, Richard.   Little Osborn (Ouseburn) Yorks.   Smith
and farrier.   JT.   4 yrs.   Jam.   27.   S.   25 Sept.   1730
123

409   BURNELL, Charles.   Chichester, Sussex.   JG.   4 yrs.   Jam.
20.   S.   25 May, 1725   93

410   BURNET, William.   St. Botolph, Aldersgate (London)   JT.
4 yrs.   Md.   24.   S.   1 June, 1739   83

411   BURNETT, James.   St. Marys, Shrewsbury, Salop.   P Si.
7 yrs.   Md.   17.   S.   8 Dec. 1731   288

BURNINGHAM.   See 406

412   BURRELL, Ann.   St. James, Westminster, Mddx.   Spinster.
CV.   5 yrs.   Va.   19.   S.   23 July, 1720   96

413   BURRITT, Richard.   Peterborough, Northants.   Groom.
NM.   4 yrs.   Jam.   23.   M.   4 Oct. 1736   81

414   BURT, Elias.   Upton Nr. Slough? Bucks.   CV.   4 yrs.   Va.
20.   S.   20 April, 1720   78

415   BURTON, David.   St. James, Westminster, Mddx.   A poor
lad.   JD.   7 yrs.   Md.   15.   S.   23 Aug. 1718   29

416   BURTON, John.   Lynn, Norfolk.   JT.   6 yrs.   Va.   16.
M.   11 April, 1720   71

417   BURTON, John.   St. James, Westminster, Mddx.   Cordwainer.   W Bu.   4 yrs.   Jam.   37.   S.   17 May, 1734. 55

418   BURWELL, Benjamin. Spalding, Lincs. Husbandman. JG
4 yrs. St. L. 23. S. 6 Oct. 1722   148

419   BUSBY John. St. James, Westminster, Mddx. Clark or
book keeper. R Wh. 5 yrs. Md. 22. S. 4 Dec. 1729
    53

420   BUSH, Thomas. Aldgate, London. Labourer. JT. 4 yrs.
St. C. or L. 40. S. 13 Aug. 1722   85

421   BUSHLIN, John. Casham (Caversham?), Oxon. Labourer.
JT. 4 yrs. Va. 20. M. 10 Sept. 1719   30

422   BUTLER, James. St. Bennet at Pauls Wharf, London.
Fanstick maker. JT. 4 yrs. Jam. 20. S. 14 Aug.
1729   2

423   BUTLER, Joseph St. Georges, Hanover Square. Labourer.
Father and mother dead. J Wh. 4 yrs. Jam. 20. S.
20 Dec. 1737   77

424   BUTLER (BUTTLER) William. Reading, Berks. and late of
St. Lukes without Cripplegate, Mddx. Drawer. W Bu.
5 yrs. Md. 20. S. 21 Jan. 1734   3

425   BUTLER, William. Hitchin, Herts. Husbandman. J Bl.
4 yrs. Jam. no age. M. 11 April, 1753   5

426   BUTT, William. Sudbury (Sodbury), Glos. Husbandman.
J Bl. 5 yrs. Md. no age. M. 21 July, 1753   17

427   BUTTENY, Jacob. St. Dunstans, Stepney. Weaver. NM
4 yrs. Jam. 23. S. 4 Nov. 1736   131

428   BUTTER, William. St. Leonards, Shoreditch, Mddx. RB
6 yrs. Jam. 16. M. 29 Nov. 1725   212

429   BUTTERFIELD, James. St. Giles Criplegate, London.
Clogg maker. WC. 4 yrs. Pa. 22. S. 10 July, 1728
    23

430 BUTTERFIELD, John. St. Clement Danes, Mddx. WC2.
4 yrs. Pa. 16. S. 23 July, 1728   44

BUTTLER. See 424

C

431 CAGE, John. St. Andrews, Holbourn, Mddx. AC. 5 yrs.
Barbados or Md. 17. S. 30 July, 1718   37

432 CAGE, William. Wareham, (Wereham) Norfolk. Husbandman. JT. 4 yrs. Jam. 17. M. 17 June, 1730   53

433 CAIN, Michael. Cobham, Hants. Labourer. JG. 4 yrs.
Pa. 19. M. 21 June, 1722   36

434 CAM, John. St. Luke, Old St . (London). Cooper.
Father Joseph Cam. SF. 4 yrs. Jam. 18. S.
8 Nov. 1739   118

435 CAMBELL, Daniel. Southerland, town of Dunrobin, N. of
Scotland. JG. 5 yrs. Md. 18. M. 26 Aug. 1720. 117

436 CAMBELL, Patrick. Edenborough, Scotland. Husbandman.
JG. 4 yrs. St. C. 18. M. 12 July, 1722   52

437 CAMPBELL, George. Manchester, Lancs. Cordwainer.
J BALL. 4 yrs. Pa. 19. S. 2 July, 1728   1

438 CAMPBELL, John. St. Botolph, Aldgate, London. JG
4 yrs. St. L. 18. S. 5 Oct. 1722   145

439 CAMRON, John. The Highlands of Scotland. Husbandman.
NM. 4 yrs. Jam. 20. M. 26 Aug, 1734   77

440 CANDY, Jacob. Clayhadon (Clayhanger?) Devon.
Husbandman. P Si. 4 yrs. Jam. 19. S. 2 Nov.1731. 256

441 CANE, Maximilian. St. Botolph, Aldgate, London. JG.
4 yrs. St. C. or L. 19. S. 13 Aug. 1722   89

442 CANNON, Edward. Ren ? (Kenn?), Somerset. Gardner.
NM. 4 yrs. Md. 28. S. 3 Dec. 1733   134

443 CANTLE (CANTLIE), Alexander. Town of Mantross
(Montrose?), Scotland. Carpenter and joyner. WT. 4 yrs.
Jam. 42. S. 2 Feb. 1730   40

CANTLIE. See 443

444 CANTWELL, Pearce. Margrove(?) Queens County, Ireland.
NM. 4 yrs. Md. 19. M. 12 Sept. 1735   80

445 CAPLES, Samuel. St. Mary Cray, Kent. JG. 5 yrs.
Va. 17. S. 20 June, 1721   44

446 CAPPER, Thomas. St. Saviour, Southwark, Surrey. JD.
5 yrs. Pa. or Md. 19. M. 24 Sept. 1723   96

447 CARDINALL, Robert. Oundle, Northants. Carpenter and
joyner. NM. 4 yrs. Jam. 21. S. 18 Sept. 1730   114

448 CAREY, John. Ammerson (Amersham?) Bucks. WC.
4 yrs. Pa. 18. S. 14 Oct. 1725   113

449 CARLILE, Charles. St. James, Westminster, Mddx.
Plaisterer. NM. 4 yrs. Md. 34. S. 17 March, 1734
9

450 CARLYANT, Edward. Falmouth, Cornwall. Cooper. JT
4 yrs. Jam. 32. S. 11 Sept. 1731   201

451 CAROUN, Jacob. St. Botolphs Bishopsgate (London).
Weaver. NM. 5 yrs. Md. 23. M. 15 Oct. 1736   91

452 CARPENTER, Benjamin. Rainham, Essex. JT. 5 yrs.
Jam. 17. M. 23 Oct. 1730   161

453 CARPENTER, Henry. St. Michael, City of Dublin, Ireland.
JL. 5 yrs. Md. 17. S. 1 Feb. 1719   27

454 CARPENTER, Henry. Portsmouth, Hants. JT. 5 yrs.
St. C. or L. 16. M. 4 Aug. 1722   84

455 CARPENTER, Job. Paulasperry (Paulerspury) Northants.
JG. 5 yrs. Pa. 18. S. 2 July, 1722   42

456 CARR, Daniel. St. Giles in the Fields. Shoemaker. J Ri.
5 yrs. Va. no age. S. 1 April, 1752   4

457 CARR, Edward. Cooper Sale, Essex. Husbandman. 4 yrs.
Jam. 18. M. 30 Dec. 1729   89

458 CARR, John. Gosport (Hants.) Gardner. JS. 4 yrs. Md.
no age. M. 11 April, 1751   43

459 CARR, Richard. Allhallows in the Wall, London. Bricklayer and plaisterer. Mother Elizabeth Carr. CV. 4 yrs.
Md. 18. S. 11 Oct. 1722   162

460 CARR, Samuel. Allhallows, London Wall. JG. 6 yrs.
Md. 16. S. 7 Oct. 1724   58

461 CARRIER, Thomas. Goodmansfield (?) London. RH. 5yrs.
Va. no age. S. 16 March, 1750   20

462 CARROLL, John. Christ Church, Spittlefields. Weaver.
NM. 3 yrs. Carolina or West Indies. over 21? M.
10 Aug. 1736   52

463 CARROLL, Patrick. Dublin, Ireland. Clerk. MW. 4 yrs.
Jam. 18. S. 2 Oct. 1738   53

464 CARTER, Edward. Exeter. Barber. Father and mother
dead. BW. 5 yrs. Antigua. 18. S. 26 Jan. 1736   31

465 CARTER, James. Stepney, Mddx. JG. 6 yrs. Va.
17. M. 4 Feb. 1720   18

466 CARTER, James. St. Botolphs, Bishopsgate, London.
Bricklayer. J Ta. 4 yrs. N.C. 25. S. 8 July, 1736. 35

467 CARTER, John. St. James, Clerkenwell, Mddx. JG.
7 yrs. Va. 17. S. 7 July, 1721 50

468 CARTER, John. St. George, Southwark. Twine spinner.
JD. 7 yrs. S.C. 18. M. 9 Dec. 1723 119

469 CARTER, Laurance. St. Peters Mounte(r)gate, Norwich.
Throwster. JT. 4 yrs. Jam. 21. M. 16 Nov. 1725. 167

470 CARTER, Robert. Skipton, Yorks. Clerk. NM. 4 yrs.
Jam. 22. S. 11 Nov. 1736 147

471 CARTER, Timothy. St. Peters(?) City of Chester. Carpenter. JT. 4 yrs. Jam. 22. S. 13 Oct. 1731 234

472 CARTER, William. Richmond, Surrey. Sawyer. JT.
5 yrs. Md. 18. S. 24 Nov. 1722 187

473 CARTER, William. St. James, Westminster, Mddx.
Sawyer. NM. 4 yrs. Jam. 30. S. 17 Aug, 1730 73

474 CARTER, William. Northampton. NM. 7 yrs. Md.
16. S. 8 Dec. 1733 145

475 CARTEY, Thomas. Cork, Ireland. Labourer. J Pr.
4 yrs. Md. 23. M. 10 Dec. 1736 196

476 CARTWRIGHT, Thomas. St. Giles in the Fields, Mddx.
Father Thomas Cartwright. JW. 7 yrs. Pa. 14. M.
11 Jan. 1738 6

477 CARTY, Rice. St. Mildred, Poultry. (London) Musician.
Father Jeremy Carty in Ireland. JP. 4 yrs. Jam. 18
S. 25 Oct. 1736 111

478 CARVER, Thomas. Portsmouth, Hants. JD. 6 yrs. Pa.
or Md. 16. M. 24 Sept. 1723 95

479 CARVILL, Benjamin. Northampton. Barber and peruke-
maker. CV. 4 yrs. Va. 20. S. 19 Jan. 1720 8

480 CASE, Chadwell. St. James, Westminster, Mddx. Apothecary. NM. 4 yrs. Jam. 21. S. 17 Jan. 1733   15

481 CASEY, Richard. Ciceter (Cirencester?) Glos. J Bl. 4 yrs. Jam. no age. M. 15 Dec. 1757   20

482 CASEY, Walter. St. Margarets, Westminster, Mddx. Coachman. JG. 4 yrs. Va. 19. S. Last Dec. 1719   117

483 CASSON, John. St. Edmund the King in Lombard St., London. Barber. NM. 6 yrs. Jam. 19. S. 8 Nov. 1731   264

484 CASTER, William. Ryegate (Reigate) Surrey. Poulterer. JT. 4 yrs. Antigua. 24. S. 3 Jan. 1733   8

485 CATTERALL, William. Worcester. Groom. JG. 4 yrs. Md. 22. S. 21 Jan. 1724   11

486 CAWWOOD Richard. St. Botolph by Aldgate, London. NM. 6 yrs. Pa. 19. S. 22 June, 1731   163

487 CHADWICK, Elias. Christ Church Spittlefields, Mddx. W Bu. 6 yrs. Pa. 19. M. 22 March 1735   15

488 CHAMBERLAINE, Thomas. St. John, Wapping, Mddx. P Si. 4 yrs. Pa. 20. S. 27 Sept. 1733   77

489 CHAMBLIT, Samuel. Killingworth (Kenilworth?), Warwicks. JG. 6 yrs. Md. 19. M. 16 Feb. 1724   70

490 CHAMNESS, Anthony. White Chappell, Mddx. J Co. 7 yrs. Md. 15. M. 9 Feb. 1724   62

491 CHAMPION, John. Breadhurst (Bredhurst), Kent. JG. 6 yrs. Va. 19. M. 6 April, 1720   67

492 CHANDLER, Henry. Maidstone, Kent. CV. 5 yrs. Md. 15. S. 5 Feb. 1723   20

493 CHAPMAN, Daniel. Oaken (Ockham?), Surrey. JK. 6 yrs.
Md. 15. M. 4 Aug. 1718. 11

494 CHAPMAN, James. Peterborough, Northants. Peruke
maker. J Di. 4 yrs. Pa. no age. S. 21 Feb. 1757. 12

495 CHAPMAN, William. Northern? Parish of Down, Kent.
Husbandman. W Th. 4 yrs. S. C. 16. S. 25 April
1751 52

496 CHARLTON, Jonathan. Reading, Berks. Cloath worker.
R Wh. 5 yrs. Md. 20. S. 1 Dec. 1729 47

497 CHARNACK, Thomas. Darlington, Durham. Apothecary.
SG. 4 yrs. Md. 22. S. 19 Nov. 1725 188

498 CHARNOCK, William. St. James, Westminster. Labourer.
NM. 4 yrs. Jam. 23. S. 25 Oct. 1736 110

499 CHARTER, Charles. Reading, Berks. Felt maker. JT.
4 yrs. Jam. 36. M. 30 Nov. 1725 215

500 CHARTER (CHATER), Henry. St. Stephen, Coleman St.
London. Tallow Chandler. CV. 4 yrs. Md. 20. S.
18 Jan, 1722 22

501 CHASE, William Hasleham. Sunbry (Sunbury?) Painter.
WJ. 4 yrs. Antigua. no age. S. 27 March, 1758 6

CHATER. See 500

502 CHATFIELD, Thomas. St. Johns, Southwark. Blockmaker.
J Bl. 3 yrs. Nova Scotia. No age. S. May, 1750 19

503 CHATT, Robert. St. Andrews, Holbourn, London. Taylor.
NM. 4 yrs. Va. 37. S. 6 Sept. 1734 82

504 CHELPS, Richard. St. Mary Magdalene, London. J Wil.
5 yrs. Md. 20. M. 22 April, 1751 51

505 CHELTUM, Andrew. Whitleberry (Whittlebury), Forrest, Northants. JT. 4 yrs. Jam. 19. M. 12 March, 1724

86

506 CHENOWETH, John. Murren (St. Merryn?), Cornwall. Cordwainer. JG. 4 yrs. St. C. or St. L. 20. S. 2 Aug. 1722

65

507 CHESHIRE, John. St. Marys, Leicester. W Bu. 4 yrs. Pa. 20. S. 24 April, 1736

22

508 CHESMAN, John. Wadhurst, Sussex. R Wh. 7 yrs. Md. 16. M. 28 Nov. 1729

40

509 CHESSOM, Thomas. Endfield, Mddx. (Enfield) Groom. Father and mother dead. SF. 4 yrs. Jam. 20. S. 21 Sept. 1739

107

510 CHEVALIER, Anthony. Late of France. Shoemaker. NM. 4 yrs. Jam. 24. M. 8 Nov. 1736

138

511 CHIELBY(?) Onesiphorus. Marlborough, Wilts. Plaisterer. Father and mother dead. NM. 4 yrs. Pa. 18. S. 19 Sept. 1738

51

512 CHINNICK, Henry. Diggit, Somerset. Labourer. JD. 4 yrs. Md. 20. M. 15 Sept. 1719

34

513 CHOLMLEY, Thomas. Aldgate, London. JD. 6 yrs. Pa. 16. M. 19 Oct. 1725

117

514 CHRISLEY, James. Selkrig (Selkirk), N. Britain. Clerk. NM. 4 yrs. Jam. 24. S. 15 Nov. 1736

160

515 CHRISTIAN, Thomas. Portsmouth, Hants. P Si. 5 yrs. Md. 19. S. 21 Nov. 1729

27

516 CHRISTOPHER, Charles. The precinct of St. Catherine. Labourer. Father and mother dead. J Wh. 4 yrs. Pa. 19. S. 27 Feb. 1738

39

42

517 CHRISTOPHER, Edward. St. James, Dukes Place, By
Aldgate, London. Book keeper. NM. 4 yrs. Jam. 33
S. 30 Aug. 1733 41

518 CHRISTOPHER, John. Broomgrove (Bromsgrove), Worcs.
Carpenter and joyner. JG. 4 yrs. St. C. 32. S.
10 Sept. 1730. 97

519 CHURCH, Charles. Sheerness, Kent. JG. 6 yrs. Va.
19. M. 14 July 1721 53

520 CHURCH, George. Deptford, Kent. Sawyer. J Ta.
4 yrs. Jam. 25. S. 20 Oct. 1736 103

521 CHURCH, James. Stepney, Mddx. CV. 5 yrs. Md.
16. S. 4 Jan. 1722 13

522 CHURCH, John. St. Olaves, Southwark, Surrey. Cordwainer. JT. 4 yrs. Jam. 20. M. 16 Oct. 1730 153

523 CHURCHILL, Thomas. St. Alphage, London. Labourer.
P Si. 4 yrs. Jam. 21. S. 20 June, 1733 19

524 CHURCHS, John. St. Thomas, Southwark, Surrey. Cordwainer. NM. 4 yrs. Md. 20. M. 15 Dec. 1730 212

CLAITON. See 556

CLARCK. See 536

525 CLARK, Benjamin. Hackney, Mddx. JC. 4 yrs. Md.
or Pa. 17. M. 17 Dec. 1722 194

526 CLARK, John. Woodston(e) Northants. Sawyer. JT.
4 yrs. Jam. 20. S. 6 Feb. 1730 60

527 CLARK, Francis. Dunstable, Beds. Brickmaker. AC
5 yrs. Va. 16. S. 16 March, 1720 32

528 CLARK, Francis. Kettering, Northants. JT. 4 yrs.
St. L. 20. M. 8 Oct. 1722   155

529 CLARK, James. St. Michaels, Coventry. J Wi. 4 yrs.
Md. 19. S. 3 Feb. 1719   32

530 CLARK, John. Gotam (Gotham,) Notts. A poor lad. EF.
7 yrs. Va. or Md. 14. M. Last March, 1720   58

531 CLARK, John. St. Martins in the Fields, Mddx. Glover.
JT. 4 yrs. Jam. 19. S. 16 Oct. 1730   150

532 CLARK, John. St. James, Clerkenwell, Mddx. Bricklayer.
W Bu. 4 yrs. Jam. 19. S. 24 Jan. 1731   2

533 CLARK, John. Markfield, Leics. JG. 4 yrs. Jam. 21.
S. 26 Oct. 1733   102

534 CLARK, John. Thor(n)ton, Cheshire. Husbandman. NW.
4 yrs. Jam. 23. S. 6 June, 1739   87

535 CLARK, John. Bristol. Wheelwright. J Pa. 4 yrs. Jam
no age. M. 8 March 1750   18

536 CLAR(C)K, Joseph. Great Burfleet (Purfleet), Essex.
Labourer. J Wh. 6 yrs. Jam. 16. S. 26 March, 1730.98

537 CLARK, Ralph. Hexham, Northumberland. Taylor. NM.
4 yrs. Jam. 25. M. 13 Sept. 1731   20:

538 CLARK, Richard. Horsham, Sussex. NM. 7 yrs. Md.
15. S. 6 Nov. 1730   171

539 CLARK, Samuel. South Betherton, Somerset PM. 7 yrs.
Va. 18. S. 2 Jan. 1718/19.   1

540 CLARK, Samuel. A native of Boston, New England and late
from Bristol. (a poor lad) JD. 8 yrs. Va. or Md. 15
M. 22 Oct. 1719   77

44

541 CLARK, Thomas. Neborth (Knebworth) Herts. Husbandman. JW. 4 yrs. Jam. 17. S. 15 Nov. 1720   168

542 CLARK, Thomas. St. Dunstans in the West, London. Clerk
JT. 4 yrs. Jam. 17. S. 22 Dec. 1729   81

543 CLARK, Thomas. St. Botolphs, Aldersgate, London.
Carpenter. JT. 4 yrs. Jam. 19. S. 20 May, 1731 135

544 CLARK, Thomas. Crayford, Kent. Butcher. P Si. 4 yrs.
Jam. 26. S. 23 Oct. 1733   95

545 CLARK, William. St. Ann, Westminster. Carpenter
and joyner. JG. 4 yrs. Md. 20. S. 25, Oct. 1725 123

546 CLARK, William. Helpringham, Lincs. NM. 6 yrs.
Jam. 17. M. 18 Aug. 1733   34

547 CLARKE (CLARK), Charles. Hatfield, Herts. Carpenter.
EP. 4 yrs. Jam. 21. S. 22 Nov. 1737   65

548 CLARKE, Daniel. St. Saviour, Southwark (Surrey).
Ivory turner. NM. 4 yrs. Jam. over 21. S.
30 Aug. 1736   66

549 CLARKE, John. Anthony (Antony), Cornwall. NM. 4 yrs.
West Indies or Jam. 31. S. 14 Dec. 1734   117

550 CLARKE, Francis (Frances). St. James Westminster.
Bricklayer. NW. 4 yrs. Jam. 21. S. 12 Sept. 1739
101

551 CLARKE, Thomas. Rowley, Warwicks. Smith. EP.
4 yrs. Md. 25. S. 12 Jan. 1737   5

552 CLARKE, Thomas. Tottenham High Cross, Mddx.
Husbandman. JW. 4 yrs. Jam. 21. M. 10 Nov. 1738
65

553 CLASSON (S), Nicholas. Sittingbourne, Kent. Brickmaker.
J. Co. 4 yrs. Md. 19. S. 26 Oct. 1725 128

554 CLAY, Henry. St. Olaves, Southwark, Surrey. Taylor.
NM. 4 yrs. N. C. 31. S. 13 July, 1736 40

555 CLAY, William. Nottingham. Labourer. NM. 5 yrs.
Jam. 17. M. 8 Nov. 1736 139

556 CLAYTON (CLAITON), Samuel. Woodbridge, Suffolk.
Carpenter. Father and mother dead. J Wh. 4 yrs. Jam.
19. S. 1 March, 1737 24

557 CLAYTON, Towers. Christ Church, Spitlefields, Mddx.
Father Francis Clayton. JG. 7 yrs. Jam. 18. S.
1 Jan. 1730 3

558 CLELAND, James. Kerk (Kirk) of Shots (now Shotts),
Lanark, Scotland. Surgeon and Apothecary. NM. 4 yrs.
Jam. 23. S. 26 March, 1735 12

559 CLEMENT, John. St. Martins in the Fields, Mddx. CV.
7 yrs. Md. 17. M. 5 Dec. 1724 87

560 CLEMENT, John. St. Giles in the Fields, Mddx. WC2.
4 yrs. Pa. 19. S. 23 July, 1728 46

561 CLEMENTS, John. St. Michael, Cornhill, London. Book-
keeper. EP. 4 yrs. Md. 22. S. 15 March, 1737 29

562 CLIFF, Edward. Tenterden, Kent. Apothecary and Surgeon. NM. 4 yrs. Jam. 24. S. 29 Aug. 1735 74

563 CLIFFORD, John. Chippingham (Chippenham), Wilts. JT.
4 yrs. Jam. 19. S. 15 Oct. 1731 242

564 CLIFTON, Mary. Spinster. Richard Bounett of Wye River,
Md. Ship Amity. 5 yrs. S. 15 Nov. 1718 62

565 CLUNE, Thomas. Munster, Ireland. Servant. J Bl. 4 yrs.
Jam. no age. S. 11 April, 1753 6

566   CLYATT, John.   St. Bartholomews by the Exchange, London, Barber and Peruke maker.   Master John Smithson.   Father Edward Clyatt.   NM.   5 yrs.   Va. or Md.   18.   S. 14 Feb. 1732   3

567   COAKER, Jonathan.   Essex.   Bricklayer.   JD.   4 yrs. Jam.   21.   S.   21 Dec. 1724   106

568   COALS, William.   Ringwood, Hants.   NM.   5 yrs.   Md. 20.   S.   9 Dec. 1729   61

569   COAT(E)S, Elizabeth.   Spinster.   Portsmouth, Hants.   JD. 6 yrs.   Md.   17.   M.   9 Oct. 1719   65

570   COBB, John.   Stepney, Mddx.   Weaver.   J BALL.   4 yrs. Pa.   30.   S.   24 July, 1728   50

571   COBB, Michael.   St. Leonards,, Shoreditch.   Bricklayer. NW.   5 yrs.   Md.   27.   S.   19 Dec. 1738   76

COBWELL.   See 577

572   COBIN, George.   St. Johns, Wapping, Mddx.   Carpenter. P Si.   4 yrs.   Jam.   22.   S.   27 Nov. 1730   193

573   COCHRAN, Mary.   St. Martins in the Fields,   Spinster. GJ.   4 yrs.   Jam.   no age.   S.   18 Dec. 1751   68

574   COCKER, Edward.   St. Lukes, Mddx.   Blacksmith.   NM. 4 yrs.   N.C.   29.   M.   8 July, 1736   36

575   COCLE, Oliver.   St. Edmunds Bury (Bury St. Edmunds) Suffolk.   Groom, husbandman.   NM.   4 yrs.   Jam.   38. S.   19 Aug. 1730   69

576   CODRY, George.   Reading, Berks.   Bricklayer.   J Se. 4 yrs.   Jam.   18.   M.   7 Feb. 1754   7

577   COGWELL (COBEWELL) Robert.   New Castle Upon Tine. Pipe maker.   NM.   5 yrs.   Md.   21.   S.   11 Dec. 1729   66

578   COLE, Charles, a native of Jamaica.   P Si.   4 yrs.   Jam.
19.   S.   14 Sept. 1733   62

579   COLE, George.   Lambeth, Surrey.   R Wh.   5 yrs.   Md.
17.   S.   14 Feb. 1729   32

580   COLE, John.   St. Clement Danes, Mddx.   AC.   6 yrs.
Va.   17.   M.   12 Dec. 1719   111

581   COLE, William.   St. Clement Danes, Mddx.   AC.   6 yrs.
Va.   18.   S.   12 Dec. 1719   110

582   COLEMAN, John.   Stepney, Mddx.   Weaver.   R Wh.
5 yrs.   Md.   20.   M.   23 Jan, 1729   11

583   COLES, Richard.   Taunton, Somerset.   Taylor.   J Gi.
5 yrs.   Philadelphia.   17.   M.   31 Aug. 1749   7

584   COLLETT, John.   Berk Hampstead, Herts.   Husbandman.
NM.   4 yrs.   Jam.   28.   S.   3 Jan. 1736   7

585   COLLETT, Thomas.   Stains, Mddx.   Bricklayer.   HE.
5 yrs.   Va.   no age.   S.   19 July, 1754   19

586   COLLEY, James.   St. Giles in the Fields, Mddx.   Smith.
W. Bu.   4 yrs.   Md.   20.   M.   14 Feb. 1729   33

COLLIER.   See 597

587   COLLINGWOOD, John.   St. Clement Danes.   Labourer.
NM.   4 yrs.   Jam.   28.   S.   7 Dec. 1736   189

588   COLLINS, John.   Barnett, Herts.   TB.   4 yrs.   St. C. or
St. L.   19.   M.   9 Aug, 1722   81

589   COLLINS, Michael.   St. Pauls, Shadwell.   Labourer.   J Bl.
5 yrs.   Va.   20.   M.   22 March, 1750   21

590   COLLINS, Richard.   Temple (?) Bristol.   Carpenter.   NM.
4 yrs.   Jam.   21.   S.   31 July, 1735   63

591 COLLINS, Samuel. St. Giles, Criplegate, London. Husbandman. J BALL. 4 yrs. Va. 25. S. 28 Sept. 1727
42

592 COLLIS, Thomas. Aldgate, London. Chair maker. Mother Lettice Collis. WC2. 6 yrs. Md. 19. S. 9 Dec. 1730
203

593 COLLNER, John. St. Mary Aldermary, London. Husbandman. MW. 4 yrs. Pa. 24. M. 7 March, 1738 51

594 COLLUE, Abraham. Stepney, Mddx. Weaver. CV. 5 yrs. Md. 19. M. 11 Feb. 1724
67

595 COLVARD, William. Nottingham. Smith. J Co. 4 yrs. Va. 24. S. 17 Nov. 1725
180

596 COLVENS, John. Chelsea, Mddx. Gardner. J Co. 4 yrs. Jam. 22. S. 29 Nov. 1725
213

597 COLLYER (COLLIER), Thomas. Newport, Salop. Taylor. 4 yrs. Jam. 20. S. 11 Aug. 1730
67

598 COMER, James. Walsam (Walsham?) Norfolk. 5 yrs. Va. or Md. WB. 18. M. 24 Nov. 1719
99

599 COMER, John. Bristol. Husbandman. CV. N. Y. or Carolina. 28. M. 16 Nov. 1724
72

600 CONNELLY, John. Edingborough, North Brittan. Taylor. W Bu. 4 yrs. Jam. 20. S. 8 Aug. 1736
46

601 CONNOR, Cornelius. St. Mary le Bone, Mddx. Groom. JT. 4 yrs. Jam. 19. S. 18 Sept. 1730
113

602 CONNOR, Lawrence (Laurence). Dublin. Husbandman. J Ri. 5 yrs. Va. no age. S. 3 April, 1752
5

603 CONRAN, Edward. St. Clement Danes, Mddx. W Bu. 4 yrs. Pa. 20. S. 8 Aug. 1728
70

604   COOK, Charles.   Bat(t)ersea, Surrey.   Gardner.   W Bu.
4 yrs. Jam.   21.   S.   15 Sept. 1731   212

605   COOK, Edward.   Stowerbridge, (Stourbridge) Worcs.   P Si.
5 yrs.   Pa.   16.   M.   10 Sept. 1730   94

606   COOK, George.   St. Lukes, Mddx.   J Bl.   5 yrs.   Md.
19.   S.   22 March, 1750   24

607   COOK, James.   Putney, Surrey.   Labourer.   P Si.   5 yrs.
Pa.   18.   S.   Last Aug. 1730   84

608   COOK, Joseph.   Wootton under Edge, Glos.   NM.   7 yrs.
Md.   18.   S.   14 Nov. 1730   180

609   COOK, Thomas.   Hereford.   P Si.   8 yrs.   Md.   16.   S.
21 Nov. 1730   184

610   COOK, Thomas.   St. Martins in the Fields, Mddx.   Smith.
P Si.   4 yrs.   Md.   17.   S.   19 Nov. 1733   113

611   COOK, William.   Stone (Stony) Stratford, Bucks.   Labourer.
WC2.   6 yrs.   Md.   19.   S.   6 Jan, 1729   4

612   COOL(L)ING, William.   Burton Peredine (Pedwardine),
Lincs.   Groom.   NM.   4 yrs.   Jam.   22.   S.
3 Nov. 1736   127

613   COOPER, Charles.   St. Margarets, Westminster.   JD.   4
4 yrs.   St. L.   19.   S.   4 Oct. 1722   160

614   COOPER, Elizabeth.   St. James, Westminster, Mddx.
Spinster.   TH.   6 yrs.   Pa.   16.   M.   18 Feb. 1723   30

615   COOPER, John.   Wiggan, Lancs.   W Bu.   7 yrs.   Jam.
15   M.   16 Sept. 1731   213

616   COOPER, John.   St. Martins in the Fields, Mddx.   Labourer.
CM.   4 yrs.   Jam.   20.   M.   16 May, 1735   38

617 COOPER, Nathanial. St. Anns, Westminster, Mddx. WB
7 yrs. Md. 16. S. 27 Aug. 1719   27

618 COOPER, Nathaniel. Windsor, Berks. JW. 7 yrs. Va.
16. S. 23 July, 1720   95

619 COOPER, Peter. Canterbury, Kent. Cordwainer. W Bu.
5 yrs. Ga. 19. M. 3 Oct. 1735   101

620 COOPER, Richard. Bromley, Kent. Carpenter. NM.
4 yrs. Jam. 27. S. 12 Dec. 1734   115

621 COOPER, Robert. Lambeth, Surrey. Taylor. NM. 4 yrs.
N. C. 30. S. 13 Oct. 1730   142

622 COOPER, Thomas. Sheerness, Kent. a poor lad. JD.
8 yrs. Md. 15. S. 9 Dec. 1719   106

623 COPELAND, Christopher. St. Martins in the Fields, Mddx.
JT. 6 yrs. Jam. 16. S. 24 Jan. 1734   4

624 COPELAND, Leonard. Buntingford, Herts. Carpenter.
EP. 4 yrs. Jam. 35. S. 11 April, 1738   32

625 COPELAND, William. Plimouth, Devon. JD. 6 yrs.
Md. 17. M. 22 Aug. 1718   28

626 COPSEY, Roger. Haisted (Halstead?) Essex. Wool comber.
4 yrs. Barb. JW. 19. M. 24 June, 1718   6

627 CORBET (CORBIN), Matthew. St. Georges, Hanover Squ.
Mddx. R Wh. 5 yrs. Md. 18. S. 27 Nov. 1729   35

628 CORBETT, Isaac. St. Giles, Criplegate, London. Carpenter. P Si. 4 yrs. Jam. 24. S. 12 Feb. 1730   57

629 CORBETT, Oswald. Walsall, Staffs. Husbandman. EP.
4 yrs. Jam. 27. S. 11 Nov. 1737   60

CORBIN. See 627

630 CORFIELD, Charles. St. Peters, Cornhill, London. Cook.
JG. 4 yrs. Md. 18. S. 24 Jan. 1722   25

631 CORMACK, William. Wick, Catons (Caithness?) Scotland.
Husbandman. JG. 4 yrs. Nevis. 20. S. 20 June, 1723. 63

632 CORNISH, Isaac. St. Andrews Holbourn. Perriwig maker.
NM. 4 yrs. Jam. 22. S. 20 Nov. 1736   168

633 CORNWALL, Thomas. Caster (Castor) Northants. Wheelwright. Not knowing where his wife is. MW. 4 yrs.
Jam. 29. S. 6 Dec. 1737   75

634 CORNWELL (WALL), Robert. Kensington, Mddx. Gardner.
W Bu. 4 yrs. Md. 20. S. 26 Feb. 1729   39

635 COSNELL, Phillip. St. Andrews Wardrobe (London) Watch
chain maker. Mother Mary Cosnell. NM. 5 yrs. Jam.
19. S. 15 Dec. 1736   203

636 COSSETT, John. Waltham Abbey, Essex. Mother Elizabeth
Tribone Thompson. CV. 4 yrs. St. C. or St. L. 16.
M. 14 Aug. 1722   96

637 COSTER, David. St. Botolphs, Aldgate, London. Labourer. NM. 4 yrs. Md. 22. S. 28 Feb. 1733   30

638 COTEL(E), Samuel. Christ Church Spittlefields, Mddx.
Weaver. NM. 4 yrs. Jam. 27. S. 24 Dec. 1733. 156

639 COTTERILL, Rebecca. St. Leonards, Shoreditch, Mddx.
Spinster. P Si. 4 yrs. Md. 17. M. 8 May, 1731. 130

640 COTTLE, Charles. Shipton Mallard (Shepton Mallet),
Somerset. Husbandman. J Pe. 4 yrs. Jam. 29. M.
18 Feb. 1737   20

641   COTTLE, John. Trowbridge, Wilts. Tallow chandler.
NM. 4 yrs. Md. 20. S. 1 Dec. 1733   128

642   COTTON, George. St. Clement Danes, Mddx. Barber.
MW. 4 yrs. Jam. 22. S. 14 Dec. 1735   115

643   COTTON, John. Allhallows, Lombard St., London. JT.
4 yrs. Md. 20. S. 10 Feb. 1724   65

644   COTTON, Joshua. Bart(h)omly, Cheshire. Husbandman.
P Si. 4 yrs. Md. 29. M. 5 Nov. 1730   170

645   COULSTON, John. Moreland (morland), Westmorland.
Taylor. P S. 4 yrs. Md. 20. S. 3 Nov. 1725   141

646   COULTMAN, Anthony. Durham. Groom. JT. 4 yrs.
Jam. 19. M. 26 July, 1731   174

647   COURT, Richard. St. James Westminster, Mddx. Footman. JG. 4 yrs. St. C. 19. S. 21 July, 1722   63

648   COURTNEY John. Posset (?) Somerset. JT. 4 yrs.
Jam. 37. M. 17 Dec. 1724   105

649   COVILL, Humphry. Holbitch (beach), Lincs. Husbandman. JG. 4 yrs. St. L. 25. M. 6 Oct. 1722   147

650   COW, John. Ware. J Bl. 4 yrs. Jam. no age. M.
Jan. 1756   2

651   COWELL, John. St Peters le Balee (Bailey) Oxford. Groom.
JT. 4 yrs. Antigua or Barb. 19. M. 22 July, 1735 .

         54

652   COWELL, Thomas. St. Botolph, Bishopsgate. J. Pa.
4 yrs. Va. 15. M. 3 Feb. 1749   6

653   COWLES, Thomas. Gloucester. CV. 7 yrs. New
England. 16. S. 16 April, 1724   48

654   COWPER, James.   St. Clement Danes, Mddx.   Taylor.
NM.   4 yrs.   Jam.   24.   S.   18 Aug. 1730   74

655   COX, John.   Trowbridge, Wilts.   Plaisterer and Tyler.
W Bu.   4 yrs.   Jam.   20.   S.   3 Nov. 1729   10

656   COX, John.   Singleton, Sussex.   Carpenter.   JT.   4 yrs.
Jam.   19.   S.   7 Nov. 1733   109

657   COX, Joseph.   Thame, Oxon.   Cooper.   NW.   4 yrs.
Jam.   21.   S.   15 Dec. 1739   127

658   COX, Samuel.   Liverpool, Lancs.   NM.   5 yrs.   Barb.
17.   S.   12 March, 1732   11

659   COX, Thomas.   Trowbridge, Wilts.   Cloath worker.   TB.
4 yrs.   St. C. or St. L.   19.   S.   13 Aug. 1722   92

660   COX, William.   Pensutt, Nr. Bristol.   EE.   5 yrs.   On
board any ship.   16.   S.   2 Sept. 1757   14

661   COYD, Thomas.   Leominster, Hereford,   Carpenter and
Joyner.   EP.   4 yrs.   Jam.   30.   S.   18 March, 1730.   97

662   CRADDOCK, George.   St. James Westminster, Mddx.   JG.
7 yrs.   Md.   16.   S.   1 Feb. 1724   39

663   CRADDOCK, Thomas.   St. Dunstans in the West, London.
Taylor.   CV.   4 yrs.   Md.   20.   S.   15 Sept. 1720.   128

664   CRAGG, Richard.   Rotherhith, Surrey.   Labourer.   Father
and mother dead.   MW.   5 yrs. Pa. or Jam.   19.   S.
19 Sept. 1739   104

665   CRAGG, Thomas.   St. Bartholomews the Great, London.
Buckle maker.   JG.   4 yrs.   Jam.   22.   S.   19 Oct. 1731
246

666   CRAKE, William.   Boyton (Beighton?) Norfolk.   Husbandman.   NM.   4 yrs.   Md.   31.   M.   14 Dec. 1730   209

667 CRANFIELD, Henry. St. James Westminster, Mddx. 4 yrs.
Va. 20. S. 27 Jan. 1720   10

668 CRANFURD, John. Irvan (Irvine) Ayrshire. Surgeon.
J Pa. 4 yrs. Jam. 20. S. 1 Sept. 1750   37

669 CRANSTONE, John. St. Botolphs Bishopsgate, London.
Cordwainer. JT. 4 yrs. Jam. 19. S. 30 Dec. 1730
                                                                   207

670 CRAVEN, James. Harrow on the Hill, Mddx. Joyner.
JT. 4 yrs. Jam. 19. S. 29 July, 1731   175

671 CRAVEN, Thomas. Stepney, Mddx. P Si. 4 yrs. Pa.
18. S. 26 July, 1728   51

672 CREAK, Joseph. St. Olaves, Southwark, Surrey. Hat-
maker. JD. 5 yrs. Md. or Pa. 17. S. 8 Feb. 1719. 56

673 CREED, Thomas. St. George, Southwark, Surrey. Sawyer.
CV. 5 yrs. Md. 21. M. 2 March, 1722   42

674 CREEK, Thomas. Market Debin (Deeping?), Lincs. J Bl.
4 yrs. Jam. no age. M. 15 Dec. 1757   18

675 CREESE, William. Bristol. Corck cutter. J Ta. 4 yrs.
Jam. 22. S. 13 Oct. 1736   90

676 CRESSE, Isaac. Bednall Green (Bethnall Green?) Mddx.
Labourer. w Bu. 4 yrs. Jam. 21. S. 5 Oct. 1736. 82

677 CREW, Humphrey. Froom (Frome) Somerset. Mason.
WT. 4 yrs. Jam. 21. S. 21 Jan. 1730.   31

678 CRICHTON, James. Glenyla (Glenisla) Shire of Angus in
Scotland. JG. 4 yrs. Va. 17. S. 16 Aug. 1721   65

679 CRICKET, John. Margate, Kent. Taylor. JJ. 3 yrs.
Va. 20. S. 27 Aug. 1718   49

680 CROFT, Edward. TV. 5 yrs. On board the Hopewell.
No age. M. 4 Jan. 1757   1

681 CRONEY, John. Penzance, Cornwall. Taylor. JG. 4 yrs.
Md. 25. S. 24 Nov. 1725   202

682 CROOKE, (CROOK), John. St. Benedict, Broad St., London.
Joyner. MW. 4 yrs. Pa. 22. S. 26 May, 1738. 45

683 CROOKSHANKS, William. St. James, Westminster.
Servant. TP. 4 yrs. Jam. no age. M. 2 Oct. 1755   10

684 CROSHOW, Hugh. Chesterfield, Derbyshire. Blacksmith
and farrier. NM. 4 yrs. Barb. 29. S. 8 Feb. 1737.
13

685 CROSS, Henry. St. Nicholas, Warwick. AC. 5 yrs. Md.
18. M. 20 Jan. 1718   2

686 CROSS, Joseph. St. Olaves, Hart St., London. Packer?
. AC. 4 yrs. Md. 20. S. 27 Sept. 1720   138

687 CROSS, Richard. North Curry, Somerset. JD. 6 yrs.
Md. 16. M. 24 Sept. 1719   45

688 CROSS, Thomas. Northampton. Shoemaker. Mother
dead. NW. 3 yrs. Md. or any other plantation. 18. M.
23 Aug. 1739   98

689 CROSSNALL, Andrew. Shenster (Shenstone) Staffs. Labourer. R Wh. 5 yrs. Md. 20. M. 26 Nov. 1729   33

690 CROSSWHART(?) Ephraim. Whitehaven (Cumberland)
Smith and farrier. MW. 4 yrs. Antigua. 23. S.
20 Dec. 1737   78

691 CULBORSON, Lawrence. St. James, Westminster, Mddx.
JT. 5 yrs. Jam. 17. M. 10 Aug. 1731   186

692 CULLEN, William. Dublin, Ireland. Taylor. JG. 5 yrs.
Md. 19. S. 3 Feb. 1723 16

693 CULLON, William. Maxfield (Mangotsfield?), Glos. JD.
5 yrs. Md. 19. S. 10 Oct. 1724 61

694 CULVER, John. Puck(e)ridge parish of Standon, Herts.
Blacksmith. JG. 4 yrs. Jam. 19. M. 22 March, 1722
46

695 CUNNINGHAM, William. Belfast, Ireland. Gardner.
J Bl. 4 yrs. Jam. 30. S. 4 July, 1750 28

696 CUNNIS, John. St. Martin at Pallace, Norwich. JD.
7 yrs. Md. 19. M. 13 Jan. 1721. 5

697 CURD, John. Stepney, Mddx. Weaver. JD. 5 yrs.
Md. 20. S. 3 Feb. 1723 15

698 CURRELL, George. Haxham (Hexham), Northumberland.
Gardner. W Bu. 4 yrs. Jam. 16. S. 1 Feb. 1730. 35

699 CURTIS, John. St. Michaels, Crooked Lane, London.
Wire worker. NM. 4 yrs. Jam. 21. S. 8 Oct. 1735
110

700 CUSHOE, John. Burntwood (Brentwood), Essex. Labourer.
SG. 4 yrs. Md. 30. M. Nov. 1725 168

701 CUTTS, Christopher (Christopear), A native of Danzick and
late of Hadley, Worcs. Gardner. NM. 4 yrs. Jam.
26. S. 30 March, 1734 38

D

702 DAGLIS, Samuel. Bear St. (?) Norfolk. RB. 6 yrs. Pa.
or Md. 17. S. 17 Feb. 1723 29

703 DALLYNER, John. St. Mary, Devizes, Wilts. CV. 6 yrs.
Md. 17. S. 15 Jan. 1724 1

704 DANDEY, Edward. Wilersey, Warwicks. J BALL. 6 yrs.
Pa. 16. M. 6 July, 1728   7

705 DANGERFIELD, Elizabeth. Aldgate, London. Spinster.
WB. 6 yrs. Pa. 19. M. 5 May, 1719.   11

706 DANIEL(E), John (Jen). Canterbury, Kent. W Bu. 4 yrs.
Antigua. 18. S. 21 Aug. 1728   92

707 DANIEL, Jonathan. Stepney, Mddx. Carpenter. Master
Robert Cofell. JG. 4 yrs. Md. 19. S. 5 Oct. 1725
                                                                  102

708 DANIEL, Thomas. Keir (Kyre?) Worcs. JD. 5 yrs. Va.
16. M. 19 Oct. 1720   155

709 DARBY, Francis. Salisbury. Husbandman. NM. 4 yrs.
Jam. 24. S. 20 Oct. 1736   101

710 DAREY, Robert. Dublin. J Bl. 5 yrs. Md. 20. S.
26 March, 1750   12

711 DARNELL, Robert. St. Mary White Chappell, Mddx.
Barber and perrywig maker. JT. 4 yrs. Jam. 21. S.
11 Oct. 1733   90

712 DASS, Thomas. St. Giles in the Fields. Servant. JS.
4 yrs. Md. no age. M. 11 April, 1751   39

713 DAVENPORT, William. Ipswich, Suffolk. J Bl. 4 yrs.
Jam. no age. S. 21 March, 1758   5

714 DAVIDSON, James. St. Martin in the Fields, Mddx.
Joyner. Father John Davidson. R Wh. 4 yrs. Md. 17.
S. 13 Feb. 1729   30

715 DAVIDSON, John. Inverness, Scotland. Accomptant.
AB. 4 yrs. Md. no age. S. 22 Jan. 1755   3

716   DAVIDSON, Thomas.   Barwick upon Tweed.   Distiller.
W Bu. 4 yrs. Jam. 25. S. 30 April, 1731   117

717   DAVIDSON, William.   Perth, Scotland.   Taylor.   W Bu.
4 yrs. Va. 20. S. 13 Nov. 1727   22

718   DAVIES, Henry.   Welsh Pool, Montgomery, Wales.   Husbandman. W Bu. 4 yrs. Jam. 33. S. 8 Dec. 1730.
              195

719   DAVIS, Benjamin.   St. Martins in the Fields, Mddx.
Smith. NM. 4 yrs. Jam. 20. S. 19 Jan. 1730   27

720   DAVIS, Daniel.   Llanneer (Llanyre) Radnor, Wales.   Husbandman. NM. 4 yrs. Jam. 28. S. 10 Nov. 1731.   271

721   DAVIS, David.   Kidwelly, Carmartham, Wales.   Labourer.
W Bu. 4 yrs. Jam. 19. S. 11 Jan. 1730   21

722   DAVIS, Francis.   Ludlow, Salop.   J BALL. 4 yrs. Md.
or Va. 15. M. 4 Dec. 1728   111

723   DAVIS, John.   L(l)angardock, Carmarthanshire, Wales.
JD. 4 yrs. Md. 20. M. 1 Feb. 1719   24

724   DAVIS, John.   St. Leonards, Shoreditch, Mddx.   Weaver.
CV. 4 yrs. Md. 20. M. 18 Sept. 1723   92

725   DAVIS, John.   Maidstone, Kent.   JT. 6 yrs. Jam. 19.
S. 16 Oct. 1730   151

726   DAVIS, John.   St. Botolph by Aldgate, London.   Sawyer.
P St. 4 yrs. Jam. 20. S. 9 Feb. 1732   1

727   DAVIS, Mary.   St. Andrews, Holborn, Mddx.   Spinster.
JD. 6 yrs. Md. 17. M. 18 Aug. 1718   15

728   DAVIS, Mary.   St. Johns, Wapping.   Spinster.   Father
dead. James Forward of London, Merchant. 5 yrs. Md.
16. S. 3 July, 1739   89

729 DAVIS, Philip. Michaelstone (stow), Cornwall. J Bl.
5 yrs. **Va.** 19. S. 11 March, 1752   2

730 DAVIS, Richard. Llanbedanvon (Llanbadarnfawr?) Cardigan,
Wales. JD. 4 yrs. Md. 19. S. 6 Sept. 1722   120

731 DAVIS, Thomas. St. Catherines, Gloucester. JT. 4 yrs.
Md. 18. S. 15 Aug. 1718   34

732 DAVIS, Thomas. Cadon (?) City of Hereford. Husbandman. JT. 4 yrs. Jam. 20. M. 4 Dec. 1732   13

733 DAVIS, Thomas. Exeter. WL at present in London.
4 yrs. **Va.** no age. S. 22 June, 1750   24

734 DAVIS, William. Taunton dean, Somerset. Cordwainer.
TB. 4 yrs. Md. 22. S. 19 Jan, 1722   24

735 DAVIS, William. St. Giles in the Fields, Mddx. Bricklayer. JT. 4 yrs. Jam. 18. M. 12 July, 1723   64

736 DAVIS, William. Ross, Herefordshire. P Si. 6 yrs.
Md. 16. S. 1 April, 1731   101

737 DAVISON, James. Cambridge, Cordwainer. NM.
4 yrs. Md. 21. S. 19 Dec. 1729   80

738 DAVIDSON (DAVISON), Thomas. St. Martins in the Fields,
Mddx. Taylor. JG. 4 yrs. Va. 18. S. 21 Jan. 1719
15

739 DAVISON, Thomas. Windsor, Berks. Cordwainer. P Si.
4 yrs. Pa. 20. M. Last July, 1728   61

740 DAVISON, William. Boston, Lincs. Baker. NM. 4 yrs.
Md. 28. S. 13 Sept. 1735   88

741 DAWKINS, Jeremiah. Epping, Essex. Barber and peruke-
maker. NM. 4 yrs. Md. no age. S. 14 Dec. 1730
208

742 DAWSON, Charles. Highgate, Mddx. J Co. 5 yrs. Md.
17. S. 4 Feb. 1724 63

743 DAWSON, John. Lambeth, Surrey. JD. 8 yrs. Md.
15. S. 28 Jan. 1724 31

744 DAWSON, John. Leeds, Yorks. MW. 5 yrs. Antigua.
16. S. 1 Nov. 1738 59

745 DAY, Anthony. Abington (don) Berks. Groom and footman. WD. 5 yrs. Va. 18. S. 10 April, 1751 38

746 DAY, James. Bishopsgate St., London. Blacksmith. JS.
4 yrs. Philadelphia. no age. S. 27 July, 1751 58

747 DAY, John. Allhallows the Great, London. CV. 5 yrs.
Md. 18. S. 28 Nov. 1722 188

748 DAY, John. Shoreditch, Mddx. Glass polisher. SG.
4 yrs. Md. 25. M. 18 Nov. 1725 185

749 DAY, Joseph. Bedford. Writer. Father and mother dead.
JT. 4 yrs. Jam. 20. S. 20 Nov. 1739 121

750 DAY, Mary. St. James, Westminster, Mddx. Widow.
P Si. 4 yrs. Md. 30. S. 6 May, 1731 129

751 DAYE, John. Scoul(t)on, Norfolk. NM. 4 yrs. Jam.
19. S. 21 Aug. 1736 58

752 DAYNES, William. St. Giles, Norwich. Weaver. JT.
4 yrs. Md. 20. S. 12 Sept. 1722 126

753 DEACRES, James. St. James, Clerkenwell. J Bl. 7 yrs.
Va. 17. S. 29 March, 1750 16

754 DEAKS, John. Salop. Cooper. S Wh. 4 yrs. Jam.
20. M. 14 Oct. 1737 52

755 DEAN, Jacob. Sapsud (probably Sawbridgeworth) Herts.
NM. 5 yrs. Va. or Md. 17. S. 28 July, 1735   58

756 DEAN, Thomas. Bishop Stafford (Bishop's Stortford), Herts.
Husbandman. NW. 4 yrs. Jam. 20. S. 9 Nov. 1738
63

757 DEEPUP, John. St. John Baptist, Peterborough, Northants.
Barber and peruke maker. JD. 4 yrs. Barb. 18. S.
22 Nov. 1720   169

758 DEICKMANN, August Gerhard. Einbeck, Hannover.
Surgeon. JS. 4 yrs. Jam. 20. S. 31 July, 1753. 20

759 DELAMAR, Peter Alexander. Stepney, Mddx. Weaver.
P Si. 4 yrs. Pa. 20. M. 16 June, 1731   156

760 DELBRIDGE, Edward. Dunster (Somerset). Taylor. J Cr.
4 yrs. Va. no age. S. 14 May, 1750   22

761 DELLEBERE, Henry. St. Sepulchers, London. Brother-in-
law Joseph Woolveston. JT. 7 yrs. Jam. 14. S.
28 Nov. 1733   121

762 DELLER, Thomas. New Win(d)sor, Berks. Labourer. SF.
6 yrs. Jam. 18. S. 5 March, 1738   48

763 DENNEVALL, Robert. Christ Church London. JT. 4 yrs.
Jam. 19. S. 9 July, 1730   59

764 DENNISWOODS, Edward. Or Edward Dennis Woods.
Low Layton (Leyton?), Essex. JD. 7 yrs. Va. or Md.
16. S. 3 Feb. 1720   16

765 DENT, James. St. Mary Magdalene, Bermondsey, Southwark, Surrey. Carpenter. JT. 5 yrs. Md. 22. S.
3 April, 1735   16

766 DENT, William. Penrith, Cumberland. Sadler. JT.
4 yrs. Jam. 19. S. 11 March, 1729   46

767 DEPLICH, Benjamin. Manchester, Lancs. Joyner and
cabinet maker. JT. 4 yrs. Jam. 19. S. 25 May, 1731
140

768 DESTER, Thomas. Lynn, Norfolk. Husbandman. NW.
4 yrs. Jam. 21. S. 31 Oct. 1739 117

769 DEVERALL, Daniel. Gloucester. Brick and tile maker.
JS. 4 yrs. Jam. no age. S. 19 Oct. 1752 8

770 DEVERELL (ALL), Jonathan. Edwarton (Edwalton), Notts.
JT. 4 yrs. Jam. 16. S. 3 Oct. 1730 131

771 DEVINE, Charles. Carlisle, Cumberland. Husbandman.
JS. 4 yrs. Philadelphia. 20. S. 27 July, 1751 59

772 DEXTER, Ann. St. James, Westminster, Mddx. Spinster.
P Si. 4 yrs. Pa. 17. S. 11 June, 1731 147

773 DEZADRE, Charles. Boulogne, France. Bricklayer.
JD. 6 yrs. Md. 19. S. 18 Nov. 1724 75

774 DICKINSON, Peter. St. Clement Danes, Mddx. Labourer.
CM. 5 yrs. Md. 27. S. 7 April, 1735 19

DICKSON. See 782

775 DIGHTON, Benjamin. St. Martins in the Fields, Mddx.
Father and mother, William and Elizabeth Dighton. IS.
7 yrs. Md. 16. S. 9 Jan. 1723 5

776 DIMMERY, Daniel. Westerly (leigh), Glos. JT. 4 yrs.
Jam. 17. M. 12 Oct. 1731 229

777 DIMORE (DYMOER), Daniel. Bristol. Barber. CV. 4 yr.
St. L. 20. S. 8 Nov. 1722 180

778 DISNEY, John. Wisbitch (Wisbech), Isle of Ely, Cambs.
JG. 4 yrs. Md. 28. S. 20 Jan. 1723 10

779   DIX, John. Abington, Berks. P Si. 4 yrs. Jam. 20.
       S. 10 Nov. 1730   175

780   DIX, Wellborn. St. Clement Danes, Mddx. Patten maker.
       J BALL. 4 yrs. Pa. 34. S. 9 July, 1728   17

781   DIXON, George. Woolwich, Kent. A poor lad. JD.
       9 yrs. Md. 12. M. Last Sept. 1719   59

782   DIXON (DICKSON), John. Dilston, Northumberland.
       Bricklayer. P Si. 4 yrs. Va. 27. S. 30 Sept. 1727
                                            43

783   DIXON, John. St. Lukes, Old St. (London). Girdler.
       J Wh. 5 yrs. Va. 21. S. 30 Dec. 1737   73

784   DIXON, Richard. Burton near (in) Kendal, Westmorland.
       JG. ·4 yrs. St. C. 17. M. 13 July, 1722   53

785   DIXON, William. St. Giles Cripplegate, Mddx. JD.
       8 yrs. Md. 15. M. 12 Sept. 1719   31

786   DIXON, William. Rochester, Kent. J Bl. 4 yrs. Jam.
       no age. S. 14 Nov. 1754   23

787   DOBBINS, Henry. St. Margarets, Westminster, Mddx.
       Callendar. NM. 4 yrs. Antigua. 23. S. 17 April,
       1734   47

788   DOBSON, James. St. Edmunds Bury (Bury St. Edmunds),
       Suffolk. Joyner. 4 yrs. Pa. 19 S. 16 June, 1731   155

789   DOBSON, Thomas. Pocklington, Yorks. Shoemaker.
       NW. 4 yrs. Jam. 23. S. 6 June, 1739   86

790   DOBSON, William. St. Peters, Colchester, Essex. Weaver.
       TB. 4 yrs. St. L. 20. M. 12 Oct. 1722   164

791   DOCHESTER William. Kennit (Kennett) Wilts. Husband-
       man. W Bu. 4 yrs. Jam. 28. S. 20 Oct. 1731   249

792 DOGGETT, Thomas. Cambridge. Plumber. NM. 4 yrs.
Jam. 18. S. 27 Nov. 1736   177

793 DOLBY, Edward. Inglesby (Ingleby) Lincs. Groom and
farrier. P Si. 4 yrs. Jam. 21. S. 1 Nov. 1733   107

794 DOLBY, John. Deptford, Kent. Sawyer. JT. 4 yrs.
Jam. 19. M. 11 Feb. 1722   34

795 DOLLTON, Obediah. Hendon, Mddx. Gardner. NM.
4 yrs. Jam. 24. S. 31 July, 1735   64

DON. See 834

796 DONALDSON, John. Kemnay, Aberdeenshire, Scotland.
JG. 4 yrs. Md. 18. S. 20 Aug., 1718   24

797 DONNIGER, Daniel. Gosport, Hants. Surgeon. CV.
4 yrs. Md. 22. S. 2 March, 1722   40

798 DORWAITE, James. Edenborough in Scotland. Cordwainer. AC. 5 yrs. Md. 20. M. 1 Dec. 1721   79

799 DOUGHTEN, Stephen. Putney, Surrey. Footman. W Bu.
4 yrs. Pa. 18. S. 30 Sept. 1730   129

800 DOUGLAS (S), Charles. Isle of Orkney, Scotland. JT.
5 yrs. Jam. 17. S. 11 Dec. 1731   291

801 DOUGLAS, George. Linton, Tiviotdele (Teviotdale, now
Roxburghshire), Scotland. Scholar. JL. 4 yrs. Va.
18. S. 3 Feb. 1721   13

802 DOUGLAS, John. Deptford, Kent. JD. 4 yrs. St. C or
St. L. 18. S. 4 Aug. 1722   82

803 DOUGLAS, John. St. James, Westminster. T Ca. 3 yrs.
Any ship. 17. M. 19 Nov. 1757   15

DOUGLASS (Robert) See 833

804 DOVER, Mary. St. Martins at Ludgate, London. Spinster.
WB. 4 yrs. Va. 17. S. 22 Sept. 1719   44

805 DOWDING, Edward. Fortinbridge (Fordingbridge), Hants.
Weaver. JG. 6 yrs. Md. 19. S. 6 Feb. 1724   57

806 DOWDY, John. St. Augustine, Norwich (Norfolk). JF.
8 yrs. Md. 16. S. 17 Dec. 1720   174

807 DOWLER, William. St. Mary, Whitechappell, Mddx.
Plaisterer. Master John Ward. WC2. 4 yrs. Antigua.
20. M. 27 Aug. 1728   99

808 DOWLING, John. St. Andrews, Holbourn, London. P Si.
5 yrs. Pa. 16. S. 16 June, 1731   154

809 DOWLING, William. Dublin, Ireland. Barber and peruke
maker. JG. 7 yrs. Jam. 17. S. 6 Aug. 1729   1

810 DOWN, William. Dublin, Ireland, and late from Spithead.
W Bu. 4 yrs. Pa. 18. M. 16 Feb. 1735   5

811 DOWNHAM, Thomas. Woodford, Essex. Leather briches
maker. W Bu. 4 yrs. Pa. 20. S. 15 April, 1735. 30
3

812 DOWNIE, Robert. Glasgow, Scotland. JT. 4 yrs. Jam.
20. S. 15 Dec. 1724   99

813 DOWNING, Arthur. St. Bennetts, Paul's Wharf (London)
Uncle John Cumming. MW. 6 yrs. Jam. 16. S.
22 Nov. 1736   170

814 DRAKE, Peter. Lynn Regis (King's Lynn), Norfolk. Butcher. NM. 4 yrs. Jam. 24. S. 20 Oct. 1736   100

815 DRAKE, Thomas. Bloxham? Nr. Banbury, Oxon. Husbandman. SG. 4 yrs. Antigua. 20. M. 4 Dec. 1728. 110

816 DRAPER, George. Deptford, Kent. Book keeper. NM.
4 yrs. Jam. 25. S. 27 Feb. 1730   96

817   DRAPER, James.   South Hardin (Harting), Sussex.   JT.   4 yrs.
Jam.   18.   M.   12 Oct. 1733   91

818   DRAPER, Thomas.   St. James, Westminster.   JD.   4 yrs.
Md.   17.   M.   20 Aug. 1718   26

819   DRAPER, William.   St. Peters, Colchester, Essex.   JD.
5 yrs.   Md.   18.   M.   15 Aug. 1718   32

820   DREW, John.   Dublin, Ireland.   SG.   7 yrs.   Va.   15.
S.   16 Nov. 1727   21

821   DREZEY, Thomas.   Bristol.   Vintner.   JT.   4 yrs.   Jam.
21.   S.   20 Dec. 1733   155

822   DRING, Francis.   Chalberry (Charlbury), Oxford.   P Si.
4 yrs.   Md.   19.   M.   6 Dec. 1733   141

823   DROSE, John.   Colchester, Essex.   Weaver.   A CASH.
4 yrs.   Nevis or St. C.   19.   M.   6 Nov. 1729   13

824   DRUCE, John.   St. Clements in the Strand.   Shoemaker.
Father and mother dead.   J Wh.   5 yrs.   Md.   17.   S.
29 March, 1739   65

825   DRUMMER, Robert.   St. Saviours, Southwark, Surrey.   JG.
8 yrs.   Va. and Md.   15.   M.   18 Aug. 1718   14

826   DRUMOND John.   North Sheils (Shields), Northumberland.
J BALL.   4 yrs.   Antig.   18.   S.   5 Dec. 1728   113

827   DUBBERLEY, (DULBERLY)William.   Sodbury? Glos. JD. 5yrs.
Md.   19.   S.   2 Feb. 1724   40

828   DUBOURDIEU, Charles.   Sa(w)bridgeworth , Herts.   Book-
keeper.   NM.   4 yrs.   Jam.   17.   S.   6 Oct. 1731.   227

829   DUCROW, Stephen.   Birmingham, Warwicks.   Cutler.
NM.   4 yrs.   Jam.   25.   S.   16 May, 1735   39

830   DUDLEY, George. Hackney, Mddx. Brickmaker. JT.
4 yrs. Md. or Va. 18. M. 29 Nov. 1733.   123

831   DUDLEY, James. Darkin (Dorking?), Surrey. P Si. 7 yrs.
Md. 16. S. 27 Sept. 1730   194

832   DUFFIN, Edward. Ayston, Rutland. Baker. JG. 4 yrs.
St. L. 23. M. 6 Oct. 1722   148

833   DUGLAS (DOUGLASS), Robert. Aberdeen, Scotland. (A
poor lad.) CV. 7 yrs. Jam. 15. S. 2 June, 1721. 38

834   DUN (DON), James. Isle of Ely, Cambs. Bricklayer.
NW. 4 yrs. Jam. 29. S. 15 Dec. 1739   125

835   DUNGAN, John. St. Philips, Bristol. Taylor. JG. 4 yrs.
Jam. 24. S. 9 March, 1724   81

836   DUNK, John. Dover, Kent. NM. 5 yrs. Md. 15.
M. 1 Dec. 1733   132

837   DUNN, Andrew. St. Andrews, Holbourn, Mddx. Cordwainer. J BALL. 4 yrs. Pa. 20. S. 11 July, 1728 33

838   DUNN, John. Whit(t)lesey, Isle of Ely, Cambs. P Si.
5 yrs. Md. 17. S. 28 Feb. 1732   9

839   DUNN, William. Dublin, Ireland. Weaver. R Wh.
5 yrs. Md. 20. S. 1 Dec. 1729   46

840   DUNSTON(E), George. St. Martins in the Fields, Mddx. Cook.
JG. 4 yrs. Md. 21. S. 3 Dec. 1729   52

841   DUPONT, Francis. A native of France. Joyner. J Co.
4 yrs. S. C. 20. M. 17 Nov. 1725   178

842   DUTY, Thomas. Hull. VM. 4 yrs. Antigua. No age.
S. 2 March, 1758   4

843   DYE, Henry. St. Giles, Norwich. Weaver. JG. 5 yrs.
Md. 21. M. 31 Dec. 1729   91

844   DYER, Robert. Wells, Somerset. JT. 5 yrs. Md. 18
M. 28 Nov. 1729   39

845   DYMER, Charles. St. James, Westminster, Mddx. Labourer. AC. 5 yrs. Va. 20. S. 12 Dec. 1721   82

DYMOER. See 777.

846   DYSON, William. St. Andrews, Holbourn, Mddx. TB.
4 yrs. St. C. or St. L. 18. S. 2 Aug. 1722   66

847   DYSON, William. Bristol. Rope maker. JG. 4 yrs.
Md. 21. S. 9 Nov. 1724   71

E

848   EADES, Laurance. Glastonbury, Somerset. Husbandman.
WC2. 4 yrs. Pa. 19. M. 29 July, 1728   55

849   EARL, Thomas. Kingston Upon Thames, Surrey. Gardner.
P Si. 4 yrs. Pa. 19. S. 21 June, 1731   162

850   EARLE, Joseph. Warrington, Lancs. W Bu. 6 yrs. Pa.
19. S. 24 April, 1735   33

851   EAST, John. East Smithfield, London. Groom. Father
and mother dead. MW. 5 yrs. Md. 15 March, 1737
                                     31

852   EASTON, Thomas. Cannongate, Edinburgh, Scotland.
Baker. JT. 4 yrs. Md. 19. S. 1 Dec. 1719.   102

853   EATON, John. St. Annes, Westminster, Mddx. Wine
cooper. NM. 4 yrs. Jam. 29 S. 13 Oct.1733. 92

854   EBBERNATHY, William. Sunderland, Durham. Glazier.
JT. 4 yrs. Md. 18. M. 16 Nov. 1723   110

855   EBISON, Thomas.   St. Mary le Strand, Mddx.   Barber
and peruke maker.   P Si.   4 yrs.   Jam.   22.   S.
31 Aug., 1733   45

856   ECCLES, Griffin.   St. Johns, Worcester.   Surgeon and
apothecary.   NM.   4 yrs.   N. C.   24.   S.   12 July, 1736
                                                   39

857   EDGAR, John.   Lanham (Langham?), Suffolk.   JD.   6 yrs.
Md.   18.   M.   5 Sept. 1720   119

858   EDGEN, Henry.   Foden Bridge (Fordingbridge,) Hants.
Barber and peruke maker.   JG.   6 yrs.   Va.   19.   S.
18 April, 1720   73

859   EDGERTON, George.   St. James, Westminster, Mddx.
Coachman.   WC2.   4 yrs.   Md.   19.   M.   31 Dec. 1728
                                                 123

860   EDIN, Thomas.   Devizes, Wilts.   Carpenter.   JT.   4 yrs.
Jam.   23.   S.   25 May, 1731   139

861   EDWARDS, Edward.   Siron Cester (Cirencester,) Glos.
Perriwigmaker.   ST.   4 yrs.   Jam.   20.   S.   8 Dec. 1736.
                                                193

862   EDWARDS, Francis.   Audlin (Audlem,) Cheshire.   W Bu.
5 yrs.   Md.   18.   S.   27 Jan. 1729   18

863   EDWARDS, Isaac.   St. Butolphs, Aldgate, London.   JT.
6 yrs.   Jam.   17.   M.   Last Oct. 1734   105

864   EDWARDS, John.   Whittington, Salop.   Taylor.   JT.
4 yrs.   Md.   18.   S.   25 Aug. 1720   114

865   EDWARDS, John.   Shrewsbury, Salop.   JG.   5 yrs.   Pa.
17.   M.   30 June, 1722   41

866   EDWARDS, John.   St. Margrets, Loathbury, London.   JT.
4 yrs.   Jam.   18.   M.   16 Jan. 1729   7

867 EDWARDS, John. Chester. JT. 4 yrs. Jam. 20. S.
30 Jan. 1729   20

868 EDWARDS, John. Covent Garden (London) Servant.
J Bl. 5 yrs. Md. no age. S. 18 Nov. 1755   11

869 EDWARDS, Mary. St. Giles in the Fields, Mddx. Spinster. P Si. 4 yrs. Pa. 20. S. 2 July, 1728   2

870 EELLS, Robert. St. Andrews, Holbourn, London. Farrier.
P Si. 4 yrs. Jam. 25. M. 25 Sept. 1733   74

871 EGELLTON, Richard. St. James, Westminster, Mddx.
Labourer. JT. 5 yrs. Jam. 19. S. 16 Nov. 1732. 12

872 EGLETON, Francis. Stepney, Mddx. Labourer. Father
and mother dead. J Wh. 5 yrs. Jam. 17. M.
12 Dec. 1739   124

873 ELAM, Thomas. St. Andrews, Holborn. Labourer.
Mother Ann Sellers. SF. 4 yrs. Jam. 17. S.
6 Sept. 1739   99

874 ELBONE, Henry. Market Harborough, Leics. JD. 7 yrs.
Md. 16. M. 15 Aug. 1718   33

875 ELLIOT(T), Thomas. New Castle Upon Tine, Northumberland. Bricklayer. J BALL. 4 yrs, Jam. 25. S.
6 Dec. 1728   115

876 ELLIS, John. Rotherham, Yorks. JG. 4 yrs. St. C.
17. S. 11 July, 1722   51

877 ELLIS, John. Little St. Bartholomew, London. JT. 4 yrs.
St. C. or St. L. 18. S. 6 Aug. 1722   73

878 ELLIS, Mark. York. Labourer. W Bu. 4 yrs. Jam.
26. S. 11 Feb. 1730   53

879 ELLIS, Samuel. St. Andrews, Holbourn, London. Gunsmith. W Bu. 4 yrs. Jam. 27. S. 18 July, 1733. 27

880 ELLIS, Thomas. Crookhorn (Crewkerne?) Somerset. JD.
6 yrs. Md. 16. M. 1 Sept. 1722   116

881 ELLIS, William. Leeds, Yorks. Cloth dresser, P Si.
5 yrs. Md. 20. S. 3 Dec. 1729   50

882 ELLISTONE, Ambrose. Ballington (don,) Essex, now in
Suffolk. Bricklayer. NM. 4 yrs. Jam. 23. S.
5 Nov. 1736   134

883 EMBERG (Y?), John. Sneed (St. Nedes or St. Neots, now
in Hunts?) Father and mother dead. JT. 4 yrs. S. C.
16. M. 20 Feb. 1737   21

EMBERY. See 883

884 EMMETT, Catherine. Bristol. Spinster. J Pa. 4 yrs.
Va. 20. M. 31 Jan. 1749   2

885 EMPEROR, Charles. St. Stephen, Norwich Weaver.
JT. 4 yrs. Jam. 20. M. 10 Nov. 1729   18

886 EMPERSFIELD. Hartley Row, Hants. Gardner. NM.
4 yrs. Jam. 21. S. 1 Jan. 1736   5

ENGEILFELD See 887

887 ENGLEFIELD, John (ENGEILFELD) St. Georges, Bloomsbury. Apprenticed to Clement Taylor of same parish,
smith. SW. 4 yrs. S. C. 15. S. 11 Oct. 1736   87

888 ENGLISH, James. St. James Dukes Place (London)
Taylor. NM. 4 yrs. Jam. over 21? M. 30 Aug. 1736
65

889 ENGLISH, Jane (Jean INGLIS) Edingburgh. MW. 4 yrs.
Md. 20. S. 24 Oct. 1738   57

890 ENZOR, John. St. Mary, White Chappell, Mddx. JD.
7 yrs. Md. 18. S. 8 Aug. 1720 100

891 ERWIN (IRVIN,) Laurence. Glascow, Scotland. Cutler.
W Bu. 4 yrs. Jam. 20. S. 4 Sept. 1735 77

892 ESSEX, James. Christchurch, Spitlefields, Mddx. P Si.
5 yrs. Pa. 17. S. 27 Sept. 1733 76

893 ESSEX, Mary. Christ Church, Spitlefields, Mddx. Spinster.
P Si. 4 yrs. Pa. 19. M. 27 Sept. 1733 75

894 ESTAPP, John. E(a)rnley, Sussex. Husbandman. JG.
4 yrs. St. C. 26. S. 1 Jan. 1722 5

895 ETHERTON, James. St. Brides, Fleet St., London. JT.
4 yrs. Jam. 18. S. 6 Nov. 1733 108

896 EVANS, Daniel. St. Margarets, Westminster, Mddx.
Labourer. P Si. 4 yrs. Ga. 20. S. 10 Sept. 1733. 52

897 EVANS, David. St. Giles, Criplegate, London. Distiller.
SS. 4 yrs. Antig. 25. S. 18 Feb. 1730 74

898 EVANS, George. Gloucester. J Bl. 4 yrs. Jam. no
age. S. 2 Jan. 1755 1

899 EVANS, Hugh. Liverpool, Lancs. Sailor. JT. 4 yrs.
Va. 20. S. 10 Oct. 1720 145

900 EVANS, John. St. Michaels, Wood St. London. Glover.
WB. 4 yrs. Md. or Va. 20. S. 8 Oct. 1719 64

901 EVANS, John. Tewksberry, Glos. Cordwainer. JT.
4 yrs. Jam. 20. S. 5 Jan. 1722 9

902 EVANS, John. Biddiford (Bideford,) Devon. P Si. 4 yrs.
Jam. 19. M. 16 Nov. 1731 282

903 EVANS, John. St. Bennets, Gracechurch St., London. Gent.
P Si. 4 yrs. Jam. 23. S. 13 April, 1734 49

904   EVANS, John. Worcester. Carpenter and joyner. HE.
       4 yrs. Va. 21. S. 19 July, 1754   18

905   EVANS, Robert. Hertford. JD. 4 yrs. St. C. or St. L.
       19. S. 9 Aug. 1722   78

906   EVE, William. Canterbury, Kent. Book keeper.
       Mother at Bridge. S Mi. on behalf of John Gale of Jam.
       4 yrs. Jam. 18. S. 25 Oct. 1737   53

907   EVENDEN, Richard. Son of James Evenden late of London.
       Marriner. R Wi. 7 yrs. St. C. No age. S.
       21 Jan. 1754   1

908   EVENS, John. St. Andrews Holeborn, Mddx. JG. 4 yrs.
       Jam. 20. M. 12 Dec. 1730   206

909   EVERETT, Robert. St. Martins in the Fields, Mddx. JD.
       7 yrs. Pa. or Md. 15. M. 18 Sept. 1723   93

910   EVERSDEN, Elizabeth. Foxton, Cambs. Spinster. P Si.
       5 yrs. Md. 27. S. 2 Dec. 1731   287

911   EVOS, John. Rumford (Romford), Essex. JD. 7 yrs. Pa.
       15. M. 15 Oct. 1725   115

912   EWIN, Joseph. St. Mary at Islington, Mddx. Labourer.
       JG. 4 yrs. Jam. 20. M. 5 May, 1731   123

913   EXLEY, George. Knasborough (Knaresborough), Yorks.
       Mason. CV. 4 yrs. Jam. 20. S. 11 Dec. 1722. 191

914   EYLES, Samuel. St. Laurence Jewry, London. Plaisterer.
       P Si. 4 yrs. Barb. 22. M. 30 Oct. 1730   165

                              F
915   FAIRFAX, William. Stanmore, Herts. (Mddx?) J Bl.
       4 yrs. Antigua. No age. M. 8 July, 1755   5

916 FALDO, Robert. St. Nioholas Cole Abbey, London. Butcher. Father John Waters. J BALL. 4 yrs. Antigua. 18. S. 22 Aug. 1728   96

917 FALKENER, John. St. James, Westminster. Labourer. Father and mother dead. NM. 5 yrs. Md. 19. S. 25 Jan, 1736   29

918 FALKNER, Obadiah. Ridgley, Staffs. MW. 4 yrs. Pa. 21. S. 6 July, 1728   12

919 FANNING, Peter. Swords, Co. Dublin, Ireland. JG. 4 yrs. Pa. 20. M. 24 Sept. 1730   122

920 FANTON, John. Lidlington, Beds. Husbandman, S Wh. 4 yrs. Jam. 21. M. 11 Nov. 1737   61

921 FAREY (FEAREY), John. Dean, Beds. Husbandman. P Si. 4 yrs. Pa. 25. S. 25 Sept. 1733   73

922 FARLEY, John. St. Anns Black Fryers, London. P Si. 7 yrs. Md. 16. M. 7 Nov. 1727   27

923 FARMER, Thomas. Stepney, Mddx. AC. 6 yrs. Va. 17. M. 29 Dec. 1721   91

924 FARNBOROW (FORMBOROW), Alexander. Watford, Herts. J BALL. 4 yrs. Pa. or Md. 19. S. 3 Aug. 1728.   64

925 FARNBOROW, Jacob. St. Michaels, Cornhill, London. Joyner and cabinet maker. J BALL. 4 yrs. Pa. 21. S. 9 July, 1728   18

926 FARNELL, Jonathan. St. Pauls, Covent Garden, Mddx. Grocer. NM. 4 yrs. Md. 23. S. 8 April, 1735   20

927 FARQUHER, Alexander. Edenbrough, Scotland. WC2. 4 yrs. Pa. 15. S. 14 Aug. 1728   82

928   FARR, Henry.   Bristol and late of Lambeth, Surrey.   Potter.
P Si.   4 yrs.   Jam.   22.   S.   19 Feb. 1732   5

929   FARR, Thomas.   Holmerry or Stolmerry (?), Herts?   J To.
4 yrs.   Antigua.   no age.   S.   5 Dec. 1756   26

930   FARR, William.   J To.   7 yrs.   Antigua.   No age.   M.
4 Dec. 1756.   25

931   FARRAN, Augustine.   St. Martins in the Fields (Mddx.)
Carpenter.   NM.   4 yrs.   Jam.   28.   S.   1 Jan, 1736.   2

932   FARREL, John.   Newington, Mddx.   Hosier.   Mother and
father dead.   J Wh.   4 yrs.   Pa.   20.   S.   13 Feb. 1738.
    18

933   FARRER, William.   Allhallows, Lombard St. London.
Cloth worker.   NM.   3 yrs.   Carolina or West Indies.
Over 21?   S.   10 Aug. 1736   49

934   FARRINGTON, John.   St. Giles, Criplegate, London.
Vintner.   P Si.   4 yrs.   Jam.   27.   S.   16 Feb. 1730.   69

935   FARROW, Henry.   Coln(e), Lancs.   JT.   6 yrs.   Jam.
17.   M.   30 Oct. 1729   8

936   FARROW, John.   Beccles, Suffolk.   Carpenter.   JT.   4 yrs.
Jam.   19.   M.   2 Feb. 1719   31

937   FARTHING, John.   Lynn, Norfolk.   AC.   7 yrs.   Va.
15.   S.   19 April, 1720   75

938   FAWSETT, Bryan.   St. James, Clerkenwell, Mddx.
Mother Elizabeth Fawsett.   P Si.   8 yrs.   Md.   15.   S.
29 March, 1730   99

939   FAYE, William.   Casham (Caversham?), Oxford.   Bricklayer.   J Se.   4 yrs.   Jam.   20.   S.   7 Feb. 1754   6

940 FEARBY, George. Borrough Bridge and from Hull, Yorks.
JT. 4 yrs. Jam. 19. S. 4 Oct. 1734   98

FEAREY. See 921

941 FEATHERSTON, John. James Deeping (Deeping St. James),
Lincs. Husbandman. JT. 4 yrs. Jam. 20. S.
18 Jan. 1724   8

942 FEBURES, Lewis. A native of France. Labourer. J Co.
4 yrs. S. C. 19. S. 19 Nov. 1725   183

943 FEDDER, Snade. Wrexham, Denbyshire, Wales. Taylor.
W Bu. 5 yrs. Md. 18. M. 16 Dec. 1730   215

944 FEEPOUND, Joseph. St. Mary White Chappell. Butcher.
Master, Thomas Kent. EP. 4 yrs. Jam. 18. S.
8 Feb. 1737   15

945 FELLOWS, Jonathan. St. Mary Woolnorth, London. Distiller. NM. 4 yrs. Jam. 31. S. 21 Aug. 1736   56

946 FELSTEAD, Richard. Dunmow, Essex. Collar maker and
rope maker. NM. 4 yrs. Jam. 26. S. 10 Nov. 1731
272

947 FENLISON, Peter. Edenborough, Scotland. Bricklayer.
JG. 4 yrs. Jam. 20. M. 15 Oct. 1723.   105

948 FENN, Robert. Harbury (Stanborough?) Herts. WD. 5 yrs.
Va. 19. S. 10 April, 1751   37

949 FENNIMORE, William. St. Clement Danes, Mddx. Distiller. JG. 4 yrs. Md. 20. S. 30 Oct. 1725   131

950 FENTON, Alexander. Dundee, North Britain. Surgeon.
Father dead. 3 yrs. Antigua. 19. S. 29 Sept. 1738
52

951 FENWICK, Mary. New Castle Upon Tine, Northumberland. Spinster. JG. 5 yrs. Md. 18. S. 2 Oct. 1723. 104

952 FERGUSON, Mary. Aldgate, London. Spinster. NM. 4 yrs. Md. 22. M. 24 Dec. 1733 157

953 FETHERSTON, Thomas. St. Peters, Colchester, Essex. Book keeper. P Si. 4 yrs. Jam. 26. S. 28 Aug. 1733 36

954 FIELD, Henry. St. Margarets, Westminster, Mddx. Mother, Mary Field. CV. 8. yrs. New England 14. M. 13 April, 1724 45

955 FIELD, John. Northampton. Husbandman. CV. 4 yrs. Md. 24. S. 14 Jan. 1722 16

956 FIELD, Samuel. Chadelwer (Chaddleworth), Berks. Labourer. EP. 4 yrs. Jam. 21. S. 30 Nov. 1737. 68

957 FIELD, William. St. Sepulchers. Cooper. NM. 4 yrs. Jam. 21. S. 25 Nov. 1736 173

958 FIELDER, William. Hembruff, Yorks. JT. 4 yrs. Jam. 18. M. 3 Jan. 1723 1

959 FINCHER, Henry. Hagget Broughton (Broughton Hackett,) Worcs. Bricklayer. P Si. 4 yrs. Pa. 25. S. 6 July, 1728 10

960 FINER, John. St. Andrews, Holbourn, Mddx. JG. 5 yrs. Jam. 17. S. 30 Nov. 1725 214

961 FINN, William. Doncaster, Yorks. Coachman. NM. 4 yrs. Md. 21. M. 3 Jan. 1733 7

962 FINNEY, George. Woolverhampton, Staffs. JG. 7 yrs. Pa. 15. M. 12 Aug. 1728 78

963 FISHER, Joseph. Stowerbridge (Stourbridge,) Worcs. Husbandman. NM. 4 yrs. Jam. 25. M. 20 Sept. 1731 218

964 FISHER, Samuel. Spitlefields   Weaver. Father
and mother dead. JT. 5 yrs. Md. 19. M. 19 Feb.
1738   21

965 FISHER, William. Dublin, Ireland. Carpenter and joyner.
NM. 4 yrs. Jam. 24. S. 26 Sept. 1730   125

966 FITZGERALD (ILD), Thomas. Bath, Somerset. JG. 5 yrs.
Md. 19. S. Last Dec. 1723   126

967 FLATMAN, Thomas. St. Georges, Colegate, Norwich.
Weaver. JG. 4 yrs. Jam. 23. S. 25 Nov. 1725. 205

968 FLEETCROFT, Thomas. St. Catherine Cree Church, London.
Vintner. EC. 4 yrs. Barb. or Md. 19. M. 9 July, 1718
                                                               8

969 FLEETT (FLEET), Abraham. Meer (Mere), Wilts. J Co.
4 yrs. Jam. 21. S. 16 Jan. 1724   5

970 FLETCHER, Charles. Wilsden (Willesden), Mddx. J Ba.
4 yrs. St. L. 18. M. 1 Oct. 1722   136

971 FLETCHER, John. London. T Hu. 4 yrs. on board ship.
no age. S. 5 Jan. 1757   4

972 FLETCHER, William. St. Martins in the Fields, Mddx.
Carpenter. JG. 6 yrs. Md. 22. S. 23 Jan, 1724. 22

973 FLETCHER, William. St. Olaves, Southwark, Surrey.
Cordwainer. 4 yrs. Va. 20. M. 26 Nov. 1730   190

974 FLORA, Thomas. St. Giles Criplegate. JL. 5 yrs. Md.
17. M. Witness Penelope Flora. 1 Feb. 1719.   29

975 FLOWER, Joseph. Windsor, Berks. Husbandman. J BALL.
4 yrs. Va. 22. M. 26 Sept. 1727   39

976 FLOYD, John. Stepney, Mddx. 4 yrs. Barb. JW. 18.
S. 24 June, 1718.   5

977 FLOYD, William. Wormsley (Mousley?) Worcs. Husbandman. P Si. 4 yrs. Jam. 18. M. 6 Aug. 1731   182

978 FLUD, John. Christ Church, Spitlefields, Mddx. Weaver.
JG. 4 yrs. Pa. 20. M. 1 Oct. 1730   130

979 FLUDD, William. St. Margarets, Westminster. Bricklayer.
NM. 4 yrs. Va. 25. M. 4 Jan. 1737   2

980 FLUX, Richard. Cirencester, Glos. Carpenter. EP.
4 yrs. Jam. 28. S. 11 May, 1738   37

981 FODDER, Isaac. Lynn, Norfolk. W Bu. 5 yrs. Pa. 15.
M. 15 April, 1735   31

982 FOLLETT, Francis. St. Mary Overs (Southwark), Surrey.
W Bu. 5 yrs. Md. 20. M. 2 April, 1731   102

983 FORBES, Alexander. White Chappel, Mddx. Butcher.
NM. 4 yrs. Jam. 19. S. 14 Sept. 1731   207

984 FORBES, Thomas. St. Mary le Bow, Cheapside, London.
Watch maker. NM. 4 yrs. Jam. 22. S. 10 Nov. 1731
268

985 FORD, Elizabeth. Canterbury, Kent. Spinster. JG.
6 yrs. Va. 19. M. 9 Aprill, 1720   70

986 FORD, Henry. St. Clement Danes, Mddx. J Bl. 7 yrs.
Md. no age. S. 10 April, 1756   10

987 FORD, John. Battersea, Surrey. Husbandman. W Bu.
5 yrs. Md. 20. M. 8 Dec. 1729   58

988 FORDRED, William. Canterbury, Kent. Tanner. W Bu.
4 yrs. Md. 25. S. 9 Dec. 1730   200

989 FOREMAN, Thomas. St. James, Westminster, Mddx. JT.
4 yrs. Jam. 19. S. 7 Oct. 1725   104

990   FORESIGHT, David. Hampstead, Mddx. JT. 5 yrs.
Jam. 18. M. 13 Feb. 1722   38

FORMBOROW. See 924

991   FORREST, James. St. Pauls, Shadwell. Husbandman.
J Ta. 4 yrs. Jam. 35. S. 20 Nov. 1736   166

992   FORSTER, George. St. Martins in the Fields, Mddx.
Father and mother Thomas and Mary Forster. NM. 7 yrs.
Jam. 15. S. 1 Jan. 1730   2

993   FOSSEY, John. Hertford. Husbandman. NM. 4 yrs.
Jam. 23. S. 20 Oct. 1736   102

994   FOSTER, Elizabeth. St. Olaves, Southwark, Surrey.
Spinster. CC. 4 yrs. Md. 19. M. 12 Oct. 1722   165

995   FOSTER, John. Exeter, Devonshire. JT. 4 yrs. Jam.
19. M. 5 Dec. 1722   189

996   FOSTER, John. Deebridge, Derbyshire. Wheelwright.
JT. 4 yrs. Jam. 33. S. 23 March, 1738   59

997   FOSTER, Joseph. Congleton, Cheshire. CV. 5 yrs. Md.
16. S. 23 Aug. 1722   110

998   FOUNTAINE, Francis. White Chappell, Mddx. SG. 6 yrs.
Jam. 17. M. 2 Nov. 1725   136

999   FOUNTAINE (FOUNTEN), John. Road(e) Northampton.
JT. 7 yrs. Jam. 17. S. 2 Nov. 1727   28

FOUNTEN. See 999

1000   FOWELL, Edmund. St. Martins in the Fields, Mddx.
Vintner. NM. 4 yrs. Jam. 25. S. 29 Dec.1736. 212

1001   FOWELL, James. St. Giles Chayfont (Chalfont St. Giles)
Herts. (Bucks?). J Bu. 4 yrs. St. L. 18. S. 3 Oct.1722
140

1002   FOWKS, William.   St. Marys, Warwick.   Bricklayer.
J Co.   4 yrs.   Jam.   21.   S.   21 Dec. 1724   107

1003   FOWLER, Richard.   Auborne (Aldbourne,) Wilts.   Husbandman.   JG.   4 yrs.   Jam.   26.   S.   9 March, 1724   78

1004   FOX, Abraham.   Christ Church, Spitlefields, Mddx.
Weaver.   NM.   4 yrs.   Md.   31.   M.   1 July, 1735   44

1005   FOX, Elizabeth.   Wombridge, Salop.   Spinster.   Mother,
Mary Clark.   JD.   6 yrs.   Md.   19.   M.   22 Aug. 1720.
111

1006   FOX, George.   St. Lukes, Mddx.   Taylor.   J Bl.   5 yrs.
Md.   no age.   S.   30 July, 1753   19

1007   FOXCRAFT, Hugh,   Peckham, Parish of Camberwell, Surrey.
Shoe maker.   JT.   4 yrs.   Md.   18.   S.   6 Oct. 1720. 143

1008   FOXWELL, Joseph.   St. John, Southwark.   Oremaker.
JW.   4 yrs.   Md.   20.   S.   30 May, 1739   79

1009   FRANCEWAY, Norwood.   Stoney Stratford, Bucks.   Taylor.
WB.   5 yrs.   Md.   17.   S.   18 Aug. 1719   23

1010   FRANCIS, Peter.   Eastlo(o)e, Cornwall.   Cooper.   JT.
4 yrs.   St. C.   19.   S.   19 July, 1722   61

1011   FRANCKLYN, Robert.   Tadnam (Toddenham) parish of
Lemington (?) Glos. Husbandman.   JG.   4 yrs.   Md.   19
M.   23 Oct. 1725   121

1012   FRANKITT, Thomas.   St. James, Westminster, Mddx.
Brickmaker.   JG.   5 yrs.   Pa. or Md.   16.   M.   17 Sept.
1723   90

1013   FRANKLYN (LIN), John.   St. Bartholomews the Great, London.
Cabinet maker.   NM.   4 yrs.   Jam.   22.   M.   28 July, 1735
56

1014 FRANKS, Henry. Feaversham (Faversham,) Kent. A poor
lad and destitute of friends.) JD. 8 yrs. Md. and Pa.
14. M. 19 Jan. 1719.   13

1015 FRANKS, Robert. Tadcaster, Yorks, late of St. Brides,
Fleet St. London. Drawer. 5 yrs. Md. 17. S. W Bu.
21 Jan. 1734   2

1016 FRASER, William. St. Andrews Holbourn, London. Silver
smith. JT. 4 yrs. Jam. 21. S. 12 Dec. 1731   292

1017 FRAZIOR, Elizabeth. St. Anns, Westminster, Mddx.
Spinster. EC. 5 yrs Barb. 19. M. 26 Aug. 1718   50

1018 FREDRICK, Henry. St. Leonards, Shoreditch, Mddx.
Gardner. W Bu. 4 yrs. Jam. 24. M. 12 Oct. 1730. 138

1019 FREEMAN, James. Aberdeen Scotland. Labourer. P Si.
6 yrs. Md. 16. S. 2 Dec. 1729   49

1020 FREEMAN, John. Stockwell, Surrey. Coachman. NM.
4 yrs. Jam. 34. S. 16 Jan. 1736   27

1021 FREEMAN, Samuel. Stepney, Mddx. Brickmaker
J Csn. 4 yrs. Md. 19. S. 18 Nov. 1719   91

1022 FREEMAN, Sarah. Stratford Upon Avon, Warwicks. Spinster. WB. 4 yrs. S. C. 17. S. 20 Oct. 1722.   169

1023 FREESEN, Charles. Wells, Norfolk. Clerk. NM. 4 yrs.
Jam. 22. S. 1 Oct. 1731   220

1024 FRENCH, John. St. Anns, Westminster , Mddx. Butcher.
JT. 4 yrs. Pa. 23. S. 5 July, 1728   5

1025 FRENCH, Joseph. Cree Church, London. W Bu. 7 yrs.
Jam. 16. S. 23 Oct. 1730   160

1026 FRENCH, Richard. Oxford. Chandler. JT. 4 yrs. Jam.
25. S. 15 Nov. 1725   163

1027 FRETWELL, William. Pontefract, Yorks. Tallow chandler. JT. 4 yrs. Jam. 21. S. 5 Aug. 1731 180

1028 FRITH, James. Worsup (Worksop?), Nottingham. Husbandman. JG. 4 yrs. Jam. 19. S. 2 Nov. 1721 70

1029 FRITZ, John Gerald. Hamburg. Surgeon. Wife at Hamburg. 4 yrs. Jam. 43. S. 28 Oct. 1737 55

1030 FROKE, Mary. Ludgate, London. Spinster. WC. 5 yrs. Pa. 19. M. 26 Oct. 1725 127

1031 FROST, Amey. Hadley(leigh), Suffolk. Spinster. JD. 5 yrs. Pa. 19. M. 20 Oct. 1725 119

1032 FROUD, John. Blackshaw, Nithsdale (in Dumfries) Scotland. CV. 4 yrs. Md. 20. S. 24 Aug. 1722. 111

1033 FRY, Edward. Lambeth, Surrey. Carpenter. Master, Edward Scruton. JD. 4 yrs. Md. 19. S. 10 Nov. 1724 74

1034 FRYDAY, John. Chiswick, Mddx. Carpenter. JG. 4 yrs. Antigua. 48. M. 20 Nov. 1725 193

1035 FULLER, Daniel. Stepney, Mddx. Silk weaver. J Co. 4 yrs. Md. 25. M. 17 Nov. 1725 175

1036 FULLER, William. Chelswood (Chelsworth?) Suffolk. J Bl. 4 yrs. Antigua. no age. M. 9 July, 1755. 6

1037 FULLKER, Mary. St. James, Westminster, Mddx. Widow. P Si. 4 yrs. Pa. 25. M. 11 June, 1731 152

1038 FURGUSON, Abel. Queens Co. Ireland. W Bu. 4 yrs. Jam. 19. M. 24 Sept. 1734 89

G

1039   GADSBY, Henry. Brickstock, (Brigstock,) Northants. J De.
5 yrs. Pa. 19. S. 2 March, 1724   76

1040   GALLOWAY, Thomas. Hensom (Ensham?) Oxon. Labourer. JW. 4 yrs. Md. 20. M. 3 March, 1719   44

1041   GAMAN, Richard. Ledbury, Herefordshire. Taylor.
W Th. 4 yrs. S. C. 16. M. 25 April, 1751   54

1042   GANTUM, James. St. Giles in the Fields, Mddx. Barber
and perrywig maker. NM. 4 yrs. Jam. 24. S.
16 May, 1735   40

1043   GANTUM, James. St. Giles in the Fields, Mddx. Barber.
CM. 5 yrs. Md. 22. S. 15 July, 1735   51

1044   GARDINER, Richard. St. Peters, Oxford. Taylor. RC.
4 yrs. Va. no age. S. 4 May, 1753   7

1045   GARDNER, John. St. James, Westminster, Mddx. Painter.
Father, James Gardner. JG. 4 yrs. Md. 19. S.
12 Nov. 1731   280

1046   GARDNER, Richard. Whitechappell, Mddx. SF. 5 yrs.
Pa. 18. M. 22 March, 1735   17

1047   GARFOOT, Jonathan. St. Brides, Fleet St., London.
JT. 5 yrs. St. L. 15. S. 9 Oct. 1722   158

1048   GARNAR, James. Spitlefields, Mddx. JT. 7 yrs. Pa.
or Md. 16. S. 19 Aug. 1735   73

1049   GARNETT, Thomas. He(l)msley, Yorks. JG. 5 yrs.
Md. 19. M. 27 Jan, 1724   29

1050   GARRAD, John. Ashton, Lancs. Smith. JG. 4 yrs.
Jam. 27. M. 11 Aug. 1730   66

1051   GARRAD, Thomas. St. Martins in the Oak, Norwich.
JD. 5 yrs. Md. or Va. 18. M. 3 Nov. 1719   85

1052   GARRAED, William. Westilton (Westleton,) Suffolk. WT.
6 yrs. Jam. 19. M. 4 Jan, 1730   7

1053   GARRETT, William. St. Margarets, Westminster, Mddx.
JT. 7 yrs. Md. 16. S. 8 Aug. 1720   102

1054   GARROTT (GARROT,) St. Giles Criplegate, London.
Needle maker. JT. 4 yrs. Jam. 18. S. 17 Dec. 1733. 152

1055   GARWOOD, Abraham. Flem(p)ton, Suffolk. Taylor.
CV. 4 yrs. Va. 19. S. 4 Sept. 1723   81

1056   GASCOYNE, Thomas. St. Giles Criplegate, London.
P Si. 4 yrs. Jam. 19. S. 26 Oct. 1733   100

1057   GATES, William. St. Mary, Lambeth, Surrey. Mason.
NM. 4 yrs. Va. 36. S. 6 April 1734   43

1058   GATTEN, Hugh. Hevetree (Heavitree,) Devon. JT.
4 yrs. Jam. 18. M. 17 Oct. 1730   155

1059   GATUS (GEATTUS), Alexander. St. Andrews, Holbourn,
London. W Bu. 5 yrs. Md. 19. S. Last Jan. 1733. 19

1060   GAULLTER, Scarlett; St. Andrews, Holborne. Labourer.
MW. 4 yrs. Pa. 22. S. 2 March, 1738   47

1061   GAZELEY, Nathaniel. Congleton, Cheshire. JD. 8 yrs.
Md. 15. M. 9 Sept. 1720   123

GEATTUS (See 1059)

1062   GEE, William. Grantham, Lincs. Cooper. NM. 4 yrs.
Jam. 27. S. 3 Jan. 1733   6

1063   GENTLE, Robert. Creef (Crieff,) Perthshire. JR. 4 yrs.
Jam. No age. S. 17 Oct. 1750   38

1064   GEORGE, Isaac. Sherborne, Hants. Labourer. P Si.
4 yrs. Va. 19. M. 14 Nov. 1730   179

1065 GEORGE, John. Oxford. TB. 5 yrs. St. C. or St. L.
18. S. 14 Aug. 1722   93

1066 GEORGE, William. St. Andrews, Holbourn, Mddx. JG.
4 yrs. Md. 20. S. Last July, 1723   66

1067 GIBB, Alexander. Lithgow (Linlithgow,) Scotland. Cordwainer. P Si. 4 yrs. Md. 31. S. 4 Nov. 1730. 169

1068 GIBBONS, William. Arnsham (Eynsham or Ensham?),
Oxon. Husbandman. JS. 4 yrs. Jam. no age. S.
17 Nov. 1752   10

1069 GIBBS, John. Bristol. Coachman. JG. 4 yrs. Va.
20. S. 22 June, 1721   47

1070 GIBBS, Thomas. Wellingborough, Northants. JD. 5 yrs.
Md. 18. M. 21 Nov. 1719   96

1071 GIBSON, Robert. Durham. Husbandman. JT. 4 yrs.
Jam. 37. S. 7 Jan. 1730   14

1072 GIBSON, Robert. Croydon, Surrey. Gardiner. NM.
4 yrs. Va. or Md. 30. S. 6 Jan, 1736   14

GILBERD. See 1073

1073 GILBERT (D). Claybrook, Leics. AC. 4 yrs. Md.
18. S. 22 Oct. 1719   79

1074 GILES, Robert. FOULSTON (Folkestone?), Kent. JD.
5 yrs. Md. 19. M. 20 Nov. 1723   111

1075 GILLINGHAM, Thomas. St. Martins in the Fields, Mddx.
Cordwainer. P Si. 4 yrs. Pa. 22. S. 9 July, 1728 21

1076 GILLSON, James. Kenton, Devon. JT. 4 yrs. Jam.
18. S. 4 Feb. 1729   22

1077   GINN, Robert. (New) Leam, Cambs. WC2. 4 yrs.
Antigua. 20. M. 21 Aug. 1728   93

1078   GINN, Thomas. St. Giles in the Fields, Mddx. Father,
Richard Ginn. NM. 7 yrs. Md. 16. M. 15 Dec. 1730
      213

1079   GITINS, Thomas. St. Chads, Shrewsbury, Salop. W Bu.
7 yrs. Pa. 18. M. 7 Sept. 1730   90

1080   GLADIN, Richard. St. Andrews, Holbourn, London.
Cordwainer. JG. 4 yrs. Antig. 19. S. 16 Aug. 1728
      85

1081   GLADING, Mary. St. Albans, Wood St. London. Spinster. W Bu. 4 yrs. Pa. 25. M. 20 Feb. 1735. 9

1082   GLADWIN, Richard. Ledbury, Hereford. Carpenter.
JT. 4 yrs. Jam. 19. S. 11 March, 1724   83

1083   GLANCE, David. Edenbrough, Scotland. Groom. SG.
4 yrs. Jam. 19. S. 12 Nov. 1725   157

1084   GLASSUP, Jonathan. Bla(c)kley, Lancs. JD. 8 yrs.
Md. 15. M. 5 Feb. 1723   21

1085   GLENN, William. Allhallows, Barking, London. Cooper.
NM. 4 yrs. Jam. 30. S. 27 Feb. 1730   95

1086   GLOD, Peter. Fulham, Mddx. Gardner. NM. 4 yrs.
Md. 24. S. 10 Feb. 1735   4

1087   GLOVER, John. St. Saviours, Southwark, Surrey. Mother,
Sarah Young. JD. 6 yrs. Md. 16. S. 7 Feb. 1723
      23

1088   GODDARD, Arthur. Richmond, Surrey. JG. 4 yrs.
Antigua. 20. S. 27 Aug. 1728   98

1089   GODFREY, Thomas.   Mary(le)bone, Mddx.   Sawyer.
J Wh.   4 yrs.   Jam.   21.   S.   28 Feb. 1738   41

1090   GODSON, John.   Colebrook, Berks.   (Bucks?)   Cordwainer.
NM.   4 yrs.   Jam.   19.   S.   27 Aug. 1733   35

1091   GODWIN, , Henry.   Sidbury (Sudbury), Derbyshire.
SF.   5 yrs.   Jam.   19.   M.   14 April, 1736   20

1092   GOGANE (GOGARE,) Dominique.   Paris, France.   JT.
4 yrs.   Md.   20.   S.   22 Oct. 1719   76

GOGARE.   See 1092

GOLDSMITH.   See 1120

1093   GONDE, John.   Leicester.   Husbandman.   P Si.   5 yrs.
Jam.   19.   M.   28 Oct. 1731   255

1094   GOOBY, Noah.   Bedford.   NM.   4 yrs.   Jam.   19.
M.   15 Nov. 1736   159

1095   GOOD, James.   Stow Markitt, Suffolk.   JD.   7 yrs.
Md.   18.   S.   Last March, 1722   31

1096   GOODAKARY (GOODAKEREY,) John.   Saklesby (Saxelby,)
Leics.   Husbandman.   JG.   4 yrs.   Jam.   20   S.
1 Aug. 1721   62

1097   GOODALL, Huddlestone.   Wandsworth, Surrey.   Book-
keeper.   Father and mother at Bentham, Yorks.   W Bu.
4 yrs.   Jam.   20.   S.   29 Dec. 1736   215

GOODBURN.   See 1106

1098   NICHOLLS (NICKOLS,) Goodfre(i)nd.   Aison (Aston?)
Bucks.   JD.   6 yrs.   St. L or St. C.   16. S. 20 Aug. 1722
      104

1099   GOODGAME, William.   St. Mary at Hill (London)
Cooper.   EP.   4 yrs. Jam. 27.   S.   8 Feb. 1737   14

1100   GOODWIN, James.   Over Norton, Oxon.   HH at Present
in London and York.   7 yrs.   Jam.   12.   S.   23 Aug. 1749
    4

1101   GOODWIN, William.   Kedlethorp (Kettlethorp) Lincs.
JD.   6 yrs.   Va.   17.   S.   12 Oct. 1720   152

1102   GOODYER, Thomas.   Bishopsgate, London.   JT.   4 yrs.
Md. or Va.   20.   M.   19 March, 1719   47

1103   GOR(R)AD, Henry.   Cher(t)sey, Surrey.   Brickmaker.
JT.   4 yrs.   Jam.   17.   S.   13 Sept. 1734   85

1104   GORAD, John.   Cher(t)sey, Surrey.   Brickmaker.   JT.
4 yrs.   Jam.   19.   S.   13 Sept. 1734   84

1105   GORDEN (GURDEN,) Henry.   Buckingham.   Tallow chandler.   NM.   4 yrs.   Md.   29.   S.   29 Nov. 1733
    125

1106   GORDON (GOODBURN,) George.   Penrith, Cumberland.
W J.   3 yrs.   Antigua.   no age.   S.   8 Dec. 1757   17

1107   GORDON, John.   The Raise of Huntly, Aberdeenshire.
Gardner.   W Bu.   4 yrs.   Jam.   24.   S.   2 Feb. 1730.   38

1108   GORDON, John.   Sh(e)ilds, Northumberland.   Labourer.
Father and mother dead.   BW.   5 yrs.   Antigua.   19.
S.   26 Jan. 1736   33

1109   GORDON, John.   Edinburgh, N. Britain.   Barber and
perriwig maker.   JT.   4 yrs.   Jam.   17.   S.   15 March, 1737
    27

1110   GOREBY, Joseph.   Ansley, Warwicks.   Labourer.   MW.
4 yrs.   Pa.   19.   M.   14 Sept. 1738   50

1111   GORHAM, Samuell.   St. Martins in the Fields, Mddx.
Carpenter.   W Bu.   4 yrs.   Jam.   23.   S.   30 Dec. 1734
                                                                       121

GORRAD.   See 1103

1112   GORWELL, Sackvild.   Fulham, Mddx.   Clerk or writer.
NM.   4 yrs.   Md.   21.   S.   10 Feb. 1735   2

1113   GOSDEN, Richard.   Croyden, Surrey.   JD.   6 yrs.   Md.
16.   M.   24 Sept. 1720   136

1114   GOSS, John.   Holbidge (Holbeach,) Lincs.   JD.   8 yrs.
Md.   15.   M.   10 Dec. 1724   91

GOTEAR.   See 1115

1115   GOTER (GOTEAR) Benjamin.   Christ Church, Hants.
JT.   4 yrs.   Jam.   18.   S.   25 Nov. 1729   31

1116   GOTHER, James.   Liverpool.   Barber and peruke maker.
J Bl.   4 yrs.   Jam.   no age.   S.   20 Nov. 1751   67

1117   GOTTEREY, William.   Middleten (Middletown,) Somerset.   JT.   5 yrs.   Jam.   15.   M.   4 Nov. 1725   152

1118   GOUIN (GOUJON,) Jeremiah.   Dublin, Ireland.   JG.
7 yrs.   Pa.   18.   S.   Last March, 1722   32

GOUJON.   See 1118

1119   GOULD, Edward.   St. Peters, Colchester, Essex.   Carpenter.   JG.   4 yrs.   Jam.   31.   S.   17 April, 1723   54

1120   GOULDSMITH (GOLDSMITH,) John.   St. Olives (Olaves,)
Southwark, Surrey.   Paviour.   JT.   4 yrs.   Jam.   20
S.   25 Feb. 1729   38

1121   GOURE, Jacob.   St. Anns Westminster, Mddx.   JW.   6 yrs.
Md. or Va.   17.   S.   4 Aug. 1720   98

1122   GOVER, John. Tiverton, Devon. J Bl. 5 yrs. Md.
no age. S. 23 Feb. 1750   10

1123   GOWER, John. Newport Pagnell, Bucks. JT. 4 yrs.
Jam. 17. M. 18 Oct. 1729   4

1124   GRAGG, Michael. Dublin, Ireland. Pin maker. JT.
4 yrs. Jam. 19. M. 11 March, 1729   45

1125   GRAHAM, Robert. Fintree, Sterlingshire. AT. 4 yrs.
Md. 20. S. 27 March, 1750   13

1126   GRAHAM, Thomas. Durham. Footman. BW. 4 yrs.
Jam. 19. M. 9 Nov. 1736   142

1127   GRANT, John. Westborough, Warwicks. Miller. JT.
4 yrs. Md. S. 19. 30 May, 1739   76

1128   GRANT, Mungo. Invernesshire. Coppersmith. J Bl.
4 yrs. Jam. no age. S. 9 May, 1753   9

1129   GRANT, Patrick. Edenburg. Book keeper. Daniel
Grant and Alexander Straton, merchants. 3 yrs. Jam. 17. S.
18 Dec. 1750   45

1130   GRAVES, Isaac. Plymouth, Devon. Barber and peruke
maker. NM. 4 yrs. Md. 34. S. 17 Dec. 1730   221

1131   GRAY, Ann. St. Giles in the Fields, Mddx. Spinster.
RJ. 4 yrs. S. C. 19. M. 17 June, 1736   23

1132   GRAY, John. Edenbrough, Scotland. Clark or writer.
W Bu. 4 yrs. Antigua. 27. S. 29 Aug. 1728   102

1133   GRAY, Joseph. Eccles, Norfolk. W Bu. 6 yrs. Md.
16. M. 14 Jan, 1729   6

1134   GRAY, Robert. St. Michael, Cornhill, London. JoB.
4 yrs. Antigua. 14. S. 14 Feb. 1749   9

1135   GRAY, Thomas. Stepney, Mddx. NM. 5 yrs. Va. or Md. 19. M. 1 Jan. 1733   3

1136   GRAY, William. Bristol. Weaver. CV. 4 yrs. Md. 21. S. 22 Jan. 1724   20

1137   GREBBELL, John. Culliton (Colyton?) Devon. Husband-man. W Bu. 4 yrs. Jam. 21. M. 22 Oct. 1731. 251

1138   GREEN, Abraham. Aldgate, London. R Wh. 5 yrs. Md. 19. S. 1 Dec. 1729   45

1139   GREEN, Edmund. Arncliff, Yorks. Smith. NM. 4 yrs. Jam. 27. S. 8 May, 1731   131

1140   GREEN (GRENE,) Giles. St. Clement Danes, Mddx. EC. 4 yrs. Va. or Md. 17. S. 16 Oct. 1719   72

1141   GREEN, Henry. Chidworth (Chedworth,) Glos. Labourer. JT. 4 yrs. Jam. 22. S. 8 Jan. 1730   19

1142   GREEN, John. St. Pauls, Bedford. Baker. JT. 4 yrs. Va. 20. S. 5 Jan. 1721   2

1143   GREEN, Jonathan. Bilper (Belper,) Derbyshire. JT. 7 yrs. Jam. 15. M. 5 Oct. 1733   83

1144   GREEN, Jonathan. Bilford (Milford?) Derbyshire. P Si. 7 yrs. Md. 15. M. 20 Nov. 1733 (See previous item)   115

1145   GREEN, Joseph. Burn (Bourne,) Lincs. Taylor. NM. 4 yrs. Jam. or Barb. 21. M. 22 Sept. 1733.   70

1146   GREEN, Martha. Bishopsgate, London. Widow. CV. 5 yrs. Md. 26. M. 4 Feb. 1724   49

1147   GREEN, Thomas. Northampton. Labourer. JT. 4 yrs. Jam. 19. S. 12 Sept. 1733   55

1148   GREEN, Thomas.   Hampton, Mddx.   Glazier and painter.
NM.   4 yrs.   Pa.   24.   S.   22 March, 1735   18

1149   GREEN, William.   St. Augustine, Bristol.   JT.   6 yrs.
New England.   17.   M.   14 March, 1721   28

1150   GREEN, William.   Worksworth, Derbyshire.   (Wirksworth)
Woolcomber.   JT.   4 yrs.   Md.   20.   M.   7 Sept. 1722
      122

1151   GREEN, William   St. Butolphs, Bishopsgate, London.
Weaver.   NM.   5 yrs.   Va. or Md.   22.   S.
17 Aug. 1734   75

1152   GREEN, William.   Blacknortley (notley,) Essex.   W Wa.
4 yrs.   On board ship.   no age.   S.   12 Dec. 1757   21

1153   GREENING, John.   Aldgate, London.   Cooper.   JT.
4 yrs.   Jam.   30.   S.   29 Jan. 1730   32

1154   GREENLAND, Richard.   St. Leonards, Shoreditch, Mddx.
JT.   7 yrs.   Jam.   14.   M.   17 Nov. 1733   111

1155   GREENWOOD, Joseph.   St. James, Bristol.   AC.   5 yrs.
Va.   18.   S.   27 Dec. 1721   90

1156   GREENWOOD, Miles.   St. Michaels a Cosney (at Coslany,)
Norwich.   Woolcomber.   JG.   4 yrs.   Md.
20.   S.   19 Aug. 1720   110

1157   GREENWOOD, Miles.   Norwich.   Woolcomber.   WT.
4 yrs.   Jam.   29.   S.   19 Jan. 1730   28

1158   GREET, John.   St. Peters, Nottingham.   Barber   H Bo.
4 yrs.   S.C.   18.   S.   8 June, 1720   84

1159   GREGERICK (GUYERICK,) Benjamin.   Litchfield.   Husbandman.   TR.   4 yrs.   Md.   no age.   M.   7 Feb. 1750.   6

1160 GREGORY, Richard. Camberwell, Surrey. Husbandman.
NM. 4 yrs. Jam. 32. M. 12 Nov. 1736   151

GRENE. See 1140

1161 GRIFFIN, John. Coventry, Warwicks. Weaver. CV.
4 yrs. Antigua or Leeward Isles. 21. S. 4 Dec. 1724. 82

1162 GRIFFIS (GRIFFITHS,) John. St. Giles in the Fields, Mddx.
P Si. 7 yrs. Jam. 15. S. 12 Oct. 1730   141

1163 GRIFFIS, John. Labourer. Burnt Wood (Brentwood,)
Essex. J St. 5 yrs. (Md?) 19. M. 1 April, 1751. 33

1164 GRIFFIS, Robert. Carnarvon, Wales. Footman. W Bu.
4 yrs. Md. 20. S. 24 Jan, 1729   14

1165 GRIFFIS, William. Ruhabbon (Ruabon,) Denbigh, Wales.
Carpenter. NM. 4 yrs. Jam. 21. S. 31 July, 1735. 62

1166 GRIFFISS, Griffith. Portalley, Kinervan (Pwllheli, Caern-
arvon?) N. Wales. SF. 4 yrs. Jam. 25. S. 6 March,
1738   49

1167 GRIFFITH, Evan. Cardigan. Husbandman. JS. 5 yrs.
Va. 20. S. 20 April, 1751   49

1168 GRIFFITH, Thomas. St. Annes Westminster. Taylor.
J BALL. 4 yrs. Va. 25. S. 27 Sept. 1727   41

1169 GRIFFITHS, Benjamin. Netherdeen (now Lower Dean,)
Beds. Husbandman. TR. 4 yrs. Md. 19. S.
7 Feb. 1750   8

GRIFFITHS, John. See 1162

1170 GRIMES, Jeremiah. Charley (Chorley,) Lancs. J BALL.
4 yrs. Antigua. 18. M. 10 Dec. 1728   117

1171   GRINDAN (EN,) Samuell. Ross, Herefordshire. JD.
5 yrs. Antigua. 17. S. 31 Jan, 1720   14

1172   GRINSLADE, John. Wyverlescom (Wiveliscombe,) Somerset. Distiller. NM. 4 yrs. Jam. 20. S. 13 April,
1731   103

1173   GRISDELL, Joseph. Blackhill (Blagill?) Cumberland.
Sawyer. His mother in Dublin. W Bu. 4 yrs. Jam.
19. S. 16 Oct. 1736   92

1174   GROVE, Benjamin. Hailsham, Sussex. Barber and perriwig maker. J Ta. 4 yrs. N. C. 24. S. 5 July, 1736.
    25

1175   GROVE, Charles. Petersfield, Hants. Husbandman.
P Si. 4 yrs. Va. 33. S. 14 Nov. 1730   178

1176   GROVE, Gazeley. St. Giles Criplegate, Mddx. Watch-
maker. JT. 4 yrs. Jam. 29. S. 6 Jan. 1730   9

1177   GRUMITT, John. Alford, Lincs. Wheel wright. NM.
4 yrs. Jam. 22. S. 19 Sept. 1730   115

1178   GUEST, Abraham. Laurance, Norwich. JD. 6 yrs.
Md. 18. S. 5 Aug. 1723   69

1179   GUEST, Job. St. Margarets, Westminster, Mddx. P Si.
5 yrs. Jam. 16. S. 27 Feb. 1730.   89

1180   GUINEADEAU, Francis (Fransois Guineandeau) Native of
France and late of Spitlefields, Mddx. Weaver. NM.
4 yrs. Jam. 22. S. 19 Sept. 1735   93

1181   GUINN, John. Monmouthshire. Husbandman. WC2.
5 yrs. Md. 20. M. 5 Jan. 1729   2

1182   GULLIVER, Thomas. Sturminster, Dorset. JT. 4 yrs.
Jam. 17. M. 4 Oct. 1734   91

1183   GUNDY, Samuel.   Great St. Helens, Bishopsgate, London.
        Carpenter and Joyner.   JT.   4 yrs.   Jam.   23.   S.
        23 March, 1738   61

1184   GUNNING, Jose.   Basingstoke, Hants.   Carpenter.   W Bu.
        4 yrs.   Jam.   23.   S.   30 Dec. 1734   123

1185   GUNTER, John.   Abergany (Abergavenny,) Mon.   J Bl.
        4 yrs.   Antigua.   20.   S.   6 March, 1754   13

1186   GUNTER, William.   Green (now Wisborough Green,)
        Sussex.   JD.   5 yrs.   Md.   17.   M. 16 Sept. 1719.   38

        GURDEN.   See 1105

1187   GUY, Isaac.   Temple, Bristol.   (A poor lad.)   JD.   7 yrs.
        Md.   16.   S.   20 March, 1719   50

1188   GUY, Isaac.   Temple, Bristol.   A poor lad.   JT.   8 yrs.
        Md.   16.   S.   30 March, 1720.   54

1189   GUY, Roger.   Windom (Wymondham?) Norfolk.   NM.
        5 yrs.   Md.   18.   M.   10 Jan. 1729   5

        GUYERICK.   See 1159

1190   GUYTON, Benjamin.   St. Martins, Norwich.   Hot Presser.
        5 yrs.   Barb. or Md.   17.   S.   17 July, 1719   17

1191   GWYNN, Josiah.   St. Saviours, Southwark.   Grocer.
        Father and mother dead.   JT.   4 yrs.   Jam.   19.   S.
        21 Nov. 1739   122

H

1191a   HABORN, Hannah.   Coventry, Warwicks.   Spinster.   EC
        5 yrs.   Md. or Pa.   20.   S.   24 Sept. 1719   48

1192   HACKENS, Henry. Hitchin, Herts. J Bl. 4 yrs. Jam.
20.   14 Jan. 1758   2

1193   HACKETT, John. Seaton, Rutland. W Bu. 5 yrs. Pa.
17. M. 11 March, 1734   8

1194   HADON, William. St. Pauls, Covent Garden, Mddx.
Distiller. P Si. 4 yrs. Jam. 19. S. 14 Sept. 1733. 61

1195   HAG(G)ER, Samuel. Spittlefields, London. Servant.
JS. 5 yrs. Md. no age. S. 11 April, 1751   41

1196   HAGUE, John. St. Andrews, Holbourn, London. Silver
smith. SG. 4 yrs. Jam. 21. S. 2 Nov. 1725 139

1197   HAINE, William. St. Martins in the Fields. Brazier.
SF. 4 yrs. Antigua. 24. S. 8 May, 1739   69

1198   HAINES (HEANES,) Henry. Eaton, Bucks. W Bu. 7 yrs.
Md. 15. S. 15 Sept. 1735   90

1199   HAINES, John. Ashon Cains (Ashton Keynes,) Wilts.
Husbandman. T Hi. 4 yrs. Jamaica. 26. M.
5 Oct. 1733   84

HAIRISON. See 1283

1200   HALE, John. St. Leonards, Shoreditch, Mddx. Cordwainer. J Ta. 4 yrs. N. C. 23. S. 8 July, 1736. 34

1201   HALES, Sarah. St. James Westminster, Mddx. Spinster.
P Si. 4 yrs. Pa. 18. S. 9 Aug. 1728   73

1202   HALES, William. Oxford. Husbandman. J Cr. 4 yrs.
Jam. 25. S. 4 July, 1750   33

1203   HALL, Daniel. No parish. Taylor. JT. 4 yrs. Jam.
19. S. 4 Oct. 1733   81

1204   HALL, Edward.   Spalding, Lincs.   Cooper.   JT.   4 yrs.
Jam.   20.   S.   18 Jan. 1724   7

1205   HALL, John.   St. Pauls, Covent Garden, Mddx.   Carpenter.   JG.   4 yrs.   Jam.   20.   S.   9 Nov. 1720   167

1206   HALL, John.   Shilburn (Shilburnhaugh?) Northumberland.
J Le.   4 yrs.   River Sherbro (Africa) 19.   15 July, 1734.   64

1207   HALL, John.   White Chappel.   Taylor.   NW.   4 yrs.
Md.   21.   S.   23 Feb. 1738   27

1208   HALL, Mary.   St. Georges in the East, Mddx.   Spinster.
NM.   4 yrs.   Md.   22.   S.   27 Dec. 1733   160

1209   HALL, Richard.   Bear St., Norwich.   5 yrs.   Md. or Va.
JD.   18.   M.   3 Nov. 1719   86

1210   HALL, Thomas.   St. Giles Cripplegate, London.   JT.
7 yrs.   Md. or Va.   14.   S.   26 Oct. 1719   81

1211   HALL, Thomas.   Stratford, Essex.   Carpenter.   JG.   4yrs.
Jam.   25.   S.   12 Feb. 1730   61

1212   HALL, William.   Canterbury, Kent.   Grocer.   AC.   4 yrs.
Md.   20.   S.   8 Oct. 1719   63

1213   HALL, William.   Sheffield, Yorks.   JG.   4 yrs.   Antigua.
17.   S.   20 Aug. 1728   91

1214   HALLIFAX, Thomas.   New Church in the Strand, Mddx.
Husbandman.   NM.   4 yrs.   Ga.   40.   S.   3 Oct. 1735
   99

1215   HALLOTT, William.   Farway, Devon.   JT.   4 yrs.   Va.
17.   M.   11 Oct. 1720   147

1216   HALSEY, John.   Little Panton, Lincs.   Butler.   NM.
4 yrs.   Jam.   22.   S.   3 July, 1736   44

HALTION. See 1217

1217 HALTON (HALTION,) George. Reading, Berks. JT.
4 yrs. St. L. 18. S. 10 Nov. 1722   182

1218 HAM, Jeremiah. Bennington, Herts. P Si. 6 yrs.
Va. or Md. 16. S. 23 March, 1733   35

1219 HAMBERRY, James. Kiltomash (Kiltormer?) Gallaway,
Ireland. Labourer. P Si. 4 yrs. Jam. 21. M.
22 Feb. 1730   83

1220 HAMBLIN, James. Kelminston, Somerset. Labourer.
W Bu. 4 yrs. Md. 18. S. 30 Dec. 1734   122

1221 HAMELTON, Joseph. Halmer End. Staffs. J To. 7 yrs.
Antigua. no age. M. 20 Jan. 1757   6

1222 HAMILTON, James. Halmer End J To. 5 yrs.
Antigua. no age. S. 20 Jan. 1757   7

1223 HAMILTON, John. Halmer End, Staffs. J To. 4 yrs.
Antigua. no age. S. Feb. 7, 1757   11

1224 HAMILTON, Thomas. St. Georges, Hanover Squ.
Father in Ireland, mother dead. NW. 5 yrs. Md. 20.
S. 19 March, 1738   53

1225 HAMILTON, William. Leith, North Britain. Cooper.
R Br. 4 yrs. Jam. 19. S. 4 Nov. 1736   129

1226 HAMLIN, Robert. Ipswich, Suffolk. Coachman. JT.
4 yrs. Jam. 20. S. 1 Jan. 1722   3

1227 HAMMILTON, John. St. Martins in the Fields, Mddx.
Taylor. W Bu. 4 yrs. Va. 28, S. 12 Feb. 1731   4

1228 HAMMOND, Corker. St. Clement Danes, Mddx. J Co.
7 yrs. Md. 15. S. 2 Feb. 1724   41

1229   HAMMOND, John. St. Clement Danes, Mddx. Coachman. Father and mother dead. NW. 5 yrs. Md.
20. M. 25 Jan. 1738   8

1230   HAMMOND, John. Limehouse. J Gr. 7 yrs. Jam.
15. S. 20 Nov. 1749   12

1231   HAMMOND, Joseph. Faringdon, Berks. JT. 4 yrs.
Pa. or N. Y. 19. S. 9 July, 1728   20

1232   HAMMOND, Joseph. Farringdon, Berks. Husbandman.
WT. 4 yrs. Jam. 22. S. 6 Jan. 1730   11

1233   HAMOND, Joseph. St. Luke, Mddx. Husbandman. NM.
4 yrs. Jam. over 21? S. 26 Aug. 1736   62

1234   HAMPTON, Richard. St. Georges by Hanover Square,
Mddx. J Co. 7 yrs. Md. 16. M. 9 Nov. 1725.   147

1235   HAMSON (HANSON,) Samuel. Manchester, Lancs.
Husbandman. NM. 4 yrs. Jam. 32. M. 23 Sept.
1730   120

1236   HANCOCK, Arnold. (Arnall.) St. Nicholas, Bristol. JG.
4 yrs. Pa. 20. S. 5 March, 1721   21

1237   HANCOCK, Henry. St. Clement Danes. Bricklayer.
EP. 4 yrs. Jam. 24. S. 24? Dec. 1737   69

1238   HANKS, Thomas. Ratley, Warwick. CV. 7 yrs. Md.
20. M. 7 Jan. 1723   3

HANSON. See 1235

1239   HAPE (HEAPE,) Richard. Manchester . Husbandman.
J Bl. 5 yrs. Md. no age. S. 21 July, 1753   15

1240   HARCOTT, Benjamin. Birmingham, Warwicks. JD.
7 yrs. S. C. 15. M. 9 Dec. 1723   120

1241   HARDCASTLE, William. Knasborough (Knaresborough,)
Yorks. Labourer. JT. 4 yrs. Jam. 19. M. 1 Aug. 1720
97

1242   HARDIMAN, Valentine. Windsor, Berks. Taylor. CV.
4 yrs. Md. 20. M. 4 Sept. 1722   117

1243   HARDING, Francis. Christ Church, Spitlefields, Mddx.
Weaver. CM. 4 yrs. Md. 39. M. 13 Aug. 1735   71

1244   HARDING, James.. St. Giles in the Fields, Mddx. JT.
7 yrs. Md. 17. S. 29 Nov. 1729   42

1245   HARDING, Peter. Bonsell (Bonsall,) Derbyshire. JG.
5 yrs. Md. 17. S. 3 Feb. 1723   17

1246   HARDING, Richard. Worcester. Weaver. AC. 6 yrs.
New England. 19. M. 4 March, 1721   26

1247   HARDING, Robert. Haslemere, Surrey. Cooper. P Si.
4 yrs. Jam. 24. M. 21 Nov. 1730   186

1248   HARDS, Ann. Fletching, Sussex. Spinster. CV. 5 yrs.
Md. 25. M. 31 (Dec.) 1724   109

1249   HARDWICK, John. Christ Church Surrey
Labourer. JT. 4 yrs. N. Y. or Carolina. 21. S.
16 Nov. 1724   73

1250   HARDY, George. Bulvan (Bulphan,) Essex. Husbandman.
JT. 4 yrs. Jam. 20. M. 5 Dec. 1722   190

1251   HARDY, Henry. Antwerp in Brabant? Upholsterer. NM.
4 yrs. Jam. 32. S. 15 Dec. 1736   205

1252   HARDY, Thomas. St. James Clerkenwell, Mddx. JD.
5 yrs. Md. 18. S. 15 Oct. 1719   71

1253   HARDYMAN, James. St. Marys, Norwich. Taylor. JT.
4 yrs. Jam. 22. M. 10 Aug. 1734   67

1254   HARE, Henry. St. Martins in the Strand, Mddx. Labourer. W Ta. 4 yrs. Pa. 19. S. 12 Feb. 1730   63

1255   HARE, William. Harwich, Essex. JD. 5 yrs. Md. 18. S. 5 Sept. 1722   119

HARES. See 1287

1256   HARFORD, Elizabeth. Maidstone, Kent. Spinster. P Si. 5 yrs. Jam. 18. S. 13 Oct. 1730   143

1257   HARGRAVE, Joseph. Sutton, Warwicks. JG. 5 yrs. Pa. 20. M. 3 Sept. 1723   79

1258   HARMAN, George. St. James in Tauntondean, Somerset (now Taunton) JD. 6 yrs. Md. 17. M. 15 Sept. 1719   35

1259   HARMAN, Peter. Stepney, Mddx. Weaver. W Bu. 5 yrs. Md. 26. S. 7 April, 1736   19

1260   HARMON, John. Allhallows, London Wall. CV. 4 yrs. St. C. 17. S. 18 May, 1723   59

1261   HARPER, Joseph. Clatford, Wilts. Husbandman. J Bl. 5 yrs. Md. no age. S. 21 July, 1753   18

1262   HARRIS, John. Aldgate, London. JG. 8 yrs. Va. 15 S. 18 Aug. 1718   13

1263   HARRIS, John. Plymouth, Devon. Labourer. JT. 4 yrs. St. L. 20. S. 22 Oct. 1722   171

1264   HARRIS, John. Town Mauldin (Malling,) Kent. WT. 6 yrs. Md. 15. S. 13 Jan. 1730   23

1265   HARRIS, John. St. Olives, Hart St. London. Wine cooper. NM. 3 yrs. Carolina or West Indies. 32. S. 5 Oct. 1734   93

1266   HARRIS, John. Crutched Friars, London. Wine cooper.
NM. 4 yrs. Jam. 29. S. 20 Oct. 1736   97

1267   HARRIS, John. St. Giles in the Fields. Hostler. NM.
4 yrs. Jam. 21. S. 3 Nov. 1736   124/5

1268   HARRISS, John. Bristol. Shoemaker. Father and mother
dead. J Wh. 4 yrs. Jam. 17. M. 3 Oct. 1739   110

1269   HARRIS, Samuel. Newberry, Berks. Cloathworker. JD.
4 yrs. Pa. 20. S. 31 Aug. 1723   78

1270   HARRIS, Samuell. St. Faiths, London. Joyner. W Bu.
4 yrs. Va. 24. S. 18 Jan. 1734   1

1271   HARRIS, Samuel. St. Sepulchers, Cambridge. Cordwainer. NM. 4 yrs. Md. 20. S. 26 March, 1734   36

1272   HARRISS, Thomas. Bristoll. Shoemaker. Father and
mother dead. J Wh. 4 yrs. Jam. 19. S. 3 Oct. 1739.112

1273   HARRIS, Thomas. Aylesbury, Bucks. AT. 4 yrs. Jam.
20. M. 30 Oct. 1750   40

1274   HARRIS, Thomas. Gloucester. Saddler. J Bl. 4 yrs.
Philadelphia. 19. S. 2 Aug. 1751   61

1275   HARRIS, William. Marlborough, Wilts. Labourer.
Father dead. J Wh. 4 yrs. Jam. 18. M. 29 Dec. 1739
    131

1276   HARRISON, Benjamin. Leeds, Yorks. Carter. JG. 4 yrs.
Jam. 19. S. 13 Oct. 1722   167

1277   HARRISON, James Lashly. St. Catherine Coleman. Clerk
or writer. W Bu. 4 yrs. Ga. 21. S. 8 Oct. 1735. 102

1278   HARRISON, Nathan. Liverpool Lancs. and late of Lambeth,
Surrey. Potter. P Si. 4 yrs. Jam. 20. S. 16 Feb.
1732   4

1279 HARRISON, Richard. Woot(t)on, Warwicks. JG. 8 yrs.
Barb. 16. M. 28 April, 1718 1

1280 HARRISON, Richard. St. Stephens, Norwich. NM. 5 yrs.
Jam. 17. M. 9 Sept. 1731 200

1281 HARRISON, Robert. Raisby (Raithby,) Lincs. JG. 4 yrs.
Md. 20. M. 2 Aug. 1723 67

1282 HARRISON, Thomas. Leeds, Yorks. JD. 7 yrs. Md.
15. M. 19 Aug. 1718 20

1283 HARRISON (HAIRISON,) William. Linton, Cambridge.
Smith and farrier. CV. 4 yrs. Md. 20. S.
26 Sept. 1722 134

1284 HARRISON, William. St. Giles in the Fields. Brickmaker.
NM. 4 yrs. Jam. 25. M. 20 Nov. 1736 167

1285 HARROD, John. Sandford (Sampford) Peverell, Devon.
Labourer. JT. 4 yrs. Md. 18. M. 25 Aug. 1718 43

1286 HARROLD, Thomas. St. John Timberhill, Norwich. W Bu.
6 yrs. Pa. 18. M. 21 Sept. 1730 117

1287 HARS (HARES,) George. Barget (Burcott?) Somerset.
Husbandman. EC. 4 yrs. Md. or Pa. 17. S.
27 Feb. 1718 4

1288 HART, Stephen. Bristol. Taylor. J Bl. 4 yrs. Philadelphia. 20. M. 2 Aug. 1751 60

1289 HARTLEY, John. Worsell, Staffs. Smith. CV. 5 yrs.
Md. 18. M. 16 Oct. 1719 73

1290 HARTLEY, Thomas. Dunessdale (Dunnerdale?) Lancs.
Clark or book keeper. H Bo. 4yrs. S. C. 20. S.
8 June, 1720 83

1291   HARTWELL, John.   Whaddon, Bucks.   Husbandman.   NM.
4 yrs.   Jam.   21.   S.   26 June 1732.   9

1292   HASHER, Henry.   Hassall, Derbyshire.   JD.   6 yrs.   Md.
16.   M.   27 Aug. 1718   51

1293   HASKINS, John.   St. Sepulchers, London.   Glass grinder.
NW.   4 yrs.   Pa.   28.   S.   22 Feb. 1738   25

1294   HASMAN, James.   St. Andrews, Holborn.   Carpenter and
joiner.   JT.   4 yrs.   Jam.   21.   S.   23 March, 1738.   60

1295   HAST, William.   Moly Swanton (Swanton Morley,)
Norfolk.   Weaver.   J Co.   4 yrs.   Md.   21.   M.
16 Nov. 1725   166

1296   HATFIELD, Thomas.   Rotherhith, Surrey.   Ship carpenter
and carver.   NM.   4 yrs.   Md.   24.   S.   13 Nov. 1734.
                                        108

1297   HATHERELL, William.   Sutton, Wilts.   Husbandman.
J BANKS.   4 yrs.   St. C. or any other.   22.   S.
10 July, 1736   38

1298   HAWES, Michael.   St. Giles Criplegate, London.   Weaver
Father William Hawes.   JT.   4 yrs.   Antigua.   18.   M.
22 Aug. 1728   94

1299   HAWKER, Richard.   St. James Westminster, Mddx.   NM.
6 yrs.   Md.   16.   S.   6 Dec. 1733   142

1300   HAWKINS, Henry.   Froom(Frome,)Somerset.   Cloath
worker.   TB.   4 yrs.   St. C. or St. L.   18.   S.
13 Aug. 1722   91

1301   HAWKINS, Sampson.   Stone, Staffs.   Taylor.   J Bl.
4 yrs.   Jam.   no age.   S.   1 Nov. 1753   28

1302   HAWKINS, William.   St. Anns Limehouse.   Clerk and
book keeper.   PP.   4 yrs.   Jam.   19.   S.   28 Jan. 1750.   1

1303   HAWKSWORTH, William. Lincoln. Carpenter and joyner. NM. 4 yrs. Jam. 25. S. 17 April, 1734. 48

1304   HAWSTEAD, Jane. St. Giles in the Fields, Mddx. Spinster. W Bu. 6 yrs. Jam. 17. S. 14 Oct. 1730. 145

1305   HAWTHORN, Charles. St. Nicholas, Gloucester. JG. 5 yrs. Md. 17. S. 16 Jan. 1721   6

1306   HAWTON, William. Birmingham, Warwicks. AC. 5 yrs Va. 19. M. 20 Sept. 1720   131

1307   HAXFORD, John. Dow(n)ton Nr. Salisbury, Wilts. Carpenter. JT. 4 yrs. Jam. 18. S. 11 Jan. 1723.   6

1308   HAY, William. East Gordon (Berwickshire) Scotland. Gardner. J Bl. 4 yrs. Md. no age. S. 4 Feb. 1754   24

1309   HAYES, John. St. Giles Criplegate, London. Mother Sarah Hayes. J COOKE. 7 yrs. Md. 15. S. 21 Jan. 1724   13

1310   HAYES, John. Walsal, Staffs. P Si. 5 yrs. Md. or Va. 20. S. 4 Feb. 1733   22

1311   HAYES, Samuel. Dublin. J Bl. 4 yrs. Antigua. No age. S. 2 Aug. 1755   8

HAYES, William. See 1314

1312   HAYNES, Edward. St. Giles in the Fields, Mddx. Mother late Ann Haynes, now Ann Wilson. SF. 7 yrs. Jam. 14 S. 24 Sept. 1736   77

1313   HAYNES, George. Bath, Somerset. Cooper. P Si. 4 yrs. Jam. 28. S. 10 Sept. 1734   83

1314   HAYS (HAYES,) William. Waterford in Ireland. Cooper. J BALL. 4 yrs. Pa. or N.Y. 17. S. 23 July, 1728. 47

1315   HAYTON, John.   Beadall (Bedale,) Yorks.   Husbandman.
W Bu.   4 yrs.   Jam.   27.   S.   20 Oct. 1731   248

1316   HAYWARD, William.   St. Giles in the Fields, Mddx.
Cordwainer.   JG.   4 yrs.   Md.   20.   S.   25 Nov. 1725.   204

1317   HEAD, Jonathan.   St. James,Bristol.   Mason.   JG.   4 yrs.
Antigua.   20.   No S or M.   5 June, 1723   62

HEANES.   See 1198

HEAPE.   See 1239

1318   HEATH, George.   Sheilds, Northumberland (Shields)
Tayler.   CV.   4 yrs.   Va.   20.   M.   27 Oct. 1720.   160

1319   HEATH, John.   Froom (Frome,) Somerset.   JD.   5 yrs.
St. C. or St. L.   17.   M.   7 Aug. 1722   76

1320   HEATH, John.   Wassell (Walsall,) Staffs.   Buckle maker.
JT.   4 yrs.   Jam.   21.   M.   30 Nov. 1725   215

1321   HEATH, John.   St. Mary Steps, Exeter, Devon.   P Si.
5 yrs.   Pa.   16.   S.   25 Aug. 1730   82

1322   HEATH, John.   St. Giles Cripplegate, London.   Husbandman.   WD.   5 yrs.   Va.   19.   S.   17 April, 1751.   48

1323   HEATH, Robert.   St. Giles in the Fields, Mddx.   Brickmaker.   J Gar.   4 yrs.   Jam.   19.   M.   27 March, 1723
   48

1324   HEATH, Thomas.   St. Leonards, Shorditch.   Weaver.
Father and mother dead.   NW.   4 yrs.   Md.   20.   S.
30 May, 1739   75

1325   HEATH, William.   Low Leckcome, Berks.   (Letcomb
Basset or Regis?)   P Si.   6 yrs.   Jam.   16.   M.   22 Feb.
1730   84

1326   HEBBERD, John. Richmond, Surrey. Carpenter. CV.
4 yrs. Jam. 26. S. 5 Dec. 1724   88

1327   HEBDIN, Thomas. Churchdenton (Church Fenton,) Yorks.
Husbandman. NM. 5 yrs. Jam. 17. S. 22 Nov. 1736
     176

1328   HECKSTALL, Abraham. St. Mary le Bone. Father
Thomas Heckstall. RF on behalf of Dr. Wm. Young of
Antigua. 3 yrs. Antig. 19. S. 24 Nov. 1736.   171

1329   HEDGE, John. Mutch Okley (Great Oakley,) Essex.
Smith and farrier. NM. 4 yrs. Jam. 30. S.
22 Oct. 1730   155a

1330   HEELING, William. Newport, Salop. Mother dead and
knows not where father is. EP. 6 yrs. Md. 17. M.
16 Dec. 1737   81

1331   HEIRON, William. Litleton, Worcs. Cordwainer. JG.
4 yrs. Antigua. 20. S. 15 Aug. 1728   84

1332   HELBURN, William. South Petherton, Somerset. JG.
4 yrs. Jam. 19. M. 16 Jan. 1722   18

1333   HELSBY, Richard. Robey (Roby,) Lancs. JT. 4 yrs.
Jam. 19. M. 20 Aug. 1731   190

1334   HENDERSON, James. St. Olives, Southwark. Brass founder. J St. 5 yrs. Md. 20. S. 30 March, 1751.   34

1335   HENDERSON, Robert. St. Giles Criplegate, London.
Book keeper. JT. 4 yrs. Barb. 22. S. 15 July, 1735
     52

1336   HENLEY, John. St. Giles Criplegate, Mddx. JT. 5 yrs.
Jam. 19. M. 16 Sept. 1734   87

1337   HENNECUS, Michael. A native of Portugal. P Si. 7 yrs.
Jam. 15. M. 29 April, 1731   112

1338   HENN(E)Y, Thomas. Trentham, Staffs. Husbandman.
J Bl. 4 yrs. Antig. 18. S. 6 March, 1754   11

1339   HART, John. St. Edmunds, Norwich. Worsted weaver.
RB. 5 yrs. New England. 20. S. 28 March, 1724.   38

1340   HERBERT, John. Ware, Herts. JT. 6 yrs. Jam. 16.
S. Last Oct. 1729   9

1341   HERBY, Thomas. Uppingham. Mason. J Cr. 4 yrs.
Va. no age. S. 2 Feb. 1750   2

1342   HERWOOD, Robert. Horsington, Lincs. JT. 5 yrs. Va.
17. M. 16 Dec. 1734   119

HESELTON. See 1343

1343   HESLETINE (HESELTON,) William. Berndsey? Yorks.
Barber. CV. 4 yrs. Md. 32. S. 26 Nov. 1724.   78

1344   HESSEL, Edward. York. Sawyer. NW. 4 yrs. Jam.
27. S. 23 Nov. 1738   68

1345   HESTER, William. Taunton dean, Somerset. Woolcomber. CV. 4 yrs. Md. 17. S. 8 Oct. 1722   157

1346   HEWESON, Hugen. Wimlinton (Wimblington,) Isle of
Ely, Cambs. Husbandman. JG. 4 yrs. Jam. 26. M.
14 Jan. 1722   14

1347   HEWITSON, Thomas. Sedg(e)field, Durham. Surgeon.
JT. 4 yrs. Jam. 24. S. 17 Dec. 1724   101

1348   HEWITT, Charles. Nun Eaton, Warwicks. W Bu. 8 yrs.
Va. 14. M. 6 Dec. 1733   139

1349   HEWITT, Joseph. Chislehurst, Kent. P Si. 4 yrs. Md.
18. S. 10 Nov. 1727   24

1350   HEWITT, Joshua.   Carrington (Cardington,) Beds.   Bricklayer.   JG.   6 yrs.   Md.   25.   M.   23 Jan. 1724   22

1351   HEWITT, Richard.   St. James Westminster, Mddx.   Groom.
J Co.   6 yrs.   Md.   19.   S.   1 Oct. 1725   96

1352   HEWS, James.   St. Olaves, Southwark, Surrey.   JD.
4 yrs.   Md.   19.   M.   19 Aug. 1718   23

1353   HEWS, Lancelot.   Dissert (Dyserth?) Flintshire, Wales.
JD.   7 yrs.   Md.   18.   M.   11 Nov. 1719   88

1354   HEWSTER, James   Sherborn, Dorset.   JD.   5 yrs.   Va.
17.   M.   15 Dec. 1719   112

1355   HEY, John.   St. Paul, Shadwell, Mddx.   Weaver.   JD.
5 yrs.   Md.   21.   S.   4 Dec. 1724   86

1356   HICKS, William.   Whitney (Witney,) Oxon.   JG.   4 yrs.
Pa.   15.   M.   1 Aug. 1728   62

1357   HICKSON, Joseph.   Grantham, Lincs.   Grocer.   CV.
5 yrs.   Md.   21.   S.   3 Feb. 1724   46

1358   HIDE, Thomas.   Risely, Beds.   CV.   5 yrs.   Md.   17.
S.   23 Aug. 1722   109

1359   HIGGINS, Robert.   St. Botolph, Aldersgate, London.
Cordwainer.   W Bu.   4 yrs.   Antigua.   19.   M.
30 Aug. 1728   104

1360   HIGGINS, Thomas.   Wellington, Salop.   JT.   4 yrs.
Jam.   20.   S.   9 Nov. 1731   265

1361   HIGGINS, William.   St. Martins in the Fields.   Plaisterer.   Father and mother dead.   NW.   4 yrs.   Jam.   17.
M.   25 July, 1739   90

1362   HIGHBARGIN, John.   St. Giles in the Fields, Mddx.   4 yrs.
Jam.   EC.   18.   S.   12 June, 1718   4

1363   HILL, James. Childridge (Childerditch?) Nr. Rumford
(Romford,) Essex. RB. 6 yrs. Jam. 16. M.
3 Nov. 1725   142

1364   HILL, James. St. James, Bristol. Husbandman. NM.
4 yrs. Jam. 21. S. 8 Oct. 1734   95

1365   HILL, John. Oakham, Rutland. Baker. JG. 4 yrs.
Va. 20. S. 22 June, 1721   45

1366   HILL, John. Allhallows, Barking, London. JG. 4 yrs.
Md. 21. S. 27 Jan. 1724   30

1367   HILL, John. Melton (Milton,) Somerset. Waggoner.
NM. 4 yrs. Jam. 29. M. 16 March, 1735   11

1368   HILL, John. Wells. Husbandman. Father and mother
dead. BW. 5 yrs. Antigua. 18. M. 26 Jan. 1736
32

1369   HILL, Margrett. Dublin. AT. 4 yrs. S. C. 20. M.
4 Sept. 1749   10

1370   HILL, Peter. Stepney, Mddx. Coachman. JT. 4 yrs.
Jam. 29. M. Dec. 1724   104

1371   HILL, Richard. St. Botolph, Bishopsgate. Plaisterer.
MW. 4 yrs. Pa. 25. S. 17 May, 1738   39

1372   HILL, Robert. St. Botolphs, Aldersgate, London. WC.
4 yrs. Jam. 20. S. 12 Nov. 1725   155

1373   HILL, Thomas. St. Leonards, Shoreditch, Mddx. NM.
5 yrs. Md. 19. S. 1 Feb. 1730   33

1374   HILL, Thomas. St. Mary Magdalene, Bermondsey, Surrey.
Chair maker. NM. 4 yrs. Jam. 23. M. 3 Aug. 1731
178

1375 HILL, William. Kensington, Mddx. JT. 6 yrs. Jam.
16. M. 2 Nov. 1725 140

1376 HILLIARD, James. London. T Hu. 3 yrs. On board
ship. 18. M. 5 Jan. 1757 3

1377 HILLYARD, Simon. St. Marys, Whitechapel, Mddx.
8 yrs. Barb. 15. M. 5 May, 1718. 3

1378 HINDE, John. St. Leonards, Shoreditch, Mddx. Barber.
NM. 4 yrs. Jam. 23. S. 22 Sept. 1733 69

1379 HINDSON, Joseph. Allhallows, London Wall. Cordwainer.
NM. 4 yrs. Jam. 22. M. 20 July, 1733 29

1380 HINOIOSSA, George. St. Giles in the Fields, Mddx.
JT. 4 yrs. Jam. 20. S. 6 Jan. 1720 3

1381 HINSOM, Colby. Edminton (Edmonton,) Mddx. SG.
4 yrs. Jam. 18. S. 21 Nov. 1727 16

1382 HINSON, Henry. Chelsea, Mddx. JT. 5 yrs. Jam.
18. S. 9 Feb. 1722 32

1383 HISS, Samuel. St. Martins, Worcester. JT. 5 yrs.
Va. 19. M. 17 Sept. 1718 57

1384 HISSEY, Charles. Newnham, Oxon. J Csn. 5 yrs. Md.
17. S. 6 Jan. 1719 6

1385 HITCHFIELD, George. Taunton, Somerset. Weaver.
JT. 5 yrs. Md. or Pa. 19. M. 15 Sept. 1719 33

1386 HOARE, Christopher. Chatham, Kent. Shipwright.
Father dead, mother at Horsham, Sussex. W Bu. 6 yrs.
Pa. 18. S. 10 Feb. 1737 16

1387 HOBBS, Joseph. Amersham, Bucks. R Wh. 4 yrs.
Nevis or St. C. 19. M. 8 Nov. 1729 17

1388 HODSON, Thomas. Presten (Preston,) Herefordshire. NM.
5 yrs. Md. 16. S. 9 Dec. 1729 62

1389 HOGG, John. Harrigate, parish of Knasborough (Knaresborough,) Yorks. JG. 5 yrs. Pa. 16. M. 7 July,
1722 46

1390 HOGG, Robert. St. Brides, Fleet St, London. NM.
4 yrs. Pa. 21. S. 22 March, 1735 16

1391 HOLBIRD, Samuel. St. Martins, Ludgate, London. Late
master, John Kendall. CV. 5 yrs. New England. 17.
S. 14 April, 1724 46

1392 HOLDEN, Robert. Ratcliff, Notts. J Bl. 4 yrs. Jam.
no age. S. 16 Aug. 1753 25

1393 HOLDER, Henry. Mansfield, Notts. Shoemaker. Father
and mother dead. NW. 4 yrs. Jam. 20. S. 5 Feb.
1738 14

1394 HOLDING, John. Cree Church, Leadenhall St., London.
J Co. 7 yrs. Md. 16. M. 4 Feb. 1724 50

1395 HOLDWAY, Mary. St. Margarets, Westminster, Mddx.
Spinster and cook. P Si. 4 yrs. Jam. 19. M.
7 Oct. 1731 228

1396 HOLIOAKE, John. New Windsor, Berks. Gardner. NM.
4 yrs. Jam. 26. S. 5 Nov. 1736 133

1397 HOLLAND, James. Spittlefields London. Shoemaker.
J Bl. 5 yrs. Md. no age. S. 23 Feb. 1750 11

1398 HOLLIER, Stephen. Woodford, Essex. P Si. 7 yrs.
Jam. 16. S. 14 Oct. 1730 147

1399 HOLLINGSHED, Francis. Maxfield (Macclesfield?)
Cheshire. NM. 5 yrs. Va. 19. M. 8 Jan. 1733. 10

1400   HOLLOWAY, James. Reading, Berks. Weaver. NM.
4 yrs. Jam. 26. S. 11 Nov. 1736   148

1401   HOLLOWAY, John. Epsom (Surrey) J Bl. 5 yrs. Va.
no age. M. 2 March, 1750   14

1402   HOLLOWAY, William. Windsor, Berks. JD. 7 yrs.
Pa. 15. S. 3 Sept. 1723   80

1403   HOLM, Andrew. Stockholm (Sweden.) Weaver. JD.
4 yrs. Md. 21. M. 12 Dec. 1724   93

1404   HOLM(E), Thomas. Cartmel, Lancs. Weaver. JT.
4 yrs. Md. 35. S. 1 June, 1739   84

1405   HOLMES, Henry. Wanstead, Essex. Vintner. NM.
4 yrs. Jam. 21. S. 1 Jan. 1736   1

1406   HOLMES, John. Comes (Combs,) Suffolk. Carpenter and
joyner. JD. 4 yrs. Jam. 20. S. 2 Dec. 1724   80

1407   HOLMES, John. Hertford. Bricklayer. NM. 4 yrs.
Jam. 29. S. 20 Nov. 1733   114

1408   HOLMES, Thomas. St. Mary, Islington, Mddx. Carpenter. P Si. 4 yrs. Pa. 27. S. 9 July, 1728   22

1409   HOLT, William. St. Johns, Westminster. Mother,
Elizabeth Forster, late Holt. BW. 6 yrs. Jam. 16.
M. 21 Oct. 1736   106

1410   HOMAN, William. St. Botolphs, Aldersgate, London.
AC. 5 yrs. Md. 18. M. 8 Aug. 1720   103

1411   HOME, Catharine   Liverpool, Lancs. Spinster.
P Si. 4 yrs. Pa. or N. Y. 19. M. 10 July, 1728 26

1412   HOMES, Richard. London. J Cr. 7 yrs. Jam. no age.
M. 10 April, 1756   12

1413   HOOD, Richard.   Froom (Frome,) Somerset.   Brasier.
        J Co. 4 yrs. Jam. 19. S. 7 Oct. 1725   110

1414   HOOPER, William.   Whitechappell, Mddx.   Cordwainer.
        J Lo. 4 yrs. Pa. 20. S. 17 March, 1735   13

1415   HOPE, Josiah.   Christ Church, London.   Carpenter.   AC.
        4 yrs. Jam. 20. S. 13 Dec. 1721   84

1416   HOPKINS, Mary.   St. Mathews, Friday St. London.   Spin-
        ster. JM. 5 yrs. Pa. 17. M. 15 Feb. 1723   27

1417   HOPKINS, Robert.   Manchester, Lancs.   Bricklayer.
        W Bu. 4 yrs. Jam. 19. S. 1 June, 1734   56

1418   HOPKINS, Thomas.   Wotton Hundrigge (Under Edge?)
        Glos. Weaver. NM. 5 yrs. Md. 21. S. 25 Jan.
        1736   28

1419   HOPKINS, William.   St. Martins in the Fields, Mddx.
        Cordwainer. AC. 4 yrs. Va. 18. S. Last Sept.
        1719   58

        HOPPAT. See 1468

1420   HORENDEN, Thomas.   Town Malden (Malling?) Also
        called West Malling, Kent. J Bl. 5 yrs. Va. 17.
        M. 2 March, 1750   13

1421   HORN, John.   Oxford.   Hostler. W Bu. 5 yrs. Pa.
        20. M. 11 Sept. 1730   99

1422   HORSBURGH, John.   St. James, Westminster, Mddx.
        Labourer. WC. 4 yrs. Jam. 30. S. 20 Nov. 1725. 191

1423   HORSEY, George.   St. Saviours, Southwark.   Chairmaker.
        SF. 4 yrs. Jam. 21. S. 7 Dec. 1736   190

1424   HORSLEY, George.   Newcastle Upon Tine, Northumberland
        Carpenter. JT. 4 yrs. Va. 19. S. 12 April, 1720 72

1425   HORTH, John. St Johns, Timber Hill, Norwich. Weaver.
JT. 4 yrs. Jam. 23. S. 27 Dec. 1733   158

1426   HOSIER, Charles. St. Giles in the Fields, Mddx. Carpenter. W Bu. 7 yrs. Barb. 21. S. 29 April, 1731. 113

1427   HOSKINS, William. St. Martins in the Fields, Mddx.
WB. 5 yrs. Pa. 17. S. 27 May, 1719   15

1428   HOUGH, John. Roston (Rostherne,) Cheshire. Smith.
W Bu. 4 yrs. Barb. 28. S. 18 Dec. 1730   223

1429   HOUGHTON, John. St. Martins in the Fields, Mddx.
Coachman. Mother and father dead. JT. 5 yrs. Jam.
19. S. 30 Nov. 1738   73

1430   HOW, Matthew. St. Anns, Blackfryers, London. Mother,
Sarah Wombell. CV. 6 yrs. Md. 17. S. 27 Dec. 1723
    123

1431   HOWARD, George. St. Georges, Southwark, Surrey.
JD. 4 yrs. Md. 19. M. 3 Feb. 1724   47

1432   HOWARD, George. St. Buttolphs, Aldgate. Labourer.
Father, William Howard. MW. 6 yrs. Antigua.
19 (crossed out) S. 2 Dec. 1737   74

1433   HOWARD, Henry. Walt(h)amstow, Essex. Gardner. EP.
4 yrs. Jam. 30. M. 28 April, 1738   35

1434   HOWARD, James. Stoke Underham (Stoke sub Hamdon,)
Somerset. JG. 4 yrs. Va. 19. M. 26 Jan. 1729. 16

1435   HOWARD, James. St. Giles Criplegate Without, Mddx.
Husbandman. W Bu. 4 yrs. Jam. 23. S. 8 Dec. 1730
    197

1436   HOWARD, John. Culliton Rawley (Collaton Rawleigh,)
Devon. Carpenter. JT. 4 yrs. Pa. or Md. 20. S.
4 Feb. 1723   19

1437 HOWARD, John. Lanton, (Laindon?) Essex Shoemaker. Father and mother dead. J Wh. 5 yrs. Pa. 19. S. 9 Feb. 1738   16

1438 HOWARD, Robert. St. Margaret, Westminster, Mddx. Cordwainer. EC. 4 yrs. Md. 19. S. 18 Feb.1720   24

1439 HOWARD, Thomas. Preston, Lancs. Husbandman. W Bu. 4 yrs. Jam. 23. M. 19 Feb. 1730   75

1440 HOWARD, William. Kingston, Surrey. JD. 4 yrs. Md. 20. M. 10 Sept. 1722   125

1441 HOWELL, Abraham. Temple Street, Bristol. J BALL. 4 yrs. Antigua. 20. M. 11 Dec. 1728   118

1442 HOWELL, John. St. Martins in the Fields, Mddx. Joyner. W Bu. 4 yrs. Jam. 25. S. 3 May, 1731   120

1443 HOWELL, Jonathan. Chelsea, Mddx. Mother, Rachael Davis. P Si. 7 yrs. St. C. 15. S. 24 Oct. 1730. 162

1444 HOYLAND, Benjamin. Sheffield. Tallow chandler. JT. 4 yrs. Jam. 19. S. 23 Feb. 1738   33

1445 HUBBARD, Edward, Jnr. St. Margarets, Westminster, Mddx. Father and mother Edward and Mary Hubbard. CV. 4 yrs. Md. 18. S. 16 Oct. 1724   64

1446 HUBBARD, John. St. Giles in the Fields, Mddx. Labourer. JT. 4 yrs. St. L. 31. M. 6 Oct. 1722   154

1447 HUDSON, Jeremiah. Bloxham, Oxon. Husbandman. JG. 4 yrs. Jam. 24. S. 6 May, 1731   127

1448 HUDSON, John. Addingham, Yorks. MR. 4 yrs. Jam. no age. S. 10 Dec. 1756   28

1449 HUDSON, Thomas. Malling (Malden?) Surrey. Husbandman. WB. 5 yrs. Md. or Pa. 19. S. 4 Sept. 1719   29

1450   HUDSON, William. Lynn, Norfolk. Husbandman. NM.
4 yrs. Jam. 30. M. 17 Aug. 1730   70

1451   HUGGINS, John. St. Augustine, Norwich. Weaver.
JG. 5 yrs. Md. 19. M. 25 Dec. 1723   122

1452   HUGGINS, William. Longner. Salop. Husbandman.
JS. 4 yrs. Jam. no age. M. 29 June, 1750   26

1453   HUGHES, Barzillai. St. Margarets, Westminster. Mddx.
Cordwainer. Father Basill Hughes. JG. 4 yrs. Md.
20. S. 24 Sept. 1724   55

1454   HUGHES, Edward. Greenwich, Kent. Coachman. JG.
4 yrs. Va. 42. S. 18 Dec. 1729   76

1455   HUGHES, Henry. Ruthin, Denbigh, Wales. Carpenter.
JT. 4 yrs. Jam. 20. S. 30 May, 1724   50

1456   HUGHES, John. St. Martins in the Fields Mddx. Dancing
Master. JT (for John Forster of Jamaica.) 4 yrs. Jam.
20. S. 14 Dec. 1721   86

1457   HUGHES, Thomas. Newtown, Montgomeryshire, Wales.
WT. 7 yrs. Jam. 16. M. 25 Feb. 1730   88

1458   HUGHS, William. Westbury, Glos. Writer. JT. 4 yrs.
Jam. 20. S. 10 May, 1731   132

1459   HUMFREY, Thomas. St. Margarets, Westminster, Mddx.
Father Thomas Humfrey. NM. 7 yrs. Md. 13. S.
17 Dec. 1730   219

1460   HUMPHERES, Thomas. Dublin, Ireland, J Bl. 4 yrs.
Md. no age. M. 22 April, 1756   13

1461   HUMPHREYS, John. Molton in Mash (Moreton in Marsh,)
Glos. Butcher. J Wh. 4 yrs. Jam. 27. S. 17 Nov.
1737   64

1462 HUMPHRYS, John. Worcester. Groom. JT. 4 yrs.
Md. 25. M. 31 May, 1739   80

1463 HUNT, John. Downley, Bucks. JD. 7 yrs. St. L.
16. M. 21 Sept. 1722   130

1464 HUNT, Joseph. St. Mary, Newington, Surrey. P Si.
6 yrs. Md. 19. M. 8 Dec. 1731   289

1465 HUNT, Richard. St. James, Clerkenwell, Mddx. Iron
monger. NM. 4 yrs. Md. 21.. S. 10 July, 1735. 49

1466 HUNTER, John. Garstang Church Town, Lancs. Clerk.
JE. 7 yrs. Jam. 14. S. 1 March, 1753   1

1467 HUNTER, William. Garstang Church Town, Lancs. WH
7 yrs. Jam. 15. S. 23 Oct. 1751   66

1468 HUPPERT (HOPPAT,) Robert. Basingstoke, Hants. Gardner. NM. 4 yrs. Jam. 33. S. 3 Jan. 1736   8

1469 HUSSEY, Benjamin. Wapping, Stepney, Mddx. Watch-
maker. J BALL. 4 yrs. Pa. 27. S. 6 July, 1728. 6

1470 HUSSEY, William. St. Marys, White Chapel. Taylor.
NM. 4 yrs. Va. 21. S. 24 Dec. 1736   210

1471 HUTCHIN, William. St. Giles, Cripplegate. Labourer.
Mother Ann Hutchin. NM. 6 yrs. Antig. 17. S.
21 Dec. 1737   82

1472 HUTCHINSON, John. St. Ann Blackfryers, London.
Tayler. W Bu. 4 yrs. Jam. 21. S. 2 Sept. 1736. 71

1473 HUTCHINSON, Joseph. St. Giles, Criplegate, London.
Book binder. JT. 4 yrs. Pa. 21, S. 5 July, 1728. 5

1474 HYDE, John. West Chester. Footman. JG. 4 yrs.
St. C. 19. S. 6 July, 1722   45

1475 HYMOSS, Caron. Tinmouth (Tynemouth,) Northumberland. JT. 4 yrs. Jam. 18. S. 18 Aug. 1719 22

I

1476 IBINGFIELD, Richard. Osprinch (Ospringe,) Kent. Husbandman. NW. 4 yrs. Jam. 26. M. 19 Dec. 1738
74

1477 ILLABY, John. West Chester. JD. 7 yrs. Md. 16.
M. 15 Aug. 1723 73

1478 ILLING, Walter. Bruton, Somerset. Shoemaker. NM.
4 yrs. Jam. 19. S. 3 Jan. 1736 11

INGLIS. See 889

1479 INKSON, William. Lynn Regis (King's Lynn.) Norfolk.
Perriwig maker. NM. 4 yrs. Jam. 22. S. 10 Nov.
1736 145

IRVIN. See 891

1480 ISAAC, Joseph. St. Andrews, Holbourn, London. WC2.
7 yrs. Md. 20. S. 26 Jan. 1729 17

1481 IVES, John. York. Carpenter. JG. 4 yrs. Jam.
19. S. 30 March, 1723 49

1482 IVEY, John. St. James, Clerkenwell, Mddx. Taylor.
AC. 5 yrs. Md. or Va. 18. S. 4 Jan, 1721 4

J

1483 JACKSON, Jane. St. Giles, Criplegate, London. Spinster. Aunt Jane Bennet. CV. 7 yrs. Md. 16. S.
29 Dec. 1721 93

1484   JACKSON, John. St. Giles in the Fields, Mddx. Coachman. Mother and father dead. JT. 4 yrs. Jam. 20
S. 30 Nov. 1738   72

1485   JACKSON, Joseph. St. Marys, Nottingham. Wool comber. AC. 4 yrs. Va. 20. S. Last Sept. 1719.   57

1486   JACKSON, Robert. Nottingham. Stocking weaver.
JT. 5 yrs. Md. 20. M. 24 Nov. 1721   77

1487   JACKSON, Richard. Stone, Staffs. JT. 4 yrs. Jam.
20. S. 12 Nov. 1729   20

1488   JACKSON, Samuel. St. Giles, Criplegate, London.
Schoolmaster. P Si. 4 yrs. Pa. 23, S. 6 July, 1728
    9

1489   JACKSON, William. Redman (Redmile?) Leics. JD.
6 yrs. Md. 15. M. 25 Aug. 1718   45

1490   JACKSON, William. Edenborough, Scotland. Carpenter and Joyner. NM. 4 yrs. Jam. 22. S. 28 Oct. 1731
    254

1491   JACKSON, William. Pe(e)bles, Tweeddale (now Peeblesshire,) Scotland. Husbandman. NM. 4 yrs. Md. 22
S. 13 Sept. 1735   83

1492   JACKSON, William. St. Botolphs, Aldersgate. Coach maker. Mother, Elizabeth Croft. Master, John Ollive.
S Wh. 4 yrs. Jam. 19. S. 21 March, 1736   41

1493   JAMES, Abraham. St. Leonards, Shoreditch, Mddx.
J BALL. 7 yrs. Pa. or N. Y. 17. M. 10 July, 1728   28

1494   JAMES, Henry. New Brentford, Mddx. Barber and perrywig maker. JT. 4 yrs. Jam. 20. S. 16 July, 1733
    23

1495   JAMES, Isaac. Mayersfield (Mangotsfield?) Glos. Carpenter. J Co. 4 yrs. Jam. 20. S. 7 Oct. 1725.   108

1496   JAMES, John. St. Georges, Bloomsberry, Mddx. P Si. 5 yrs. Va. 18. S. 29 Dec. 1733   162

1497   JAMES, John. St. Marylebone. Bricklayer. J Cr. 4 yrs. Jam. no age. M. 31 Dec. 1754   25

1498   JAMES, Samuel. A native of the East Indies and late of parish of Lincolns Inn Chappell. JG. 4 yrs. Md. 20. M. 3 Feb. 1724   48

1499   JAMES, William. Risely, Beds. Husbandman. JT. 4 yrs. Pa. or N. Y. 19. S. 9 July, 1728   19

1500   JAMESON(E,) Philip. Edenborough, Scotland. Book keeper. NM. 4 yrs. Md. 23. S. 12 Dec. 1730.   204

JARDINE. See 1590

1501   JARVIS, Abraham. St. Katherine Cree Church, London. Book keeper. W Bu. 5 yrs. Jam. 25. S. 8 Dec. 1730   198

1502   JARVIS, Henry. Willington, Salop. TB. 7 yrs. St. C or St. L. 17. S. 17 Aug. 1722   102

1503   JARVIS, Robert. St. James Clerkenwell, Mddx. Butcher. Father John Jarvis. R Wh. 4 yrs. Jam. 19. S. 11 March, 1729   47

1504   JARVIS, Thomas. Shrewsbury, Salop. Taylor. JG. 4 yrs. Jam. 21. S. 19 Aug. 1730   76

1505   JARVIS, William. St. Clement Danes. Labourer. Father William Jarvis. NM. 5 yrs. Jam. 19. S. 31 Dec. 1736   219

1506   JEFFERY, Joseph.   Thorkim (Thorncombe?) Devon.
Cloathier. Father and mother dead. J Wh. 4 yrs. Pa.
18. M. 28 Feb. 1738   43

1507   JEFFERY, Josias. Winchester, Southampton. T Bo (For
James Bowles of Md. Merchant.) 7 yrs. Md. 16. S.
19 Dec. 1723   121

JEFFERYS. See 1508

1508   JEFFOYS (JEFFERYS,) William. Dartford, Kent.
Labourer. RB. 4 yrs. Md. 20. S. 30 Oct. 1725   132

JEFFRES. See 1509

1509   JEFFRYS (JEFFRES,) Charles. St. Georges, Southwark,
Surrey. JD. 6 yrs. Md. 16. S. 1 Feb. 1724   35

1510   JEM(M), Rice. Mansfield, Notts. Shooemaker. NM.
4 yrs. Jam. 25. S. 23 Oct. 1736   109

1511   JENKINS, Francis. St. Giles Criplegate, London. JT.
7 yrs. Jam. or Md. 16. M. 27 Nov. 1733   118

1512   JENKINS, George. Gosport, Hants. JT. 4 yrs. Jam.
17. M. 19 Dec. 1729   77

1513   JENNINGS, John. St. Anns, Blackfryers, London. Printer.
P Si. 4 yrs. Jam. 22. S. 19 April, 1734   50

1514   JENNINGS, Robert. Reading. Blacksmith. J Bl. 5 yrs.
Md. No age. S. 21 July, 1753   14

1515   JERVIS, Peter. Market Weeton (Weighton,) Yorks.
Cooper. JT. 4 yrs. Jam. 21. S. 7 Aug. 1735   68

1516   JOASLIN, George. Ingerstone (Ingatestone,) Essex. Dyer.
SG. 4 yrs. Md. 21. S. 17 Nov. 1725   181

1517   JOBSON, Robert.   Great Aclife (Aycliffe,) Durham.
Bricklayer and mason.   NM.   4 yrs.   Jam.   45.   M.
21 Aug. 1736   54

1518   JOHNSON, Charles.   St. James, Westminster, Mddx.   JT.
4 yrs.   Jam.   19.   S.   12 Dec. 1722   192

1519   JOHNSON, Henry.   Wowton In the Nais (Walton-on-the-
Naze,) Essex.   JD.   8 yrs.   Md.   15.   M.   6 Oct. 1724
        56

1520   JOHNSON, James.   St. Andrews, Holbourn, London.
Vintner.   P Si.   4 yrs.   Jam.   25.   S.   23 Oct. 1733   96

1521   JOHNSON, John.   St. Ethelbergs, Bishopsgate St., London.
WB.   6 yrs.   Md. or Pa.   17.   S.   Last Sept. 1719.   56

1522   JOHNSON, John.   Rumford (Romford,) Essex.   Labourer.
JG.   4 yrs.   Md.   29.   S.   13 Nov. 1725   158

1523   JOHNSON, John.   Peterborough, Northants.   Coachman.
W Bu.   4 yrs.   Pa.   31.   S.   10 Sept. 1730   95

1524   JOHNS(T)ON, John.   Rokeley (Rockcliffe?) Cumberland.
Smith and farrier.   NM.   4 yrs.   Jam.   19.   S.
27 March, 1731   100

1525   JOHNSON, Prestman.   Deptford, Kent.   Husbandman.
NM.   4 yrs.   Jam.   20.   S.   21 Oct. 1736   107

1526   JOHNSON, Richard.   Ware, Herts,   JD.   6 yrs.   Md.
16.   M.   29 Aug. 1718   52

1527   JOHNSON, Robert.   St. Peters, Nottingham.   JG.   4 yrs.
Jam.   18.   S.   20 June, 1720   88

1528   JOHNSON, Samuel.   Thornton, Chester.   Husbandman.
NM.   4 yrs.   Jam.   32.   S.   26 June, 1732   10

JOHNSON, Samawel. See 1595

1529   JOHNSON, Thomas. Sunderland, Durham. Shipwright and sawyer. JT. 4 yrs. Jam. 20. S. 5 Feb. 1721. 14

1530   JOHNSON, Thomas. Yexley (Yaxley,) Hunts. JG. 4 yrs. Va. 16. M. 17 June, 1721   41

1531   JOHNSON, Thomas. Bury St. Edmunds. Husbandman. NM. 4 yrs. Jam. 20. M. 6 Dec. 1736   184

1532   JOHNSON, William. Greenwich, Kent. JW. 4 yrs. Va. 18. S. 30 Sept. 1720   130

1533   JOHNSON, William. Dumfriese, Scotland. Taylor. J Pa. 4 yrs. Jam. 20. M. 5 April, 1750   16

1534   JOHNSON, William. Barrawill (Barwell,) Leics. J Bl. 4 yrs. Antigua. no age. M. 1 July, 1755   4

JOHNSTON, John. See 1524

1535   JOHNSTON (JOHNSON,) Mary. Horsleydown,(London.) Widow. J Pa. 4 yrs. Va. 19. S. 31 Jan. 1749   3

1536   JOHNSTON, William. Cirencester. Barber and peruke maker. J Hal. 4 yrs. Jam. no age. S. 6 March, 1750   17

1537   JOLLIFF, William. Holy Trinity, Coventry. Weaver. JD. 4 yrs. Md. 20. S. 15 Jan. 1719.   11

1538   JOMPSON (JOMSON,) William. St. Katherine Creed Church, London. Coachman. CV. 4 yrs. Va. 33. S. 19 ? 1725   95

1539   JONES, Abraham. Ruthen (Ruthin,) Denbigh, Wales. Labourer. JG. 4 yrs. Jam. 36. S. 11 Feb. 1730. 52

1540   JONES, Charles Henry. Chealsea, Mddx. Gardner.
W Bu. 4 yrs. Va. 21. S. 2 Feb. 1737   7

1541   JONES, Cornelius. St. Clement Danes, Mddx. JT. 4 yrs
Jam. 18. S. 21 May, 1731   137

1542   JONES, David. Lay Hall, Parish of Preson Goburn (Preston
Gubbals?) Nr. Shrewsbury, Salop. AC. 6 yrs. Va. or
Md. 17. M. 11 Dec. 1719   109

1543   JONES, David. Mouthey, Merionethshire, Wales
(Llanam Mouthwy?) Husbandman. W Bu. 4 yrs. Pa.
21. M. 10 Sept. 1730   96

1544   JONES, Diana. St. Dunstans, Fleet St. JDB. 4 yrs.
Jam. 17. S. 31 Jan. 1749   4

1545   JONES, Edward. St. James, Westminster, Mddx. JD.
4 yrs. Pa. 20. S. 25 Oct. 1725   124

1546   JONES, Edward. St. James, Westminster, Mddx. Stay
maker. JG. 4 yrs. Jam. 20. S. 12 Nov. 1729.   19

1547   JONES, Elizabeth. Spinster. St. Clement Danes, Mddx.
SG. 5 yrs. Va. 16. M. 16 Nov. 1727   20

1548   JONES, Evan. Filey (Tilley?) Salop. Husbandman.
Father and mother dead. NW. 5 yrs. Md. 17. S.
19 March, 1738   52

1549   JONES, Francis. St. James, Bristol. NM. 5 yrs. Md.
19. S. 5 April, 1735   17

1550   JONES, George. Chester (Chichester?) Sussex. Stay
maker. P Si. 4 yrs. Jam. 38. S. 1 Oct. 1731.   221

1551   JONES, Isaac. Lambeth, Surrey. Looking glass grinder.
P Si. 4 yrs. Pa. 29. S. 21 Sept. 1733   66

1552   JONES, John.   Painswick, Glos.   CV.   6 yrs.   Va. or Md.
17.   S.   21 Sept. 1720   132

1553   JONES, John.   Ailsbury (Aylesbury,) Bucks.   AC.   6 yrs.
Md.   19.   S.   25 Jan. 1721   12

1554   JONES, John.   Lannon (Llannon,) Carmarthen, Wales.
JD.   5 yrs.   St. C. or St. L.   16.   M.   3 Aug. 1722   70

1555   JONES, John.   Barnet, Herts.   BG.   4 yrs.   St. L.   18.
M.   1 Nov. 1722   177

1556   JONES, John.   Oswestry, Salop.   Husbandman.   WC2.
4 yrs.   Pa.   20.   M.   16 Aug. 1728   86

1557   JONES, John.   Ilminster, Somerset.   Book keeper.   W Bu.
4 yrs.   Jam.   34.   S.   27 Feb. 1730   91

1558   JONES, John.   St. Georges. Hanover Square, Mddx.   NM.
4 yrs.   Jam.   18.   S.   18 July, 1733   28

1559   JONES, John.   Abergavenny, Mon. Wales.   Husbandman.
NM.   3 yrs.   S. C. or West Indies.   25.   S.   5 Oct. 1734
                                          92

1560   JONES, John.   St. Margarets, Westminster, Mddx.   CM.
5 yrs.   Va. or Md.   15.   M.   30 June, 1735   42

1561   JONES, John.   Greenwich, Kent.   JT.   4 yrs.   Jam.   17.
S.   16 Sept. 1735   91

1562   JONES, John.   Carwis (Caerwys,) Flint, N. Wales.
House carpenter.   NM.   4 yrs.   Jam.   22.   S.   8 Oct. 1735
                                       114

1563   JONES, John.   Putney, Surrey.   Gardner.   Father and
mother dead.   JT.   4 yrs.   Md.   18.   S.   1 March, 1738
                                       46

1564   JONES, Joseph.   St. Botolphs, Aldersgate, London.   Carpenter and joyner.   P Si.   4 yrs.   Pa.   23.   S.   6 July, 1728. 11

1565   JONES, Joseph. Whitchurch, Salop. Bricklayer. R Wa.
4 yrs. Jam. 30. S. 4 July 1750   32

1566   JONES, Lewis. Merionethshire, N. Wales. JT. 4 yrs.
Jam. 19. M. 19 Sept. 1734   88

1567   JONES, Margaret. St. Martins in the Fields, Mddx.
Spinster JT. 4 yrs. S. C. 17. M. 2 June, 1732. 6

1568   JONES, Owen. Anglesea, Wales. CV. 5 yrs. Md.
19. M. 25 Jan, 1724   23

1569   JONES, Patient Job. St. James, Westminster, Mddx.
Spinster. JG. 6 yrs. Va. 18. M. 7 Feb. 1720   21

1570   JONES, Peter. Pasanfraid (Llansantfraid,) Danbyshire
(Denbigshire.) Blacksmith. JT. 4 yrs. Jam. 20.
S. 5 Jan, 1730   8

1571   JONES, Ralph. Chester. Taylor. JG. 4 yrs. Jam.
22. S. 11 Aug. 1730   66

1572   JONES, Richard. St. Gillians, Shrewsbury, Salop. JD.
5 yrs. Md. 18. M. 30 Sept. 1720   139

1573   JONES, Richard. Branier (Brynare,) Mon. Labourer.
NM. 4 yrs. Pa. 22. S. 5 Sept. 1730   89

1574   JONES, Richard. St. Leonards, Shoreditch, Mddx. Butcher. JG. 4 yrs. Jam. 23. S. 6 May, 1731   126

1575   JONES, Robert. St. Botolphs without Bishopsgate, London.
JG. 5 yrs. Md. or Pa. 19. S. 18 Feb. 1723   32

1576   JONES, Robert. St. Giles in the Fields. Sawyer. JT.
4 yrs. Jam. 23. S. 23 March, 1738   56

1577   JONES, Roger. Frodesham (Frodsham,) Cheshire. Barber.
JT. 3 yrs. S. C. 18. S. 24 Feb. 1737   23

1579 JONES, Samuel. Bissill Castle, Chester. J Wh. 5 yrs.
Jam. 17. M. 4 Jan, 1739   2

1580 JONES, Thomas. Carmarthon, Wales. Taylor. JD.
6 yrs. Md. 19. S. 30 July, 1718   39

1581 JONES, Thomas. Halloway (Holywell?) Flintshire. Brickmaker. NM. 4 yrs. Jam. 22. M. 19 Sept. 1730. 115

1582 JONES, Thomas. Hammersmith, Mddx. W Bu. 5 yrs.
Va. or Md. 18. S. 30 July, 1735   60

1583 JONES, Thomas. L(l)annon, Carmarthen, Wales. Surgeon. EP. 4 yrs. Jam. 25. S. 23 May, 1738.   42

1584 JONES, William. St. Margarets, Westminster, Mddx.
J Co. 6 yrs. Md. 16. S. 5 Feb. 1724   54

1585 JONES, William. Brentwood, Essex. Plaisterer. SG.
4 yrs. Antigua. 20. S. 24 Nov. 1727   8

1586 JONES, William. Landboyde (LLanboidy,) Carmarthenshire
Wales. Taylor. J BALL. 4 yrs. Pa. 25. S.
24 July, 1728   49

1587 JONES, William. St. James, Westminster, Mddx.
Weaver. JT. 5 yrs. Md. 24. M. 10 April, 1735.   22

1588 JONSON, John. Worksop, Notts. Carpenter. W Bu.
4 yrs. Jam. 21. S. 15 Sept. 1736   74

1589 JORDAN, Richard. Stonedon (Stondon,) Essex. Husbandman. J Bl. 4 yrs. Antigua. no age. S. 6 March, 1754
                                                              12

1590 JORDINE (JARDINE,) William. Yarmouth, Norfolk. Tin
plate worker. W Bu. 4 yrs. Jam. 22. S. 30 April,
1731   116

1591   JORN(E)S, John. Wooburn (Woburn,) Beds. Butcher.
        P Si. 4 yrs. Va. 19. S. 28 Dec. 1733   161

1592   JO(U)RDAIN, Francis, a native of France. Joyner. J Co.
        4 yrs. S.C. 30. S. 17 Nov. 1725   176

1593   JOY, Joseph. Bristol. Book keeper. WT. 4 yrs. Jam.
        19. S. 7 Oct. 1732   11

1594   JOYNSON, Joseph. Chester. Gardner. J Bl. 4 yrs.
        Jam. 19. S. 2 March. 1753   2

1595   JOYNSON (JOHNSON,) Samawel. Sut(t)on, Cheshire.
        J St. 5 yrs. Md. 16. S. 30 March, 1751   35

1596   JUDKIN, Elizabeth. St. Giles in the Fields, Mddx. Spin-
        ster. W Bu. 5 yrs. Md. 18. M. 25 Nov. 1727.   4

                            K

KAIRKMAN. See 1639

1597   KANE, Lesley. Morton, Lincs. Schoolmaster. JG.
        4 yrs. Jam. 18. S. 30 June, 1720   90

1598   KATE (KEATE,) Edmund. St. Johns, Westminster. NM.
        4 yrs. Jam. over 21? S. 31 Aug. 1736   70

1599   KATES, James. Isleworth, Mddx. Glover. P Si. 4yrs.
        Jam. 21. S. 3 Sept. 1734   80

1600   KAY, William. Sow(e) Nr. Coventry, Warwicks. CV.
        6 yrs. Md. 17. M. 19 Jan. 1724   12

1601   KAY, William. Mansfield Woodhouse, Notts. Saddler.
        NM. 4 yrs. Jam. 39. S. 7 May, 1735   35

1602   KEACH, Thomas. St. James, Norwich. AC. 6 yrs.
        Md. 16. M. 15 Aug. 1720   104

1603   KEARTLAND, Ann.   Chatham, Kent.   Widow.   CV.
5 yrs.   St. C. or Antigua.   19.   M.   16 May, 1723   58

KEATE.   See 1598

1604   KEEP, George.   Sturry, Nr. Canterbury, Kent.   JT.   4 yrs.
St. C.   18.   S.   17 July, 1722   57

1605   KELLEY, James.   Turue (Turoe,) Galloway, Ireland.
Mason.   JT.   4 yrs.   Jam.   19.   M.   22 Jan. 1729   10

1606   KELLITT, Matthew.   St. Mary le Strand, Mddx.   JT.
5 yrs.   Jam.   16.   S.   11 Dec. 1729   68

1607   KELLSON, Isaac.   St. Giles, Criplegate, London.   Cordwainer.   NM.   4 yrs.   Md.   23.   S.   1 Dec. 1733   131

1608   KELLSON, Jacob.   Trowbridge, Wilts.   Cordwainer.   NM.
4 yrs.   Md.   20.   S.   1 Dec. 1733   129

1609   KELLY, John.   Armagh, Ireland.   Cooper.   J Bl.   4 yrs.
Ga. or any other place.   20.   S.   9 June, 1752   6

1610   KELLY, Lawrence (Laurence.)   Dublin, Ireland.   Vintner.
Father dead.   J Wh.   4 yrs.   Jam.   18.   S.   16 Oct. 1739
                                                    114

1611   KELSEY (RELSEY,) John.   Luddington (Luddenden,) Yorks.
Groom.   JS.   4 yrs.   Jam.   18.   S.   2 Dec. 1752   11

1612   KELVIE, William.   Kilabright (Kirkudbright?) North Britain.
HUSBANDMAN.   JT.   4 yrs.   Md.   25.   S.   May 31, 1739
                                                    81

1613   KEM, Robert.   Chisleton (Chiseldon,) Wilts.   JG.   5 yrs.
Md.   18.   M.   15 Nov. 1721   75

1614   KEM, Samuel(l.)   High Cross, Warwicks.   Labourer.   NW.
4 yrs.   N. C.   25.   S.   31 July, 1738   49

1615   KEMP, John. Kin(g)ston, Notts. JT. 5 yrs. Jam. 15.
M. 26 April, 1731   110

1616   KENADY (KENNEDY,) Alexander. Trinity, Chester.
Cloath worker. P Si. 4 yrs. Va. 23. S. 16 Sept. 1727
   36

KENNEDY. See 1616

1617   KENNETT, Robert. St. Andrews, Holbourn, London.
Carpenter and joyner. P Si. 4 yrs. Jam. 22. S.
1 June, 1734   58

1618   KENNEY, Thomas. Cork, Ireland. CV. 4 yrs. Md.
19. M. 7 Jan. 1722   10

1619   KENSEY, Thomas. St. Clements, Cornwall. Plaisterer.
CV. 4 yrs. Md. 25. S. 15 Jan. 1724   2

1620   KENT(T,) Andrew. Galloway, Scotland. Dyer. 38.
TB. 4 yrs. Plantations. S. Sept. 1722   131

1621   KENT, Ishmael. Watham, Lincs. Linnen weaver. JT.
4 yrs. Md. 24. M. 26 Jan. 1724   26

1622   KENTING, John. St. Gregorys. London. Sawyer. EP.
4 yrs. Pa. 25. S. 14 Feb. 1737   17

1623   KERSHE, Edward. West Chester. W Bu. 5 yrs. Md.
16. S. 18 Feb. 1729   34

1624   KETTLEWELL Thomas. St. James, Clerkenwell, Mddx.
Cabinet maker. NM. 4 yrs. Md. 23. S. 13 Sept. 1735
   86

1625   KEY, John. Bolton, Lancs. Shoemaker. MW. 4 yrs.
Jam. 33. M. 13 Oct. 1738   55

1626   KEY, William. St. James, Colchester, Essex. Husbandman. JT. 4 yrs. Jam. 19. M. Last. Oct. 1733   104

1627   KEYS, John. St. Martins in the Fields, Mddx. J Co.
        4 yrs. Jam. 20. S. 7 Oct. 1725   109

1628   KILLET(T,) Samuel(1) Towcester, Northants. TB. 4 yrs.
        St. C. 20. S. 20 July, 1722   62

1629   KING, George. St. Martins in the Fields, Mddx. JT.
        4 yrs. Jam. 18. S. 24 Oct. 1733   97

1630   KING, Jasper. St. Neots, Hunts. JT. 4 yrs. Md.
        20. S. 1 Oct. 1723   102

1631   KING, John. Portsmouth, Hants. Sailor. EC. 4 yrs.
        Md. 20. M. 27 Feb. 1718   3

1632   KING, John. St. Giles, Criplegate , London. JT. 5 yrs.
        Jam. 16. S. 9 Feb. 1719   40

1633   KING, Thomas. St. Thomas, Southwark, Surrey. Cord-
        wainer. NM. 4 yrs. Md. 23. S. 13 Aug, 1735   72

1634   KINGHAM, Robert. Tingary(?) Beds. GK. 7 yrs. Va.
        15. S. 13 May, 1723   57

1635   KINSINGTON, Jeffery. Salisbury, Wilts. Coach harness
        maker. NM. 4 yrs. Jam. 24. S. 10 Nov. 1731.   267

1636   KIRBY, Thomas. Lample (?) Somerset. J Bl. 6 yrs.
        Md. no age. M. 23 Aug. 1756   20

1637   KIRK, Thomas. Barton? Oxon. Husbandman. Father
        and mother dead. MW. 5 yrs. Pa. 18. M. 7 Feb.
        1738   23

1638   KIRK, William. Stoughton, Leics. Husbandman. NM.
        4 yrs. Jam. no age. M. 20 Aug. 1736   64

1639   KIRKMAN (KAIRKMAN.) Richard. St. James, Westminster,
        Mddx. WC. 4 yrs. Pa. 19. S. 25 Oct. 1725   126

1640 KIRSHAW, James. St. Giles, Criplegate, London. Cordwainer. J Wi. 4 yrs. Md. 20. S. 6 July, 1720. 92

1641 KITCHIN, Joseph. St. Leonards, Shoreditch, Mddx. Kallendar. NM. 4 yrs. Md. 24. S. 1 Dec. 1733. 133

1642 KITCHINER, Joseph. St. Sepulchers, London. Joyner and carpenter. JT. 4 yrs. Jam. 27. S. 13 Oct. 1731
233

1643 KNIGHT, Francis. St. Gregorys, London. Cloath drawyer. JT. 4 yrs. Jam. 24. S. 24 Dec. 1724 108

1644 KNIGHT, Henry. St. Olaves, Southwark, Surrey. Wheelwright. W Bu. 4 yrs. Jam. 22. M. 24 Aug. 1730. 79

1645 KNIGHT, James. St. Andrews, Holbourn. W Bu. 5 yrs. Pa. or Md. 17. S. 9 Aug. 1728 71

1646 KNIGHT, Robert. St. Michaels, Dublin. Farowster. WB. 4 yrs. Md. or Pa. 19. S. 16 Sept. 1719. 39

1647 KNIGHT, Thomas. St. Giles, Criplegate, Mddx. Cordwainer. JG. 4 yrs. Jam. 21. 15 Jan. 1730. 25

1648 KREBS, Rachel. Christ Church, London. Spinster. AC. 5 yrs. Va. 19. S. 12 Oct. 1720 150

L

1649 LACON, Thomas. Tewksberry, Glos. NM. 7 yrs. Md. 16. S. 7 Dec. 1733 144

1650 LADLEY, Walter. Langholm, Roxbrough (now Dumfries.) Scotland. 4 yrs. Jam. WT. 20. S. 15 Feb. 1730 66

1651 LAKE, Walter. Exmouth, Devon. Gardner. 4 yrs. Jam. NM. 27. M. 9 Oct. 1730 135

1652   LALAM, William. Newcastle Upon Tine, Northumberland.
Labourer. JD. 4 yrs. Md. 19. M. 12 Sept.1720.   124

1653   LAMPARD, William. South Farnham, Surrey. Gardner.
W Th. 4 yrs. S.C. 19. S. 25 April, 1751   53

1654   LANCASHIRE, John. St. Giles in the Fields, Mddx. Carpenter and joiner. J Wh. 4 yrs. Jam. 30. S. 23 March,
1738   58

1655   LANDER, Henry. Gloucester. Baker and maltster. P Si.
4 yrs. Pa. 20. S. 3 Sept. 1730   86

1656   LANE, Jonathan. Dublin, Ireland. Carpenter. JT.
4 yrs. Jam. 45. S. 6 Nov. 1730   172

1657   LANE, Samuel. St. Marys in the Savoy, Mddx. Druggist.
JT. 3 yrs. Jam. 19. S. 4 Oct. 1720   141

1658   LANE, Samuel. Prickellwell (Prittlewell,) Essex. Barber.
RB. 4 yrs. Jam. 35. S. 26 Nov. 1725?   208

1659   LANE, Stephen. Bristol. JG. 4 yrs. Va. 19. S.
3 Feb. 1720   17

1660   LANE, Thomas. Chiswick, Mddx. JG. 4 yrs. St. C.
19. M. 16 June, 1722   34

1661   LANGDON, Henry. late of Boston N. E. Baker. P Si.
4 yrs. Pa. 25. S. 6 July, 1728   10

1662   LANGTON, John. St. Margarets, Westminster. RP.
4 yrs. Jam. no age. S. 8 Jan. 1755   2

1663   LARG, Joseph. St. Georges by Hanover Square. J Co.
7 yrs. Md. 16. M. 9 Nov. 1725   149

1664   LARKIN, John. Dublin, Ireland. Starch maker. WC.
4 yrs. Md. 20. M. 17 Nov.1725   171

1665 LARKIN, Thomas. Bengeo, Herts. Husbandman. NM.
4 yrs. Jam. 21. M. 15 Nov. 1736   157

1666 LA SALL(E,) John. St Anns, Westminster, Mddx. Watch-
maker. W Bu. 4 yrs. Va. or Md. 21. S. 18 Feb. 1730
     73

1667 LASLEY, James. Swansey, Carmarthen, Wales. Labourer.
JD. 5 yrs. Va. 19. S. 18 Jan. 1720   6

1668 LATHEM, Thomas. Penrith. Cumberland. Painter.
Father and mother dead. NW. 4 yrs. Jam. 20. S.
1 Aug. 1739   94

1669 LATON, John. Edmundsbury (Bury St. Edmunds,) Suffolk.
JD. 5 yrs. Va. 18. S. 4 April, 1720   59

1670 LATTER, John. St. Michaels, Cornhill, London. Sword
cutter. JT. 4 yrs. Jam. 27. S. 14 Sept. 1727.   32

1672 LAURIE, James. Selkirk, N. Britain. Tailor. Father
and mother dead. NM. 4 yrs. Md. 20. S. 7 Jan. 1736
     22

1673 LAVER (LEVER,) John. Blackfryers, London. Taylor.
JG. 4 yrs. Va. 35. S. 18 Dec. 1729   76

1674 LAWRENCE, John. Brockworth, Glos. W Bu. 7 yrs. Md.
15. S. 13 Sept. 1735   87

1675 LAWRENCE, John. Holbourn, London. J Bl. 5 yrs.
S. C. no age. S. 23 Aug. 1756   19

1676 LAWRENCE, Thomas. Madeley, Salop. Husbandman.
P Si. 4 yrs. Pa. 19. M. 26 Aug. 1730   83

1677 LAWRENCE, Rutter. Cunsfer? Norwich. Weaver. JT.
5 yrs. Barb. or Md. 18. S. 4 Aug. 1719   18

1678   LAWS, William. Dunstable, Beds. Husbandman. JG.
        4 yrs. Jam. 20. M. 23 March, 1722   47

1679   LAWSON, James. Edmonton, Mddx. Footman and groom.
        P Si. 4 yrs. Jam. 19. M. 11 Sept. 1730   98

1681   LAWSON, Richard. Kickey (Kirkby?) Yorks. Baker. NM
        3 yrs. Carolina or W.I. No age. S. 10 Aug. 1736   48

1682   LAWSON, Thomas. Chester. Surgeon. NM. 4 yrs.
        Jam. 25. S. 28 July, 1735   57

1683   LAYSINBY, Thomas. Bruton, Somerset. Groom. J Bl.
        4 yrs. Jam. no age. S. 12 March, 1753   3

1684   LAZELL, Clement. Rumford (Romford,) Essex. Poulterer.
        NM. 4 yrs. Md. 22. S. 13 Sept. 1735   82

1685   LEA, Francis. Elsmore (Ellesmere?) Salop. J Co. 5 yrs.
        Va. 23. S. 19 Nov. 1725   187

1686   LEADBEATER, William. Old Fish St. , London. Haber-
        dasher. SF. 4 yrs. Jam. 23. S. 3 Nov. 1736.   119/20

1687   LEAK, William. Silesbey, Leics. Taylor. P Si. 4 yrs.
        Md. 21. S. 27 May, 1727   45

1688   LEE, Abraham. Stepney, Mddx. JD. 4 yrs. Md. 20.
        M. 31 Oct. 1724   68

1689   LEE, George. St. Pauls, Shadwell. JS. 5 yrs. Md.
        18. S. 22 March, (1750)   22

1690   LEE, Robert. White Chappell, Mddx. J BALL. 7 yrs.
        Pa. or N.Y. 17. S. 19 July, 1728   42

1691   LEE, Sherwood. St. Giles in the Fields, Mddx. JD.
        5 yrs. Md. 18. S. 25 Jan. 1723   9

1692 LEE, Thomas. Carlton, Leics. Groom. WB. 5 yrs.
Md. or Va. 17. S. 3 Dec. 1719   104

1693 LEE, William. Limerick, Ireland. Taylor. JW. 4yrs.
Jam. 19. S. 3 Jan. 1738   1

1694 LEECH, Henry. Monkland, Herefordshire. Taylor.
SW. 4 yrs. Jam. 21. S. 23 March, 1736   42

1695 LEES, John. Allhallows, Lombard St., London. W Bu.
4 yrs. Jam. 17. S. 7 Oct. 1735   107/8

1696 LEES, William. Willan (Willington?) Derbyshire. P Si.
4 yrs. Jam. 19. M. 12 Aug. 1731   188

1697 LEIVESLEY. Robert. Chester. Barber and perrywig maker.
NM. 4 yrs. Jam. 31. S. 8 Oct. 1735   111

1698 LEO, Samuel. Blunham, Beds. SG. 4 yrs. Md. 19.
M. 17 Nov. 1725   177

1699 LEONARD, John. Whitechappell, Mddx. JT. 7 yrs.
Jam. 15. S. 11 June, 1720   85

1700 LEPPER, John. St. Butolphs, Aldgate, London. Butcher.
NM. 4 yrs. Va. 22. S. 1 Jan. 1733   2

1701 LEP(P)INGTON, Barber. York. P Si. 4 yrs. Pa. or
N. Y. 20. S. 18 July, 1728   40

1702 LESTER, Joseph. Thame, Oxon. Sawyer. JT. 4 yrs.
Jam. 21. M. 17 Dec. 1724   104

1703 LESTER, Samuel. St. Leonard, Shoreditch. J Bl. 4 yrs.
Md. No age. S. 22 April, 1756   15

1704 LETTINEAR, Daniel. Christ Church, Mddx. Labourer.
JT. 4 yrs. Jam. 22. M. 10 Aug. 1734   68

1705   LEVANIER, Louis. Calais, France. Book keeper. EC.
4 yrs. Barb. 17. S. 19 Aug. 1718   48

LEVER. See 1673

1706   LEVIN, Abraham. Luthgow (Linlithgow?) North Britain.
Taylor. Father dead. NW. 4 yrs. Md. 18. S.
23 May, 1739   73

1707   LEVINS, Thomas. Portsmouth, Hants. JG. 5 yrs. Md.
17. M. 8 Sept. 1722   124

1708   LEWEN (LEWIN,) Abraham. St. Anne Soho. Sawyer.
NW. 4 yrs. Md. 33. S. Dec. 19, 1738   79

LEWIN. See 1708

1709   LEWING, Richard. St. Botolph, Aldgate. Father dead,
mother Elizabeth Lewing. W Be. 7 yrs. Jam. 15. S.
18 May, 1739   ·   70

1710   LEWIS, Christopher. Trafthin (Trevethan,) Monmouth,
Wales. JG. 7 yrs. Jam. 18. M. 19 July, 1731   170

1711   LEWIS, David. Olive St. J St. 7 yrs. Md. 18. M.
6 April, 1751   28

1712   LEWIS, James. Glamorganshire, Wales. Husbandman.
JG. 4 yrs. Jam. 21. S. 16 Jan, 1724   4

1713   LEWIS, James. Stafford. JG. 4 yrs. Jam. 18. S.
15 Sept. 1730   105

1714   LEWIS, John. St. Dunstans in the West, London. Mother
Sarah Cotton. JT. 8 yrs. Pa. 15. S. 10 Sept. 1723
                                                         84

1715   LEWIS, John. Rowell? Glos. Gardner. NM. 5 yrs.
Pa. 19. S. 20 July, 1731   172

1716   LEWIS, Joseph. Lambeth, Surrey. SG. 4 yrs. Jam.
17. S. 2 Nov. 1725   135

1717   LEWIS, William. Abergenny, Mon. Wales. A CASH.
4 yrs. Nevis or St. C. 20. M. 6 Nov. 1729   12

1718   LEWIS, William. Hereford. JT. 4 yrs. Jam. 18. S.
18 Nov. 1730   182

1719   LEWIS, William. Welchpoole, Montgomery. Groom.
NM. 5 yrs. Antig. 20. S. 28 Dec. 1737   83

1720   LIFLEY (LIFLIY,) Edmund. St. James, Westminster, Mddx
Smith. P Si. 4 yrs. Jam. 27. S. 31 Dec. 1733. 163

LIFLIY. See 1720

1721   LIGHT, John. Tewksberry, Glos. Mother, Mary Clements.
JG. 5 yrs. St. C. or St. L. 14. M. 3 Aug. 1722. 69

1722   LIGHT, Joseph. St. James Colchester, Essex. Husbandman. JT. 4 yrs. Jam. 19. M. 25 Oct. 1733   98

1723   LILL(E)Y, Joseph. Allhallows the Great, London. Labourer. JT. 4 yrs. Jam. 20. S. 30 Oct. 1730.   168

1724   LILLY, John. Barkin, Essex. JD. 4 yrs. St. L. 18.
M. 25 Sept. 1722   132

1725   LILLY, Thomas. Windham, Norfolk. Husbandman. NM.
4 yrs. Jam. 22. M. 17 Aug. 1730   72

1726   LIMES, John. St. Margaret, Westminster, Mddx. Hatter.
P Si. 4 yrs. Jam. 20. S. 12 Nov. 1730   176

1727   LINDSEY, Edward. Christ Church, Spitlefields, Mddx.
Taylor. JT. 4 yrs. Jam. 17. S. 13 April, 1734. 44

LINEN. See 1729

1728   LINNELL, Mary. St. Giles, Criplegate, London. Spinster
P Si. 4 yrs. Jam. 20. M. 15 Oct. 1730   149

1729   LINNEN (LINEN,) Daniel. Kilriss (Kilrush?) Co. Clare,
Ireland. Labourer. P Si. 4 yrs. Jam. 25. S.
22 Feb. 1730   81

LITTEL. See 1730

1730   LITTLE, (LITTEL.) Andrew. Canaby (Cannonby,) Cumberland. CV. 4 yrs. Antigua or any Leeward Isles.
20. S. 27 Nov. 1724   79

1731   LITTLE, John. St. Giles, Mddx. Smith. JW. (for
Wm. Hill of Antegoa.) 4 yrs. Antegoa. 19. S.
7 Dec. 1721   81

1732   LITTLE, William. Newcastle. Carpenter. J Wh.
4 yrs. Pa. 20. M. 28 Feb. 1738   44

1733   LLOYD, John. Rithen (Ruthin?) Denbighshire. Shoemaker
EP. 4 yrs. Jam. 21. M. 28 April, 1738   36

1734   LLOYD, Philip. Chester. Carpenter. SG. 4 yrs.
Jam. 22. S. 29 Nov. 1725   211

1735   LLOYD, Sarah. Fullham, Surrey (?) Spinster. NM. 4yrs.
Md. 22. S. 13 Sept. 1735   85

1736   LLOYD, William. Henthan(?) Denby, Wales. Husbandman. JG. 4 yrs. Jam. 22. S. 1 Jan, 1722   1

1737   LLOYD, William. St. Nicholas, Worcester. Taylor.
JT. 4 yrs. Jam. 19. S. 14 Oct. 1734   100

1738   LOCK, Peter. Exeter, Devon. Smith and farrier. JT.
4 yrs. Jam. 19. S. 20 Nov. 1729   26

1739   LODGE, Jane. East Tower (Stour,) Dorset. Spinster
JD. 6 yrs. Pa. 20. M. 10 Sept. 1723   87

1740   LOMAN, Joshua.   Taunton dean, Somerset.   A poor lad.
JD.   6 yrs.   Md.   17.   M.   22 March, 1719   49

1741   LOMAX, Stephen.   St. Botolphs, Bishopsgate, London.
AC.   5 yrs.   Md.   17.   S.   26 Aug. 1719   26

1742   LOMAX, Thomas.   St. Leonards, Shoreditch, Mddx.   JL.
7 yrs.   Md.   18.   M.   1 Feb. 1719   26

1743   LONDON, Richard.   Stepney, Mddx.   WB.   7 yrs.   Pa.
14.   M.   27 May, 1719   14

1744   LONG, Jacob.   St. Martins le Grand, parish of Christ
Church, London.   Stay maker.   JT.   4 yrs.   Jam.
26 Nov. 1730   191

1745   LONG, John.   Rumsey (Romsey,) Hants.   Coachman.
NM.   4 yrs.   Jam.   27.   S.   5 Oct. 1733   86

1746   LONG, Richard.   St. James, Westminster, Mddx.   Carpenter.   JT. (for Hon Edward Pinnant of Jam.)   3 yrs.   Jam.
20.   S.   5 Dec. 1723   117

1747   LONGFORD, Joseph.   St. James, Clerkenwell, Mddx.
Chair maker and joyner.   J Ta.   4 yrs.   N. C.   23.   S.
8 July, 1736   30

1748   LONSDALE, George.   New Castle Upon Tine, Northumberland.   Smith.   CV.   4 yrs.   St. C.   20.   S.   2 Jan. 1722
     5

1749   LOTTS, John.   Boston, Lincs.   Mercer.   WC.   4 yrs.
Md.   22.   S.   17 Nov. 1725   172

1750   LOVE, Abraham.   Arrundell, Sussex.   Carpenter.   JT.
Jam.   23.   S.   16 Nov. 1733   110

1751   LOVEE, Peter.   Stepney, Mddx.   Weaver.   SG.   4 yrs.
Md.   20.   M.   20 Nov. 1725   196

1752   LOVEMORE, Charles.   St. James, Westminster,   Upholsterer.   J Bl.   4 yrs.   Jam.   no age.   S.   27 Aug. 1754
   22

1753   LOVELIDGE, Thomas.   St. Leonards, Shoreditch   Mddx.
W Bu.   4 yrs.   Jam.   20.   S.   24 Sept. 1734   90

1754   LOVELOCK, Daniel.   St. Botolphs, Aldgate. London.
Father, Nicholas Lovelock.   WC2.   7 yrs.   Pa.   16.   S.
23 July,   1728   45

1755   LOVETT, William.   Felton (Fouldon?) Norfolk.   R Wh.
5 yrs.   Md.   18.   M.   10 Feb. 1729   23

1756   LOWE, Joshua.   Derby.   Taylor.   JT.   4 yrs.   Jam.
19.   M.   11 Jan. 1722   14

1757   LOWNSDILL, John.   Ferry-bridge, Yorks.   Husbandman.
W Bu.   4 yrs.   Jam.   20.   M.   23 April, 1731.   109

1758   LOYELL, Anthony.   Native of the East Indies.   Labourer.
NM.   4 yrs.   Antigua.   26.   M.   31 Dec. 1730.   226

1759   LOYTE, William.   Lidlidge (Lydlinch,) Dorset.   NM.
6 yrs.   Va.   17.   S.   10 Jan. 1733   14

1760   LUCAS, William.   St. Albans, Herts.   Packthread spinner.
AC.   6 yrs.   Va. or Md.   18.   S.   21 Dec. 1720   176

1761   LUCK, Joseph.   Moulton, Northants.   Husbandman.   NM.
4 yrs.   Jam.   21.   M.   3 Jan. 1736   10

1762   LUING, Elizabeth.   Criplegate, London.   Spinster.   CV.
5 yrs.   Md.   23.   M.   4 Feb. 1724   49

1763   LUNN, Benjamin.   Chelmsford, Essex.   Baker.   NM.
4 yrs.   Md.   21.   S.   5 July, 1735.   46

1764   LUTTON, Sidney.   St. Andrew, Holborne.   Carpenter.
Father and mother dead.   JW.   4 yrs.   Jam.   20.   S.
9 Dec. 1738   75

1765   LYNCH, John.   St. Clement Danes, Mddx.   Clerk or
        writer. JG. 4 yrs. Jam. 18. S. 30 Aug. 1733   43

1766   LYNN, Edward.   St. Martins in the Fields. NM. 4 yrs.
        Jam. 21. S. 26 Oct. 1736   113

1767   LYON, Isaac.   Nephew of Mary Lyon of Christ Church,
        Spittlefields, Mddx., widow. RT. 9 yrs. Md. or Va.
        no age. M. June 1749   1

1768   LYON, John.   North St., Chichester, Sussex.   Carpenter.
        JT. 4 yrs. Jam. 23. S. 18 Oct. 1731   232

                              M

1769   MACCALLY, James.   Galloway (now Wigtown and Kirk-
        udbright,) N. Britain.   JT. 4 yrs. Jam. 17. M.
        15 March, 1737   28

1770   MACCLEAN (MACKLEN,) William.   Portsey (Portessie?)
        Bam (Banff) Scotland.   Cooper. NM. 5 yrs. Va. or
        Md. 22. S. 17 Aug. 1734   74

1771   MACDANIEL, Edward.   St. James, Clerkenwell, Mddx.
        Mother Eliner MacDaniel. JD. 7 yrs. Md. 16. S.
        20 Aug. 1723   76

1772   MACDONALD, Christopher.   Chester.   Taylor. NM.
        4 yrs. Va. 21. S. 6 Sept. 1734   81

1773   MACFARLANE, George.   Scotland. J Bl. 4 yrs. Md.
        no age. M. 7 April, 1756   9

1774   MACGRATH, Henry.   Edenburgh, Scotland.   Husbandman.
        W Bu. 4 yrs. Va. 22. S. 19 Oct. 1734   102

1775   MACKAY (McKay,) Daniel.   Co Entrem (Antrim,) Ireland.
        Husbandman. JG. 4 yrs. Jam. 17. S. 12 Dec. 1730
                                                             205

1776   MACKBENE, Robert. Inverness, N. Britain. Barber.
NM. 6 yrs. Jam. 16. S. 1 Nov. 1736   116

MACKDONALD. See 1864

1777   MACKE, William. Aberdeen, Scotland. NM. 4 yrs.
Antigua. 19. S. 18 Oct. 1731   245

1778   MACKENEY. James. Atholl, Perthshire, Scotland. P Si.
4 yrs. Pa. 19. M. 28 Sept. 1733   79

1779   MACKENNY (McKINZIEY?) Argyle, Scotland. JD. 4 yrs.
Md. 20. S. 4 Feb. 1724   64

1780   MACKENSEY, Mary. Bamf (Banff,) N. Scotland. Spinster. J Ta. 4 yrs. N. C. 22. M. 8 July, 1736.   33

MACKENZIE. See 1867

1781   MACK(I)E, Alexander. Aberdeen, Scotland. Groom.
NM. 4 yrs. Antigua. 22. S. 18 Oct. 1731   244

1782   MACKIER (McKEIR,) William. Carnock, Fife, Scotland.
Gardner. W Bu. 4 yrs. Jam. 22. S. 15 Sept. 1731. 209

1783   MACKKENSEY, Kenney. St. Margarets, Westminster,
Mddx. JT. 5 yrs. Jam. 16. M. 9 Jan. 1733   13

1784   MACKLAKEN, John. Kirkoven, Galway, North Britain.
Husbandman. NM. 4 yrs. Jam. 20. M. 8 Oct. 1736. 86

MACKLELAND. See 1869

MACKQUEEN. See 1789

1785   MACKWAY, William. Galloway, Scotland. Schoolmaster. AC. 4 yrs. Md. 20. S. 12 April, 1721.   33

1786   MACLARAN, John. Edinburg. N. Britain. Barber.
EP. 5 yrs. Md. 31. S. 20 Dec. 1737   79

1787 MACNEAL (McNell,) Daniel. Leverpool (Liverpool,)
Lancs. JG. 4 yrs. Md. 19. S. 11 Nov. 1731 276

1788 MACNEAL, Francis. Leverpool (Liverpool,) Lancs. Husbandman. JG. 4 yrs. Md. 21. M. 11 Nov. 1731 277

1789 MACQUEEN (MACKQUEEN,) Alexander. Banff, Scotland.
Barber. JT. 4 yrs. Jam. 17. S. 22 March, 1722. 45

1790 MACQUELIN, James. Bellamano, Co. Antrim, N. Ireland.
(Ballymena?) JG. 6 yrs. Md. 16. M. 15 Aug. 1720.
105

1791 MADDISON, James. St. Dunstons, London. Vintner.
NW. 4 yrs. Jam. 23. S. 10 March, 1738 45

1792 MADDOCKS, Thomas. Glamorganshire, Wales. Husbandman. JG. 4 yrs. Jam. 21. S. 16 Jan. 1724. 4

MAGIOR. See 1794

1793 MAHEW, Joseph. Hanslup (Hanslope,) Bucks. CV. 4yrs.
Md. 19. M. 30 Jan. 1723 12

1794 MAJOR (MAGIOR,) John. Greensnorton, Northants. Scale
beam maker. JT. 4 yrs. Pa. 20. S. 11 July, 1728. 32

1795 MAJOR, John. Southampton. AD. 5 yrs. Md. 18.
M. 29 March, 1750 15

1796 MALBERN, Cornelius. St. Olaves, Southwark, Surrey.
JL. 7 yrs. Md. 17. M. 1 Feb. 1719 28

1797 MALONE, John. Dublin. Cooper. J Bl. 4 yrs. Jam.
26. M. 4 July, 1750 35

1798 MALOON, Daniel. St. Martins in the Fields, Mddx.
Butcher. JG. 5 yrs. Md. 19. S. 3 Dec. 1729 51

1799   MAN, Henry. Wilsden (Willesden,) Mddx. P Si. 6 yrs.
Pa. 16. M. 11 June. 1731   151

1800   MAN, James. Dunkell (Dunkeld,) Perthshire, Scotland.
JT. 4 yrs. Jam. 18. S. 2 Oct. 1725   98

1801   MAN, William. St. Johns, Bristol. JoW. 5 yrs. Pa.
or anywhere in America. 16. S. 13 June. 1734   61

1802   MANDERFIELD, Paul. Claines, Worcester. JT. 4 yrs.
Jam. 18. S. 12 Nov. 1729   21

1803   MANGON, John. A native of Switzerland and late of
Chelsea, Mddx. Footman. NM. 4 yrs. Md. 22. S.
10 April, 1735   27

1804   MANNEKE, James Cason. St. Giles, Criplegate Without,
Mddx. To serve James Manneke his father, weaver.
5 yrs. Md. 18. M. 18 July, 1720   93

1805   MANNING, Benjamin. Muchadam (Much Hadham,) Herts.
J Go. 5 yrs. Antigua. no age. S. 28 Feb. 1758.   3

1806   MANNING, Joseph. London. J Bl. 5 yrs. Md. no
age. M. 7 April, 1756   7

1807   MANSER, Joshua. Bristol. Labourer. Father and mother
dead. NW. 4 yrs. Jam. 20. S. 25 July, 1739   91

1808   MANSFIELD, Jonathan. St. Martins in the Fields, Mddx.
Twister. JT. 5 yrs. N. E. 19. S. 7 March, 1721   24

1809   MANTLE, Richard. Longhope, Glos. Wheelwright. EP.
4 yrs. Jam. 25. S. 11 May, 1738   38

1810   MAROT, Reny. St Martins in the Fields, Mddx. Barber
and peruke maker. J GEE. 5 yrs. Md. or Va. 20. S.
9 Feb. 1722   33

1811 MANTON, Lawrence (Larrance.) Leddington (Liddington,)
      Rutland. Wheeler. NM. 4 yrs. Jam. 34. S.
      8 April, 1737   43

1812 MARRAS, John. Whalesby (Walesby,) Lincs. T Cr.
      3 yrs. On board ship. 25. S. 28 Jan, 1757   10

1813 MARSDEN, Christopher. St. Martins in the Fields, Mddx.
      Carver. JT. 4 yrs. Jam. 22. S. 3 Jan. 1722   7

1814 MARSH, Stayfield. St. Clement Danes, Mddx. P Si.
      5 yrs. St. C. 18. S. 9 Feb. 1730   49

1815 MARSH, William. St. Giles in the Fields, Mddx. Plais-
      terer. JT. 4 yrs. Jam. 19. S. 19 June, 1730   54

1816 MARSHALL, George. St. James, Westminster. Taylor.
      NM. 4 yrs. Va. or Md. 27. S. 1 Dec. 1736   183

1817 MARSHALL, James. St. Anns, Westminster, Mddx.
      Groom. NM. 4 yrs. Md. 22. S. 10 April, 1735.   25

1818 MARSHALL, John. Nottingham. Wool comber. JT.
      4 yrs. Jam. 20. S. 12 March, 1732   12

1819 MARSHALL, Richard. Whitchurch, Hants. Taylor.
      Father in Newberry, Berks. W Bu. 4 yrs. Va. 20. S.
      15 Dec. 1736   206

1820 MARSHALL, Susanah. Shrewsbury. Spinster. RH. 4 yrs.
      Va. no age. M. 16 March, 1750   19

1821 MARSHEL, Jonathan. Ingham, Norfolk. Carpenter.
      Father at Horning, Norfolk. J Wh. 4 yrs. Jam. 19. S.
      3 Nov. 1737   57

1822 MARSTON, Gilbert. Slawston, Leics. JG. 4 yrs. St. L.
      21. S. 6 Oct. 1722   149

1823   MARTEN (MARTINE,) Alexander. Inverness, Scotland.
NM. 5 yrs. Jam. 16. S. 29 Aug. 1733   37

1824   MARTIN, Philip. Chelsie (Chelsea,) Mddx. Butcher.
MW. 4 yrs. Pa. 21. M. 21 Feb. 1738   24

1825   MARTIN, Ralph (Robert.) Cannon St., London. Labourer. Father and mother dead. W Bu. 5 yrs. Md. 16.
M. 10 Jan. 1736   25

1826   MARTIN, Walter. Salisbury and late of Southampton,
Hants. Taylor. JT. 5 yrs. Va. or Md. 17. S.
6 Aug. 1734   66

1827   MARTIN, William. St. Andrews, Holbourn, Mddx. JW.
7 yrs. Va. 16. S. 23 April, 1720   79

MARTINE. See 1823

1828   MASON, Edward. Chatteris, Isle of Ely, Cambs. Glover.
JD. 5 yrs. Va. 18. M. 23 April 1720   80

1829   MASON, Grace. St. Margarets, Westminster, Mddx.
Widow. JG. 5 yrs. Barb. 21. M. 29 Jan. 1724.   33

1830   MASON, James. Dorchester, New England. Labourer.
JD. 4 yrs. Md. 19. M. 19 Aug. 1720   107

1831   MASON, John. Prestidge (Prestwich,) Nr. Manchester,
Lancs. Joyner. AC. 5 yrs. New England. 20. S.
9 March, 1721   25

1832   MASON, Thomas. Bath, Somerset. Cordwainer. P Si.
4 yrs. Jam. 20. S. 9 June, 1733   14

1833   MASON, Thomas. St. Mary Magdalene, Bermondsey,
Southwark, Surrey. Painter. NM. 4 yrs. Md. 28.
S. 25 March, 1735   11

1834   MASSEY, Elizabeth. St. Olaves, Southwark, Surrey.
Spinster. P Si. 4 yrs. Md. 21. M. 1 Nov.1733. 106

1835   MASSEY, John. Chelsea, Mddx. Joyner. P Si. 4 yrs.
Md. 45. S. 26 Nov. 1730   189

1836   MATHEWS, John. St. Martins in the Fields, Mddx.
Mother, Ann King. W Bu. 7 yrs. Jam. 15. S.
22 Oct. 1730   156

1837   MATHEWS, Robert. Betsworth (Betchworth,) Surrey.
Groom. J Br. 4 yrs. Jam. 16. M. 14 Aug.1749. 3

1838   MATTHEWS, Arnold. Whitefryers. Distiller. NM.
4 yrs. Jam. 38. S. 24 Dec. 1736   209

1839   MATHEWS, Benjamin. Litchfield, Staffs. JD. 8 yrs.
Md. 15. M. Last Jan. 1723   14

1840   MATTHEWS, Benjamin. St. Botolphs, Aldgate, London.
JD. 7 yrs. S. C. 16. S. 9 Dec. 1723   118

1841   MATTHEWS, James. St. Clement Danes, Mddx. CV.
5 yrs. Md. 19. S. 16 Jan. 1724   6

1842   MATTHEWS, John. St. Leonards, Shoreditch, Mddx.
JT. 6 yrs. S. C. 17. S. 6 June, 1732   8

1843   MATTHEWS, Sarah. St. James, Clerkenwell, Mddx.
Spinster. AC. 5 yrs. Va. 19. M. 12 Oct. 1720   151

1844   MATTHEWS, William. Abergaveny, Mon. Wales. TB.
4 yrs. St. C. 20. M. 16 July, 1722   54

1845   MATTHEWS, William. Landil Parthole (Llantilio Pertholey,) Mon. Wales. Husbandman. JD. 5 yrs. Md.
20. M. 26 Sept. 1723   100

1846   MATTHEWS, William. Hertford. W Bu. 4 yrs. Jam.
19. S. 16 Oct. 1736   93

1847   MATTREVERS, William.   St. Magnus the Martyr by
London Bridge.   Vintner.   JT.   4 yrs.   Jam.   22.   S.
18 Oct. 1733   93

1848   MAULE, James.   Chessey (Chertsey?) Surrey.   SF.   18.
M.   6 Dec. 1736   185

1849   MAULE, Nathaniel.   St. Giles in the Fields, Mddx.   Cordwainer.   JT.   4 yrs.   Md.   26.   S.   27 Jan. 1724   32

1850   MAWD, John.   Leeds, Yorks.   Cloth worker.   JD.   5 yrs.
Va.   18.   S.   18 Oct. 1720   154

1851   MAXWELL, John.   St. Sepulchers, London.   Distiller.
NM.   4 yrs.   Jam.   25.   S.   2 Aug. 1735   66

1852   MAY, James.   Portsmouth, Hants.   JG.   7 yrs.   Md.
17.   S..   29 Jan. 1724   34

1853   MAY, John.   Kings North, Kent.   Husbandman.   JT.
4 yrs.   Jam.   20.   M.   2 April, 1724   41

1854   MAY, William.   Lin (King's Lynn?) Norfolk.   Cooper.
Father and mother dead.   J Wh.   4 yrs.   Jam.   19.   S.
17 Feb. 1738   20

1855   MAY, William.   Reading, Berks.   TN.   5 yrs.   Va. or
on board ship.   No age.   S.   14 Dec. 1756   29

1856   MAYES, Robert.   Allhallows, Barkin(g,) London.   Groom.
NM.   4 yrs.   Pa.   20.   S.   22 June, 1731   164

1857   MAYNARD (MAYNERD,) John.   Taunton, Somerset.   Bricklayer.   EP.   4 yrs.   Va. or Md.   21.   S.   19 April, 1737.   45

1858   MAYNERD (MAYNARD,) Laurence.   Ashby de la Zouche,
Leics.   NM.   5 yrs.   Md.   20.   S.   29 Dec. 1729   87

1859   MAYSEY, John.   Chiswick, Mddx.   W Bu.   5 yrs.   Va.
or Md.   19.   S.   17 Feb. 1730   71

1860 MAYSTON, Robert. Yarmouth, Norfolk. Smith. JT.
4 yrs. Jam. 20. S. 22 Feb. 1730 86

1861 McBETH. James. Edenborough, Scotland. NM. 5 yrs.
Antigua. 15.. S. 16 Oct. 1731 243

1862 McCLAREN, Alexander. Muthell (Muthill,) Perthshire,
Scotland. Cook and butcher. JT. 4 yrs. Jam. 24.
S. 7 Aug. 1731 184

1863 McCURR, Daniell. Edingburgh. R Br. 7 yrs. Jam.
12. M. 4 Nov. 1736 130

1864 McDONALL (MACKDONALD,) James. St. Botolph,
Bishopsgate. Dyer. Father John Mackdonald. W Bu.
4 yrs. Pa. 19. S. 23 Feb. 1738 29

1865 McGIBBON, Robert. Strowan, Perthshire, N. Britain. Husbandman. JS. 4 yrs. Jam. 17. S. 31 July, 1753 21

1866 McILROY, John. Inch, Galloway (now Wigtownshire,)
Scotland. Husbandman. JT. 4 yrs. Jam. 18. S.
26 Aug. 1731 192

McKEIR. See 1782

1867 McKENZIE (MACKENZIE) Collin (Colin) Inverness.
WS. 4 yrs. Antigua. no age. S. 30 March, 1754. 15

1868 McKENZIE, David. Auldearn, Scotland. CK. 6 yrs.
N. Y. no age. S. 16 Aug. 1754 21

McKINZIEY. See 1779

1869 McLELAND (MACKLELAND,) James. Stepney, Mddx.
P Si. 5 yrs. Pa. 18. S. 19 June, 1731 159

1870 McMIN, John. Andover. WJ. 3 yrs. Antig. no age.
S. 7 Dec. 1757 16
McNELL. See 1787

1871   McPHERSON, James. Kengusey (Kingussie) Invernesshire, Scotland. Printer. JT. 4 yrs. Jam. 19. S. 14 Sept. 1727   35

1872   MEAD, Matthew. Enfield. Mddx. JG. 4 yrs. Md. 21. S. 23 Nov. 1722   186

1873   MEAD, Samuel. Malden, Essex. P Si. 6 yrs. Pa. 15. M. 20 Sept. 1733   64

1874   MEAGHER, James. Clonmell, Tipperary, Ireland. EP. 4 yrs. Jam. 18. S. 5 Nov. 1731   260

1875   MEARS, James. Grafton, Warwicks. Husbandman. J Bl. 4 yrs. Jam. no age. S. 23 Jan, 1754   2

1876   MEBBISON, John. Leicester. JT. 7 yrs. Jam. 16. S. 4 Nov. 1734   106

1877   MEED(E,) John. Stutly (Stewkley?) Bucks. Footman. Mother Grace Meed. JT. 4 yrs. Jam. 20. S. 24 March, 1721   30

1878   MEEK, John. Kendall, Westmorland. Bricklayer. J Ta. 4 yrs. Va. 21. S. 29 Nov. 1736   180

1879   MEGINISS, Anthony. Clain (Clane,) Co. Kildare, Ireland. Husbandman. NM. 4 yrs. Jam. 23. M. 30 Sept. 1730.   127

1880   MELTON, Richard. Lambeth, Mddx. Cordwainer. J Wi. 4 yrs. Md. 20. S. 4 July, 1720   91

1881   MEMBERY, Charles. Porbury, (Panborough?) Somerset. Husbandman. NS. 4 yrs. Philadelphia. 18. S. 21 April, 1750   17

1882   MEORCY, George. St. Giles, Criplegate, London. Joyner. P Si. 4 yrs. Jam. 31. M. 10 Sept. 1730.   93

1883   MERCER, John. Nottingham. Wool comber. JT. 4 yrs.
Jam. 20. M. 12 Sept. 1733   57

1884   MERDITH, John. Holt, Worcs. Gardner JS. 4 yrs.
Md. no age. S. 11 April, 1751   40

1885   MEREFIELD, Robert. Hewish, Somerset. Taylor. 4 yrs.
Jam. 19. S. 7 Dec. 1724   89

1886   MERIDITH, Elizabeth. Cardiff. Glam. Wales. Spinster.
CV. 5 yrs. Va. 16. M. 5 April, 1720   63

1887   MERIDITH, Hestor. (MERDITH, Easter.) Widow. NC.
5 yrs. Md. 20. S. 3 Sept. 1718   30

1888   MERITON, Thomas. St. Saviours, Norwich. Weaver.
JG. 4 yrs. Md. 19. S. 29 Sept. 1718   58

1889   MERRISON, Henry. Rayner, Norfolk. WC. 4 yrs.
Jam. 16. M. 11 Nov. 1725   154

1890   MERVEN (MERWIN,) Nicholas. Alhallows, Lombard St.
Joyner. J Ta. 4 yrs. Jam. 29. S. 13 Oct. 1736.   89

MERWIN. See 1890

1891   MESSER, Theodore. Spitlefields, Mddx. Labourer.
P Si. 5 yrs. Md. 18. M. 2 Jan. 1730   4

1892   MICHELL, Barnard. A native of High Garmaney. W Bu.
5 yrs. Va. or Md. 19. S. 21 Dec. 1730   224

1893   MICKANNEY, Timothy. Dublin, Ireland. JD. 7 yrs.
St. L. 16. M. 5 Nov. 1722   179

1894   MIDDLEBROOK, Theophilus. Cambridge. Labourer.
NM. 4 yrs. Md. 21. S. 2 Feb. 1733   21

1895   MIDDLETON, George. Aberdeen, Scotland. RB. 4 yrs.
Jam. 18. S. 1 April, 1724   40

1896   MIDWINTER, George.   St. Saviours, Southwark, Surrey.
Carpenter.   JT.   4 yrs.   Jam.   32.   S.   17 March, 1724
   85

1897   MIL(L)BOURN, John.   St. Saviours, Southwark, Surrey.
Box maker.   J BALL.   4 yrs.   Pa.   27.   S.   6 July, 1728.   8

1898   MILES, Richard.   Pressen (Preston?) Herefordshire.   NM.
5 yrs.   Md.   18.   S.   9 Dec. 1729   63

1899   MILES, William.   Emley (Elmley) Castle, Worcs.   Husbandman.   JD.   4 yrs.   Va.   19.   M.   17 Sept. 1722   129

1900   MILLARD, Henry.   Stroud, Glos.   JD.   6 yrs.   Md.   16.
M.   20 Dec. 1720   175

1901   MILLER, Edith.   St. Catherines by the Tower, London.
Spinster.   NM.   4 yrs.   Jam.   17.   S.   2 Aug. 1731.   176

1902   MILLER, Francis.   St. Johns, Dublin, Ireland.   Joyner.
JW.   4 yrs.   Md.   20.   S.   30 Sept. 1720   140

1903   MILLER, James.   St. Clement Danes, Mddx.   Taylor.
P Si.   4 yrs.   Md.   21.   S.   29 Aug. 1733   38

1904   MILLER, John.   Edenbrough, Scotland.   J BALL.   4 yrs.
Pa. or N. Y.   18.   S.   17 July, 1728   38

1905   MILLER, Joseph.   Burbridge (Burbage,) Leics.   JT.   5 yrs.
St. L.   16.   M.   12 Oct. 1722   5

1906   MILLER, Richard.   St. Dunstans, Canterbury.   JD.   7 yrs.
St. C or St. L.   15.   M.   4 Aug. 1722   83

1907   MILLER, Theophilus.   St. James, Westminster.   Labourer.
Mother Ann Miller.   NM.   5 yrs.   Md.   19.   M.   1 Feb.
1736   34

1908   MILLER, Thomas.   St Anns, Blackfryers, London.   JG.
5 yrs.   Jam.   20.   S.   22 April, 1731   107

1909   MILLESON, Thomas. St. Martins in the Fields, Mddx.
P Si. 4 yrs. Jam. 20. S. 16 Sept. 1730   108

1910   MILLOT, Daniel. Stepney, Mddx. Weaver. Father and
mother dead. NW. 4 yrs. Pa. 19. S. 27 Feb. 1738. 37

1911   MILLS, Ann. St. Georges, Bloomsbury. JH. 4 yrs.
Jam. No age. S. 14 Oct. 1731   239

1912   MILLS, Daniel. St. Botolphs, Aldersgate, London. Weaver. P Si. 5 yrs. Pa. 18. M. 17 June, 1731   158

1913   MILLS, David. Gibralter. Shoemaker. Siker? of London,
Marriner. 4 yrs. Philadelphia. No age. S. 2 May,
1750   21

1914   MILLS, Francis. St. Andrews, Holbourn, London. Gardner. Father Benjamin Mills. NM. 4 yrs. Jam. 19.
S. 19 Aug. 1730   75

1915   MILLS, Leonard. Bishopsgate St., London. J Bl. 5 yrs.
Md. 17. M. 29 March, 1751   26

1916   MILLS, Mary. St. Pauls, Covent Garden, Mddx. Spinster. NM. 4 yrs. Jam. 19. M. 2 Aug. 1731   177

1917   MILLS, Peter. Chester (le Street?) Durham. JD. 6 yrs.
St. L. 16. S. 5 Oct. 1722   144

1918   MILLS, Robert. Woodbridge, Suffolk. Gardner. R Wh.
5 yrs. Md. 20. S. 23 Jan. 1729   12

1919   MILLS, Robert. Woodbridge, Suffolk. Patton maker.
W Bu. 4 yrs. Md. 22. S. 16 Dec. 1730   216

1920   MILLS, Simon. Isham, Notts. Carpenter. BW. 4 yrs.
Jam. 18. S. 9 Nov. 1736   143

1921   MILLWARD, Joseph. Ails Owen (Halesowen,) Warwicks.
Husbandman. NM. 4 yrs. Jam. 30. S. 23 Sept. 1735
95

1922   MINNILLEY, Robert.   Wisbitch (Wisbech,) Isle of Ely, Cambs. Labourer. JD. 5 yrs. Va. 19. M. 18 Jan. 1720
7

1923   MITCHELL, Henry.   Norwich.   W Bu.   4 yrs.   Antigua. 18. S. 30 April, 1734
45

1924   MITCHELL, John.   St. Brides, Fleet St. , London.   Sawyer P Si. 5 yrs. Md. 20. S. 8 Nov. 1727
25

1925   MITCHELL, John.   St. Clement Danes,   Labourer.   Father Michael Betthon. J Wh. 6 yrs. Jam. 15. M. 25 Oct. 1739
115

1926   MITCHELL, Richard.   Paulton, Somerset.   Husbandman. MW. 5 yrs. Jam. 19. S. 11 Nov. 1736
149

1927   MITCHELL, Robert.   Edenborough, Scotland.   To serve in the employment of a school master. JG. 4 yrs. Md. 19. S. 13 Nov. 1723
107

1928   MITCHELL, Thomas.   St. Andrews Wardrobe, London. Felt maker. P Si. 4 yrs. Pa. 36. S. 31 May, 1731.
145

1929   MITCHELL, Thomas.   Maidstone, Kent.   Bricklayer. NW. 4 yrs. Jam. 27. S. 12 Sept. 1739
102

1930   MITCHELL, William.   St. Giles Criplegate, London. Dyer. W Bu. 5 yrs. Md. 22. S. 14 Feb. 1731.
5

1931   MITCHENER, Mary.   St. Mary Ax, London.   Spinster. P Si. 3 yrs. Jam. 33. S. 25 Sept. 1730
124

1932   MOAD, James.   St. Albans, Herts.   Taylor.   JT.   4 yrs. Barb. 22. S. 16 July, 1735
53

1933   MOLONEY, John.   Munster.   Book keeper.   AT.   4 yrs. Jam. 20. S. 15 Dec. 1749
14

1934   MONGGOMERY (MOUNTGOMERY,) Jonathan. Christ
Church, Spitlefields, Mddx. Turner. EP. 4 yrs. Jam.
25. S. 17 Nov. 1731   283

1935   MONTAU (MONTAUR,) Sarah. St. Giles in the Fields,
Mddx. Spinster. JT. 5 yrs. Md. 19. S. 30 Jan.
1719   21

MONTAUR. See 1935

1936   MOODY, William. Lambeth, Surrey. Gardner. P Si.
4 yrs. Montserrat. 19. M. 22 Oct. 1729   5

1937   MOON, Samuel. St. Johns, Waping, Mddx. Carpenter.
R B. 4 yrs. Jam. 23. S. 17 Feb. 1730   72

1938   MOOR, Edward. New Castle Upon Tine, Northumberland.
Husbandman. JT. 4 yrs. St. Christ. 18. S. 10 July,
1722   49

1939   MOOR, Robert. Beverly, Yorks. Gardner. JT. 4 yrs.
Jam. 23. S. 20 Dec. 1724   102

1940   MOOR(E,) Robert. St. James, Westminster, Mddx. W Bu.
4 yrs. Pa. 19. S. 13 Aug. 1728   79

1941   MOORE, Charles. St. Pauls, Covent Garden, Mddx.
Grocer. NM. 4 yrs. Md. 36. S. 16 Nov. 1734. 110

1942   MOORE, John. St. James, Westminster, Mddx. CV.
5 yrs. Va. 18, S. 4 Aug. 1723   71

1943   MOOR(E,) Lewis. Clerkenwell, Mddx. Ribbon weaver.
P Si. 4 yrs. Jam. 19. S. 28 Sept. 1730   126

1944   MOORE, Nathaniel. Snels(t)on, Derbyshire. Taylor.
NM. 4 yrs. Md. 26. M. 14 Dec. 1730   210

1945   MOOR(E,) Richard. Reading, Berks. JT. 4 yrs. Pa.
19. S. 26 Feb. 1724   73

1946   MOOREFIELD (MOREFIELD,) Joseph.   Ireland.   Labourer.
JD. 7 yrs. Md. 16. M. 3 Jan. 1720   2

MOREFIELD. See 1946

1947   MORELAND, Christopher.   Winton, Westmorland.   Husbandman. EP. 4 yrs. Md. 20. S. 13 March, 1737. 25

MORELL. See 1958

1948   MORGAN, John. St. Martins in the Fields, Mddx. Husbandman. NM. 4 yrs. Md. 24. S. 13 Sept. 1735 84

1949   MORGAN, John. Wuesley? Nr. Kendal, Westmorland.
Gardner. J WIL. 5 yrs. Jam. no age. S. 7 Oct.
1751   64

1950   MORGAN, Mercer. St. Lawrence Jewry, London. Book keeper. W Bu. 5 yrs. Md. 20. S. 19 Nov. 1729. 24

1951   MORGAN, Richard. Cowbridge, Glam. Wales. JT.
4 yrs. Jam. 16. M. 21 Aug. 1731   191

1952   MORGAN, Roger. Berr(i)ew, Montgomery, Wales. JG.
5 yrs. Md. 17. M. 27 May, 1723   61

1953   MORGAN, Simon. Slapton, Northants. Tanner. JT.
4 yrs. Jam. 19. S. 30 Oct. 1730   167

1954   MORGAN, Thomas. St. Sepulchers, London. Joyner.
JT. 5 yrs. Md. 20. S. 4 Feb. 1724   51

1955   MORGAN, William. St. Botolphs, Aldersgate, London.
Labourer. CM. 5 yrs. Md. or Va. 26. S. 1 July,
1735   43

1956   MORGAN, William. Marbeth, Pembroke. Husbandman.
NM. 4 yrs. Jam. over 21. S. 21 Aug. 1736 57

1957 MORLEY, James. Richmond, Surrey. AC. 8 yrs. Md.
or Pa. 14. M. 1 Feb. 1719 25

1958 MORREL (MORRELL,) Anthony. Lee, Essex. Husbandman.
Father at Hunsdeane (Hunsdon,) Herts. SF. 4 yrs. Jam.
20. S. 24 Feb. 1738 34

1959 MORRIS, Richard. Aberistwith, Wales. Taylor. EP.
4 yrs. Jam. 26. S. 25 May, 1738 43

1960 MORRIS, Thomas. Hayes, Mddx. Footman. JT. 4 yrs.
Jam. 21. S. 18 Sept. 1730 112

1961 MORRIS, Thomas. Bristol and later of Tower Hill, London.
P Si. 7 yrs. Pa. 17. S. 11 June, 1731 148

1962 MORRIS, Thomas. St. John the Evangelist, Westminster,
Mddx. JT. 4 yrs. Ga. 19. S. 27 Sept. 1733 78

1963 MORRIS, William. Rackley, Bristol. Cooper. JT. 4yrs.
Jam. 20. S. Last May, 1721 37

1964 MORRIS, William. St. Margarets, Westminster, Mddx.
SF 6 yrs. Jam. 16. S. 5 Dec. 1734 114

1965 NORTON, John. Ashby, Norfolk. P Si. 5 yrs. Pa.
19. M. 11 June, 1731 150

1966 MORTON, Richard. Wolverhampton, Staffs. Buckle
maker. SG. 4 yrs. Jam. 20. M. 12 Nov. 1725. 156

1967 MORTON, Robert. Mar Chin (Mauchline?) Ayreshire,
Scotland. Husbandman. W Bu. 4 yrs. Jam. 19. S.
5 May, 1731 125

1968 MOSES, Richard. Carlisle, Cumberland. Weaver. NM.
4 yrs. Md. 24. S. 6 Dec. 1733 140

1969 MOSELEY, Thomas, Nottingham. Stockingmaker. JD.
5 yrs. Md. 19. S. 3 Jan. 1720/21 1

1970   MOULD, Hester. St. Margarets, Westminster, Mddx. Spinster. P Si. 4 yrs. Jam. 25. S. 18 Sept.1730. 111

1971   MOUNCEY, Thomas. Newbican (Newbiggin,) Cumberland. JT (for Thos. Walker of the Bahama Soc.) 4 yrs. Bahamas or Providence. 20. S. 8 Aug. 1721. 64

MOUNTGOMERY. See 1934

1972   MUIRHEAD, Alexander. New Castle Upon Tine, Northumberland. Cork cutter. P Si. 4 yrs. Pa. 19. S. Last May, 1731 144

1973   MULFORD, Thomas. Guildford, Surrey. Husbandman, W Bu. 4 yrs. Jam. 23. S. 9 Jan. 1730 20

MULLIKEN. See 1974

1974   MULLIKIND (MULLIKEN,) Robert. Lisburn, Co. Antrim, N. Ireland. Glazier. JT. 4 yrs. Pa. 18. S. 13 June, 1720 86

1975   MULLINS, Thomas. Gravesend, Kent. P Si. 4 yrs. S. C. 19. S. 13 Sept. 1733 60

1976   M(O)UNCKTON, William. Pocklington, Yorks. Drawer. Father dead, mother at York. NW. 4 yrs. Jam. 17 S. 14 Sept. 1739 103

1977   MUNTER, John. St. Dunstans, Stepney. Weaver. NM. 4 yrs. Jam. 27. M. 17 Nov. 1736 163

1978   MURRAY, Benjamin. St. Giles in the Fields, Mddx. WD. 7 yrs. Va. 16. M. 12 April, 1751 45

1979   MURRAY, David. Cockermouth, Cumberland. Husbandman. Father and mother dead. J Wh. 5 yrs. Md. 18. M. 27 Oct. 1737 54

1980   MUSSON, John. Fusdack (Fosdyke?) Lincs. Servant.
TP. 4 yrs. Jam. no age. S. 2 Oct. 1755   9

1981   MYNAT(T,), Richard. Billiter Lane, London. Cook.
TL. 4 yrs. Va. 20. S. 12 Feb. 1749.   8

N

1982   NASH, John. St. Botolph, Aldersgate, London. Cordwainer. NM. 4 yrs. Jam. 19. S. 16 July, 1733. 24

1983   NASH, Joseph. St. Magnus, London Bridge. Brickmaker.
Father and mother dead. SF. 5 yrs. Md. 20. S.
18 Feb. 1736   37

NEAILE. See 1987

1984   NEAL, William. Harpingham (Erpingham,) Norfolk. JG.
5 yrs. Jam. 20. M. 23 April, 1731   108

1985   NEALE, Francis. St. Catherines by the Tower, London.
W Bu. 6 yrs. Jam. 17. S. 24 Dec. 1730   225

1986   NEALE, Gideon. March, Cambs. TV. 3 yrs. Any of
his ships. 16. S. March 4, 1957   13

1987   NEALE, (NEAILE.) Robert. Portsmouth, Hants. JD.
5 yrs. Md. 18. S. 23 Aug. 1720   113

1988   NEALE, Robert. Oundle, Northants. J Bl. 4 yrs. Jam.
20. S. 21 Feb. 1754   10

1989   NEALL, Nicholas. Broadworthy (Bradworthy,) Devon.
Taylor. JT. 4 yrs. Va. 23. S. 9 Sept. 1727   31

1990   NELSON, James. Glasgow, Scotland. Husbandman, JG.
4 yrs. Antigua. 31. S. 12 Feb. 1722   36

1991   NELSON, Joshua.   Penrith, Cumberland.   Schoolmaster.
CV.   4yrs.   Va.   19.   S.   11 Oct. 1720   148

1992   NESS, Peter.   Ta(u)nton, Somerset.   Weaver.   NW.
4 yrs.   Md.   35.   S.   30 May, 1739   77

1993   NEVILLE, Robert.   Portsmouth, Hants.   Carpenter.   WC.
4 yrs.   St. C.   25.   S.   4 Dec. 1725   85

1994   NEVITT, William.   St. Giles in the Fields, Mddx.
Shop joiner.   JT.   4 yrs.   Md.   20.   S.   23 Jan. 1724   21

1995   NEW, George.   St. Mary Magdalen, Bermondsey, Southwark, Surrey.   Master, David Bennister.   Cordwainer.
JT.   7 yrs.   Md.   15.   S.   10 April, 1735.   28

1996   NEW, John.   Portsmouth, Hants.   JD.   7 yrs.   Md.   16.
S.   3 Feb. 1724   44

1997   NEWBERRY, William.   St. Margarets, Westminster, Mddx.
Labourer.   P Si.   5 yrs.   Md.   20.   M.   28 Nov. 1729.
38

1998   NEWBY, Edward.   St. Giles without Cripplegate, London.
CV.   7 yrs.   Md.   15.   S.   1 Oct. 1723   103

1999   NEWMAN, Matthew.   Finchley, Mddx.   Brazier.   Mother,
Mary Newman, now Mary Bolton.   J Ta.   4 yrs.   Jam.
19.   S.   19 Oct. 1736   96

2000   NEWMAN, William.   St. Olaves, Southwark, Surrey,
J Co.   7 yrs.   Md.   15.   S.   9 Feb. 1724   60

2001   NEWSTEAD (STED,) Mary.   St. Giles in the Fields, Mddx.
Spinster.   Mother Mary Newstead.   CV.   5 yrs.   New
England.   20.   S.   16 April, 1724   47

2002   NEWTON, Samuel.   Waddington, Lincs.   JT.   6 yrs.
Jam.   15.   S.   17 March, 1729   50

2003 NICHOLLS, Ann. Stepney, Mddx. Spinster. WP. 8yrs.
S. C. 17. M. 25 July, 1723   65

2004 NICHOLLS, Hannah. St. Anns, Westminster, Mddx.
Spinster. HB. 4 yrs. New England. 20. M.
29 Aprill, 1721.   34

2005 NICHOLLS, John. Kaisher, Northants. NM. 6 yrs. Jam.
16. M. 8 Nov. 1731   262

2006 NICHOLLS, Richard. Ewell, Surrey. Mother, Mary
Nicholls. J BALL. 7 yrs. Va. 17. S. 26 Sept. 1727.
    40

2007 NICHOLLS, Richard. St. Martins in the Fields, Mddx.
NM. 5 yrs. Jam. 16. S. Last Aug. 1733.   46

2008 NICHOLO, Charles. A native of Spain and late of St.
James, Westminster, Mddx. JG. 4 yrs. Jam. 18. M.
5 Dec. 1720.   172

2009 NICHOLS, John. St. Mary, Newington, Surrey. Weaver.
4 yrs. Jam. 22. S. 16 Aug. 1733   33

2010 NICHOLS, Nathaniel. Southwark. JS? 5 yrs. Md.
16. M. 12 April, 1751   44

2011 NICHOLS, Thomas. Rickmansworth, Herts. J Bl. 4 yrs.
Philadelphia. 20. S. 2 Aug. 1751   62

2012 NICHOLS, Zachariah. Goswell St. Shoemaker. WD.
5 yrs. Va. 20. S. 3 May, 1751   57

2013 NICHOLSON, Jeremy. White Chappell, Mddx. Distiller.
W Bu. 4 yrs. Antigua. 19. S. 27 Aug. 1729.   3

2014 NICHOLSON, Pycroft. Manchester, Lancs. Book keeper.
NM. 4 yrs. Jam. 28. S 10 Nov. 1731   269

2015   NICHOLSON, Richard. St. Saviours, Southwark. (A poor lad.) J Wi. 7 yrs. Va. 14. M. 6 April, 1720. 65

2016   NICKALSON (NICKELSON,) John. Mary Magdalene in Old Fish St., London. W Bu. 4 yrs. Md. 28. S. 5 Feb., 1730 45

2017   NICKOLLS, Elizabeth. Stepney, Mddx. Spinster. Mother, Susanna Nickolls. MC. 4 yrs. Pa. 18. M. 12 June, 1719 16

2018   NICLO, Martin. A native of Bengal in East India and late from Aberdeen in Scotland. Cook. P Si. 5 yrs. Jam. 18. S. 30 June, 1730 56

2019   NICOLL, Lewis. Edenborough, Scotland. JT. 4 yrs. Jam. 20. S. 17 Aug. 1730. 68

2020   NOBBS, Henry. St. Clement Danes, Mddx. Taylor. P Si., 4 yrs. Jam. 18. M. 16 June, 1733 17

2021   NOBLE, James. Stafford. Husbandman. JT. 4 yrs. Ga. 20. S. 21 Oct. 1734 103

2022   NOBLE, Mark. St. Ives, Hunts. Cordwainer. JW. 5 yrs. Va. or Md. 19. S. 31 March, 1720. 57

2023   NOLAN, Eleanor. Charlton, Kent. Spinster. Father, Thomas Nolan. WF. 5 yrs. Md. 12. S. 22 Dec., 1736 207

2024   NONSETTE, Peter. A native of Italy. W CASH 4 yrs. Pa. 16. M. 4 Aug. 1728 76

2025   NORGATE, Thomas. St. Thomas, Southwark, Surrey. Writing master. W Bu. 4 yrs. Barb. 27. S. 2 Feb., 1730 36

2026   NORGATE, Thomas. St. Thomas, Southwark, Surrey. Writing master. W Bu. 4 yrs. Jam. 27. S. 4 Feb. 1730 44

2027   NORRIS, Arthur. Southampton, Hants. JT. 7 yrs. Md.
16. M. 29 Nov. 1729   43

2028   NORRIS, John. St. Catherine by the Tower, Mddx. Surgeon and apothecary. T Ba. 4 yrs. Jam. 26. S.
4 Oct. 1731   225

2029   NORRIS, John. Rotherhithe, Surrey. Labourer. Mother,
Sibella Pooley, late Norris. NM. 5 yrs. Jam. 17. S.
30 Dec. 1736   218

2030   NORRIS, William. Lew(i)sham, Kent. Husbandman.
W Bu. 5 yrs. Md. 19. S. 22 Dec. 1729.   83

2031   NORTH, George. Tower Hamlets in Mddx. Barber and
peruke maker. P Si. 5 yrs. Md. or Va. 22. S.
2 Feb. 1733   20

2032   NORTH, Henry. Bicker, Lincs. P Si. 5 yrs. Md. 18
M. 7 Dec. 1733   143

2033   NORTON, William. Stepney, Mddx. Weaver. WC.
4 yrs. Pa. 22. S. 10 July, 1728   41

NOTTER. See 2036

2034   NOWBULL, William. Upminster, Essex. Husbandman.
JG. 4 yrs. Md. 19. M. 21 Sept. 1719.   43

2035   NURSE, Peter. St. Johns, Maddermarket. JJ. 4 yrs.
Md. 19. M. 16 Sept. 1718   56

2036   NUTTER (NOTTER,) Robert. Burroughbridge, Yorks.
Labourer. CV. 4 yrs. Md. 20. S. Last Aug. 1722. 115

O

2037   OATES, Thomas. South Kirby, Yorks. Blacksmith. JS.
4 yrs. Jam. 18. S. 19 Jan. 1749   1

2038   OBRYAN, Thomas.   Whetstone, Herts.   Taylor.   P Si.
5 yrs.   Jam.   18.   M.   18 Nov. 1731   284

2039   O'Cahan, Barnet.   St. Brides, Dublin, Ireland.   JT.
4 yrs.   Md.   20.   S.   24 Aug. 1719   25

2040   OCKFORD, William.   Stroud, Glos.   Broad weaver.   JT.
5 yrs.   Va.   19.   M.   20 Oct. 1720   157

2041   ODDY, John.   St. Saviours, Southwark.   JS.   5 yrs.   Md.
16.   S.   19 Dec. 1752   12

OGALBY.   See 2042

2042   OGILBY (OGALBY,) David.   Ingatestone, Essex.   Gardner.
NM.   4 yrs.   Md.   29.   S.   19 Dec. 1729   79

2043   OLDFIELD, Edward.   St. Dunstans in the Wall, London.
Book keeper.   JG.   4 yrs.   Jam.   20.   S.   29 July, 1730. 64

2044   OLDFIELD, Leonard.   Marsfield? Lancs.   Husbandman.
NM.   4 yrs.   Jam.   21.   S.   8 Oct. 1735   112

2045   OLIPHANT, Robert.   St. Margarets, Westminster, Mddx.
Mother, Margaret Oliphant.   JT.   5 yrs.   Jam.   16   S.
9 Jan. 1733   12

2046   OLIVER, Edmund.   Swalwin, Northumberland.   Farrier,
smith.   JT.   4 yrs.   Barb.   20.   S.   18 Feb. 1724   72

2047   OLIVER, Frances.   St. James, Westminster, Mddx.   Spinster.   P Si.   5 yrs.   Md.   18.   M.   6 May, 1731.   128

2048   OLIVER, Richard.   Hodnett, Salop.   Farmer.   NM.   4yrs.
Jam.   31.   S.   13 Dec. 1736   200

2049   OLIVER, Samuel(l.) St. Johns, Worcester.   CV.   4 yrs.
Md.   19.   S.   19 Jan, 1722   23

2050   OLIVER, Sarah. Fulham, Mddx. Spinster. Mother Sarah
Oliver. BF. 3 yrs. Jam. 16. S. 16 Sept. 1736.   75

2051   ONEY, Benjamin. Wellingborough, Northants. Weaver.
JD. 5 yrs. Md. 20. M. 21 Nov. 1719   94

2052   ONYON, Robert. St. Botolphs, Aldgate, London. JT.
5 yrs. Jam. 18. S. 13 Feb. 1722   37

2053   ORP, William. Barmin(g) Kent. Carpenter. CV. 4yrs.
Va. 20. M. 25 Oct. 1720   159

2054   ORRED, Aaron. St. Giles in the Fields, Mddx. JT. 4yrs.
Jam. 18. M. 7 Sept. 1733   50

2055   OSBORN(E,) Henry. St. Martins in the Fields, Mddx.
Founder. P Si. 4 yrs. Pa. 22. S. 6 July, 1728.   10

2056   OSBORNE, James. Tilehurst (Ticehurst?) Sussex. Carter.
NM. 4 yrs. Jam. 27. S. 20 Oct. 1736   98

2057   OSBORN, John. Hampton, Mddx. Plaisterer. NM.
4 yrs. Jam. no age. S. 21 Aug. 1736   53

2058   OSBORNE, John. St. Giles in the Fields. Bricklayer.
NM. 4 yrs. Jam. 25. S. 13 Nov. 1736   153

2059   OSMONT, William. Brandford (Bridford?) Devon.
Groom. JT. 4 yrs. Jam. 18. S. 25 Sept. 1731.   216

2060   OVER, Thomas. The Temple, London. Labourer. JT.
4 yrs. Md. 20. S. 14 Sept. 1720   126

2061   OVERY, John. Stepney, Mddx. Weaver. 4 yrs. Va.
20. S. 3 Aug. 1721   63

2062   OWEN, Thomas. Cambridge. Carpenter. NW. 4 yrs.
Jam. 33. S. 31 Jan. 1738   12

2063 OWENS, Richard. Crislinton (Christleton,) Cheshire.
W Bu. 4 yrs. Pa. 16. M. 7 April, 1735   18

2064 OXEHAM, William. Buckland Manna Corum (Monachorum)
Devon. Footman. SG. 4 yrs. Md. 20. S.
20 Nov. 1725   195

P

2065 PACE, (PAICE,) William. Sheerfield (Sherfield,) Hants.
Carpenter. J Ha. 4 yrs. Jam. 31. S. 23 June, 1738.
     47

2066 PACKER, Richard. Newberry, Berks. Smith. NM.
4 yrs. Md. 27. S. 13 Feb. 1733   26

2067 PACTON, James. Cambridge. Gardner. P Si. 4 yrs.
Md. 20. M. 23 Nov. 1727   13

2068 PAGE, Thomas. St. Mary le Bow, Cheapside, London.
Mother, Elizabeth Crouch. CV. 4 yrs. St. L. or St. C.
17yrs. S. 17 Aug. 1722   101

2069 PAGE, Thomas. St. Olaves, Southwark, Surrey. Smith.
WC. 4 yrs. St. C. 23. S. 17 Nov. 1725   170

PAICE. See 2065

2070 PAIN, John. Portsmouth Hants. P Si. 4 yrs. Pa.
18. S. 29 May, 1731   143

PAIN, Wm. See 2074

2071 PAINE, George. Endfield (Enfield,) Herts. (now in Mddx.)
Brickmaker. JT. 4 yrs. Jam. 19. M. 23 July, 1730. 62

2072 PAINE, John. St. James, Clerkenwell, Mddx. JG. 5yrs.
Jam. 18. S. 9 March, 1723   36

2073 PAINE, Sarah. St. Olave, Southwark, Surrey. Spinster. WB. 6 yrs. Pa. 18. M. 5 May, 1719   10

2074 PAINE (PAIN,) William. St. Albans, Herts. JG. 7 yrs. Jam. 16. S. 18 March, 1729   51

2075 PAINE, William. Ellesmere, Salop. Smith. W Bu. 4 yrs. Jam. 22, M. 4 Nov. 1731   259

2076 PAINTER, John. Oxford. Barber and perriwig maker. NW. 4 yrs. Jam. 27. S. 9 Nov. 1738.   64

2077 PAINTER, Thomas. St. Giles, Criplegate, London. CV. 5 yrs. Md. 18. S. 25 Feb. 1722   39

2078 PAISE, William. Basingstoke, Hants. Labourer. JT. 4 yrs. Md. 20. M. 26 March, 1720   52

2079 PALLET, William. Chesson (Cheshunt?) Herts. JD. 7 yrs. Pa. 16. M. 25 June, 1722   38

PALLOTAU   See 2082

2080 PALMER, Mary. St. Martins in the Fields, Mddx. Spinster. WB. 6 yrs. Pa. 19. M. 5 May, 1719   9

2081 PALMES, Guy. Melton Mowbray, Leics. Surgeon. VH. 4 yrs. Jam. 24. S. 13 Feb. 1730   65

2082 PALUTO (PALLOTAU,) John Baptist. A native of Tholoun (Toulon?) in Provence, France. Barber. JG. 5 yrs. Pa. 19. S. 5 Sept. 1723   82

2083 PAMPLIN, William. Trotton, Sussex. Husbandman. NW. 4 yrs. Antigua. 27. S. May 4, 1739.   67

2084 PANTON, Alexander. Aberdeenshire, Scotland. Book keeper. NM. 4 yrs. Jam. 19. S. 13 Sept. 1733   58

2085 PANVERLIN, John. St. Giles in the Fields, Mddx. JG. 5 yrs. Pa. 17. M. 27 June, 1722   39

2086   PARENTS, John. Kennington, Surrey. Brickmaker. JT.
        4 yrs. Jam. 20. S. 22 Oct. 1730   157

2087   PARK, John. Horndon in parish of Lydkirk (Ladykirk,)
        Berwicks. N. Britain. Schoolmaster. NM. 4 yrs. Jam.
        28. S. 13 Nov. 1736   155

2088   PARKER, James. St. Giles, Criplegate without, London.
        Throwster. P Si. 4 yrs. Md. 19. M. 30 Nov. 1733.
                                                                     127

2089   PARKER, Joshua. Sunbury, Mddx. Barber. J Cr. 5yrs.
        Va. No age. S. 5 Feb. 1750   4

2090   PARKER, Robert. Knowston(e,) Devon. SG. 6 yrs.
        Jam. 17. M. 6 Nov. 1725   145

2091   PARKER, Thomas. St. Giles Criplegate, London. JT.
        4 yrs. Jam. 20. S. 9 Dec. 1724   90

2092   PARLER, George. Low Layton (Leyton,) Essex. P Si.
        4 yrs. Pa. 19. M. 11 June, 1731   149

2093   PARMAN, Thomas. St. Faiths, London. Taylor. J Ball.
        4 yrs. Va. 28. M. 18 Dec. 1728   119

2094   PARNELL, John. Cambridge, Labourer. JG. 4 yrs.
        Jam. 22. S. 15 Nov. 1725   162

2095   PARR, Joseph. Westleigh, Lancs. Husbandman. W Bu.
        4 yrs. Jam. 27. S. 11 Feb. 1730   54

2096   PARRINGAS (PERRINGES,) John. Kidderminster, Worcs.
        Weaver. W Bu. 4 yrs. Md. 18. S. 24 Nov. 1727.   6

2097   PARROTT, George. Yar(n)ton, Oxon. Husbandman. JT.
        4 yrs. Jam. 20. M. 12 July, 1723.   72

2098   PARSONS, John. Bradford, Somerset. Weaver. EC.
        5 yrs. Md. and Pa. 19. M. 18 Sept. 1719   40

2099   PARSONS, Thomas. Wansworth, Surrey. JD. 4 yrs.
Md. 20. S. 7 Sept. 1722   122

2100   PARTRIDGE, Thomas. J Bl. 4 yrs. Antigua. No age.
S. 10 May, 1756.   7

2101   PARTRIDGE, William. Fulham, Mddx. JT. 4 yrs.
St. L. 18. M. 22 Oct. 1722   170

2102   PASCALL, Robert. Enfield, Herts. (now Mddx.) JD.
6 yrs. St. L. 17. S. 5 Oct. 1722   142

2103   PASHLER, John. Cambridge. Cook. A Lo. 2 yrs.
St. L. 19. S. 1 Oct. 1722   135

2104   PAST, William. Colchester. Husbandman. NM.
4 yrs. Jam. 20. M. 15 Nov. 1736   158

2105   PATE, Richard. St. Martins in the Fields, Mddx. Writer.
SF. 5 yrs. Antigua. 18. S. 8 May, 1739   68

2106   PATERSON, James. St. Pauls, Covent Garden. Shooemaker. J Ta. 4 yrs. Jam. 20. S. 27 Dec. 1736. 211

2107   PATTERSON (PATTISON,) John. St. Botolph. Bishopsgate.
Husbandman. Father and mother dead. NW. 6 yrs.
Pa. 18. S. 3 Jan. 1738   2

2108   PATTISON, Edward. St. Peter Pancraft (Mancroft,)
Norwich. P Si. 7 yrs. Pa. 15. M. 16 June, 1731. 153

2109   PATTISON, John. Great Stainton, Durham. JD. 5yrs.
Md. 18. S. 6 Jan. 1719   7

PATTISON, John. See 2107

2110   PATON, Joseph. East Mugland (Haughland?) Lenrick
(Lanark?) Scotland. NM. 4 yrs. Jam. 30. S.
28 March, 1735   14

2111   PATTON, William.   St. James, Westminster, Mddx.
       Taylor.   JG.   4 yrs.   Va.   18.   S.   7 May, 1723.   56

2112   PAUL, John.   St. Botolph, Bishopsgate.   Carpenter.   EP.
       4 yrs.   Jam.   27.   S.   11 April, 1738   33

2113   PAYNE, Thomas.   Tunbridge Wells.   J Cr.   4 yrs.   Ant-
       igua.   17.   S.   27 Nov. 1755   12

2114   PEACH (PEECH,) Thomas.   Hull, Yorks.   JT.   4 yrs.
       Jam.   19.   S.   3 March, 1723   35

2115   PEACOCK, Edward.   Greenwich, Kent.   Carpenter.   NM.
       4 yrs.   Jam.   24.   S.   4 Jan. 1736   12

2116   PEACOCK, James.   St. Anns, Black Fryers, London.   RB.
       7 yrs.   Md.   18.   S.   25 Oct. 1723   106

2117   PEACOCK, James.   Bemestry (Bemister, now Beaminster,)
       Dorset.   Husbandman.   J Bl.   5 yrs.   Md.   no age.
       M.   21 July, 1753   16

2118   PEACOCK, Joseph.   St. Dunstan in the East.   London.   JT.
       5 yrs.   St. L. or St. C.   17.   M.   22 Aug. 1722   107

2119   PEACOCK, Richard.   St. Giles, Criplegate, London.
       W Bu.   5 yrs.   Md.   18.   S.   19 Feb. 1729   35

2120   PEACOCK, Thomas.   Bishopsgate, London.   Carpenter.
       JT.   4 yrs.   Jam.   20.   S.   16 Jan. 1720   5

2121   PEAK, Mathias.   St. Sepulchers, London.   CV.   4 yrs.
       Md.   19.   S.   30 Jan. 1723   11

2122   PEARCE, John.   Wilton, Wilts.   Labourer.   W Bu.   5 yrs.
       Md.   20.   M.   29 Dec. 1729   85

2123   PEARCE, William.   St. Martins in the Fields, Mddx.
       Cordwainer.   TB.   4 yrs.   Md.   21.   S.   19 Jan. 1722.   24

2124 PEARSALL, Joseph. St. Mary Overs, Southwark. Labourer. Mother Sarah Pearsall. HB. 5 yrs. Va. or Md.
18. S. 22 Feb. 1737 22

2125 PEARSON, Michael. Stoke Newington, Mddx. Husbandman. JD. 4 yrs. Md. 18. M. 18 Aug. 1718. 18

2126 PEASEY, Edmund. Stuston, Suffolk. JD. 5 yrs. Md.
17. M. 19 Aug. 1718 22

2127 PECK, Elizabeth. Spinster. Maudlin, Oxford. JD.
5 yrs. Pa. 17. M. 26 May, 1719 13

2128 PECK, Elizabeth. St. Peters in the East, Oxford. Spinster.
CV. 5 yrs. Va. or Md. 19. S. Last July, 1721. 61

2129 PECK, Elizabeth. St. Peters, Oxford. Spinster. CV.
4 yrs. Antegoa. 19. S. 9 Nov. 1721 72

2130 PECK, Thomas. Oxford. Barber. CV. 4 yrs. Antigua. 18. S. 9 Nov. 1721 73

PEECH. See 2114

2131 PEGG, William. St. Ives, Huntingdon. JW. 5 yrs. Md.
19. S. 19 Nov. 1719 92

2132 PEIGNIE, James. St. Ann, Westminster. Barber.
Apprentice to John Regnier. Mother, Magdalen Howell
(Houfell,) late Peignie. W Bu. 5 yrs. Jam. 17. M.
2 Nov. 1736 117

2133 PELL, Charles. St. Christophers, Threadneedle St., London. Blacksmith. NM. 4 yrs. Jam. 38. S.
1 Jan. 1736 3

2134 PELLHAM, Nicholas. St. Leonards, Shoreditch, Mddx.
Labourer. JG. 4 yrs. Md. 19. M. 22 Oct. 1725 120

2135   PEN, William. Banbury, Oxon. Husbandman. NM.
4 yrs. Pa. 21. M. 5 Sept. 1730   89

2136   PENNELL, Carfinch. St. Olaves, Southwark. Mother at
Tenterton, Kent. NM. 4 yrs. Jam. 20. M.
7 Dec. 1736   186

2137   PENNEY, Solomon. St. Clement Danes, Mddx. P Si.
5 yrs. Md. 18. S. 20 Nov. 1733   116

2138   PENNINGTON, George. Burton Leonard, Yorks. Groom.
NW. 4 yrs. Md. 33. S. 29 May, 1739   74

2139   PENNOCK, William. Seamore (Seamer?) Yorks. Clark
or Book keeper. P Si. 4 yrs. Pa. 20. S. 10 Aug. 1728
         77

2140   PERKINS, John. Woolverhampton, Staffs. Clerk. R Wh.
4 yrs. Md. 20. S. 11 Feb. 1729   26

2141   PERKINS, Joseph. Denton, Bucks. Husbandman. W Bu.
4 yrs. Jam. 21. S. 19 Feb. 1730   76

2142   PERKINS, Samuel. St. Botolphs without, Bishopsgate,
London. JD. 8 yrs. Md. 15 S. 12 Dec. 1724   92

PERREY. See 2143

PERRINGES. See 2096

2143   PERRY (PERREY,) Ambrose. Taunton Dean, Somerset.
Wool comber. J Csn. 4 yrs. Md. 20. S. 4 Jan.
1719   3

2144   PERRY, George. Gloucester. JG. 4 yrs. St. L. 18.
S. 24 Oct. 1722   172

2145   PERRY, James. St. Olaves, Southwark, Surrey. Line
maker. JT. 4 yrs. Pa. 19. M. 17 July, 1728   37

2146   PERRY, Thomas. Westhanvil (W. Hanningfield?) Essex.
Husbandman. NM. 4 yrs. Jam. 21. M. 29 Dec.1736
213

2147   PERRY, William. Taplow, Bucks. Gardner. JW. 4yrs.
Md. 20. S. 26 Jan. 1719   17

2148   PERRY, William. Evesham, Worcs. A poor lad. JD.
8 yrs. Md. 13. M. 22 Oct. 1719   78

2149   PESTANA, Samuel. Aldgate London. Schoolmaster.
NM. 4 yrs. Jam. 21. S. 16 March, 1735   12

2150   PETER, John. A native of Marsales in France. JT.
4 yrs. Jam. 19. M. 9 Jan. 1722   11

2151   PETERS, Nathaniel. Hackney, Mddx. Barber. JT.
4 yrs. Md. or Va. 19. S. 29 Nov. 1733   122

2152   PETERS (PETTERS,) William. Bodmin, Cornwall.
Shoemaker. MW. 4 yrs. Pa. 20. S. 14 Feb.1737. 18

PETTERS. See 2152

2153   PETTY, George. St. Paul, Shadwell. Cooper. Mother,
Eleanor Petty. RoW. 4 yrs. Jam. 18. S. 9 Sept. 1736
72

2154   PEW, James. Copthorne, Sussex. JD. 7 yrs. Md. 18.
S. 14 Dec. 1724   96

2155   PFINGST, Conrad. Marport, Nr. Frankfort. EJ. 4 yrs.
St. C. 19. S. 19 Dec. 1753   29

2156   PHILIPS John. Bristol. Husbandman. NW. 4 yrs.
Md. 25. M. 30 May, 1739   78

2157   PHILLIMORE, Jacob. Oxford. W Bu. 6 yrs. Va. 16
S. 18 Sept. 1727   37

2158   PHILLIPS (PHILIPPS,) Elizabeth. St. Andrews, Holbourn,
        London. Victuler. P Si. 5 yrs. Md. 49. S. 11 Feb.
        1730   55

2159   PHILLIPS, Henry. St. Giles in the Fields, Mddx. JG.
        7 yrs. Md. 17. M. 18 Jan. 1723   8

2160   PHILLIPS, Martha. St. Andrews Holborn. Mddx.
        Spinster. IK. 5 yrs. Md. 16. M. 30 July, 1718.   41

2161   PHILLIPS, Thomas. St. Martins in the Strand, Mddx.
        JT. 5 yrs. Jam. 17. S. 26 Feb. 1719.   42

2162   PHIPPS, William. East Ham, Essex. Book keeper.
        Father and mother dead. J Wh. 4 yrs. Jam. 20. S.
        3 Oct. 1739   111

2163   PICKERING, John. St. Leonards, Shoreditch, Mddx.
        CV. 4 yrs. St. L. 19. M. Last Oct. 1722   176

2164   PICKERING, Richard. Spittlefields, Stepney, Mddx.
        Clark. W Bu. 4 yrs. Antig. 19. S. 8 Nov. 1729.   15

2165   PICKERSKILL, John. Spenephern (Spennithorne?) Yorks.
        Weaver. NM. 4 yrs. Jam. 20. S. 25 Oct. 1733.   99

2166   PICKIN, John. St Saviours, Southwark, Surrey. EC.
        4 yrs. Md. or Pa. 16. M. 31 Aug. 1719   28

2167   PIERSON, Charles. Margaretts Overton (Market Overton,)
        Leics. (now in Rutland.) Shoemaker. NM. 4 yrs. Jam.
        24. S. 26 Nov. 1736   174

2168   PILBOROUGH, Daniel. St. James, Colchester, Essex.
        J Csn. 8 yrs. Va. or Md. 14. M. 15 Dec. 1719.   113

2169   PILGRIM, Amos. Ipswich. JD. 5 yrs. Md. 16. S.
        6 Feb. 1724   58

2170   PILKIN, Henry. St. Georges, Southwark, Surrey. Vintner. NM. 4 yrs. Md. 25. S. 12 Dec. 1733   146

2171   PILKIN(G)TON, Edward. St. James, Westminster, Mddx. Footman. CV. 4 yrs. Md. 26. S. 31 Dec. 1724. 110

2172   PIMBLE, William. St. Leonards, Shoreditch. Brickmaker. NM. 4 yrs. Jam. 21. M. 29 Dec. 1736   214

2173   PIMM, John. Beckley, Oxon. Labourer. JT. 4 yrs. Jam. 19. M. 16 Jan. 1721   9

2174   PINCH, John. Knighton, Leics. JD. 5 yrs. St. L. 18. S. 5 Oct. 1722   143

2175   PINDLETON, Thomas. Thame, Oxon. JT. 5 yrs. Va. or Md. 15. M. 17 Dec. 1720   173

2176   PIPER, Edward. Stepney, Mddx. JT. 4 yrs. Jam. 20. S. 3 Dec. 1728   109

2177   PITCHER, Thomas. St. Peters, Norwich. Taylor. W Bu. 4 yrs. Va. 20. S. 4 Oct. 1731   226

2178   PITCHLAND (PITCHTON,) Isaac. Portsmouth. Groom and footman. WD. 5 yrs. Va. 15. S. 10 April, 1751   36

PITCHTON. See 2178

2179   PITTS, Henry. Fulham, Mddx. Brickmaker. JT. 4 yrs. Jam. 20. M. 26 Nov. 1729   34

2180   PIX, Thomas. St. Martins in the Fields, Mddx. Cordwainer. P Si. 5 yrs. Pa. 19. S. 22 July, 1731.   173

2181   PLATT, Richard. Whetston, Mddx. JD. 6 yrs. Pa. 19. S. 8 Oct. 1725   111

2182   POCKOCK, John.   St. Botolph, Al(d)gate.   Labourer.
Father and mother dead.   JT.   6 yrs.   Md.   19.   M.
2 Feb. 1738   13

2183   POCOCK, William.   Warren? Yorks (Wharram le Street?)
JT.   4 yrs.   Jam.   17.   S.   11 Nov. 1731   275

2184   PODDEY, William.   Stepney, Mddx.   Joyner.   J BALL.
4 yrs.   Pa.   27.   S.   9 July, 1728   18

2185   POLLY, Ebenezer.   St. Giles, Criplegate, London.   Gardner.   W Bu.   4 yrs.   Antigua.   23.   S.   20 Aug. 1728.   101

2186   POMLIN, John.   St. Pauls Churchyard.   Writer.   EP.
4 yrs.   Va. or Md.   23.   S.   19 April, 1737   44

2187   POOBJOY, Walter.   Frome, Somerset.   JT.   6 yrs.   Jam.
16.   M.   27 Oct. 1729   6

2188   POOLE, John.   Bartonley, Cheshire.   WC2.   4 yrs.   Pa.
17.   S.   30 July, 1728   59

2189   PORRIS, Thomas.   Ham(p)stead Marshall, Berks.   Blacksmith.   W Bu.   4 yrs.   S.C.   22.   S.   24 July, 1733.   30

PORT.   See 2191

2190   PORTAWAY, Abraham.   Faringhill? Essex.   (Feering?)
P Si.   4 yrs.   S.C.   18.   S.   13 Sept. 1733   59

2191   PORTE (PORT,) Peter.   Hanover.   Sugar baker.   J Br.
4 yrs.   Jam.   no age.   S.   4 July, 1750   36

2192   PORTER, Aaron.   St. Mary Magdalene, Bermondsey,
Southwark.   Pin maker.   WC2.   5 yrs.   Md.   19.   M.
26 Jan. 1729   15

2193   PORTER, Aaron.   St. Mary Magdalene, Bermondsey,
Southwark.   Pin maker.   A CASH.   4 yrs.   Nevis or St. C.
19.   M.   6 Nov. 1729   11

2194   PORTER, Catharine. St. Mary Magdalene, Old Fish St.
        London. Mother Ann Porter. P Si. 4 yrs. S. C. 18
        M. 11 Sept. 1733   53

2195   PORTER, Isaac. Guildford, Surrey. Groom. NM. 4yrs.
        Jam. 36. M. 5 Oct. 1733   85

2196   PORTER, Thomas. St. Mary Magdalene, Bermondsey,
        Southwark. JD. 6 yrs. Md. 17. M. 26 Jan. 1724. 24

2197   POSTON, Henry. St. Andrews, Bristol. JT. 4 yrs.
        St. C or St. L. 20. S. 3 Aug. 1722   68

2198   POTETE, John. Christ Church Spitlefields Mddx. Weav-
        er. WT. 4 yrs. Jam. 22. M. 13 Feb. 1730   64

2199   POTTER, John. Marsworth, Bucks. J Csn. 5 yrs. Md.
        18. S. 28 Jan. 1719   19

2200   POTTER, William. St. Leonards, Shoreditch, Mddx.
        J Co. 7 Yrs. Md. 17. M. 4 Feb. 1724   53

2201   POTTERELL, George. Apstell,? Herts. JT. 6 yrs. Jam.
        17. S. 27 Nov. 1733   119

2202   POULTER, Abraham. Ash. Surrey. Sawyer. JG. 4yrs.
        Jam. 19. S. 16 April, 1723   52

2203   POVEY, Thomas. Cannock, Staffs. Distiller. W Bu.
        4 yrs. Jam. 31. S. 5 Feb. 1730   46

2204   POWELL, Edmund. St. Martins in the Fields, Mddx. JG.
        7 yrs. Jam. 19. S. 7 Oct. 1730   134

2205   POWELL, George Reading, Berks. JD. 6 yrs. Pa.
        18. S. 4 July, 1722   44

2206   POWELL, George. Dilverton (Dulverton,) Somerset.
        Bricklayer. P Si. 4 yrs. Jam. 25. M. 1 Nov. 1727. 29

2207 POWELL, John. St. Anns, Westminster, Mddx. Cordwainer. P Si. 4 yrs. Pa. 20. M. 15 July 1728. 35

2208 POWELL, Richard. St. Catherines by the Tower, London.
JT. 4 yrs. Jam. 19. M. 10 Nov. 1731 274

2209 POWELL, William. Chelton (Cheltenham?) Glos. NM.
5 yrs. Md. 18. M. 13 Dec. 1733 147

2210 POWIS, Joseph. St. Dunstans in the West, London. Book
keeper. P Si. 4 yrs. Pa. 20. S. Last Aug. 1730. 85

POWNEY. See 2376

2211 POWRIE, Peter. Artrith (Artruth, now Arthuret,) Cumberland. NM. 4 yrs. Jam. 20. S. 21 May, 1735. 41

2212 POYNER, David. St. Sepulchers, London. Cordwainer.
WC2. 4 yrs. Va. 19. S. Last Aug. 1728 105

2213 PRATT, John. Barkin, Essex. Schoolmaster. CV.
4 yrs. Md. 18. S. 21 March, 1719 48

2214 PRATT, Thomas. Broadfare, St. Lawrence, Reading,
Berks. Gardner. NM. 4 yrs. Va. or Md. 21. S.
7 Feb. 1737 12

2215 PRESTON, Richard. Allcester. (Alcester,) Warwicks.
Husbandman. JG. 4 yrs. Jam. 19. M. 30 June, 1720. 89

2216 PRESCOTT, William. Ormskirk, Lancs. Glazier. NM.
4 yrs. Jam. 22. S. 6 June, 1736 17

2217 PRICE, Abednego. St. Margrets (Margarets,) Herefordshire. Husbandman. NM. 4 yrs. Pa. 21. S.
26 June, 1731 169

2218 PRICE, John. St. Giles in the Fields, Mddx. Butler.
P Si. 4 yrs. Jam. 26. M. 2 Jan. 1730 6

2219   PRICE, John. St. Martins in the Fields, Mddx. JT.
6 yrs. Md. 17. S. 7 Sept. 1731   195

2220   PRICE, Joseph. Bristol. Tyler and plaisterer. JG. 4yrs.
Jam. 20. S. 16 Sept. 1730   106

2221   PRICE, Robert. Bristol. Labourer. JD. 4 yrs. Md.
19. S. 19 Oct. 1724   66

2222   PRICE, Thomas. St. Martins in the Fields, Mddx. JG.
5 yrs. Pa. 18. S. 3 July, 1722   43

2223   PRICE, Thomas. Hollywell(Holywell,) Flintshire. Wales.
NM. 4 yrs. Jam. 17. M. 13 May, 1731   133

2224   PRICE, Thomas. Lansomfraid (Llansantfraid,) Radnorshire,
Wales. Taylor. NM. 4 yrs. Jam. 27. S. 13 Sept. 1731
        206

2225   PRICE, William. St. James, Westminster. Mddx. EC.
6 yrs. Md. or Pa. 18. M. 3 March, 1718   6

2226   PRICE, William. St. Martins in the Fields, Mddx. Cordwainer. SG. 4 yrs. Md. 32. S. 20 Nov. 1725. 197

2227   PRICHARD, Rice. Oxford. Cordwainer. JT. 4 yrs.
Jam. 17. S. 14 Sept. 1731   208

2228   PRICHARD, William. Hemingford, Hunts. NM. 4 yrs.
Jam. 22. S. 13 Sept. 1731   204

2229   PRIDE, Shadrack. Liverpool, Lancs. Clerk. W Bu.
4 yrs. Md. 20. S. 28 Dec. 1731   294

2230   PRIDGEN, Thomas. Lincoln. Barber. JT. 4 yrs.
Jam. 19. M. 30 Nov. 1725   216

2231   PRIDGEN, Thomas. Lincoln. Labourer. P Si. 4 yrs.
Jam. 19. M. 1 Oct. 1731   222

2232   PRIEST, Ruth. Rotherhithe, Surrey. Spinster. HD.
4 yrs. Ga. 18. M. 1 Aug. 1735   65

2233   PRIGG, Thomas. Melford, Suffolk. Cooper. J BALL.
4 yrs. Va. 21. S. 27 Sept. 1727   -   41

2234   PRIMMER, William. St. Botolphs, Bishopsgate, London.
Labourer. JT. 4 yrs. N. Y. or Carolina. 23. S.
16 Nov. 1724   73

2235   PRINCE, William. St. Mary le Savoy in the Strand, Mddx.
Cordwainer. CV. 5 yrs. Md. 21. S. 16 Jan. 1724.   3

2236   PRIOR, John. Clapham, Surrey. W Bu. 4 yrs. Antigua.
17. S. 23 Aug. 1728   97

2237   PRITCHARD, John. Leominster, Herefordshire. NM.
4 yrs. Jam. 17. S. 4 Oct. 1733   82

2238   PRITCHARD, Thomas. St. Giles in the Fields, Mddx.
JG. 4 yrs. Jam. 21. S. 3 Aug. 1728   63

2239   PRODUCK, John. Lothbury, London. Blacksmith. JT.
4 yrs. Jam. 26. M. 17 Dec. 1724   104

2240   PROSSER, Mary. Aldgate, Mddx. Spinster. JT. 5yrs.
Va. 17, M. 21 Nov. 1719   93

2241   PROSSER, Richard. Stretton, Herefordshire. Husbandman.
JG. 4 yrs. Jam. 20. S. 8 March, 1720   30

2242   PROTHERS, Thomas. St. Georges in the East, Ratclife,
Mddx. Bricklayer. NM. 4 yrs. Jam. 24 S.
27 Feb. 1730   94

2243   PROTHORO, Thomas. Warwick. Hemp dresser. WB.
4 yrs. Md. or Va. 18. M. 10 Dec. 1719   108

2244   PRUYS, John (Jan.) Naarden, Holland. NM. 4 yrs.
Jam. 21. S. 15 Nov. 1736   156

2245   PRYOR, John.   Armagh, Ireland.   Peruke-maker and
        barber. FS. 4 yrs. Jam. no age. M. 5 May, 1753. 8

2246   PUDSEY, Ambrose.   St. Martins in the Fields, Mddx.
        Book keeper. NM. 4 yrs. Md. 23. S. 9 March, 1733. 33

2247   PULL (PUTT,) William.   St. James, Westminster.   Barber
        and peruke maker. W Bu. 4 yrs. Antigua. 26. S.
        1 Jan. 1730/31   1

2248   PUMMERY, Robert.   Taunton dean, Somerset.   JT.
        5 yrs. Md. or Pa. 20. M. 29 Sept. 1719   53

2249   PURCELL, Peter, Jnr.   St. Georges, Southwark, Surrey.
        Smith. P Si. 4 yrs. Jam. 19. S. 9 Feb. 1730.   50

2250   PURCELL, Peter, Jnr.   St. Georges, Southwark.   Smith.
        EP. 4 yrs. Jam. 19. S. 2 Sept. 1731   194

        PUTT. See 2247

                                R

2251   RADE, John.   Stowerbridge (Stourbridge,) Worcs. Smith.
        W Bu. 5 yrs. Md. 17. M. 22 Feb. 1730   79

2252   RADFORD, John.   Silforton (Silverton,) Devon.   Weaver.
        WB. 6 yrs. Md. or Pa. 17. M. 24 Sept. 1719.   49

2253   RADFORD, William.   Silforton (Silverton,) Devon.   Weav-
        er. WB. 5 yrs. Md. or Pa. 19. M. 24 Sept. 1719. 47

2254   RADWELL, William.   Redb(o)urn, Herts.   Carpenter.
        W Bu. 4 yrs. Jam. 22. S. 18 Dec. 1735   117

2255   RAHIND (REHIND,) William.   Preston Pans, Midlowden
        (Midlothian,) Scotland. NM. 4yrs. Pa. 18. S.
        19 July, 1731   171

2256   RAINTON, Thomas.   Hinginham (Hingham,) Norfolk.
J BALL.   7 yrs.   Pa.   16.   M.   17 Aug. 1728   88

2257   RAMISH, Robert.   St. Giles, Criplegate, London.   Cordwainer. 4 yrs.   Va. or Md.   29.   M.   1 Jan. 1733.   1

RAMSAY.   See 2258

2258   RAMSEY (RAMSAY,) John.   Dalry, Galloway, Scotland.
CV.   4 yrs.   Md.   20.   S.   Last Sept. 1721.   68

2259   RAMSEY, Robert.   St. Anns Westminster, Mddx.   NM.
4 yrs.   Jam.   20.   S.   6 Oct. 1735   105

2260   RAND, John.   St. Clement Danes, Mddx.   Sister, Sarah
Rand.   JT.   8 yrs.   Va.   13.   M.   25 July, 1721   55

2261   RAND, William.   Kennington, Surrey.   Brickmaker.   JT
4 yrs.   Jam.   20.   S.   22 Oct. 1730   159

2262   RANDALL, Francis.   Marlington (Arlington?) Devon.
Cooper. NM. 4 yrs.   Jam.   32.   S.   13 Oct. 1731.   237

2263   RANDALL, Mary.   St. Anns Westminster, Mddx.   4 yrs.
Va.   JJ.   15.   M.   26 Aug. 1718   47

2264   RANKIN, (RANKEN,) William.   Edenburgh (Edinburgh,)
Turner.   JS.   4 yrs.   Jam.   18.   S.   4 Feb. 1754   5

2265   RATHWELL, John.   Dublin.   Taylor.   J Wil.   4 yrs.
Philadelphia.   20.   S.   5 Aug. 1751.   63

2266   RATTARY (RATTRAY,) James.   Benathue? Angus? Scotland. J BALL. 4yrs. Antigua. 15. S. 28 Aug. 1728.   100

2267   RATTENBURY, Thomas.   Temple Street, Bristol.   CV.
6 yrs.   Md.   15.   S.   28 Aug. 1722   112

RATTRAY.   See 2266

2268 RAVENELL, Henry. St. Martins in the Fields, Mddx. NM.
4 yrs. Md. 18. M. 4 Dec. 1733   137

2269 RAYNER, Thomas. Wakefield, Yorks. Coachman. JJ.
4 yrs. Va. 17. M. 30 Aug. 1718   55

2270 READ, Thomas. Aldgate, London. Labourer. P Si.
4 yrs. Md. 20. S. 18 Nov. 1727   19

2271 READ, William. St. Botolph, Aldgate, Mddx. Cook.
P Si. 4 yrs. St. C. 29. M. 6 Feb. 1730   47

2272 READER, John. Marden, Kent. Carpenter. P Si. 4 yrs.
Jam. 20. S. 12 Oct. 1730   139

2273 RED, Jeremiah. A native of Genna (Jena?) JD. 5 yrs.
Md. 19. M. 5 Jan. 1722   8

2274 REDDALL, Thomas. St. Philips, Birmingham, Warwicks.
Weaver. JT. 4 yrs. Va. 20. S. 10 Oct. 1720. 146

2275 REDHEAD, William. Corbridge, Northumberland.. Carpenter. WC. 4 yrs. St. C. 27. S. 4 Dec. 1725. 85

2276 REED, George. Londen? (Clifton?) Bristol. JD. 7 yrs.
Md. or Pa. 16. M. 6 Feb. 1719   38

2277 REED, Martha. Rochester, Kent. Widow. WW. 4yrs.
Pa. 21. S. 9 Aug. 1728   75

2278 REEVES, Bartholomew. Oxford. Painter. W Bu. 4 yrs.
Jam. 19. S. 2 Feb. 1730   41

2279 REEVES, James. Portsmouth. Hants. Butcher. NM.
4 yrs. Md. 19. S. 29 Nov. 1733   124

2280 REEVES, John. Cane (Calne,) Wilts. JD. 6 yrs. Md.
16. M. 27 Aug. 1722   27

2281 REEVES, Susanna. Didbrook. CV. 5 yrs. Md. 18. S.
12 Oct. 1724   62

2282 REHIND, William. Preston Pans, Midlowden (Midlothian,) Scotland. P Si. 4 yrs. Jam. 19. S. 14 Aug. 1733. 31

REHIND, William. See 2255

RELSEY. See 1611

2283 RENWOOD, Thomas. Worcester. Gardner. NM. 4yrs. Jam. 21 S. 13 Sept. 1731   205

2284 RERDON, Joseph. Ratclife, Bristol. Labourer. NM. 4 yrs. Md. 25. M. 17 Dec. 1733   150

2285 REST, Robert. St. Martins, Leicester. Labourer. W Bu. 4 yrs. Va. 19. S. 22 Oct. 1734   104

2286 RESTALL, Jones. St. James, Westminster, Mddx. Bricklayer. SG. 4 yrs. Md. 25. S. 20 Nov. 1725 197

2287 REVISS, Henry. St. Martins in the Fields, Mddx. Smith. CV. 4 yrs. St. L. 20. S. 9 Nov. 1722   181

2288 REYNOLDS, John. Rotherhith(e,) Surrey. Carpenter. JT. 4 yrs. Jam. 23. S. 18 April, 1723   55

2289 REYNOLDS, John. Brentwood, Essex. Labourer. Father in Salop. mother dead. EP. 4 yrs. Jam. 18. S. 9 Nov. 1737   59

2290 REYNOLDS, Martha. Wansworth, Surrey. Chambermaid. NW. 4 yrs. Jam. 22. S. 23 Feb. 1738   32

2291 REYNOLDS, Thomas. Wrexham, Denbigh, Wales. NM. 4 yrs. Jam. 23. S. 30 Sept. 1730   128

2292 REYNOLDS, Thomas. St. Sepulchers, London. Labourer. Father and mother dead. NM. 5 yrs. Va. or Md. 19 S. 30 Dec. 1737   71

2293   REYNOLDS, William. Hertford. Butcher. P Si. 4 yrs.
Pa. or N. Y. 16. S. 12 July, 1728   34

2294   REYNOLDS, William. Kings Parish, Dublin, Ireland.
WC2. 7 yrs. Pa. 16. M. 20 July, 1728   43

2295   RICE, Benjamin, the Younger. St. Georges in the East,
Mddx. Father and mother, Benjamin and Ann Rice. W Bu.
6 yrs. Pa. 16. S. 24 April, 1735   32

2296   RICE, Bennet. Best St., Norwich. Spinster. SG. 4yrs.
Va. 18. M. 22 Nov. 1727   15

2297   RICE, John. Kensington, Mddx. Baker. NM. 4 yrs.
Pa. 22. S. 21 Sept. 1733   67

2298   RICE, Michael. Winsham (Windlesham?) Surrey. Husbandman. EP. 4 yrs. Va. or Md. 30. S. 19 April,
1737   49

2299   RICE, Richard. Isleworth, Mddx. Turner. MW. 4yrs.
Pa. 21. S. 18 May, 1738   40

2300   RICHARDS, Charles. St. Margrets, Westminster, Mddx.
Father, John Richards. JG. 5 yrs. Md. 20. S.
8 Sept. 1731   197

2301   RICHARDS, Hugh. St. Erm(e) Cornwall. Taylor and
stay maker. JG. 4 yrs. Jam. 28. S. 9 March, 1724
                                  79

2302   RICHARDS, John. Wem, Salop. Husbandman. NM.
4 yrs. Pa. 26. M. 26 June, 1731   168

2303   RICHARDSON, Charles. St. James, Westminster. Groom.
Mother, Mary Richardson at Bishops Stortford, Herts. NM.
4 yrs. Jam. 20. S. 5 Jan. 1736   13

2304   RICHARDSON, George. Bugbrook, Northants. Woolcomber. JG. 5 yrs. Pa. 20. S. 29 June, 1722.   40

2305 RICHARDSON, John. St. Pauls, Shadwell. Farmer.
J Bl. 5 yrs. Va. 20. M. 22 March, 1750   23

2306 RICHARDSON, Robert. Kirton, Lincs. Carpenter and
joyner. JT. 4 yrs. Jam. 20. S. 12 Feb. 1730.   59

2307 RICHARDSON, Thomas. Toft, Cambs. Husbandman.
JT. 4 yrs. Jam. 19. M. 21 Nov. 1723   112

2308 RICHARDSON, Thomas. Woot(t)on Lincs. J St. 7 yrs.
Md? 15. M. 3 April, 1751   29

2309 RICKARDS, William. St. James Westminster, Mddx.
Whip maker. JT. 4 yrs. Jam. 21. S. 11 Sept. 1730.   100

2310 RICKETTS, Edward. Stroud, Glos. Cloth worker. JD.
5 yrs. Md. 18. S. 3 Nov. 1721   71

2311 RICKETTS, James. St. Michaels, Gloucester. J Co.
5 yrs. Md. 16. M. 9 Feb. 1724   59

2312 RICKETTS, William. St. Michaels Queenhith(e) London.
Joyner and carpenter. J Co. 4 yrs. Md. 25. S.
19 Nov. 1725   182

2313 RICKEY, James. St. Margarets, Norwich. Weaver.
JT. 4 yrs. Md. 20. M. 25 Sept. 1723   99

2314 RIDLEY, Humphrey. St. Andrews, Holbourn. Labourer.
P Si. 4 yrs. Pa. 26. S. 6 July, 1728   10

2315 RIGBY, Nicholas. St. Martins in the Fields, Mddx. JT.
4 yrs. Md. 21. S. 20 Dec. 1721   88

2316 RIGHTING, George. St. Giles in the Fields, Mddx. CV.
4 yrs. Md. 17. S. 13 Nov. 1722   186

2317 RILEY, John. St. Botolphs without Bishopsgate. CV.
5 yrs. St. C. or St. L. 19. S. 17 Aug. 1722   100

2318   RILEY, Jonathan. St. Anns, Soho. Footman. MW.
4 yrs. Antigua. 25. S. 30 Dec. 1737   72

2319   RINGWOOD, Thomas. St. Georges, Hanover Square,
Mddx. Coachman. NM. 4 yrs. Md. 21. S.
4 Dec. 1733   136

2320   RIPPER, Robert. Hampstead, Mddx. SG. 4 yrs. Md.
21. S. 18 Nov. 1725   186

2321   RISLEY, William. Wiggan, Lancs. Dancing master.
NM. 4 yrs. Jam. 19. S. 14 April, 1731   104

2322   RIVERS, James. St. Brides, Fleet St., London. P Si.
4 yrs. Antigua. 18. S. Last Aug. 1728   106

2323   RIVIS, Robert. Newport Pagnell, Bucks. Carpenter and
joiner. JD. 4 yrs. Md. 18. S. 20 Aug. 1718.   25

2324   ROADS, William. Hyam (Higham,) Kent. Husbandman.
NM. 4 yrs. Jam. 25. S. 6 Nov. 1736   137

ROBBERDS. See 2331

2325   ROBBINS, John. Westborough, Wilts. Weaver. JD.
5 yrs. Md. 17. M. 15 Aug. 1720   106

2326   ROBBINS, John. Faversham, Kent. Baker. NW. 4 yrs.
Jam. 27. S. 3 May, 1739   66

2327   ROBERTS, Edward, Junr. St. Sepulcher, London. JG.
5 yrs. St. C. or St. L. 16. No S or M. 6 Aug. 1722. 72

2328   ROBERTS, Edward. Whittington, Salop. SG. 5 yrs.
Jam. 19. M. 1 Nov. 1725   134

2329   ROBERTS, Edward. St. Margarets, Westminster. Mddx.
Butler. J BALL. 4 yrs. Pa. 28. S. 6 July, 1728. 6

2330 ROBERTS, John. Dolgellthe (Dolgelly,) Merioneth, Wales.
Glover. JW. 5. Pa. 20. S. 15 May. 1721   36

2331 ROBERTS (ROBBERDS,) John. Stamford, Lincs. NM.
4 yrs. Jam. 17. S. 4 Oct. 1735   103

2332 ROBERTSON (ROBINSON,) Hugh. Inverness, N. Britain.
Labourer. Mother and father in Scotland. NM. 5 yrs.
Md. 18. S. 26 Jan, 1736   30

ROBESON. See 2344

2333 ROBINS, James Francis. St. Margarets, Westminster.
Husbandman. EP. 4 yrs. Va. or Md. 21. S.
19 April, 1737   47

2334 ROBINSON, Charles. Woodstock. Servant. JS. 5 yrs.
Jam. No age. S. 29 Dec. 1755   13

2335 ROBINSON, George. Hunnington, Lincs. Turner and
glazier. NM. 4 yrs. Md. 25. S. 10 Feb. 1735   3

ROBINSON, Hugh. See 2332

2336 ROBINSON, James. St. Georges, Southwark. Cordwainer. J Co. 4 yrs. Md. 21. M. 10 Feb. 1724   66

2337 ROBINSON, James. Diss, Norfolk. P Si. 5 yrs. Jam.
19. S. 19 June, 1733   18

2338 ROBINSON (ROBISON,) James. Aberdeen. Servant. GP.
4 yrs. Jam. 18. S. 23 Nov. 1750   43

2339 ROBINSON, John. Foredice (dyce,) Bamf (Banff,) Scotland
JG. 6 yrs. Md. 16. M. 15 Feb. 1724   69

2340 ROBINSON, John. Chatham, Kent. WC2. 5 yrs. Md.
19. M. 5 Jan. 1729   3

2341   ROBINSON, John.   Barnstable, Devon.   Gardner.   NM.
5 yrs.   Md.   20.   S.   18 Dec. 1729   74

2342   ROBINSON, John.   Rawclif(f)e, Yorks.   Miller.   NM.
4 yrs.   Pa.   21.   M.   17 March, 1735   14

2343   ROBINSON, John.   St. Botolphs, Bishopsgate.   Coppersmith.   MW.   4 yrs.   Jam.   21.   S.   6 Jan. 1736.   15

2344   ROBINSON (ROBESON,) John.   St. Johns, Wapping.   Tail-
or.   Father Alexander Robinson.   NM.   4 yrs.   Md.
20.   S.   11 Jan. 1737   3

2345   ROBINSON, John.   Stansted.   J Bl.   4 yrs.   Jam.   No
age.   M.   1 Jan. 1756   1

2346   ROBINSON, Joseph.   Essex.   Gardner.   BF.   3 yrs.   Jam.
36.   S.   23 Sept. 1736   76

2347   ROBINSON, Mary.   Crayfoot (Crayford,) Kent.   Spinster.
J Ta.   4 yrs.   Jam.   17.   M.   18 Oct. 1736   94

2348   ROBINSON, Richard.   Wandsworth, Surrey.   Schoolmaster
and book keeper.   W Bu.   4 yrs.   Jam.   20.   S.   30 Dec.,
1736   216

2349   ROBINSON, Robert.   St. Augustines, Norwich.   Weaver.
JT.   3 yrs.   Barb.   18.   S.   16 March, 1719   46

2350   ROBINSON, Samuel(1.)   Spalden (Spalding,) Lincs.
Coachman and gardner.   CV.   4 yrs.   Md.   40.   S.
3 Dec. 1723   114

2351   ROBINSON, Thomas.   St. Martins in the Fields.   Smith.
JD.   4 yrs.   Md.   19.   S.   9 Jan, 1719   9

2352   ROBINSON, Thomas.   Spalding, Lincs.   JT.   4 yrs.
Jam.   17.   S.   17 Dec. 1733   153

2353   ROBINSON, Walter. Edenbrough, Scotland. JT. 5 yrs.
Jam. 18. S. 4 Sept. 1730   88

2354   ROBINSON, William. Edenborough, Scotland. Carpenter.
JT. 4 yrs. Jam. 20. S. 16 Jan. 1721   8

2355   ROBINSON, William. Tamworth, Warwicks. Labourer.
NM. 6 yrs. Md. 16. M. 8 Dec. 1729   59

ROBISON. See 2338

2356   ROBSON, Winifred. St. James, Westminster, Mddx.
Spinster. P Si. 4 yrs. Pa. 17. S. 9 Aug. 1728.   72

2357   ROCKLEY, George. Warsop, Notts. Husbandman. BR,
at present in London. 4 yrs. Va. no age. M. 12 May,
1753   10

2358   ROGERS, Charles. Stepney, Mddx. JD. 7 yrs. Md.
15. M. 14 Dec. 1724   98

2359   ROGERS, George. Lincoln. Smith. J BALL. 4 yrs.
Pa. or Md. 19. S. 3 Aug. 1728   65

2360   ROGERS, Thomas. Butteton, Salop. (Butterton, Staffs?)
Husbandman. JD. 4yrs. Pa. or Md. 20. M. 11 Feb. 1723. 25

2361   ROKBEY, Richard. Aldgate, London. Carpenter. AC.
4 yrs. Jam. 20. S. 2 Dec. 1721   80

2362   ROSE, Daniel. Stanton, Suffolk. JD. 8 yrs. Md.
14. S. 24 Sept. 1719   46

2363   ROSE, John. Inverness, Scotland. Pewterer. NM.
4 yrs. Jam. 21. S. 14 Oct. 1730   148

2364   ROSE, William. Boscomb(e,) Wilts. AC. 5 yrs. Md.
17. S. 9 Jan. 1721   3

2365   ROSS, Agnes. Kircawdey, Fifeshire, Scotland. Spinster.
J Ta. 4 yrs. N. C. 21. M. 8 July, 1736   32

2366   ROSS, David. Inverness, N. Britain. Distiller. NM.
4 yrs. Jam. 27. M. 3 Jan. 1736   9

2367   ROSS, Sarah the Younger. St. Butolphs, Aldgate, London.
Spinster. SM. 4yrs. Purisburg(Purrysburg,)S. C. 26. M.
20 July, 1734   65

2368   ROSS (ROSE,) Thomas. St. Georges in the East. Barber.
NW. 4 yrs. Jam. 24. S. 27 Feb. 1738   35

2369   ROSS, William. Cutleshin, N. Britain. (Cuttlehill,
Fifeshire?) Father and mother dead. MW. 4 yrs. Jam.
18. M. 28 Nov. 1738   71

2370   ROW, Robert. St. Philips, Bristol. J Wi. 6 yrs. Md.
19. M. 4 Feb. 1719   35

2371   ROWE, Michael. Stepney. Weaver. JT. 4 yrs. Jam.
20. M. 5 March, 1729   43

2372   ROWELL, Ann. Stepney, Mddx. Spinster. JG. 6 yrs.
Va. 16. M. 7 Feb. 1720   22

2373   ROWLAND, John. St. Martins in the Fields, Mddx. Cabinet maker. NM. 4 yrs. Md. 22. S. 2 March, 1732
         10

2374   ROWLES, John. Wooton Basset. Wilts. Husbandman.
SV. For Major John Marshall of Jamaica. 4 yrs. Jam.
20. M. 27 Aug. 1720   115

2375   ROWLETT, Thomas. Giddington (Geddington,) Northants.
Husbandman. NM. 4 yrs. Va. or Md. 21. S.
1 April, 1734   40

2376   ROWNEY (POWNEY,) James. Rickmansworth, Herts.
Writer. NM. 4 yrs. Jam. 20. S. Oct. 1736? 108
No date given.

2377 ROYSTON, John. Spitlefields, Mddx. Groom. W Bu.
5 yrs. Jam. 21. S. 2 Feb. 1730   37

2378 RUBY, George. Shrewsbury, Salop. J Co. 7 yrs. Md.
15. S. 1 Feb. 1724   36

2379 RUDD, John. St. Margarets, Westminster. Mercer.
Father and mother dead. W Bu. 5 yrs. Md. 19. S.
28 Sept. 1736   79

2380 RUDDACK, Robert. North Froddingham, Yorks. Coachman. NM. 4 yrs. Antigua. 30. S. 13 Oct. 1731. 236

RUDG. See 2381

2381 RUDY (RUDG?) Edward. St. Martins in the Fields, Mddx.
Coach founder. J Co. 4 yrs. Jam. 28. M.
18 Nov. 1725   184

2382 RUNDALL (RUNDLE,) Warwick. St. Winnow, Cornwall.
Cordwainer. JD. 4 yrs. Md. 19. S. 19 Oct. 1724. 65

2383 RUSSELL, John. Pookle Church (Pucklechurch,) Glos.
Husbandman. NM. 4 yrs. Jam. 23. M. 20 Oct.
1736   99

2384 RUSSELL, John. London. J Bl. 4 yrs. Jam. No age
S. 2 Jan. 1756   4

                                   S

2385 ST. JOHN, Thomas. Shadwell. J St. 5 yrs. Md.
20. M. 5 April, 1751   27

2386 SALES, Thomas. Pluckley, Kent. RB. 6 yrs. Jam.
16. S. 17 Feb. 1730   77

2387 SALISBURY, John. Denbeigh (Wales.) Accomptant.
WS. 4 yrs. Jam. No age. S. 19 Sept. 1756.   23

2388 SALISBURY, Thomas. Denby (Denbigh,) Wales. Accomptant. JS. 4 yrs. Jam. 17. S. 19 Jan. 1754   9

2389 SALLARD, John. St. Giles in the Fields, Mddx. Taylor. NM. 5 yrs. Jam. 18. S. 15 Feb. 1730   68

2390 SAMLER (SEMLER,) Charles. St. Peters, Liverpool. SG. 7 yrs. Va. 14. S. 23 Nov. 1727   12

2391 SAMPSON, Edward. St. Martins in the Fields, Labourer. Father, Abraham Sampson. CR. 7 yrs. Md. 16. S. 9 Dec. 1737   76

2392 SAMPT, George Anthony. St. Martins in the Fields, Mddx. Turner. Father John Sampt. JT. 4 yrs. Jam. 19. S. 22 Oct. 1730   158

2393 SAMSON, John. St. Giles, Cambridge. Gardner. NM. 4 yrs. Pa. 20. M. 12 Sept. 1730   101

2394 SANDELLS (SANDELL,) Joseph. Coventry, Warwicks. Weaver. JG. 4 yrs. Md. 20. M. 15 Aug. 1718   31

2395 SANDERS, John. St. Stephens, Bristol. Sawyer. W Bu. 4 yrs. Jam. 20. M. 2 Oct. 1731   224

2396 SANDERS, William. Worcester. Weaver. JG. 4 yrs. Md. 23. S. 3 Feb. 1724   45

2397 SANDERSON, Joseph. Selby, Yorks. Taylor. JT. 4yrs. Md. 20. M. 27 Oct. 1720.   165

2398 SAPHTON (SEPHTON,) William. Wiggin (Wigan,) Lancs. Barber. JG. 4 yrs. St. L. 19. S. 30 Oct, 1722   173

2399 SARVENT (SERVANT,) William. St. Michaels, Dublin, Ireland. JD. 4 yrs. Md. 20. S. 20 Nov. 1719.   95

2400 SAVAGE, Bartholomew. Dublin. Gardner. J Bl. 4yrs. Jam. 26. s. 4 July, 1750   27

2401   SAVILL, Joseph. Malpas, Cheshire. Husbandman.
Mother and father dead. BW. 5 yrs. Va. or Md. 18
S. 13 Jan, 1736   26

2402   SAVILL, Robert. Southwell, Notts. Husbandman. RB.
4 yrs. Jam. 19. M. 8 June, 1724   51

2403   SAWLEY, William. Marton, Yorks. Book keeper.
W Bu. 4 yrs. Jam. 28. S. 22 Oct. 1731   250

2404   SAXTON, Edmund. St. James, Westminster, Mddx.
W Bu. 4 yrs. Ga. 18. S. 22 Sept. 1735   94

2405   SAYTH, John. Andover, Hants. Weaver. JT. 4 yrs.
Md. or Pa. 20. S. 15 Sept. 1719   32

2406   SCARLETT, John. St. Butolphs Aldersgate, London.
Labourer. P Si. 4 yrs. Jam. 17. S. 15 Aug. 1733.   32

2407   SCARROTT, George. Bodnam (Bodenham,) Hereford.
Husbandman. JCr. 4 yrs. Jam. 19. S. 5 Aug. 1749. 2

2408   SCORYER, Richard. Sherborn, Dorset. Schoolmaster.
NM. 4 yrs. Antigua. 22. S. 13 Oct. 1731   235

2409   SCOTT, Edward. Portsmouth, Hants. Husbandman.
JG. 4 yrs. Md. 21. S. 19 Jan. 1724   10

2410   SCOTT, Henry. Morpeth, Northumberland. Labourer.
NM. 4 yrs. Barb. or Jam. 18. S. 10 Sept. 1733   51

2411   SCOTT, Isaac. New Castle Upon Tine, Northumberland.
JD. 4 yrs. St. L. 18. S. 10 Nov. 1722   10

2412   SCOTT, Robert. Berwick upon Tweed. Husbandman.
NM. 4 yrs. Md. 28. M. 7 Jan. 1736   23

2413   SCOTT, Samuel. Canterbury, Kent. Labourer. WT.
6 yrs. Jam. 19. M. 8 Jan. 1730   18

2414   SCOTT, Thomas.   Carisle. Northumberland (Carlisle, Cumberland?) JD. 8yrs. Md. 15. M. 30 Nov. 1719   100

2415   SCOTT, Thomas.   Selkirk, Scotland. JT. 5 yrs. Pa. 16. S. 27 Feb. 1721   15

2416   SCOTT, William.   Stepney, Mddx. Weaver. P Si. 4 yrs. Pa. or Md. 18. M. 3 Aug. 1728   66

2417   SCOTT, William.   Yarmouth, Norfolk. JT. 7 yrs. Md. 15. M. Last Jan. 1731   3

2418   SCRAGGES, William.   West Ham, Essex. JG. 4 yrs. St. Christophers. 19. M. 9 July, 1722   48

2419   SCURRIER, James.   St. Dunstans in the West, London. W Bu. 5 yrs. Md. 21. S. 31 Jan. 1733   18

2420   SEAGROVE, William.   St. Stephen, Coleman St., London. JG. 4 yrs. Jam. 19. S. 3 May, 1731   121

2421   SEALE(Y,) John.   Late of Hannover. Doctor. SF. 4yrs. Jam. 22. S. 28 Oct. 1736   115

2422   SEALE, Robert.   St. Dunstans, Stepney. Hempdresser. NM. 4 yrs. Jam. 22. M. 25 Nov. 1736   172

SEALEY.   See 2421

2423   SEAMER, Thomas.   Chatham, Kent. Sawyer. JT. 4 yrs. Jam. 24. S. ? December (1728?)   107

2424   SEAWELL, John.   St. Margarets, Westminster, Mddx. Cordwainer. P Si. 4 yrs. Va. 26. S. 1 Feb. 1730.   34

2425   SEDDON, Richard.   St. Giles in the Fields, Mddx. Painter. Mother, Hannah Seddon. JT. 4 yrs. Jam. 19. S. 14 Jan. 1723   7

2426 SEDGLEY, Thomas. Wall Wotton, Warwicks. (Hill Wootton or Wootton Wawen?) JT. 4yrs. Barb. or Md. 16. M. 24 Sept. 1733   72

2427 SEDGWICK, Frances. Criplegate, London. Widow. CV. 5 yrs. Md. 25. M. 4 Feb. 1724   49

2428 SEEMER, Richard. Wanste(a)d, Essex. Coachman. JT. 4 yrs. Jam. 20. M. 25 Sept. 1731.   215

2429 SELBY, Mary. St. Giles in the Fields, Mddx. P Si. 4 yrs. Pa. or N. Y. 19. M. 10 July, 1728   27

2430 SELBY, Thomas. Circencester, Glos. Smith. JG. 4 yrs. Jam. 21. S. 9 March, 1724   80

2431 SELLY (SELLEY,) Hugh. Southmolton, Devon. Husband-man. J Cr. 5 yrs. Va. No age. S. 16 Feb. 1750. 9

SEMLER. See 2390

2432 SENGALL, John. St. Margrets, Westminster, Mddx. WT. 5 yrs. Jam. 18. M. 12 Feb. 1730   62

SEPHTON. See 2398

2433 SERLE, Ann. St. Dunstans in the West. Spinster. Father and mother dead. MW. 4 yrs. Md. 19. M. 22 Jan. 1738   7

SERVANT. See 2399

2434 SETREE, Joseph. St. Paul, Covent Garden. J Br. 4 yrs. Jam. 19. S. 23 Oct. 1751   65

2435 SEYMORE, Alexander. Stoke Dabon (d'Abernon,) Surrey. Husbandman. JT. 4 yrs. Jam. 36. S. 20 Nov. 1725.   192

2436 SEYMOUR, George. St. Andrews, Holbourn, London. Cooper. NM. 4 yrs. Jam. 24. S. 3 Jan. 1733. 5

2437   SEYS, John. St. Georges, Southwark, Surrey. JG. 5yrs.
        Md. 17. S. 2 Feb. 1724   42

2438   SHACKLEDGE, Thomas. St. Clement Danes, Mddx.
        P Si. 5 yrs. Pa. 19. S. 25 Aug. 1730   81

2439   SHADELOE, John. St. Michaels a(t) Thorne, Norwich.
        Weaver. RB. 4 yrs. Md. 23. M. 17 Nov. 1725   174

2440   SHAKEMAPLE, Mary. St. Sepulchers, London. Spinster.
        JD. 5 yrs. Md. 19. S. 18 Aug. 1718   16

2441   SHANNON, John. Dublin, Ireland. Leather dresser, JT.
        4 yrs. Va. or Md. 19. S. 1 April, 1734   39

2442   SHAP, Noah. Hurley, Berks. Labourer. Father and
        mother dead. W Ch. 4 yrs. Jam. 18. S. 8 Jan. 1736
                                                                 24

2443   SHARP, George. St. Mary, Gate(s)head, Durham. JT.
        4 yrs. St. C. or any part of W. I. 20. S. 23 July, 1722.
                                                                 64

2444   SHARP, James. Hanslup (Hanslope,) Bucks. Labourer.
        R Wh. 5 yrs. Md. 20. M. 26 Nov. 1729   32

2445   SHARP, Robert. Selby, Yorks. J Bl. 3 yrs. Jam. 17.
        S. 17 Sept. 1756   22

2446   SHARPE, George. Hertford. Sawyer. JG. 4 yrs. Md.
        19. S. 5 Feb. 1724   55

2447   SHARPE, Thomas. St. Bennet, Grace Church, London.
        Carpenter and joyner. J Co. 4 yrs. Md. 21. S. 19 Nov.
        1725   182

        SHARWOOD. See 2458

2448   SHAW, David. Edenbrough, Scotland. Carpenter and
        joyner. NM. 4 yrs. Jam. 23. S. 1 May, 1731.   119

2449 SHAW, Francis. Deptford, Kent. JG. 4 yrs. Jam.
19. M. 15 Nov. 1725   159

2450 SHAW, James. Trinity in the Minories Mddx. Labourer.
JT. 4 yrs. Jam. 20. S. 12 Dec. 1731   293

2451 SHAW, John. Thorn(e), Yorks. Labourer. WT. 4yrs.
Jam. 20. S. 3 Feb. 1730   43

2452 SHAW, Thomas. St. Leonards, Shoreditch. Broom
maker. Father and mother dead. S Wh. 4 yrs. Md.
19. M. 16 March, 1736   40

2453 SHEAT(E,) George. Whitchurch, Hants. Labourer. JG.
4 yrs. Jam. 20. S. 18 Jan, 1730   26

2454 SHELLMERDINE, John. St. Martins in the Fields, Mddx.
Mother, Grace Tanner. RB. 4 yrs. Jam. 18. S.
24 Nov. 1725   200

SHELTON (Catherine.) See 2462

2455 SHELTON Thomas. Mansfield Woodhouse, Notts. Carpenter and joyner. W Bu. 4 yrs. Jam. 28. S.
4 Feb. 1734   6

2456 SHEP(P)HERD, William. Conisford? City of Norwich.
RB. 4 yrs. Md. 20. S. 15 Nov. 1725   160

2457 SHERPIN, John. Ollessham (Aylsham?) Norfolk. Husbandman. WT. 4 yrs. Md. 36. M. 6 Jan. 1730   10

2458 SHERWOOD (SHARWOOD,) Daniel. St. Botolph, Al(d)gate,
London. NW. 4 yrs. Jam. 24. S. 20 Feb. 1738.   22

2459 SHERWOOD, Thomas. St. Swithins, Norwich. JG.
7 yrs. Md. 17. S. 9 Aug. 1723   70

2460 SHILL, Mary. St. Brides, Fleet St. , London. Spinster.
JT. 5 yrs. Md. 19. M. 29 March, 1720   53

2461   SHILLING, John.   Southampton.   Baker.   Father and
mother dead.   J Wh.   4 yrs.   Jam.   17.   M.   31 Dec.
1739   132

2462   SHILTON (SHELTON,) Catherine.   St. Paul, Covent Garden.
Spinster.   Mother and father dead.   JT.   4 yrs.   Md.
17.   S.   29 June, 1738   48

2463   SHIPLEY, Sarah.   St. Mary Whitechapell, Mddx.   Spinster.   JT.   5 yrs.   Md.   17.   M.   29 Sept. 1719   55

2464   SHITTLETON, William.   Stepney, Mddx.   Weaver.   CV.
4 yrs.   Va.   19.   S.   12 Dec. 1721   83

2465   SHREVE, Joseph.   St. Albons, Wood St. London.   Cooper.
NM.   4yrs.   Jam.   35.   S.   8 Oct. 1735   109

2466   SHORD, John.   Stepney, Mddx.   Weaver.   CV.   4 yrs.
Antigua or Leeward Isles.   23.   S.   4 Dec. 1724   84

2467   SHORE, Richard.   Mansfield, Notts.   Stocking maker.
Alias frame work knitter.   JT.   4 yrs.   Md.   20.   S.
29 Nov. 1721   78

2469   SILK, Edward.   Cosell (Coleshill?) Warwicks.   Smith and
farrier.   J Ta.   4 yrs.   N. C.   23.   M.   7 July, 1736.   29

2470   SILK, Joseph.   Birmingham.   Warwicks.   Forkmaker.
NM.   4 yrs.   Jam.   24.   M.   4 Nov. 1736.   132

2471   SILLITO, Thomas.   Wybunbury, Cheshire.   Butcher.   J Wh.
6 yrs.   Va.   18.   S.   30 Nov. 1739.   120

2472   SILLS, William.   Henley Upon Thames.   Book keeper.
J Bl.   4 yrs.   Va.   No age.   S.   23 June, 1750.   25

2473   SIMMON(D)S, Jane.   Wansworth, Surrey.   Chambermaid.
NW.   4 yrs.   Jam.   23.   M.   23 Feb. 1738   31

SIMMS.   See 2684

2474   SIMPSON, George.   Edenburgh.   Book keeper.   J Cr.
4 yrs.   Jam.   17.   S.   31 Aug. 1749   8

2475   SIMPSON, Mordicai.   Wethersfield, Essex.   JW.   5 yrs.
Md.   18.   S.   2 Jan. 1719/20   1

2476   SIMPSON, Richard.   Scarborough, Yorks.   JD.   4 yrs.
Pa. or Md.   20.   S.   11 Feb. 1723   26

2477   SIMPSON, Thomas.   Dartford, Kent.   Plow boy.   BW.
6 yrs.   Jam.   17.   S.   10 Nov. 1736   146

2478   SIMPSON, William.   Kirby Moor(side.) Yorks.   JT.
3 yrs.   Barb.   19.   M.   16 March, 1719   45

2479   SIMS, Thomas.   Kings Clere, Hants.   Butcher.   SG.
4 yrs.   Jam.   27.   S.   Nov. 15, 1725   165

2480   SINCLAIR, James.   North Britain.   J Bl.   4 yrs.   Antig.
or Montserratt.   No age.   S.   7 May, 1756   16

2481   SINCLAIR, John.   St. Margarets, Westminster.   J Bl.
5 yrs.   Va.   18.   M.   2 March, 1750   12

2482   SINGERS, John.   Bath, Somerset.   Gardner.   JG.   4 yrs.
Jam.   19.   S.   15 May, 1725   92

2483   SINGLETON, John.   St. Margarets, Westminster.   Mddx.
Goldsmith.   NM.   4 yrs.   Va. or Md.   31.   S.   3 April,
1734   41

2484   SKELTON, William.   St. Giles, Mddx.   JT.   4 yrs.
St. C.   18.   M.   17 July, 1722   56

2485   SKELTON, William.   Leeds, Yorks.   Husbandman.   JT.
        4 yrs. Jam. 20. M. 8 Oct. 1733   88

2486   SKINNER, Charles. Whitchappell, Mddx. Mother, Lydia
        Skinner. MW. 6 yrs. Pa. 17. S. 13 Feb. 1738.   17

2487   SKINNER, John. Rotherhith(e) Surrey. P Si. 4 yrs.
        Md. 20. S. 17 Dec. 1733   154

2488   SKINNER, John. Branford (Brentford,) Mddx. Sawyer.
        NM. 4 yrs. Jam. 21. S. 7 Dec. 1736   188

2489   SKINNER, John. Rygate (Reigate,) Surrey. J Bl. 4yrs.
        Md. No age. S. 7 April, 1756   8

2490   SKINNER, Michael. Winscombe (Winchcomb,) Glos.
        Tanner. NM. 5 yrs. Md. 18. M. 1 Feb. 1736.   35

2491   SLATER, John. Stortford (Bishops Stortford,) Herts.
        School master. JG. 4 yrs. Va. 19. S. 28 Oct. 1719.   82

2492   SLEIGHTHOLME, John. Middle Temple, London. Clerk.
        JG. 4 yrs. Jam. 18. S. 18 March, 1729   52

2493   SLIGHT, Thomas. Nottingham. R Wh. 5 yrs. Md.
        16. M. 27 Nov. 1729   37

2494   SLUCE, John. Stepney, Mddx. Weaver. J Co. 5yrs.
        Md. 20. M. 21 Jan. 1724   17

2495   SMALL, Ellison. Market Drayton, Salop. Gardner.
        P Si. 4 yrs. Va. 23. M. 7 Oct. 1734   94

2496   SMALL, Joseph. St. Andrews, Holbourn, London. Taylor.
        P Si. 4 yrs. Va. 20. S. 22 Nov. 1729   28

2497   SMALLBURN, William. Litchborough, Northants. Carp-
        enter. JT. 4 yrs. Jam. 23. M. 24 Aug. 1730.   80

2498   SMALLEY, John. Gt. St. Hellens, London. JT. 4 yrs.
Jam. 18. S. 1 Jan. 1722   2

2499   SMALLEY, Thomas. Croydon, Surrey. JT. 8 yrs. Pa.
16. S. 6 Sept. 1723   83

2500   SMALLPEACE, William. Halstead, Essex. Husbandman.
JD. 4 yrs. Md. 28. M. 22 Nov. 1724   76

2501   SMART, Margaret. Spinster. St. James, Westminster.
HR. 5 yrs. Va. 18. M. 2 Oct. 1719   61

2502   SMART, Richard. Reading, Berks. Bricklayer. P Si.
4 yrs. Jam. 25. S. 2 Jan. 1730.   5

2503   SMART, William. Christ Church, Spitlefields, Mddx.
smith. 4 yrs. Jam. 21. S. ˙5 May, 1731   124

2504   SMIRK. William. St. Anns, Blackfryers, London. Cordwainer. P Si. 4 yrs. Pa. 21. S. 6 July, 1728   11

2505   SMITH, Abraham. Barnet, Herts. TB. 5 yrs. St. C. or
St. L. 18. M. 4 Aug. 1722   85

2506   SMITH, Abraham. Canterbury. Husbandman. J Bl.
5 yrs. Va. 15. M. 22 March, 1750   25

2507   SMITH, Ambrose. Milner (Milden?) Suffolk. JT. 4 yrs.
Jam. 18. M 8 May 1735   37

2508   SMITH, Ann. St. Anns, Westminster, Mddx. Spinster.
JT. 4 yrs. Pa. 19. M. 26 Feb. 1724   74

2509   SMITH, Casper. Late of Nemvigo? Germany. Labourer.
NM. 4 yrs. Jam. 35. M. 26 Nov. 1736   175

2510   SMITH, Christopher. Castlegate, York. P Si. 5 yrs.
Md. 19. S. 30 Dec. 1729.   90

2511   SMITH, Daniel.   St. Edmonsbury (Bury St. Edmunds,) Suffolk. Husbandman. J Bl. 4 yrs. Philadelphia. No age. S. 13 March, 1754   14

2512   SMITH, Edward. Bushey, Herts. JD. 5 yrs. Md. 17 M. 9 Oct. 1719   67

2513   SMITH, Edward. Eckington (Heckington,) Lincs Butcher. AC 7 yrs. New England. 16. S. 6 March 1721.   23

2514   SMITH, Edward. Chester. Husbandman. P Si. 4 yrs. Jam. Md. both crossed out. 29. S. 12 Dec. 1729   69

2515   SMITH, Edward. St. Sepulchers, London. Distiller. NM. 4 yrs. Jam. 30. S. 27 Feb. 1730   92

2516   SMITH Elizabeth. Brandford (Brentford,) Mddx. Spinster JoG. 5 yrs. Md. 17. M. 30 Aug. 1718   54

2517   SMITH, Elizabeth. Amport, Hants. Spinster. JT. 5 yrs. Va. or Md. 20. S. 2 Nov. 1719   83

2518   SMITH, Elizabeth. Greenwich, Kent. Spinster. J BALL. 5 yrs. Md. 20. M. 24 Nov. 1727   9

2519   SMITH, Francis. St. Giles Criplegate, London. Mother, Margret Smith. JD. 6 yrs. Md. 20. S. 5 Feb. 1723.22

2520   SMITH, Francis. Saul (Sawley?) Derbyshire. Taylor. NW. 4 yrs. Jam. 24. S. 3 Nov. 1738   60

2521   SMITH, Gabriel. Milton next Sittingbourn. Kent. RB. 5 yrs. Jam. 20. M. 1 Nov. 1725   133

2522   SMITH, Henry. Haver (Over?) Cambs. WC2. 4 yrs. Jam. 18. M. 5 March, 1729   42

2523   SMITH, Henry. Salisbury, Wilts. P Si. 4 yrs. Jam. 18. S. 10 Nov. 1730   174

2524   SMITH, Henry. St. Giles in the Fields. Carpenter.
NM. 4 yrs. Jam. 22. S. 3 Nov. 1736   123

2525   SMITH, Jacob. A native of Sweden and late from Old
Ross, Wexford, Ireland. JT. 4 yrs. Jam. 19. M.
11 Jan, 1722   15

2526   SMITH, James. Oxford. AC. 7 yrs. Md. 20. S.
25 Sept. 1721   67

2527   SMITH, James. Portsmouth, Hants. JD. 7 yrs. Md.
15. M. 14 Dec. 1724   97

2528   SMITH, James. Air in the North of Scotland. (Airor,
W. Inverness?) WC2. 7 yrs. Md. 17. M. 27 Jan. 1729.
      19

2529   SMITH, James. Harding (now Harpendon,) Herts. P Si.
6 yrs. Md. 17. M. 18 Dec. 1729   75

2530   SMITH, James. St. Annes, Westminster, Mddx. Painter. NM. 4 yrs. Jam. 25. S. 10 Nov. 1731   273

2531   SMITH, John. Withbey (Westbie?) Lancs. Husbandman.
JG. 4 yrs. Jam. 20. S. 28 Jan. 1720.   11

2532   SMITH, John. Penrin(ryn,) Cornwall. JT. 5 yrs. Pa.
17. S. 1 March, 1721   17

2533   SMITH, John. Boston, Lincs. Husbandman. JT. 5yrs.
Va. 19. M. 19 July, 1721   54

2534   SMITH, John. St. Andrews, Holbourn, Mddx. Cordwainer. JG. 4 yrs. St. C. or St. L. 19. S. 16 Aug.
1722   74

2535   SMITH, John. Woolverhampton, Staffs. J Gar. 4 yrs.
Jam. 17. S. 5 April, 1723   51

2536   SMITH, John.   Christ Church, London.   Mother, Mary
Monk.   JD.   7 yrs.   S. C.   15.   M.   9 Dec. 1723   116

2537   SMITH, John.   St. Saviours, Southwark, Surrey.   WC2.
8 yrs.   Md.   15.   M.   3 Jan. 1729/30   1

2538   SMITH, John.   St. Brides, Fleet St., London.   Cooper.
P Si.   4 yrs.   Jam.   23.   S.   18 Sept. 1730   110

2539   SMITH, John.   Halifax, Yorks.   Woolcomber.   WC2.
5 yrs.   Jam.   18.   S.   6 Oct. 1730   133

2540   SMITH, John.   Edenborough, N. Britain.   Husbandman.
NM.   4 yrs.   Jam.   23.   S.   1 May, 1731   118

2541   SMITH, John.   Killam (Kilham,) Yorks.   JT.   5 yrs.
Jam.   17.   M.   20 May, 1731   136

2542   SMITH, John.   St. Giles in the Fields, Mddx.   P Si.
5 yrs.   Pa.   19.   S.   2 Oct. 1733   80

2543   SMITH, John.   St. Botolphs, Aldgate, London.   Smith.
Father, Benjamin Smith.   P Si.   4 yrs.   Md.   18.   M.
19 Nov. 1733   112

2544   SMITH, John.   St. Margarets, Westminster.   Book keeper.
J Ta.   4 yrs.   Jam.   20.   S.   30 Dec. 1736   217

2545   SMITH, Joseph.   Coventry.   Weaver.   W Bu.   5 yrs.
Md.   20.   M.   7 Dec. 1731   296

2546   SMITH, Joshua.   West Ham, Essex.   Gardner.   P Si.
4 yrs.   St. C.   42.   S.   28 Oct. 1730   164

2547   SMITH, Mary.   Durham.   Spinster.   J Jones.   5 yrs.
Md.   19.   M.   2 Oct. 1725.   97

2548   SMITH, Nathan.   St. Paul at Shadwell, Mddx.   Bricklayer.   P Si.   4 yrs.   Jam.   24.   S.   22 Nov. 1731   285

2549   SMITH, Richard.   East Tilbury, Essex.   Carpenter.   JT.
4 yrs.   Jam.   24.   M.   20 Dec. 1724   102

2550   SMITH, Robert.   Lanham (Langham?) Suffolk.   Weaver.
JD.   4 yrs.   Md.   19.   M.   5 Oct. 1720   142

2551   SMITH, Robert.   Carlisle, Cumberland.   JT.   4 yrs.
Jam.   18.   M.   14 Nov. 1729   22

2552   SMITH, Robert.   Camberwell? Surrey.   Gardner.   MW.
4 yrs.   Jam.   24.   S.   16 Feb. 1738   19

2553   SMITH, Thomas.   Faversham, Kent.   Tanner.   JT.
4 yrs.   Jam.   20.   S.   4 Feb. 1719   34

2554   SMITH, Thomas.   St. James, Westminster, Mddx.   JT.
5 yrs.   Jam.   18.   M.   9 Feb. 1722   31

2555   SMITH, Thomas.   Little Waringfield (Waldingfield?)
Suffolk.   RB.   4 yrs.   Jam.   18.   M.   4 Nov. 1725.   153

2556   SMITH, Thomas.   Colchester, Essex.   Carpenter.   JT.
4 yrs.   Jam.   20.   S.   14 Sept. 1727   34

2557   SMITH, Thomas.   St. Marys, Nottingham.   NM.   7yrs.
Jam.   15.   M.   11 Jan. 1730   22

2558   SMITH, Thomas.   Stroud, Glos.   Butcher.   W Bu.   4yrs.
Md.   25.   S.   17 Dec. 1730   222

2559   SMITH, Thomas.   Walton (Waltham?) Hants.   Father
and mother dead.   J Wh.   4 yrs.   Jam.   18.   M.
14 March, 1737   26

2560   SMITH, Thomas.   Lemster (Leominster?) Herefordshire.
Fisherman.   JS.   4 yrs.   Md.   No age.   M.   11 April, 1751
       42

2561   SMITH, William.   St. Leonards Shoreditch, Mddx.
Labourer.   JG.   4 yrs.   Jam.   23.   M.   1 Jan. 1722.   4

2562 SMITH, William. St. Andrews, Holbourn, Mddx. JT.
5 yrs. Pa. or Md. 18. S. 1 May, 1725   88

2563 SMITH, William. Dublin, Ireland. P Si. 5 yrs. St. C.
16. S. 11 Feb. 1730   56

2564 SMITH, William. St. Martins in the Fields, Mddx.
Bricklayer. P Si. 4 yrs. Jam. 34. M. 21 Nov. 1730. 185

2565 SMITH, William. Hollywell, Flintshire. Husbandman.
W Bu. 4 yrs. Jam. 19. M. 28 Oct. 1731   252

2566 SMITH, William. St. Giles in the Fields. Father and
mother John and Lidia Smith. RS. 7 yrs. Jam. 14.
M. 30 Sept. 1736   73

2567 SMITH, William. Wisbidges (Wisbech,) Cambs. Bricklayer. BW. 4 yrs. Jam. 18. S. 19 Nov. 1736   165

2568 SMITH, William. Cowlei (Cowley) Glos. Smith and
farrier. NW. 4 yrs. Jam. 29. M. 27 Feb. 1738   38

2569 SMITH, William. Lambeth, Surrey. Boat builder.
J Wh. 4 yrs. Jam. 22. S. 28 Feb. 1738   42

2570 SMITH, William. Salisbury, Wilts. Weaver. Father
and mother dead. NW. 4 yrs. Md. 18. S. 19 Dec.
1738   80

2571 SNAGNALE, Ralph. Stepney, Mddx. JD. 8 yrs. Md.
14. M. 12 Oct. 1719   69

2572 SNEAL, Thomas. Beverley, Yorks. JD. 4 yrs. Md.
20. M. 23 Nov. 1719   97

2573 SNEATH, William. Rowell, Northants. Bricklayer.
JG. 4 yrs. Jam. 29. S. 1 Jan. 1722   1

2574 SNOWDEN, Richard. York. Book keeper. RW. 4 yrs.
Barb. 21. S. 4 Nov. 1725   143

2575   SOAN, Ann.   Lambeth, Surrey.   Spinster.   P Si.   4 yrs. Pa.   20.   S.   16 Aug. 1728   87

2576   SOARE, Richard.   Loughborough, Leics.   JT.   5 yrs. Barb. or Md.   18.   S.   15 July, 1735   50

2577   SOMERS (SUMMERS,) William.   St. Margarets, Westminster.   Cooper.   J Wh.   4 yrs.   Jam.   25.   S.   23 March, 1738   57

2578   SOON, John.   Wrexham, Denbighshire, Wales.   Hemp dresser.   JT.   5 yrs.   Va.   16.   S.   15 Dec. 1719.   114

2579   SOUTHERTON, Richard.   Burlescom(be,) Devon.   Tayler. SG.   4 yrs.   Jam.   35.   S.   24 Nov. 1725   203

2580   SPALDING, Thomas.   St. Mary, White Chapple.   Brickmaker and bricklayer.   HE.   4 yrs.   Va.   No age.   S. 11 July, 1754   17

2581   SPAR, Stephen (Steven.)   Hamburg, Holland(?) JT. 7 yrs.   Md.   16.   S.   8 Aug. 1720   101

2582   SPARKS, Richard.   Bristol.   Carpenter.   NM.   4 yrs. Jam.   34.   S.   12 Aug. 1734   71

2583   SPARROW, Anthony.   Borough Bridge, Yorks.   Gardner. JG.   4 yrs.   Md.   24.   S.   19 Jan. 1724   9

2584   SPARROW, John.   St. Edmunds Bury (Bury St. Edmunds,) Suffolk.   JT.   4 yrs.   Jam.   17.   S.   30 March, 1724.   39

2585   SPARROW, John.   Burford, Oxon.   Labourer.   JT.   4yrs. Jam.   19.   S.   26 Nov. 1734   112

2586   SPARROW, Joseph.   St. Martins in the Fields, Mddx. Coachman.   JT.   4 yrs.   Jam.   25.   M.   17 Dec. 1724   105

2587   SPEAR, Mary.   St. Margarets, Westminster, Mddx.   Spinster. Mantua maker.   CV.   5 yrs.   Md.   19.   S.   14 Dec. 1721.   85

2588   SPENCE, Andrew. Stow Markit, Suffolk. Schollar. JG.
5 yrs. Va. 17. S. 16 March, 1720   31

2589   SPENCER, James. Isleworth, Mddx. Gardner. W Bu.
4 yrs. Pa. 20. S. 1 Sept. 1727   30

2590   SPENCER, Samuel. St. Giles, Cripplegate, London.
Smith. NS. 4 yrs. Phila. No age. S. 2 May, 1750   20

2591   SPENCER, Thomas. St. Mary, Rotherhithe. J Bl. 5yrs.
Va. 18. M. 2 March, 1750   15

2592   SPENCER, William. St. Pauls, Covent Garden, Mddx.
Uncle, William Stavely. JT. 6 yrs. Md. 17. S.
14 Nov. 1723   109

2593   SPENDER, John. St. Giles in the Fields, Mddx. Writer.
CM. 4 yrs. Jam. 22. S. 11 Sept. 1735   78

2594   SPENSER, Elizabeth. St. James, Westminster, Mddx.
Spinster. WT. 7 yrs. Jam. 15. M. 7 Jan. 1730.   17

2595   SPICER, James. St. Mary Aldermary, London. Tayler.
JB. 4 yrs. Va. 23. S. 24 Nov. 1727   10

2596   SPICER, Richard. St. James, Westminster, Mddx. Smith.
J Co. 4 yrs. Md. 24. S. 27 Feb. 1724   75

2597   SPIRING, John. West Harptree, Somerset. Carpenter.
NM. 4 yrs. Jam. 22. S. 21 Nov. 1738   66

2598   SPRAGGS, Edward. Dover, Kent. JT. 4 yrs. Jam.
19. M. 28 Feb. 1723   34

2599   SPRAKE, William. Crookhorn (Crewkerne,) Somerset.
Glover. WC2. 4 yrs. Pa. 19. S. 29 July, 1728.   56

2600   SPRAY, Thomas. Abbington(don,) Berks. Smith and
farrier. JT. 4yrs. St. C. or St. L. 20. S. 2 Aug. 1722. 67

2601   SPRIGG, Thomas.   Over Kibworth, Leics.   (Kibworth
Beauchamp or Harcourt?)   W Bu.   4 yrs.   Antigua.   20.
M.   19 Oct. 1731   247

2602   SPRIVER, George.   St. Mary, Hundred of How (Hoo,) Kent.
Husbandman.   RB.   4 yrs.   Jam.   30.   M.   15 Nov. 1725.
                                                                            161

2603   SROTTEN (STOTTEN?) Samuel.   Coventry.   Labourer.
Father and mother dead.   JT.   7 yrs.   Md.   16.   M.
3 Feb. 1737   8

2604   STACE, Richard.   St. Andrews, Holbourn, London.   Clerk.
W Bu.   4 yrs.   Va.   31.   S.   3 Dec. 1731   298

2605   STAGG, Edward.   St. Larence, City of London.   JG.
4 yrs.   Va.   19.   S.   27 Oct. 1720   161

2606   STAINING, Crisp(a)in.   St. Olaves, Southwark.   Master,
Thomas Bullock.   SG.   7 yrs.   Md.   15.   S.   20 Nov.
1725   190

STANARD.   See 2613

2607   STANBUREY, John.   Croydon, Surrey.   Bricklayer.
W Bu.   4 yrs.   Jam.   25.   S.   22 Sept. 1731   214

2608   STANBURY, John.   White Chappell, Mddx.   Bricklayer.
NM.   4 yrs.   N. C.   44.   S.   8 July, 1736   37

2609   STANDFORD, Thomas.   Stutley (Stewkley?) Bucks.   Husbandman.   R Wh.   5 yrs.   Md.   22.   M.   4 Dec. 1729.   54

2610   STANDIDGE (STINDIG,) Thomas.   St. Olaves, Southwark,
Surrey.   Blacksmith.   CV.   4 yrs.   Md.   20.   S.
30 March, 1720   55

2611   STANFORD, William.   Stutley (Stewkley?) Bucks.   W Bu.
5 yrs.   Md.   20.   S.   6 Sept. 1735   76

2612 STANHOPE, Thomas. Marlow, Bucks. Dyer. JT.
4 yrs. Jam. 21. S. 21 Nov. 1730 187

2613 STANNARD (STANARD,) William. Wonhouse (Onehouse,)
Suffolk. TB. 4 yrs. St. L. 17. S. 2 Oct. 1722 137

2614 STANSELL, John. St. Thomas Appo(s)tle, London. Cordwainer. AC. 5 yrs. Va. 19. S. 3 Jan. 1721/2 1

2615 STANTON, John. Northampton. Baker. NM. 4yrs.
Md. 25. S. 5 July, 1735 45

2616 STANTON, William. Stow, Glos. J Bl. 4 yrs. Jam.
18. S. 14 March, 1753 4A

2617 STANWAY, Ralph. (Nantwich?) Cheshire. Husbandman.
NM. 4 yrs. Jam. 23. S. 14 Dec. 1736 192

2618 STAPER, Charles. Hackney, Mddx. JD. 4 yrs. Md.
18. S. 5 Aug. 1718 12

2619 STAPLES, Ann. Lambeth, Surrey. Spinster. SG.
4 yrs. Va. 16. M. 28 Nov. 1727 2

2620 STAPLETON, George. Edminton (Edmonton,) Mddx. JT.
4 yrs. Md. 18. M. 7 Sept. 1720 121

2621 STAPLETON, William. Marlborough, Wilts. JD. 7yrs.
Pa. 16. S. 13 Sept. 1723 89

2622 STARKEY, Richard. Camberwell, Surrey. Gardner.
NM. 4yrs. Jam. 21. S. 21 Oct. 1736 104

2623 STARLING, Robert. St. Georges, Norwich. JD. 7 yrs.
Va. 15. S. 17 Sept. 1722 128

2624 STARR, Richard. Standon, Herts. Husbandman. Father
and mother dead. W Bu. 4 yrs. Jam. 19. S.
2 Nov. 1737 56

2625　STEAN, Edward.　Harton (Haughton? Horton?) Staffs.
JS.　4 yrs.　Md.　20.　S.　5 April, 1753　　　　4B

2626　STEDMAN, John.　Kingsbury, Mddx.　Printer.　NW.
4 yrs.　Jam.　26.　M.　3 Nov. 1738　　　　61

2627　STEEL, Edward.　Doncaster, Yorks.　P Si.　5 yrs.　Pa.
17.　M.　4 Sept. 1730　　　　87

2628　STEEN, Roger.　Shrewsbury, Salop.　CV.　8 yrs.　Pa.
or Md.　14.　S.　4 Jan. 1719/20　　　　2

2629　STEPHENS (STEPHIN,) George.　Aberdeen, N. Britain.
Taylor.　NM.　4 yrs.　Jam.　No age.　S.　21 Aug. 1736.
　　　　55

2630　STEPHENS, Mordecai.　Sheely (Shirley?) Derbyshire.　P Si.
4 yrs.　Jam.　18.　S.　9 June, 1733　　　　13

2631　STEPHENS, William.　Brandford (Brentford,) Mddx.
Bricklayer.　JD.　4 yrs.　Md.　23.　M.　31 Dec. 1722. 196

2632　STEPHENSON, John.　Wisbitch (Wisbech,) Isle of Ely,
Cambs.　Smith and farrier.　JG.　4 yrs.　Antigua.　26.
M.　18 Feb. 1722　　　　30

2633　STEPHENSON, Joseph.　Durham.　Gent.　JH.　4 yrs.
Jam.　No age.　S.　13 July, 1753　　　　11

STEPHIN.　See 2629

2634　STEUART, Thomas.　Dublin, Ireland.　Mason.　JT.
4 yrs.　Jam.　24.　S.　26 May, 1731　　　　142

2635　STEVENS, Bedey (Badey.) Bexley, Kent.　Widow.　Mantua
maker.　NM.　4 yrs.　Jam.　26.　S.　30 Aug. 1733.　42

2636　STEVENS, Henry.　St. Vedast alias Foster, London.
Carpenter.　P Si.　4 yrs.　Jam.　42.　S.　10 Oct. 1734　99

2637   STEVENS, Henry.   Shoemaker.   Father and mother dead. JT.   7 yrs.   Md.   17.   S.   3 Feb.1737   9

2638   STEVENS, John.   St. Margarets, Westminster.   Labourer. NM.   4 yrs.   Jam.   28.   S.   1 Jan.1736   4

2639   STEVENSON, Robert.   Edenbrough, Scotland.   Book binder.   JT.   4 yrs.   Antigua.   20.   S.   30 Aug.1728   103

2640   STEVENSON, Samuel.   Huntingdon (and late of Wapping) Cordwainer.   NM.   4 yrs.   Md.   18.   S.   10 April, 1735.   23

2641   STEVENSON, William.   Southampton.   Labourer.   JT. 4 yrs.   Md. or Va.   20.   M.   22 Feb. 1733   27

2642   STEWARD(T,) Benjamin.   White Chappell, Mddx.   JD. 8 yrs.   St. C. or St. L.   15.   S.   11 Aug. 1722   87

2643   STEWARD (STUARD,) Benjamin.   Kidderminster, Worcs. Weaver.   W Bu.   5 yrs.   Md.   18.   S.   24 Nov.1727.   5

2644   STEWARD, Charles.   St. Andrews, Holbourn, London. Cordwainer.   NM.   4 yrs.   Md.   19.   M.   21 Jan.1730. 30

2645   STEWART, James.   St. James Westminster, Mddx.   Book keeper.   P 'Si.   4 yrs.   Md.   24.   S.   4 Dec.1733.   135

2646   STEWART, John.   New Church, Argyle, Scotland.   JD. 5 yrs.   Pa.   18.   M.   11 Sept. 1723   88

2647   STIFF, Dubartus.   St. James, Westminster, Mddx.   Joyner. P Si.   4 yrs.   SC.   24.   S.   23 Sept. 1730   118

STINDIG.   See 2610

2648   STINTON, William.   St. Georges, Hanover Square. Bricklayer and mason.   NM.   4 yrs.   Jam.   26.   S. 13 Nov.1736   152

2649 STISTED, Lawrence. Rumford (Romford,) Essex. Cook.
NM. 4 yrs. Jam. 28. S. 30 Aug.1733 44

2650 STOCK, Thomas. Axbridge, Somerset. J Bl. 4 yrs.
Jam. No age. S. 1 Nov.1753 27

2651 STOCKDON, James. St. James Westminster, Mddx.
WC2. 4yrs. Antigua. 18. S. 22 Aug.1728 95

2652 STOCKTON, Edmund. St. James, Westminster, Mddx.
Baker. NW. 4 yrs. Jam. 22. S. 26 Oct.1738 58

2653 STOKES, William. Reading, Berks. Bricklayer. W Bu.
4 yrs. N.C. 21. S. 5 July, 1736 26

2654 STONE, Elias. Knowle St. Giles, Somerset. Carpenter.
W Bu. 4 yrs. Jam. 24. S. 9 Nov.1731 266

2655 STONE, George. Wandser (Wandsworth?) Surrey. Husbandman. SG. 4 yrs. Md. 26. S. 19 Nov.1725. 189

2656 STONE, James. Abington, Berks. Vintner. NM. 4yrs.
Jam. No age. S. 30 Aug. 1736 67

2657 STONE, Samuel. Canterbury, Kent. Taylor. JG.
4 yrs. Va. 24. S. 24 Oct. 1724 67

2658 STONE, William. St. Botolphs, Aldgate. Upholsterer.
NM. 4 yrs. Md. 30. S. 7 Jan.1736 20

2659 STOPPER (TOPPER,) George. Billingborough, Lincs.
Husbandman. TB. 4 yrs. St.L. 20. S. 6 Oct.1722.151

STOTTEN. See 2603

2660 STOW, Alexander. Buckingham. Weaver. NM. 4yrs.
Md. 26. M. 29 Nov.1733 126

2661 STRAFFORD, John. St Peters Cornhill, London. NM.
4 yrs. Antigua. 30. S. 3 May, 1734 52

2662 STRAINGER (STRANGER,) John. Oxford. Joyner and carpenter. NM. 4 yrs. Jam. 22. S. 13 April, 1734   46

STRANGER. See 2662

2663 STRATTON, John. Kettering, Northants. JT. 5 yrs. Jam. 16. S. 12 Sept. 1730   102

2664 STREETS, Edward. St. Ives, Huntingdon. JD. 7 yrs. Md. 14. S. 15 Sept. 1719   36

2665 STRINGER, Henry. Queenhith(e) London. Chimney sweeper. JT. 4 yrs. Jam. 20. M. 28 Nov. 1733.   120

2666 STRINGER, James. St. Saviours, Southwark, Surrey. Carpenter and joyner. W Bu. 4 yrs. Jam. 21. S. 25 Jan. 1733   16

2667 STRINGFELLOW, John. Stepney, Mddx. Carpenter. J Co. 4 yrs. Va. 28. S. 17 Nov. 1725   179

2668 STRONG, James. Stepney, Mddx. Mother, Lidia Strong. Late master, Robert Stocker. JT. 6 yrs. Md. 16. M. 14 Nov. 1723   108

2669 STRONG, William. West Lavington, Wilts. Gardner. SA. 4 yrs. Md. 20. S. 18 Jan, 1719   12

2670 STRONG, William. Exeter. Bricklayer. NW. 4 yrs. Jam. 36. S. 15 Dec. 1739   126

STUARD. See 2643

2671 STUART, John. Strinrow (Stranraer?) Galloway, Scotland. Soap boyler. NM. 4 yrs. Jam. 19. S. 6 Nov. 1731. 261

2672 STUCKBURY, Edward. Anno (Aynho?) Northants. Carpenter and sawyer. NW. 4 yrs Jam. 19. S. 20 Feb. 1738   30

2673   STURGIS (STURGES,) Phillip; St. Paul, Covent Garden. Gunsmith. MW. 4 yrs. Jam. 22. S. 13 Oct. 1738.   54

2674   SUCH, George. Brailes, Warwicks. JD. 5 yrs. Pa. 18. M. 5 March, 1721   22

SUMMERS. See 2577

2675   SUMPTER, George. St. Brides, Fleet St., London. Brickmaker. JG. 5 yrs. Va. 19. S. 22 June, 1721   46

2676   SURREDGE, Francis. St. Paul, Shadwell, Mddx. Upholder. NW. 4 yrs. Jam. 28. S. 31 Jan. 1738.   11

2677   SUTHARD, John. Stansfield, Yorks. JT. 5 yrs. Md. 16. M. 24 Oct. 1720   158

2678   SUTTON, Francis. Wells, Norfolk. Carpenter. NM. 4 yrs. Jam. 29. S. 13 Nov. 1736   154

2679   SUTTON, John. Bristoll. Carter. NM. 4 yrs. Jam. 23. M. 27 Oct. 1736   114

2680   SUTTON, Samuel. Peterboro, Northants. Taylor. NM. 4 yrs. Jam. 26. M. 1 May, 1731   118

2681   SWAN, Jacob. London. Watch case maker. J Bl. 4 yrs. Md. No age. S. 4 Aug. 1756   18

2682   SWIFT, William. North Biddick, Northumberland (Durham) P Si. 7 yrs. Pa. 15. S. 27 July, 1728   54

2683   SWITHIN, Thomas. Southampton, Hants. JT. 7 yrs. Md. 17. M. 29 Nov. 1729   44

2684   SYMMS (SIMMS,) Philip. St. Martins in the Fields, Mddx. Ingraver. A Lo. 1 yr. St. L. 20. S. 15 Sept. 1722   127

2685   SYMONDS, Robert. Soam (Soham?) Cambs. JT. 5yrs. Va. 20. M. 12 Oct. 1720   149

TANCROD. See 2686

2686   TANKROD (TANCROD,) John.   Wakefield, Yorks.   JD.
        5 yrs. Md. 19. S. 3 Dec. 1719   103

2687   TANNER, John. Faversham, Kent.   Founder.   TB.
        4 yrs. St. L. or St. C. 20. M. 20 Aug. 1722   106

2688   TASSELL, George. Whittlesey, Cambs. JD. 6 yrs.
        Md. 15. M. 31 July, 1718   42

2689   TAYLER, John. Dartford, Kent. JT. 4 yrs. Jam.
        19. M. 8 Feb. 1722   29

2690   TAYLER, John. Littlethorp, parish of Narb(o)rough, Leics.
        JG. 4 yrs. Jam. 17. M. 15 Nov. 1725   164

2691   TAYLER, Thomas. Whitechappel, Mddx. AC. 7 yrs.
        Va. 15. S. 6 Sept. 1720   120

2692   TAYLER, Thomas. North Summer Coats (Somercotes,)
        Lincs. Labourer. SG. 4 yrs. Md. 35. S. 20 Nov. 1725
                                                             194

2693   TAYLER, William. Hambleton(den,) Bucks. CV. 4 yrs.
        Md. 19. S. 7 Sept. 1722   123

2694   TAYLER, William. St. Clements, Oxford. Distiller.
        W Bu. 4 yrs. Jam. 19. M. 8 Sept. 1730   91

2695   TAYLIOR (TYLIOR,) Robert. Eversham (Evesham,) Worcs.
        J Bl. 5 yrs. Md. No age. M. 23 Aug. 1756.   21

2696   TAYLOR, Daniel. St. Georges at Colgate, Norwich.
        Weaver. JG. 5 yrs. Pa. 18. M. 4 Sept. 1723   85

2697   TAYLOR, Daniell. Chelsea, Mddx. Gardner. NM.
        4 yrs. Jam. 26. M. 5 Nov. 1736   135

2698 TAYLOR, Elizabeth. St. Mary Magdalene, Bermondsey, Surrey. Spinster. 5 yrs. Va. 19. S. First Oct. 1719 60

2699 TAYLOR, George. Dublin. Apothecary and Surgeon. Father and mother dead. NW. 4 yrs. Pa. 20. S. 7 Feb. 1738 15

2700 TAYLOR, James. Arieth (Earith,) Hunts. JG. 4 yrs. Va. 18. M. 17 June, 1721 40

2701 TAYLOR, John. Montrose, Meirns (now Forfarshire,) Scotland. JT. 4 yrs. Barb. 18. S. 24 Feb. 1720 41

2702 TAYLOR, John. Newton Toney, Wilts. Gardner. NM. 4 yrs. Jam. 22. M. 12 Oct. 1731 281

2703 TAYLOR, John. Tarperley (Tarporley,) Cheshire. W Bu. 5 yrs. Va. or Md. 19. S. 30 July, 1735 61

2704 TAYLOR, John. Lineham (Lyneham,) Wilts. Husbandman. J Bl. 4 yrs. Jam. 16. M. 2 Feb. 1754 3

2705 TAYLOR, Matthew. St. Saviours, Southwark. Hatter. J Ta. 4 yrs. Jam. 24. M. 21 Oct. 1736 105

2706 TAYLOR, Ralph. Rochdale, Lancs. Gun smith. W Bu. 4 yrs. Jam. 33. S. 24 Jan. 1731/2 1

2707 TAYLOR, Richard. Southampton, Hants. JG. 4 yrs. Va. 18. S. 27 Oct. 1720 162

2708 TAYLOR, Thomas. Ashby de la Zouche, Leics. Joyner. JT. 4 yrs. Bahamas or Providence. 20. S. 29 July, 1721 59

2709 TAYLOR, Thomas. St. Mary Islington, Mddx. JT. 5 yrs. Jam. 19. S. 6 Oct. 1735 104

2710 TAYLOR, William. St. Andrews, Holbourn, London. Carpenter and joyner. JT. 4 yrs. Jam. 24. S. 30 Oct. 1730 166

2711 TAYLOR, William. St. George the Martyr, Mddx. W Bu.
4 yrs. Va. or Md. 20. S. 14 Oct. 1734 101

2712 TEBBS, Nathaniell. Leicester. Plow boy. NM. 5yrs.
Jam. 18. M. 30 Nov. 1736 182

2713 TEEBOT, Nathaniel. Oundell, Northants. Taylor. P Si.
4 yrs. Md. 25. M. 27 May, 1727 46

TEED. See 2754

2714 TEMPLE, John. St. Margarets, Westminster, Mddx.
Bricklayer. JB. 4 yrs. Md. 25. M. 6 Oct. 1722 153

2715 TEMPLEMAN, Edward. St. Olaves, Southwark, Surrey.
J Co. 7 yrs. Md. 16. M. 4 Feb. 1724 52

2716 TEMPLEMAN, John. St. Georges, Southwark, Surrey.
W Bu. 5 yrs. Md. 17. M. 13 Feb. 1729 29

2717 TENNISON, William. Kenningham (now Keyingham,)
Yorks, (E. R.) Labourer. CV. 4 yrs. Jam. 20. M.
2 June. 1721 39

2718 TERRY, Robert. Southampton. Husbandman. NM.
4 yrs. Va. or Md. 30. S. 4 April, 1734 42

2719 THATCHER, Edward. St. Botolphs, Bishopsgate, London.
WC2. 7 yrs. Pa. 15. M. 30 July, 1728 58

2720 THATCHER, James. St. James, Westminster, Mddx.
Vintner. SG. 4 yrs. Md. 23. S. 17 Nov. 1725 173

2721 THATCHER, William. St. Thomas, Bristol. JD. 5yrs.
Md. 19. M. 11 Aug. 1719 19

2722 THELWALL, Ethelston. Thelwall, Cheshire. Taylor.
AC. 5 yrs. Md. 18. M. 28 Nov. 1720 170

2723 THOMAS, Henry. Spitlefield, Mddx. Weaver. NM.
4 yrs. Md. 31. S. 10 April, 1735   26

2724 THOMAS, Hugh. Partpibor (?) Montgomeryshire, Wales.
Labourer. JT. 4 yrs. Md. 20. M. 25 Oct. 1718   60

2725 THOMAS, Hugh. Carus (Caerwys?) Flintshire. Taylor.
JT. 4 yrs. Jam. 20. S. 11 March, 1724   84

2726 THOMAS, John. Hembury (Henbury,) Glos. Coachman.
JG. 4 yrs. Barb. 25. M. 28 Jan. 1722   28

2727 THOMAS, John. St. Giles in the Fields. Painter. NM.
4 yrs. Md. 23. S. 11 Feb. 1736   36

2728 THOMAS, James. St. Giles, Criplegate, London. Cooper.
JT. 4 yrs. Jam. 21. S. 12 Feb. 1730   58

2729 THOMAS, Joseph. Shrewsbury, Salop. Hat maker. J Co.
5 yrs. Md. 18. M. 4 Oct. 1725   99

2730 THOMAS, Joseph. St. Wasenburg (Werburgh?) Bristol.
Cooper. W Bu. 4yrs. Va. 19. S. 2 Dec. 1731   297

2731 THOMAS, Morgan. Limster (Leominster) Hereford. CM.
4 yrs. Jam. 17. M. 21 March, 1734   10

2732 THOMAS, Sarah. St. James, Westminster, Mddx. Spinster
JD. 5 yrs. Md. 18. S. 15 Oct. 1724   63

2733 THOMAS, Timothy. St. Andrew, Holbourn, Mddx. EC.
6yrs. Md. or Pa. 16. M. 3 March, 1718   5

2734 THOMAS, William. St. Sepulchers, London. Master,
James Smith. JT. 4 yrs. St. L. 17. S. 30 Oct. 1722.
                                                    175

2735 THOMAS, William. St. Sepulchers. Pinmaker. Father,
Matthew Thomas. J Ta. 4 yrs. Jam. 20. S. 20 Nov.
1736   169

2736   THOMPSON, Alexander. St. John, Wapping, Mddx.
Mother, Clarinda Thompson. W Bu. 4 yrs. Va. or Md.
16. S. 22 Feb. 1730   80

2737   THOMPSON, George. St. Giles Criplegate, London.
Gardner. NM. 4 yrs. Md. 27. S. 5 Dec. 1733. 138

2738   THOMPSON (THOMSON,) John. New Castle Upon Tine,
Northumberland. JG. 4 yrs. St. C. 25. S. 12 March,
1722   43

2739   THOMPSON, John. St. Botolph Without, Bishopsgate,
London. JD. 8yrs. Md. 15. S. 12 Dec. 1724   94

2740   THOMPSON, John. St. Georges, Southwark, Surrey. Cordwainer. P Si. 4 yrs. St. C. 32. S. 10 Feb. 1730   51

2741   THOM(P)SON, Joseph. St Lucks (Lukes,) London. Husbandman. MW. 4 yrs. Pa. 26. S. 7 March, 1738. 50

2742   THOMPSON, James. St. James, Westminster, Mddx.
P Si. 4 yrs. Pa. 20. S. 20 Sept. 1733   63

2743   THOMPSON, Lawrence. St. Swithin by London Stone in
Cannon St. London. Bricklayer. R Wh. 5 yrs. Md.
19. S. 23 Jan. 1729   13

2744   THOMPSON, Laurence. Lewis (Lewes,) Sussex. Bricklayer. NM. 4 yrs. Jam. 22. S. 2 Oct. 1735   96

2745   THOMPSON, Thomas. St. Giles Criplegate, London.
Cooper. JT. 4 yrs. Jam. 23. S. 10 Aug. 1734.   69

2746   THOMPSON, Thomas. Spilsby, Lincs. Husbandman. NM.
5 yrs. Jam. 16. M. 6 Jan, 1736   18

2747   THOMSON, John. Langer, Notts. Gardner. NM. 4yrs.
Jam. No age. S. 24 Aug. 1736   59

THOMSON, John. See 2738

2748 THOMSON, Richard. Falkirk, Sterlingshire, Scotland.
Surgeon. NM. 4 yrs. St. C. or Jam. 21. S.
13 Aug. 1734 72

2749 THORN, Daniel. Cro(s)combe, Somerset. Cooper. SG.
4 yrs. Jam. 32. S. 29 Nov. 1725 210

2750 THORNTON, John. St. Giles in the Fields, Mddx. Carpenter and joyner. W Bu. 4yrs. Jam. 34. S. 9 Dec.
1731 290

2751 THORNTON, William. Clipston(e,) Notts. Husbandman.
JD. 4 yrs. Md. 31. S. 20 Aug. 1723 77

2752 THRUSTON, George. Woolverhampton, Staffs. JD.
6yrs. Md. 18. S. 15 Nov. 1721 74

2753 TIBBY, Robert. Chilton, Bucks. JT. 4yrs. Jam. 19
M. 23 Nov. 1725 198

2754 TIDD (TEED,) Samuel. Wapping, Mddx. Carpenter.
JT. 4 yrs. Jam. 27. S. 18 April, 1723 55

2755 TILNEY, Stephen. Tickleburg (Dickleburgh,) Norfolk.
Husbandman. JT. 4yrs. Jam. 20. M. 27 April, 1731. 111

2756 TILT, John. St. Martins in the Fields. Baker. Father
at Worcester, mother dead. J Be. 6 yrs. Pa. 17.
M. 10 Jan. 1738 5

2757 TIMS, John. St. Pulkers (Sepulchres?) Labourer. J St.
7 yrs. (Md?) 16. M. 1 April, 1751 32

2758 TIPLER (TIPLAR,) John. Osbornby (Osbournby,) Lincs. NM.
4 yrs. Jam. 19. S. 7 Oct. 1735 106

2759 TIPLER, Laurance. St. Giles Cripplegate, London. JD.
5 yrs. Md. 19. M. 30 Aug. 1718 53

2760 TIRRY, William. St. Thomas Without the Gates, City of Exon(?) JD. 8 yrs. Pa. 16. M. 2 March, 1721. 19

2761 TISDALE, James. St. Catherines by the Tower, London. WC. 4 yrs. Pa. 20. M. 25 Oct. 1725   125

2762 TODD, Andrew. Erwin (Irvine?) Ayreshire, Scotland. Carpenter. NM. 4yrs. Jam. 19. S. 4 Nov. 1731   258

2763 TODD, Jonathan. Hunslett, Yorks. Tanner. NM. 4yrs. Jam. 23. S. 6 Nov. 1736   136

2764 TOFIELD, Charles. Tickhill, Yorks. Accomptant. NM. 4 yrs. Jam. 31. S. 6 Oct. 1736   85

2765 TOFTS, William. St. Botolphs, Aldgate, London. Labourer. P Si. 5yrs. Barb. or Md. 20. S. 20 Feb. 1732
                                                                                                            7

2766 TOMSON, William. Barkin(g,) Essex. JT. 4 yrs. Md. 18. S. 30 Jan. 1720   13

2767 TOOBY, John. Burton Upon Trent, Staffs. Husbandman. P Si. 4yrs. Md. 34. S. 12 Dec. 1729   70

2768 TOOLS, James. St. Marys, Dublin, Ireland. Baker. AC. 4yrs. Va. 19. S. 23 April, 1720   81

2769 TOOLY, John. Oakingham (now Wokingham,) Berks. Shoemaker. J Bl. 4yrs. Jam. No age. S. 10 Jan. 1752
                                                                                                            1

2770 TOOMER, George. Dunhead, Wilts. Baker. J Cr. 5 yrs. Va. No age. S. 5 Feb. 1750   3

2771 TOOTH, Joseph. Colton, Staffs. Sawyer. W Bu. 4 yrs. Jam. 38. S. 26 Oct. 1730   163

2772 TOPP, William. Ashby de la Zouche, Leics. Baker. JT. 4 yrs. Jam. 19. S. 27 Sept. 1731.   217

TOPPER. See 2659

2773   TOUSEY, Bazill (Basile.) St. James, Westminster, Mddx.
Carver and gilder. R Wh. 4 yrs. Md. 20. S. 19 Feb.
1729   37

2774   TOWNDENE(?) Thomas. Salisbury, Wilts. 7yrs. Md.
JD. 15. M. 9 Oct. 1719   66

2775   TOWNING, John. Nottingham. W Bu. 4 yrs. Pa.
19. M. 11 March, 1734   7

2776   TOWNSEND, William. Chirrell, Wilts. 5yrs. Md. or
Va. WB. 16. M. 10 Dec. 1719   107

2777   TRANTER, Thomas. Tashell? Staffs. TC. 7 yrs.
New England. 16. S. 2 April, 1724   43

2778   TRAVIS, John. White Chappell, Mddx. JT. 5 yrs.
Jam. 16. M. 4 March, 1729   41

2779   TRESELER, Mary. Badbey, Northants. Spinster. P Si.
4 yrs. Pa. 16. M. 2 July, 1728   3

2780   TREWEEKS, George. St. Clement Danes, Mddx. Surgeon. NM. 4 yrs Jam. 25. S. 17 May, 1734   54

2781   TRIBET, Simon. St. James Westminster, Mddx. P Si.
4 yrs. Pa. 20. M. 26 July, 1728   52

2782   TROUT, Adam. St. James, Westminster, Mddx. Labourer. AC. 4 yrs. Va. 20; S. 8 April, 1720   68

2783   TRUEMAN, William. Barkin(g,) Essex. P Si. 5yrs.
Pa. or Md. 16. M. 8 Aug. 1728   69

2784   TRUNLEY, William. St. Andrews, Holbourn, London.
Brickmaker. JT. 4 yrs. Jam. 20. S. 30 Oct. 1729.   7

2785   TUCKER, Joseph. Devizes, Wilts. Cordwainer. NM.
4yrs. Md. 23. S. 17 Dec. 1733   149

2786   TUNKES, Alice. St. Sepulchers, London. Spinster.
Mother, Elizabeth Tunkes. CV. 5 yrs. Md. 17. M.
16 Jan. 1722   21

2787   TURNER, George. Dullingham, Cambs. JT. 4 yrs.
Antigua. 19. S. 3 Jan. 1733   9

2788   TURNER, George. Stutley (Stukeley?) Hunts. Husbandman. NM. 4 yrs. Jam. 22. S. 19 April, 1736   21

2789   TURNER, James. Widenbury (Wybunbury?) Cheshire.
JT. 6 yrs. Jam. 17. S. 13 Dec. 1723   115

2790   TURNER, James. St. Clement Danes, Mddx. Labourer,
WC. 4 yrs. Jam. 21. S. 18 Nov. 1730   183

2791   TURNER, John. Aldgate, London. A poor lad. JD.
5 yrs. Md. 16. S. 14 Aug. 1718   36

2792   TURNER, John. Dunnun (Dunoon,) Argyll, Scotland. JT.
4 yrs. Jam. 19. M. 21 Feb. 1732   8

2793   TURNER, John. St. Edmunds Bury (Bury St. Edmunds,)
Suffolk. Labourer. JT. 6yrs. Jam. 18. M. 28 Nov.
1738   70

2794   TURNER, Robert. St. Mary White Chappell, Mddx. Butcher. NW. 4 yrs. Pa. 22. S. 5 Jan. 1738   3

2795   TURNER, Thomas. St. Brides, Fleet St. London. Clerk
or writer. P Si. 4yrs. Pa. 19. S. 21 Aug. 1730.   78

2796   TURNER, Thomas. Great Chelper (Shelford?) Cambs.
Husbandman. P Si. 4 yrs. Md. 22. M. 17 Dec. 1733.
148

2797 TURNER, William. St. John, Southwark. Weaver. NW.
4 yrs. Md. 22. S. Dec. 19, 1738 78

2798 TURTON, James. Beighton, Derbyshire. Button maker.
JT. 4 yrs. Jam. 18. M. 21 Jan. 1729 9

2799 TURVILL, John. Leicester. JT. 4 yrs. Jam. 17.
S. 28 Feb. 1729 40

2800 TUSTEN, Robert. St. Magnus, London Bridge. Barber
surgeon. NM. 4 yrs. Jam. 36. S. 26 Oct. 1736. 112

2801 TYLER, John. St. Thomas, Bristol. JM. 5yrs. Pa.
19. S. 15 Feb. 1723 28

2802 TYRRELL, Timothy. Leatherhead, Surrey. JD. 5yrs.
Va. 17. S. 19 Oct. 1720 156

2803 TYRRELL, William. Walthamstow, Essex. JD. 7 yrs.
Va. or Md. 15. S. Last Feb. 1720 27

2804 TWISLETON, Richard. Leeds, Yorks. Baker. NM.
4 yrs. Jam. 25. S. 10 Oct. 1733 89

TYLIOR. See 2696

U

2805 UNDERWOOD, Richard. Ludlow, Salop. Husbandman
and groom. NM. 4 yrs. Jam. 25. S. 19 Sept. 1730
116

2806 UNDERWOOD, William. Drayton, Mddx. Groom. JT.
4 yrs. Jam. 33. S. 17 Dec. 1724 103

2807 UNDERWOOD, William. Stafford. Husbandman. JT.
4yrs. Jam. 20. M. 30 Nov. 1725 217

2808   UNDERWOOD, William. St. Leonards, Shoreditch, Mddx. Brickmaker. JT. 4 yrs. Jam. 18. S. Last Oct. 1733
          103

2809   UPHAM, Isaac. St. Sepulchers, London. NW. 4 yrs. Pa. 23. S. 22 Feb. 1738   26

2810   UPHILL, William. Froom (Frome,) Somerset. JD. 6yrs. Md. 18. M. 22 Jan. 1724   19

2811   UPSTILL, Thomas. Gosport, Hants. Labourer. J Wh. 4 yrs. Pa. 19. S. 27 Feb. 1738   40

2812   USE, Henry. Richmond, Surrey. NM. 4 yrs. Jam. 20. S. 16 July, 1730   61

2813   USHER, Robert. Stepney, Mddx. JD. 8 yrs. Md. 14 S. 20 Aug. 1719   24

2814   UXLEY, Catharine. St. Leonards, Shoreditch, Mddx. Spinster. JD. 5 yrs. Pa. 17. M. 20 Oct. 1725.   118

V

VAIL. See 2827

2815   VALET, Joseph. St. Anns, Westminster, Mddx. Stay maker. NM. 4 yrs. Jam. 22. S. 31 July, 1736. 42

2816   VALLEY, Ann. Stepney, Mddx. Spinster. BD. 5 yrs. Pa. 18. M. 22 Sept. 1720   133

2817   VALLIE, Peter. Spitlefields in Tower Liberty, London. Weaver. P Si. 4 yrs. Jam. 22. S. 16 Feb. 1730. 70

2818   VANDALL, Lucy. St. Mary Whitechapell, Mddx. Spinster. JT. 5 yrs. Md. or Pa. 19. S. 29 Sept. 1719. 54

2819 VANDENHURCK, Anne. St. Luke, Old St., Mddx. Spinster. Father and mother dead. SF. 4 yrs. Pa. 18. S. 3 Aug. 1739   95

2820 VAN DORSTON, Gloudrenus. A native of Holland and late of Suffolk St. Mddx. Cook. NM. 4 yrs. Ga. 33. S. 3 Oct. 1735   98

2821 VANE, George. St. Annes Westminster, Mddx. Jeweler. JT. 4 yrs. S. C. 21. S. 6 June, 1732   7

2822 VARNEY, John. Mark Lane, London. Labourer. WC2 6 yrs. Md. 18. S. 9 Dec. 1730   202

2823 VARNIER, Peter. St. James, Westminster. Book keeper. J Co. 4 yrs. Va. 22. S. 17 Nov. 1725   179

2824 VAUGHAN, Philip. St. Lukes, Old St. Clogg maker. J Ta. 4 yrs. Jam. 20. S. 29 Nov. 1736   179

2825 VAUGHTON, George. Woolverhampto(n) Staffs. Iron monger. NM. 4 yrs. Jam. 26. S. 31 July, 1736.   45

2826 VAUX, Leonard. White Chappell, Mddx. Taylor. H Bo. 4 yrs. Va. or Md. 19. M. 26 Sept. 1720   137

2827 VEIL (VAIL,) William. Westminster. Carpenter and joyner. J Cr. 4 yrs. Jam. 36. S. 4 July. 1750   34

2828 VICARS (VICKERS,) John. Wellingborough, Northants. TB. 4 yrs. St. L. 19. S. 11 Oct. 1722   163

VICKERS, John. See 2828

2829 VICKERS, William. St. Sepulchers, London. Labourer. SG. 4 yrs. Jam. 20. S. 9 Nov. 1725   150

2830 VISSAGE, Thomas. St. Georges, Southwark, Surrey. Labourer. JD. 4 yrs. St. C. 20. M. 18 July, 1722. 60

W

WADDELL.   See 2923

2831   WADDILOVE, Richard.   Bradford, Yorks.   MR.   4 yrs.
Jam.   No age.   S.   10 Dec. 1756   29

2832   WADE, Giles.   Berling (Barling,) Essex.   JT.   4 yrs.
Jam.   16.   M.   29 Jan. 1734   5

2833   WADSWORTH, Thomas.   St. James, Clerkenwell, Mddx.
P Si.   5 yrs.   Md.   19.   S.   22 Nov. 1733   117

2834   WAGSTAFF, John.   St. Anns, Aldersgate, London.   Labourer.   W Bu.   4 yrs.   Md.   25.   M.   8 Feb. 1730.   48

2835   WAINSCOTT, Richard.   St. George, Southwark, Surrey.
JT.   7 yrs.   Md.   17.   M.   10 July, 1728   29

2836   WAITE, Joseph.   St. Andrews, Holbourn.   Book keeper.
P Si.   4 yrs.   Jam.   22.   S.   18 Sept. 1730   109

2837   WAKE. John.   Bromley Near Bow   Mddx   JS   7 yrs
Philadelphia.   15.   S   4 April   1754   16

2838   WAKENHAM, John.   St. Martins in the Fields, Mddx.
Painter.   JG.   4 yrs.   St. L or St. C.   48.   S.   18 Aug.
1722   103

2839   WALDEN, John.   St. Leonards, Foster (Lane,) London.
P Si.   5 yrs.   Jam.   18.   S.   11 Nov. 1731   278

2840   WALDRON, Richard Christopher.   St. Margarets, Westminster.   Callico printer.   JG.   4 yrs.   Md.   21.   S.
24 Jan. 1722   26

2841   WALKER, Humphrey.   Bromsgrove, Worcs.   Cordwainer.
W Bu.   4 yrs.   Md.   27.   S.   14 Jan. 1730.   24

2842 WALKER, John. Pocklington, Yorks. P Si. 5 yrs.
Md. or Va. 19. S. 5 Feb. 1733 24

2843 WALKER, Joseph. Leeds, Yorks. JG. 5 yrs. Va. 16.
S. 20 June, 1721 43

2844 WALKER, Joseph. Stanehive, Aberdeenshire (Stonehaven,
Kincardineshire?) J BALL. 4 yrs. Pa. 20. S. 8 July,
1728 16

2845 WALKER, Michael. St. Luke Old St., Mddx. Watch-
maker. Father and mother dead. JW. 4 yrs. Jam.
19. M. 20 Sept. 1739 105/106

2846 WALKER, Richard. Brotherton, Yorks. JT. 6 yrs. Jam.
15. S. 10 March, 1729 44

2847 WALKER, Robert. Lincoln. Sadler. JT. 4 yrs. Jam.
20. S. 1 May, 1725 89

2848 WALKER, Samuel. Mars(t)on, Lincs. JD. 6 yrs. St. L.
15. S. 25 Sept. 1722 133

2849 WALKER, William. Northallerton, Yorks. Husbandman.
CV. 5 yrs. Va. 18. S. 18 April, 1720 74

2850 WALKER, William. Darland, Kent. Butcher. JT.
4 yrs. Jam. 21. S. 17 Dec. 1724 103

2851 WALKER, William. Aldgate, London. P Si. 5 yrs.
Pa. 16. M. 8 July, 1728 15

2852 WALKER, William. Ackeny (Hackney?) J St. 7 yrs.
Md? 18. M. 2 April, 1751 31

2853 WALL, John. St. James, Westminster, Mddx. JT.
4 yrs. Jam. 19. M. 9 Jan. 1723 4

2854 WALLER, John. Great Tottham, Essex. J Bl. 7 yrs.
Md. 16. M. 13 July, 1752 7

2855   WALLETT, William.   St. Saviours, Southwark.   R Bu.
4 yrs.   Pa.   27.   S.   4 July, 1750   31

2856   WALLEY, Mary.   St. Mary Over, Southwark.   Housemaid.
J Den.   4 yrs.   Va.   22.   M.   23 March, 1738   62

2857   WALLIS, Thomas.   Frome, Somerset.   CV.   4 yrs.   Md.
18.   S.   19 Aug. 1720   109

2858   WALLIS, William.   Appleby, Derbyshire (now Appleby
Magna in Leics.)   Cordwainer.   J BALL.   4 yrs.   Antigua.
21.   S.   6 Dec. 1728   114

2859   WALMSLEY, Thomas.   Boston, Lincs.   Husbandman.
AT.   4 yrs.   Jam.   20.   S.   14 Dec. 1749   13

2860   WALSON, William.   Wardington, Oxon.   Husbandman.
NM.   4 yrs.   Jam.   22.   S.   13 Dec. 1736   201

2861   WALTER, John.   St. Anns, Heldbourn (Holborn?) Mddx.
W Bu.   5 yrs.   Md.   17.   M.   12 Feb. 1729.   27

2862   WALTER, John.   Reading, Berks.   Weaver.   W Bu.
6 yrs.   Md.   18.   S.   20 Jan. 1730   29

2863   WALTON, Christopher.   Scarborough, Yorks.   JT.   6yrs.
Jam.   18.   M.   21 Jan. 1720   9

2864   WALTON, Hugh.   Kingsdale, Ireland (Kinsale, Co Cork?)
Rope maker.   NM.   5 yrs.   Md.   21.   S.   20 Feb. 1732
6

2865   WALTON, John.   Henley upon Thames, Oxon.   Baker.
NM.   4 yrs.   Antig.   22.   S.   13 Oct. 1731   231

2866   WALTON, Joseph.   Shrewsbury, Salop.   Painter.   JT.
4 yrs.   Jam.   20.   S.   25 Nov. 1734   111

2867   WALTON, William.   Freeson (Freiston?) Lincs.   JG.
5 yrs.   Va.   15.   M.   17 June, 1721   42

2868   WALWYN, Charles.   Brompton, Kent.   R Sc.   4 yrs.
Jam.   No age.   S.   14 March, 1759   1

2869   WALWYN, John.   Woolwich, Kent.   JD.   6 yrs.   Pa.
or Md.   15.   M.   24 Sept. 1723   97

2870   WANSELL, Thomas.   St. Martins in the Fields, Mddx.
P Si.   4 yrs.   Pa. or Md.   18.   S.   7 Aug. 1728.   68

2871   WARD, Daniel.   Northampton.   J Co.   6 yrs.   Md.
17.   M.   6 Feb. 1724   56

2872   WARD, George.   Stepney, Mddx.   Mother, Rachael Ward.
JT.   6 yrs.   Jam.   17.   S.   23 Feb. 1730   87

2873   WARD, John.   Salisbury, Wilts.   Wool comber.   CV.
4 yrs.   Md.   19.   M.   18 Aug. 1718   17

2874   WARD, John.   St. Sepulchers, London.   Carpenter.   WC.
4 yrs.   Md.   24.   S.   ? July, 1728   4

2875   WARD, John.   A native of Lisle in Flanders.   JT.   7 yrs.
Jam. or Md.   15.   M.   3 Dec. 1728   108

2876   WARD, Luke.   Waybridge (Weybridge,) Surrey.   Labourer.
NM.   4 yrs.   Jam.   20.   M.   12 Nov. 1730.   177

2877   WARD, Richard.   St. Brides, Fleet St. , London.   Mother
Margaret Ward.   JD.   5 yrs.   Md.   17.   S.   22 Aug.
1722   108

2878   WARD, Richard.   Castleford (Castlethorpe?) Lincs.   Groom
NM.   4 yrs.   Jam.   22.   M.   3 Nov. 1736   128

2879   WARD, Richard.   Norwich.   T Hu.   3 yrs.   On board
ship.   17.   M.   5 Jan. 1757   2

2880   WARD, Sarah.   Stafford.   Spinster.   JT.   4 yrs.   Barb.
Leeward Isles.   21.   S.   14 Aug. 1731   189

2881   WARD, Thomas.   Coventry, Warwicks.   Clerk or writer.
W Bu.   7 yrs.   Jam.   20.   S.   9 Oct. 1730   136

2882   WARD, Thomas.   St. Austell, Cornwall.   Ironmonger.
NM.   4 yrs.   Jam.   23.   S.   3 Nov. 1736   118

2883   WARD, William.   London.   J Bl.   4 yrs.   Md.   No age.
M.   22 April, 1756   14

2884   WAREHAM, James.   Lower Swell, Glos.   Gardner.   NM.
4 yrs.   Jam.   30.   S.   8 Oct. 1734   97

2885   WARNER, Henry.   Hitchen, Herts.   Shoemaker.   NM.
4 yrs.   Jam.   24.   S.   29 Nov. 1736   178

2886   WARNER, John.   St. Giles in the Fields, Mddx.   Labourer.
EP.   4 yrs.   Jam.   22.   S.   12 Nov. 1731   279

2887   WARNER, Mary.   St. Sepulchers, London.   Spinster.
P Si.   5 yrs.   Md.   20.   S.   23 Nov. 1730   188

2888   WARREN, Thomas.   St. Giles Criplegate, London.   P Si.
4 yrs.   Va.   25.   S.   20 Sept. 1727   38

2889   WARREN, Thomas.   St. Leonards, Foster Lane, London.
Book keeper.   NM.   4 yrs.   Jam.   29.   S.   10 Nov. 1731
270

2890   WARREN, William.   St. James, Westminster, Mddx.
Joyner and Carpenter.   W Bu.   4 yrs.   Jam.   23.   S.
8 Dec. 1730   196

2891   WARRICK, Thomas.   Chicherley, Bucks.   JD.   6 yrs.
Md.   18.   M.   31 Dec. 1719   116

2892   WARWICK, Edward.   St. Mary at Hill, London.   Box-
maker.   NM.   4 yrs.   Jam.   24.   S.   30 Aug. 1733.   40

2893   WARWICK, Samuel.   St. Martins in the Fields, Mddx.
Labourer.   NM.   4 yrs.   Jam.   31 S.   23 Sept. 1730.   119

2894   WASS, Sarah.   Northallerton, Yorks.   Spinster.   JT.
4 yrs.   Jam.   20.   S.   25 Jan, 1722   27

2895   WATERS, William.   Stepney, Mddx.   Weaver.   NM.
4 yrs.   Jam.   35.   S.   27 Feb. 1730   93

2896   WATKINS, Edward.   Chepstow, Mon.   Book keeper.
J Bl.   4 yrs.   Jam. No age. S. 4 Dec. 1754   24

2897   WATKINS, John.   Bristol.   Apothecary.   NM.   4 yrs.
Md.   19.   S.   8 Sept. 1731   196

2898   WATKINS, Joseph.   Bristol, late of Hammersmith, Mddx.
NM.   4 yrs.   Jam.   17.   S.   12 Sept. 1735   79

2899   WATTS, Elizabeth.   Deal, Kent.   Spinster.   JG.   4 yrs.
Va.   19.   S.   23 Nov. 1727   14

2900   WATTS, Joseph.   Cheddar Somerset.   Husbandman.
Father and mother dead.   SF.   6 yrs.   Md.   18.   S.
1 June, 1739   82

2901   WATSON, Elizabeth.   St. Andrews, Holbourn.   Spinster.
Mother Ann Shittel.   Father dead.   W Bu.   7 yrs.   Pa.
13.   M.   25 Feb. 1736   38

2902   WATSON, George.   St. John, Wapping, Mddx.   JD.
6 yrs.   Md.   20.   M.   26 Jan. 1724   27/28

2903   WATSON, Jacob.   St. Giles, Colchester, Essex.   WC2
4 yrs.   Pa.   18.   S.   27 July, 1728   53

2904   WATSON, John.   St. Clement Danes, Mddx.   Grocer.
TB.   4 yrs.   St. L.   27.   S.   6 Oct. 1722   150

2905   WATSON, John.   St. Johns, Westminster, Mddx.   Carpenter.   P Si.   4 yrs.   Jam.   23.   S.   18 July, 1733.   26

2906   WA(T)TSON, John.   Greenwich.   Mason and bricklayer.
J Cr.   4 yrs.   Md.   No age.   S.   30 April, 1750.   18

2907   WATSON, Robert. Wickham (Whickham,) Durham. Husbandman. NM. 4 yrs. Jam. 26. S. 15 Oct. 1731. 240

2908   WATSON, William. Muscom (Muskham?) Notts. JD. 5 yrs. Md. 18. M. 19 Sept. 1719   41

2910   WAT(T)SON, William. St. Pauls, Shadwell, Mddx. R Wh. 7 yrs. Md. 18. S. 13 Feb. 1729   31

2911   WATSON, William. Thurnham, Yorks. (Lancs? or perhaps Thornholm, Yorks.) Husbandman. NM. 5 yrs. Md. 20. S. 8 Dec. 1729   57

2912   WAY, Rebecca. Lambeth, Surrey. Spinster. J Pa. 4 yrs. Jam. 20. M. 20 Oct. 1750   39

2913   WAYLETT, William. Kingston, Surrey. Potter. JG. 5 yrs. Va. 20. S. 25 July, 1721   56

2914   WEARTER, John. Bradford, Yorks. Husbandman. JG. 4 yrs. Jam. 18. M. 9 July, 1730   60

2915   WEAVER, George. Foundhope (Fownhope,) Herefordshire. J Co. 4 yrs. Md. 16. S. 5 Oct. 1725   103

2916   WEAVER, Mary. Bristoll. Spinster. J Pa. 4 yrs. Va. 20. M. 31 Jan. 1749   5

2917   WEBB, Edmund. Richmond, Surrey. J Co. 7 yrs. Md. 16. M. 9 Feb. 1724   61

2918   WEBB, John. Bedford Watton (Wootton) Beds. JT. 6yrs. Jam. 16. M. 16 March, 1729   48

2919   WEBB, Richard. Haislemere, Surrey. Bricklayer. JG. 4 yrs. Jam. 20. S. 8 Nov. 1720   166

2920   WEBB, Robert. St. Georges, Hanover Square. Peruke maker. J Bl. 4 yrs. Jam. No age. S. 7 Aug. 1753. 23

2921   WEBB, Thomas. Newport Pagnell, Bucks. Cordwainer.
J BALL. 4 yrs. Va. 29. M. 18 Dec. 1728   119

2922   WEBSTER, Francis. Eden, Yorks. J Cr. 7 yrs. Jam.
No age. M. 10 April, 1756   11

2923   WEDDELL (WADDELL,) William. Dover, Kent. Carpenter. W Bu. 4 yrs. Jam. 20. S. 10 Dec. 1729   65

2924   WEEDON, James. Great Tew, Oxon. Husbandman. JG.
4 yrs. Md. 20. M. 19 Aug. 1718   21

2925   WEEKES, Jeremiah. Wircompton (West Compton?)
Somerset. JD. 7yrs. Md. 15. M. 15 Aug. 1719   20

2926   WEER, Thomas. Bristol. Labourer. J St. 7 yrs. Md.
16. M. 2 April, 1751   30

WELCH. See 2937

2927   WELLER, Henry. St. Georges, Southwark, Surrey. Carpenter. NM. 4 yrs. Jam. 23. S. 19 Sept. 1730. 115

2928   WELLING, William. St. Philips, Bristol. Cordwainer.
JG. 4 yrs. Jam. 19. S. 4 May, 1731   122

2929   WELLMAN, William. Cureville, Somerset. Husbandman
Father and mother dead. S Wh. 4 yrs. Ga. 19. S.
4 Oct. 1737   51

2930   WELLS, George. Bromley, Kent. Shoemaker. NM.
4 yrs. Va. 21. M. 4th Jan. 1737   1

2931   WELLS, Henry. Tring, Herts. Cordwainer. J Ti.
4 yrs. Md. 23. S. 1 Jan. 1733   4

2932   WELLS, Isaac. Stratford Upon Avon, Warwicks. J Co.
4 yrs. Md. 18. S. 5 Oct. 1725   101

2933   WELLS, Samuel. Hatfield, Herts. Blacksmith and farrier. J Cr. 4 yrs. Jam. 20. M. 31 Oct. 1749. 11

2934   WELLSTEAD, Peter. Downton, Wilts. JT. 6 yrs. Jam. 16. M. 2 July, 1730   57

2935   WELLTON, Henry. Hamnet (Hampnett,) Sussex. P Si. 4 yrs. Jam. 19. S. 11 July, 1733   21

2936   WELLYCOM, John. Bam(p)ton, Oxon. AC. 5 yrs. Va. 16. M. 7 Oct. 1720   144

2937   WELSH (WELCH,) George. St. Giles Criplegate, London. Cordwainer. P Si. 4 yrs. Pa. 21. S. 20 Aug. 1734   76

2938   WELSH, Edward. Aldgate, London. Horn turner. NM. 4 yrs. Md. 29. M. 12 Aug. 1735   70

2939   WELSH, John. Oxford. Taylor and stay maker. P Si. 4 yrs. Jam. 21. S. 1 Oct. 1731   223

2940   WESLEY, Thomas. Leicester. Labourer. JT. 4 yrs. N. Y. or Carolina. 26. M. 16 Nov. 1724   73

2941   WEST, John. Bedford. Husbandman. J Bl. 4 yrs. Jam. 24. S. 4 July, 1750   29

2942   WEST, Matthew. St. Clement Danes, Mddx. Drawer. NW. 4 yrs. Pa. 30. S. 12 Sept. 1739   100

2943   WEST, Thomas. Stepney, Mddx. J Co. 8 yrs. Md. 16. M. 2 Feb. 1724   43

2944   WESTLEY, Richard. Bromfield, Essex. JD. 6 yrs. Md. 16. M. 6 Sept. 1722   121

2945   WHALEY (WHEALLY,) John. St. Andrews, Dublin, Ireland. EC. 4 yrs. Jam. 17. S. 12 Jan, 1719   10

IMMIGRANTS TO AMERICA, 1718-1759

2946   WHARTON, Robert.   Cambridge.   A poor lad and destitute of friends.   JD.   8 yrs.   Md. and Pa.   15.   M.
23 Jan. 1719   16

WHEALLY.   See 2945

2947   WHEATLEY, Charles.   St. Mary White Chappell.   Weaver.   Father James Wheatley.   J Wh.   4 yrs.   Jam.   18.
S.   22 Sept. 1739   108

2948   WHEATLEY, John.   St. Sepulchers, London.   Cooper.
Father Benjamin Wheatley.   JT.   4 yrs.   Jam.   19.   S.
9 Sept. 1730   92

2949   WHEELER, Elizabeth.   Deptford, Kent.   Widow.   NM.
4 yrs.   Ga.   26.   M.   3 Oct. 1735   100

2950   WHEELER, John.   Stockwell, Surrey.   Coachman and
farmer.   NM.   4 yrs.   Jam.   27.   S.   15 Dec. 1736   204

2951   WHEELER, Ruth.   St. Stephens, Bristol.   Spinster.   AL.
5 yrs.   Md.   19.   S.   25 Sept. 1723   98

2952   WHEELEY (WHIELEY,) Francis.   Warsell (Walsall,) Staffs.
JG.   4 yrs.   Jam.   19,   S.   12 Sept. 1730   103

WHIELEY.   See 2952

2953   WHIKES (WIKS,) William.   Tuxberry (Tewksbury,) Glos.
JD.   7 yrs.   Md.   16.   S.   21 Jan. 1724   15

2954 .   WHIPPO, George.   Falmouth, Cornwall.   JT.   5 yrs.
Pa.   18.   M.   1 March, 1721   16

2955   WHITAKER, James.   Shoreditch, Mddx.   Weaver.   Father
and mother John and Elizabeth Whitaker.   NM.   5 yrs.
Jam.   17.   S.   24 Aug. 1736   61

2956   WHITAKER (WHITTIKAR,) John.   Sheffield, Yorks.   P Si.
4 yrs.   Jam.   17.   S.   13 July, 1733   22

242

2957   WHITAKER (WHITTEKAR,) John.   Sheffield, Yorks.   P Si.
4 yrs.   S. C.   17.   S.   15 June, 1733   15

2958   WHITAKER, Nathaniel.   St. Anns, Westminster, Mddx.
Carpenter and joyner.   JT.   4 yrs.   Jam.   30.   S.
13 Dec. 1734   116

2959   WHITBY, William.   Blackshall (Blaxhall,) Suffolk.   Miller.
NM.   4 yrs.   Md.   29.   S.   13 Sept. 1735   89

2960   WHITCRAFT (WHEATCROFT,) Richard.   Wirksworth,
Derby.   NM.   6 yrs.   Jam.   18.   S.   8 Nov. 1731.   263

2961   WHITE (WIGHT,) Edward John.   St. Georges by Queen
Square, Holbourn, Mddx.   NM.   5 yrs.   Md.   17.   S.
3 April, 1735   15

2962   WHITE, James.   Brook(e) Norfolk.   P Si.   4 yrs.   Ga.
or S. C.   18.   S.   15 June, 1733   16

2963   WHITE, John.   Longberry, Dorset.   Labourer.   JT.
4 yrs.   Jam.   19.   M.   9 Oct. 1730   137

2964   WHITE, John.   Chelsea,   Fisherman.   NM.   3 yrs.
Carolina or W. I.   No age.   S.   10 Aug. 1736   50

2965   WHITE, John.   Southampton.   Baker.   Father and mother
dead.   J Wh.   5 yrs.   Jam.   20.   S.   31 Dec. 1739   133

2966   WHITE, Robert.   Falkirk, Sterling, Scotland.   Sawyer.
NM.   4 yrs.   Jam.   30.   S.   16 April, 1731   105

2967   WHITE, Solomon.   St. Botolphs, Bishopsgate.   CV.
4 yrs.   Jam.   22.   S.   27 Dec. 1722   195

2968   WHITE, William.   Emsworth, Hants.   JD.   5 yrs.   Pa.
19.   M.   2 March, 1721   18

2969   WHITECHURCH, William.   Waltham Abbey, Essex.
Breeches maker.   Mother Sarah Whitechurch.   NM.   4yrs.
Jam.   20.   M.   9 Nov. 1736   141

2970   WHITE, William.   Fareham, Hants.   J Bl.   7 yrs.   Va.
         16.   S.   11 March, 1752   3

        WHITEACRE.   See 2958

2971   WHITEFOOT, Powys.   Tenbury, Worcs.   Cooper.   NW.
         4 yrs.   Jam.   21.   S.   25 Nov. 1738   67

2972   WHITEFOOTT, John.   St. Paul, Covent Garden.   Carpenter and joiner.   NM.   4 yrs.   Jam.   No age.   S.
         31 Aug. 1736   69

2973   WHITEFORD (WHYTFORD,) James.   Lanrick (Lanrig?)
         Scotland.   Husbandman.   P Si.   4 yrs.   Md.   29.   S.
         4 Nov. 1730   169

2974   WHITEHEAD, John.   St. James, Westminster, Mddx.
         JG.   7 yrs   Pa.   16.   S.   27 Oct. 1725   129

2975   WHITEHOUSE, Benjamin.   Newport, Salop.   Taylor.
         JT.   4 yrs.   Jam.   19.   S.   11 Sept. 1733   54

2976   WHITMAY, Thomas.   Eas(t)on, Northants.   Cook.   JT.
         4 yrs.   Jam.   18.   S.   13 May, 1724   49

2977   WHITMILL, Joseph.   Basingshaw (St. Michael Bassishaw?)
         Bow Lane, London.   Bricklayer.   P Si.   4 yrs.   Jam.
         21.   S.   27 Nov. 1730   192

2978   WHITMORE, Samuel.   Birmingham. Warwicks.   Toy
         maker.   J Co.   4 yrs.   Jam.   20.   M.   7 Oct. 1725.   107

        WHITTEKAR.   See 2957

        WHITTIKAR.   See 2956

2979   WHITTLE, William.   St. Johns, Southwark.   Cooper.
         Father and mother dead.   Brother, Thomas Whittle.   S Wh.
         4 yrs.   Jam.   20.   S.   20 July, 1737   50

2980   WHITTON, Samuel. St. Saviours, Southwark, Surrey. Tobacconist. P Si. 4 yrs. Jam. 21. S. 1 July, 1734.62

WHYTFORD. See 2973

2981   WIGGINS, Isaac. St. Magnus by London Bridge. Trunk maker. W Bu. 4 yrs. Md. 24. S. 9 Dec. 1730. 201

2982   WIGGMORE, John. St. Andrew, Holborne. Mother Hannah Jones. NW. 6 yrs. Pa. 17. M. 25 Jan. 1738.
9

WIGHT. See 2961

WIKS. See 2953

2983   WILCHINGHAM, Bartholomew. Yarmouth, Norfolk. JD. 7 yrs. Md. 15. M. 12 July, 1718   9

2984   WILCOCKS, Thomas. Carton in Moreland (Carlton-le-Moorland,) Lincs. Husbandman. J Bl. 4 yrs. Jam. 18. S. 22 Nov. 1750   42

2985   WILD, Jonathan. Aldgate, London. Labourer. W Bu. 4 yrs. Md. 25. S. 16 Dec. 1730   214

2986   WILDER, John. Walsall, Staffs. Apothecary and surgeon. W Bu. 4 yrs. Jam. 21. S. 15 Sept. 1731   210

2987   WILDER, William. St. Martins in the Fields, Mddx. P Si 4 yrs. Jam. 21. S. 15 Oct. 1731   241

2988   WILKEY, William. St. Giles in the Fields. Baker. Father and mother dead. W Bu. 6 yrs. Md. 20. S. 27 Jan. 1737   6

2989   WILKINS, Anthony. Westbury Under the Plain, Wilts. JT. 5 yrs. Jam. 18. M. 5 Nov. 1725   144

2990   WILKINSON, John. Saxmundham, Suffolk. Husbandman.
SF. 4 yrs. Jam. 21. S. 7 Feb. 1737   11

2991   WILKINSON, Joseph. Great Ashby (Asby,) Westmorland.
Labourer. W Bu. 4 yrs. Pa. 28. S. 10 Sept. 1730. 96

2992   WILKINSON, Samuel. Wellingborough, Northants. JD.
8 yrs. Md. 15. M. 15 Aug. 1723   74

2993   WILKINSON, Thomas. St. Brides, Fleet St., London.
Joyner. J BALL. 4 yrs. Pa. 27. S. 9 July, 1728   18

2994   WILLDIX, Joseph. St. Georges, Southwark, Surrey.
Weaver. JG. 4 yrs. Va? 20. S. 22 June, 1721   48

2995   WILLET, Samuel. Taunton Dean, Somerset. Husbandman. NM. 4 yrs. Pa. 24. S. 26 June, 1731   165

2996   WILLETT, James. Nutfield, Surrey. W Bu. 5 yrs. Va.
16. M. 13 Nov. 1727   23

2997   WILLIAMS, Charles. Wincanton, Somerset. JD. 7yrs.
Md. 17. S. 8 Aug. 1720   99

2998   WILLIAMS, Francis. New Castle Upon Tine, Northumberland. JG. 5 yrs. Md. 17. M. 3 Feb. 1723   18

2999   WILLIAMS, Henry. Landooilick (Llandefeilog?) Carmarthanshire, Wales. JD. 5 yrs. Md. or Pa. 16. S.
8 Feb. 1719   39

3000   WILLIAM, Hugh. Bilmer (?) Merioneth. Husbandman.
TR. 4 yrs. Md. 20. M. 7 Feb. 1750   7

3001   WILLIAMS, James. Brimmer (Breamore?) Hants. Labourer. J Ta. 4 yrs. Jam. 18. S. 12 Nov. 1736   150

3002   WILLIAMS, John. Stepney, Mddx. J Csn. 7 yrs. Md.
15. S. 2 Feb. 1719   30

3003   WILLIAMS, John. Asby de la Zouch, Leics. JT. 3 yrs.
Barbados. 20. M. 3 March, 1719   43

3004   WILLIAMS, John. Stalbridge, Dorset. Husbandman.
AC. 4 yrs. **Va.** 18. S. 14 Jan. 1720   4

3005   WILLIAMS, John. Lanroost (Llanrwst,) Debighshire, Wales
Glover. JW. 5 yrs. Pa. 18. S. 15 May, 1721.   35

3006   WILLIAMS, John. St. Botolphs, Aldgate. London. Goldsmith. John Newlin of Barbadoes, goldsmith. 4 yrs.
Barbadoes. 20. S. 5 Oct. 1721   69

3007   WILLIAMS, John. Yardley, Warwicks. JG. 5 yrs. Md.
19. S. 27 May, 1723   60

3008   WILLIAMS, John. Gloucester. JD. 7 yrs. Md. 15.
M. 22 Jan. 1724   18

3009   WILLIAMS, John. St. James, Bristol. Sawyer. RB.
4 yrs. Jam. 31. M. 26 Nov. 1725?   208

3010   WILLIAMS, John. St. James, Westminster, Mddx. P Si.
5 yrs. Md. 18. S. 13 Dec. 1729   72

3011   WILLIAMS, John. Monmouth. Cooper. NM. 4 yrs.
Jam. 27. S. 17 Dec. 1733   151

3012   WILLIAMS, John. Kensington, Mddx. Gardner. EP.
4 yrs. Jam. 21. M. 22 Nov. 1737   66

3013   WILLIAMS, Jonathan. L lanferring(?) Monmouthshire,
Wales. JD. 5yrs. Md. 19. M. 23 Sept. 1720.   135

3014   WILLIAMS, Richard. Tiverton, Devon. NM. 4 yrs.
Jam. 20. M. 9 Dec. 1736   194

3015   WILLIAMS, Thomas. St. Pauls, Norwich. JD. 5 yrs.
Pa. 19. M. 2 March, 1721   20

3016   WILLIAMS, Thomas. St. Martins in the Fields, Mddx.
Carpenter. JG. 4 yrs. Jam. 36. S. 7 April. 1723   53

3017   WILLIAMS, Thomas. Bangor, Wales. Labourer. WC2
4 yrs. Jam. 20. S. 16 March, 1729   49

3018   WILLIAMS, Thomas. Oswestry, Salop. JG. 7 yrs. Jam.
18. M. 16 Sept. 1730   107

3019   WILLIAMS, Thomas. Swansey, Glam. Wales. Silver
smith(?) NM. 4 yrs. N.C. 21. S. 8 July, 1736   31

3020   WILLIAMS, Walter. Growby, (Groby,) Leics. JD. 5yrs.
Md. 18. M. 21 Sept. 1719   42

3021   WILLIAMS, William. Glascome (Glascwm,) Radnor,
Wales. JD. 4 yrs. St.L. 20. M. 3 Oct. 1722   141

3022   WILLIAMS, William. Stepney, Mddx. JT. 4yrs. Jam.
20. S. 16 Sept. 1734   86

3023   WILLIAMSON, George. Yorkham (Yarcombe,) Devon.
Husbandman. P Si. 6 yrs. Jam. 17. S. 6 Aug. 1731.
     183

3024   WILLIAMSON, Thomas. Liverpool. Husbandman.
Mother and father dead. JT. 4 yrs. St. C. or Monserrat
18. M. 27 March, 1739   64

3025   WILLIAMSON, William. St. Giles in the Fields, Mddx.
JG. 8 yrs. Barb. 26. S. 5 May, 1718   2

3026   WILLIAMSON, William. Stockers(t)on, Leics. Bricklayer. JW. 4 yrs. Barb. 19. M. 15 Dec. 1721.   87

3027   WILLIAMSON, William. Kent (Kenchurch?) Herefordshire.
JD. 5 yrs. Md. 20. M. 9 Oct. 1724   60

3028   WILLINGHAM, John. Spittlefields, London. WD. 7 yrs.
Va. 18. M. 12 April, 1751   46

3029 WILLIS, Joseph. St. Saviours, Southwark, Surrey. Weaver. JT. 4 yrs. Jam. 20. S. 1 May, 1725 87

3030 WILLS, Theophilus. St. James, Clerkenwell, Mddx. Gardner. JC. 4 yrs. Va. 25. S. 25 Nov. 1725 207

3031 WILLSHER, Edward. Bradford, Wilts. JT. 8 yrs. Md. 15. M. 11 Nov. 1719 87

   WILLSHIRE. See 3051

3032 WILLSON, Francis. Leicester. Carpenter. J Bl. 3 yrs. Nova Scotia. No age. S. 18 May, 1750 23

3033 WILLSON, James. Dumfres(?) Ayreshire, Sootland. Husbandman. NM. 4 yrs. Jam. 22. S. 12 Aug. 1734. 70

3034 WILLSON, John. St. Andrews, Holbourn. Curryer. P Si. 4 yrs. Pa. 25. S. 6 July, 1728 9

3035 WILLSON (WILSON,) John. Christ Church, London. JT. 4 yrs. Jam. 17. S. 14 Oct. 1730 146

3036 WILLSON, Joseph. Stainland, Parish of El(l)and, Yorks. Weaver. JT. 4 yrs. Jam. 20. S. 8 Nov. 1729. 16

3037 WILLSON, Mary. St. Martins in the Fields, Mddx. Spinster. JW. 4 yrs. St. C. 20. S. 19 Sept. 1720. 129

3038 WILLSON (WILSON,) Thomas. Chester. Gardner. P Si. 5 yrs. Md. 19. S. 13 Dec. 1729 71

3039 WILLSON, Thomas. St. Saviours. Southwark, Surrey. P Si. 5 yrs. Va. 19. S. 25 Feb. 1733 28

3040 WILLSON, William. Moore Green, Notts. Husbandman. S Wh. 4 yrs. Jam. 26. M. 11 Nov. 1737 62

3041 WILSFORD, Henry. Dublin, Ireland. Book keeper. NM. 4 yrs. Md. 25. S. 12 Nov. 1734 107

3042 WILSON, David. Edenborough, Scotland. Clerk. JG.
4 yrs. Va. 20. S. 27 June, 1721 49

3043 WILSON (WILLSON,) James. Hackney, Mddx. Hat maker.
JW. 4 yrs. Md. 19. S. 18 Nov. 1719 90

3044 WILSON. John. St. Georges, Southwark, Surrey. P Si.
4 yrs. Pa. 15. S. 16 July, 1728 36

3045 WILSON, John. Carli(s)le. Husbandman. BW. 4 yrs.
Md. 25. S. 12 Oct. 1736 88

3046 WIL(L)SON, Leonard. Oakley, Essex. JT. 4 yrs. Jam.
18. S. 19 Dec. 1728 120

3047 WILSON, Mary. St. James, Clerkenwell, Mddx. Spinster. JD. 6 yrs. Md. 16. M. 19 Oct. 1719 74

3048 WILSON, Richard. Spalding, Lincs. JG. 7 yrs. Md.
17. S. 30 Dec. 1723 124

3049 WILSON, Robert. Brunt Island (Burntisland, Fifeshire,)
Scotland. Apothecary and surgeon. SC. 3 yrs. S. C.
No age. S. 20 Sept. 1753 26

3050 WILSON, William. Spalden (Spalding,) Lincs. JD.
4 yrs. St. C. 17. S. 17 July, 1722 59

3051 WILTSHIRE (WILLSHIRE) Thomas St. Sepulchers, London
W Bu 5 yrs. Md. 17. S 19 Feb. 1729 36

3052 WIMPEN(E)Y, Edmund (mond.) Almon(d)bury, Yorks.
Cloatheworker. CV. 5 yrs. Md. 22. S. 2 March, 17
1722. 41

3053 WINDON, John. Kingston, Surrey. J Bl. 5 yrs. Md.
20. M. 28 March, 1750 14

3054 WINGFIELD, Charles. St. John, Wapping, Mddx. Sugar
baker. JG. 4 yrs. Jam. 20. S. 23 Oct. 1725 122

3055   WINN, William.   R Sy.   3 yrs.   On board ship.   No age.
M.   7 Jan. 1757   5

3056   WINNERHALL, John Henry.   London.   J To.   5 yrs.
Antig.   No age.   S.   27 Jan. 1757   9

3057   WINTER, Charles.   Eaton, Nr. Windsor.   Cooper.   CV.
4 yrs.   Md.   20.   S.   16 Jan. 1722   19

3058   WINTERBOURN(E,) William.   St. Giles, Cripplegate.
Mother Elenour Winterbourne.   EP.   4 yrs.   Jam.   20.
S.   7 Nov. 1737   58

3059   WINTOWN, John.   Milton Nr. Sittingbourn, Kent.   JD.
6 yrs.   Md.   16.   S.   21 Jan. 1724   16

3060   WISE, Jane.   Stepney, Mddx.   Spinster.   CV.   6 yrs.
Md.   17.   M.   29 Dec. 1721   92

3061   WISE, John.   Stepney, Mddx.   CV.   7 yrs.   Md.   15.
S.   29 Dec. 1721   94..

3062   WITHERS, Thomas.   Nantwich, Cheshire.   JG.   4 yrs.
Jam.   19.   S.   28 Jan. 1720   12

3063   WITT, James.   Broadchalk, Wilts.   Blacksmith.   Father
and mother dead.   J Wh.   5 yrs.   Md.   18.   S.
2 June, 1739   85

3064   WITTY, William.   Lafton La Morthen (Laughton-en-le-
Morthen, Yorks.)   Coachman.   NM.   4 yrs.   Pa.   22.
S.   26 June, 1731   167

3965   WOOD, Daniel.   Reading, Berks.   Labourer.   NM.   4yrs
Antig.   25.   S.   13 Oct. 1731   230

3066   WOOD, Isaac.   Stepney, Mddx.   CV.   4 yrs.   Antig. or
Leeward Isles.   21.   S.   4 Dec. 1724   83

3067   WOOD, John.   Stepney, Mddx.   JW.   4 yrs.   Barb.   20.
S.   24 June, 1718   7

3068   WOOD. John.   St. Giles in the Fields, Mddx.   JW.   5yrs.
Md.   15.   S.   7 Jan.   1719   8

3069   WOOD, John.   St. Giles, Criplegate.   Mother, Ann Wood
JG.   7 yrs.   New England.   16.   S.   1 April, 1723   50

3070   WOOD, John.   Monson.   Annandale (Dumfriesshire.)
Scotland.   Taylor.   NM.   4yrs.   Jam.   20.   S.   30 Sept. 1731. 219

3071   WOOD, Peter.   Aldermaston, Berks.   Sawyer.   EP.
4 yrs.   Jam.   20.   S.   30 May, 1738   46

3072   WOODBRIDGE, John.   St. Gregory by St. Pauls, London.
Painter.   JT.   4 yrs.   Jam.   22.   S.   25 May, 1731.   138

3073   WOODBURN, Robert.   St. Edmundsbury (Bury St. Edmunds,)
Suffolk.   6 yrs.   Md.   16.   M.   29 Nov. 1729   41

3074   WOOLHAMS, Barton.   Little Thorndon (now West Horndon)
Essex.   Gardner.   NW.   4 yrs.   Md.   28.   S.   22 March,
1738   55

3075   WOODHEAD, Edmund.   Great.St. Helens, Bishopsgate St.
London.   JT.   6 yrs.   Jam.   18.   S.   16 June, 1724.   52

3076   WOODHOUSE, William.   London Wall.   Barber.   RB.
5 yrs.   New England.   18.   S.   28 March, 1724   37

3077   WOODHOUSE, William.   St. Leonards, Shoreditch, Mddx.
Weaver.   JT.   4 yrs.   Jam.   23.   M.   27 Dec. 1733   159

3078   WOODNY, John.   St. Peters. Cornhill, London. and late
of Virginia.   Book keeper.   NM.   4 yrs.   Jam.   32.   S.
3 Sept. 1734   78

3079   WOODROOTE, Thomas.   Bristol.   Coachman.   JG.   4yrs.
Jam.   19.   S.   15 Feb. 1730   67

WOODS, Edward Dennis. See 764

3080   WOODS, John. Norwich. Cordwainer. NM. 4 yrs.
Antigua. 19. S. 14 Oct. 1731   238

3081   WOODS, John. Godliman (Godalming,) Surrey. Husbandman. P Si. 4 yrs. Md. 19. M. 13 March, 1733. 34

3082   WOODUS, John. Charing Cross. Valet de chambre and
butler. J Wh. 4 yrs. Jam. 22. S. 17 Nov. 1737. 63

3083   WOODWARD, George. Worcester. Labourer. NM.
4 yrs. Jam. 19. M. 7 Nov. 1730   173

3084   WOLVERTON, Roger. St. Giles in the Fields, Mddx. JD.
5 yrs. St. L. or St. C. 17. M. 20 Aug. 1722   105

3085   WOOLLEY, Cornelius. Deptford. Kent. Labourer.
Father and mother dead. JT. 4 yrs. Jam. 18. M.
7 Aug. 1739   96

3086   WOOLNER, James. St. Pauls. Norwich. JT. 4 yrs.
Jam. 17. S. 14 Sept. 1727   33

3087   WOOLVERTON. Roger. St. Giles in the Fields, Mddx.
JD. 6 yrs. Pa. 17. M. 25 June, 1722   37

3088   WORKMAN, Thomas. Stroudwater. Glos. Weaver. JG.
4 yrs. Md. 20. M. 19 Aug. 1718   19

3089   WORRALL, Samuel. Penniston (Penistone,) Yorks. P Si.
5 yrs. Md. 18. M. 26 Nov. 1731   286

3090   WORRELL, John. St. Marys, White Chappell, Mddx.
Carpenter. JT. 4 yrs. Jam. 29. S. 17 May, 1731. 134

3091   WORTLEY, William. York. Baker. Father and mother
dead. JT. 4 yrs. Antigua or Jam. 20. S. 28 Dec.
1739   129

3092   WRENCH, Thomas. St. Andrews Undershaft, London.
       NM. 6 yrs. Md. 16. S. 11 Dec. 1729   67

3093   WRIGHT. Edward. Kemble, Wilts (Glos?) JG. 4 yrs.
       Va. 18. S. 18 Aug. 1721   66

3094   WRIGHT, James. St. Marys, White Chappell, Mddx.
       Glazier. JT. 4 yrs. Jam. 20. S. 25 Nov. 1724.   77

3095   WRIGHT, James. St. Anns Aldersgate, London. Founder.
       W Bu. 4 yrs. Va. 26. S. 18 Nov. 1730   181

3096   WRIGHT. James. St. Andrews Holborne. Labourer.
       Father and mother dead. JT. 4 yrs. Antigua or Jam.
       18. S. 3 Jan, 1739   1

3097   WRIGHT, Margret. St. Martins in the Fields. Mddx.
       Spinster. J BALL. 4 yrs. Pa. 19. M. 9 Aug. 1728.   74

3098   WRIGHT, Samuel. The Old Bailey. London. J Bl.
       7 yrs. Md. No age. S. 3 March, 1756   5

3099   WRIGHT, Thomas. Fordige (Fordwich,) Kent. JT.
       5 yrs. Md. 16. M. 10 April, 1735   29

3100   WRIGHT, Walter. St. James, Westminster. Mother
       late Hannah Wright, now Hannah Clarke. SF. 4 yrs.
       Jam. 18. S. 27 Sept. 1736   78

3101   WRIGHT, William. Glascow, Scotland. Postillian. JC.
       5 yrs. Pa, or Md. 18. M. 8 May, 1725   91

3102   WRIGHT, William. Bishopsgate, Mddx. Farrier. WT.
       4 yrs. Jam. 23. S. 20 Feb. 1730   78

3103   WRIGHT, William. St. Botolphs. Bishopsgate, London.
       Farrier. NM. 4 yrs. Pa. 22. S. 26 June, 1731.   166

Y

3104   YALLERE, Joseph.   Watford.   Herts.   Farrier.   NM.
5 yrs.   Md.   19.   S.   8 March, 1733   32

3105   YARRALL, William.   Barnett, Herts.   W Bu.   4 yrs.
Jam.   16.   S.   19 Sept. 1735   92

3106   YATES, Richard.   Wellington, Salop.   RB.   6 yrs.
Pa. or Md.   17.   S.   17 Sept. 1723   91

3107   YATES, Richard.   St. Vedas(t) alias Foster.   Diamond
cutter.   JG.   6 yrs.   Md.   23.   S.   4 Nov. 1724.   69

3108   YEATES, Benjamin.   Barwick (Berwick) Upon Tweed
JT.   4 yrs.   Va.   18.   M. .   9 April, 1720   69

3109   YEATS, George.   Newington, Surrey.   P Si.   6 yrs.
Jam.   16.   M.   22 Feb. 1730   82

3110   YORK, Mark.   St. Botolph, Aldgate, London.   Mother,
Ann York.   JD.   7 yrs.   Md.   14.   M.   20 Aug. 1723.   75

3111   YORK, Mary.   St. Ann, Westminster, Mddx.   Spinster.
EC.   5 yrs.   Barb.   19.   M.   26 Aug. 1718   46

3112   YOUNG, George.   Nantwich, Cheshire.   Gardner.   J Bl.
4 yrs.   Md.   No age.   S.   21 July, 1753   12

3113   YOUNG, John James.   St. Giles in the Fields.   Mother,
Mary Young.   MW.   4 yrs.   Antigua.   17.   M.   10 Oct.
1739   113

3114   YOUNG, Philip.   St. Peters in Shaftsbury, Dorset.   Labourer.   JT.   4 yrs.   Jam.   19.   M.   13 Oct. 1722   168

3115   YOUNG, Sarah.   St. Botolph, Aldersgate, London.   Spinster.   JW.   5 yrs.   Va. or Md.   20.   M.   14 Oct. 1720.
153

3116   YOUNG, Thomas.   Christ Church, Surrey.   Weaver.
JT.   4 yrs.   Jam.   20.   S.   3 Dec. 1724   81

3117   YOUNG, William.   Ridgely, Staffs.   Butcher.   R Bu.
4 yrs.   Pa.   24.   S.   4 July. 1750.   30

APPENDIX

ANALYSIS OF THE EMIGRANTS' DESTINATIONS IN THE AMERICAN COLONIES

Antigua	95	Pennsylvania	267
Antigua or Barbadoes	2	Pennsylvania or Jamaica	1
Antigua or Jamaica	3	Pennsylvania or New York	13
Antigua or Leeward Isles	4	Philadelphia	12
Antigua or Montserrat	1	Plantations	1
Antigua or St. Christophers	1	St. Christophers	38
Bahamas or Providence	2	St. Christophers or Montserrat	1
Barbadoes	31	St. Christophers or Nevis	4
Barbadoes or Jamaica	3	St. Christophers or St. Lucia	40
Barbadoes or Leeward Isles	1	St. Lucia	47
Carolina	1	South Carolina	35
Carolina or West Indies	5	South Carolina or West Indies	1
Georgia	12	Virginia	230
Georgia or South Carolina	1	Virginia or Barbadoes	1
Jamaica	1219	Aboard Ships	13
Jamaica or West Indies	1	River Sherbro in Africa	2
Jamaica or St. Christophers	1	Uncertain	1
Maryland	852		
Maryland or Pennsylvania	49		
Maryland or Virginia	77		
Maryland or Barbadoes	7		
Maryland or Jamaica	1		
Montserrat	1		
Nevis	1		
Nevis or St. Christophers	4		
New England	17		
New York	1		
New York or Carolina	4		
North Carolina	17		
Nova Scotia	2		

INDEX OF PLACES

The spelling of the place names in this index follows the spelling of the place names on the original manuscripts. Where the correct name has been added, this has been indexed also. On many occasions the same place has been spelled in several different ways, and where there is not too much variation, all have been included on the same line, but where there is a significant difference in spelling they have been indexed separately unless one is an obvious mistake.

A number of London parishes have been listed as sometimes being in London and sometimes being in Middlesex. It has been thought best therefore, as London was included in the county of Middlesex at that time, to make one entry for London and Middlesex and include all the different parishes of London and Middlesex under this heading. Parishes from other counties which have since been engulfed by London are all indexed under their own name.

Abbatston, Hants. 170
Abbersand, Hants. 170
Abbotsbury, Dorset. 45
Aberdeen, Scotland. 213 833
    1019 1777 1781 1875 2018
    2338 2629
Aberdeenshire, Scotland. 2084
Abergavenny, Mon. 1185
    1559 1777pxxvii 1844
Abergenny. 1717 1717 pxxvii
Aberistwith, Wales. 1959
Aberston, Hants. 170
Abingdon, Abington, Berks.
    745 779 2600 2656
Ackney. 2852
Addingham, Yorks. 1448
Airor, Inverness. 2528
Alberry, Surrey. 277

Albury, Surrey. 277
Alcester, Allcester, Warwicks.
    2215
Aldbourne, Auborne, Wilts.
    1003
Aldermaston, Berks. 3071
Alford, Lincs. 1177
Alginay, Moray, Scotland. 327
Aller, Somerset. 46
Almondbury, Yorks. 3052
Alton, Hants. 215
Alveley, Salop. 333
Amersham, Bucks. 448 1387
Amesbury, Wilts. 363
Amport, Hants. 2517
Andover. 1870 2405
Anglesea, Wales. 1568
Anno, Northants. 2672

INDEX OF PLACES

Ansley, Warwicks. 1110
Antony, Cornwall 549
Antrim Co. Ireland. 1775
Antwerp, Brabant. 1251
Appleby, Derbyshire. 2858
Appleby, Leics. 346
Appleby Magna, Leics. 2858
Apstell, Herts. 2201
Argyle, Scotland. 1779
Arlington, Devon. 2262
Armagh, Ireland. 1609 2245
Arncliff, Yorks. 1139
Arnsham, Oxon. 1068
Arthuret, Artruth, Artrith, Cumberland. 2211
Arundel, Sussex. 1750
Asby, Great; Westmorland. 2991
Ash, Surrey. 2202
Ashby, Norfolk. 1965
Ashby, Great; Westmorland. 2991
Ashby de la Zouche, Leics. 1858 2708 2772 3003
Ashfordby, Leics. 238
Ashton, Lancs. 1050
Ashton Keynes, Wilts. 1199
Aston, Bucks. 1098
Astwood, Bucks. 107
Atholl, Perthsire, Scotland. 1778
Atleborough, Norfolk. 70
Auldearn, Scotland. 1868
Audlin, Audlem, Cheshire. 862
Aveley, Salop. 333
Axbridge, Somerset. 2650
Aycliffe, Great; Durham. 1517
Aylesbury, Bucks. 1273 1553

Aylsham, Norfolk. 2457
Aynho, Northants. 2672
Ayston, Rutland. 832

B

Badbey, Northants. 2779
Ballington, Essex. 882
Ballymena, Antrim, Ireland. 1790
Bampton, Oxon. 2936
Banbury, Oxon. 173 815 2135
Banff, Bamf, Scotland. 90 1770 1780 1789 2339
Bangor, Wales. 3017
Barget, Somerset. 1287
Barking, Essex. 1724 2213 2746a p. xxviii 2766 2783
Barling, Berling, Essex. 2832
Barming, Kent. 2053
Barnet, Barnett, Herts. 588 1555 2505 3105
Barnstable, Devon. 2341
Barthomly, Cheshire. 644
Barton, Cheshire. 2188 pxxviii
Barton, Oxon. 1637
Barton, Warwicks. 133
Bartonley, Cheshire 2188 2188 p. xxviii
Barwell, Leics. 1534
Basingstoke, Hants. 1184 1468 2078
Bath, Somerset. 966 1313 1832 2482
Battersea, Surrey. 604 987
Beaminster, Bemister, Bemestry, Dorset. 2117
Beccles, Suffolk. 936
Beckley, Oxon. 2173
Bedale, Beadall, Yorks. 1315
Bedford. 276 749 1094 2941

Bedford.
  St. Pauls. 1142
Bedford Wootton, Watton, Beds.
  2918
Beighton, Derbyshire. 2798
Beighton, Norfolk. 666
Belfast, Ireland. 695
Bellamano, Antrim, Ireland.
  1790
Belper, Bilper, Derbyshire. 1143
Benathue, Angus, Scotland.
  2266
Bengal, East India. 2018
Bengeo, Herts. 1665
Bennington, Herts. 1218
Berkhampstead, Herts. 584
Bermondsey, Southwark, Surrey.
  St. Mary Magdalene. 765
  1374 1833 1995 2192 2193
  2196 2698
Berndsey, Yorks. 1343
Berriew, Montgomeryshire, Wales.
  1952
Berwick Upon Tweed. 716
  2412 3108
Betchworth, Betsworth, Surrey.
  1837
Betherton, South; Somerset.
  539
Beverley, Yorks. 1939 2572
Bexley, Kent. 2635
Bicker, Lincs. 2032
Biddick, North; Northumberland
  (Durham) 2682
Biddiford, Bideford, Devon.
  902
Biggleswade, Beds. 200 374
Bigglesworth, Beds. 200 374
Bilford, Derbyshire. 1144
Billingborough, Lincs. 2659

Bilmer, Merionethshire. 3000
Bingham, Notts. 190
Birmingham, Warwicks. 67 297
  301 829 1240 1306 2470
  2978
Birmingham, Warwicks.
  St. Philips. 2274
Bishops Stortford, Herts. 167
  368 756 2303 2491
Bissill Castle, Chester 1579
Blackhill, Cumberland. 1173
Blackley, Lancs. 1084
Blacknotley, Essex. 1152
Blackshaw, Nithsdale, Scotland.
  1032
Blagill, Cumberland. 1173
Blandford, Dorset. 365
Blaxhall, Blackshall, Suffolk.
  2959
Bloxham, Oxon. 815 1447
Blunham, Beds. 1698
Bodenham, Bodnam, Hereford-
  shire. 2407
Bodmin, Cornwall. 2152
Bolton, Lancs. 1625
Bonsall, Derbyshire. 1245
Borough Bridge, Burroughbridge,
  Yorks. 940 2036 2583
Boscombe, Wilts. 2364
Boston, Lincs. 110 268 740
  1749 2533 2859
Boston, N. E. 540 1661
Bourne, Burn, Lincs. 1145
Boyton, Norfolk. 666
Bradford. Somerset. 2098
Bradford. Wilts. 176 3031
Bradford, Yorks. 2831 2914
Bradworthy, Broadworthy, Devon.
  1989
Brailes, Warwicks. 2674

Braintree, Essex 48

Brandford, Devon. 2059

Breamore, Brimmer, Hants. 3001

Bredhurst, Kent. 491

Brentwood, Essex. 700 1163 1585 2289

Brewen, Cheshire. 126

Bridford, Devon. 2059

Brighthelmston, Sussex. 315

Brighton, Sussex. 315

Brigstock, Brickstock, Northants. 1039

Brimrig, Northerland. 407

Bristol. 111 257 326 535 540 590 599 675 777 821 847 884 928 1069 1136 1268 1288 1272 1593 1659 1802 1961 1963 2156 2220 2221 2276 2582 2679 2897 2898 2916 2926 3079

Bristol
  Christ Church. 198
  Rackley. 1963
  Ratcliffe 2284
  St. Andrews. 2197
  St. Augustine. 1149
  St. James. 163 1155 1317 1364 1549 3009
  St. Johns. 1801
  St. Nicholas. 1236
  St. Philips. 835 2370 2928
  St. Stephens. 354 2395 2951
  St. Thomas. 2721 2801
  St. Werburgh. 2730
  Temple. 1187 1188
  Temple St. 1441 2267

Broadchalk, Wilts. 3063

Brockworth, Glos. 1674

Bromfield, Essex 2944

Bromley, Kent. 620 2930

Brompton, Kent. 2868

Bromsgrove, Broomsgrove, Worcs. 121 518 2841

Brooke, Norfolk. 2962

Brotherton, Yorks. 2846

Broughton Hackett, Worcs. 959

Bruen, Cheshire. 126

Brunt Island, Fifeshire, Scotland. 3049

Bruton, Somerset. 1478 1683

Brynare, Monmouthshire. 1573

Buckingham. 1105 2660

Buckland Monachorum, Devon. 2064

Bugbrook, Northants. 2304

Bulphan, Bulvan, Essex. 1250

Buntingford, Herts. 624

Burbage, Leics. 1905

Burcott. Somerset. 1287

Burford. Oxon. 2585

Burgate, Kent. 226

Burham, Essex. 196

Burlescombe, Devon. 2579

Burntisland, Fifeshire. Scotland. 3049

Burntwood, Essex. 700 1163

Bursleton, Southampton. Hants. 161

Burton Leonard, Yorks. 2138

Burton Nr. Kendal, Westmorland. 784

Burton Pedwardine, Lincs. 612

Burton Upon Trent, Staffs. 2767

Bury St. Edmunds, Suffolk. 49 320 575 788 1531 1669 2511 2584 2793 3073

Bushey, Herts. 2512

Butterton, Staffs. 2360

Butteton, Salop. 2360

Byerton, Warwicks. 133

C

Caerwys, Flintshire, Wales.
1562 2725

Calne, Cane. Wilts. 2280

Camberwell, Surrey. 1007
1160 2552 2622

Cambridge. 737 792 1894
2062 2067 2094 2103
2946

Cambridge
St. Andrews. 294
St. Giles. 2393
St. Sepulchers. 1271

Cannock, Staffs. 2203

Cannonby, Canaby, Cumberland.
1730

Cannongate, Edinburgh. 852

Canterbury, Kent. 116 282
619 706 906 985 988
1212 2413 2506 2657

Canterbury
St. Dunstans. 1906

Cardiff, Glam. Wales. 1886

Cardigan. 1167

Cardington, Carrington, Beds.
1350

Carisle, Northumberland. 2414

Carleton, Norfolk. 389

Carlisle, Cumberland. 771 1968
2414 2551 3045

Carlton, Leics. 1692

Carlton-le-Moorland, Lincs.
2984

Carmarthon, Wales. 1580

Carnarvon, Wales. 1164

Carnock, Fife, Scotland. 1782

Cartmel, Lancs. 1404

Carton in Moreland, Lincs. 2984

Casham, Oxon. 421 939

Castlethorpe, Castleford. Lincs.
2878

Castor. 2005 p. xxviii

Castor, Northants. 633

Caversham. Oxon. 421 939

Chadbrough, Teviotdale. Scotland. 15

Chaddleworth. 956

Chalfont St. Giles, Herts. Bucks.
1001

Charlbury, Oxon. 822

Charlton, Kent 2023

Chatham, Kent. 1386 1603
2340 2423

Chatteris, Isle of Ely, Cambs.
1828

Cheddar, Somerset. 2900

Chedworth, Glos. 1141

Chelmsford, Essex 1763

Chelper, Great; Cambs. 2796

Chelsworth, Chelswood, Suffolk.
1036

Cheltenham, Chelton, Glos. 2209

Chepstow, Mon. 2896

Cherhill. 2776 p. xxviii

Chertsey, Surrey. 1103 1104
1848

Cheshire. 203

Cheshunt, Herts. 2079 106

Chessington, Suffolk, Surrey. 2

Chesshun, Herts. 106

Chester. 867 1571 1579
1594 1682 1697 1734
1772 2514 3038

Chester
St. Peters. 471
Trinity 1616

Chester, West. 1474 1477
  1623
Chesterfield, Derbyshire. 684
Chester le Street, Durham 1917
Chevington, Suffolk. 2
Chicherley, Bucks. 2891
Chichester, Sussex. 409 1550
  1768
Childerditch, Essex. 1363
Childwell, wall, Lancs. 54
Chillington, Devon. 91
Chilton, Bucks. 2753
Chippenham, Wilts. 563
Chirrell, Wilts. 2776 2776
  p. xxviii
Chiseldon, Chisleton, Wilts.
  1613
Chislehurst, Kent. 1349
Chorley, Lancs. 1170
Christ Church, Hants. 1115
Christ Church, Surrey 1249
  3116
Christleton, Crislinton, Cheshire.
  2063
Church Fenton, Yorks. 1327
Cirencester, Glos. 481 861
  980 1536 2430
Claines, Worcs. 1802
Clane, Clain, Kildare, Ireland.
  1879
Clapham, Surrey. 2236
Clapham, Yorks. 159
Clare, Suffolk. 218
Clatford, Wilts. 1261
Claybrook, Leics. 1073
Clayhadon, Devon. 440
Clayhanger, Devon. 440
Clipstone, Notts. 2751
Clonmell, Tipperary, Ireland.
  1874

Cobham, Hants. 433
Cockermouth, Cumberland. 1979
Colchester, Essex. 319 823
  2104 2556
Colchester, Essex
  St. Giles 236 2903
  St. James. 1626 1722 2168
  St. Peters. 790 819 953
  1119
Colebrook, Berks. Bucks. 1090
Coleshill, Cosell, Warwicks.
  2469
Collaton Rawleigh, Devon. 1436
Colne, Lancs. 935
Colton, Staffs. 2771
Colyton, Culliton, Devon. 1137
Combs, Suffolk. 1406
Congleton, Cheshire. 997 1061
Cooper Sale, Essex. 457
Copthorne, Sussex. 2154
Corbridge, Northumberland.
  2275
Cork, Ireland. 475 1618
Cortlingstock, Notts. 160
Costock, Notts. 160
Cottingwith, East. 246 p. xxvii
Coventry, Warwicks. 114 245
  529 1161 1191a 1537
  2394 2545 2603 2881
Cowbridge, Glam. Wales. 1951
Cowick, Yorks. 60
Cowley, Cowlei, Glos. 2568
Crayford, Crayfoot, Kent.
  544 2347
Crewkerne, Somerset. 880 2599
Cricklade, Wilts. 221
Crieff, Creef, Perthshire. 1063
Crookhorn. 880 2599
Croscombe, Somerset. 2749
Crostick, Notts. 160

INDEX OF PLACES

Croydon, Surrey. 1072 1113
  2499 2607
Cureville. 2929 2929 p. xxviii
Curry Rivel 2929 p. xxviii
Cuttlehill, Cutleshin, Fifeshire.
  2369

D

Dalry, Gallaway, Scotland. 2258
Danzick (Germany?) 701
Darkin, Surrey. 831
Darland, Kent 2850
Darlington, Durham. 497
Dartford, Kent. 1508 2477
  2689
Deal, Kent. 2899
Dean, Beds. 921
Dean, Lancs. 349
Dean, Lower; Beds. 1169
Deebridge. 996 996 p. xxvii
Deeping St. James, Lincs. 941
Denbeigh, Wales. 2387 2388
Denton. 2141 2141 p. xxviii
Deptford, Kent. 10 279 402
  520 794 802 816 1525
  2449 2949 3085
Derby. 1756
Devizes, Wilts.
  St. Mary. 703 860 2785
Dickleburgh, Norfolk. 2755
Didbrook. 2281
Diggitt. 512 512 p. xxvii
Dilston, Northumberland. 782
Diss, Norfolk. 2337
Ditcheat, Ditchett. 63
  512 p. xxvii
Ditton. 2141 p. xxviii
Ditton, Surrey. 227
Dolgelly, Merionethshire, Wales.
  2330

Doncaster, Yorks. 961 2627
Donhead. 2770 p. xxviii
Dorchester, Dorset. 390
Dorchester, N. E. 1830
Dorking, Surrey. 831
Douebridge. 996 p. xxvii
Dover, Kent. 836 2598 2923
Down, Kent. 495
Downley, Bucks. 1463
Downton, Wilts. 1307 2934
Dringhouses, Nr. York. 148
Droytwich, Worcs. 184
Dublin, Ireland. 14 164
  171 216 302 405 463
  602 692 710 809 810
  820 839 965 1118 1124
  1311 1369 1460 1610
  1664 1656 1797 1893 2265
  2400 2441 2563 2634
  2699 3041
Dublin
  King's Parish. 2294
  St. Andrews. 2945
  St. Brides. 2039
  St. Johns. 1902
  St. Marys. 2768
  St. Michaels. 453 1646
    2399
Duffield, Derbyshire 52
Dullingham, Cambs. 2787
Dulverton, Somerset. 2206
Dumfriese, Dumfres, Scotland.
  1533 3033
Dundee, N. Britain. 950
Dunhead. 2770 2770 p. xxviii
Dunkeld, Perthshire, Scotland.
  1800
Dunmow, Essex. 168 946
Dunoon, Dunnun, Argyll, Scot-
  land. 2792

Dunrobin.   435
Dunstable, Beds.   527   1678
Dunster.   760
Durham.   202   646   1071   1126
    1290   2547   2633
Dyserth, Flintshire, Wales.   1353

E

Earith, Arieth, Hunts.   2700
Earkups.   273
Earnley, Sussex.   894
East Ham, Essex.   2162
East Indies.   43   120   1498
    1758
Eastlooe, Cornwall.   1010
Easton, Northants.   2976
Eaton, Bucks.   1198
Eaton, Nr. Windsor.   3057
Eccles, Norfolk.   1133
Eckington, Lincs.   2513
Eden, Yorks.   2922   2922 p. xxviii
Edinborough, Edenborough, etc.
    Scotland.   119   372   436
    600   798   889   927   947
    1083   1109   1129   1132
    1490   1500   1774   1786
    1861   1863   1904   1927
    2019   2264   2353   2354
    2448   2474   2540   2639
    3042
Edwalton, Notts.   770
Einbeck, Hanover.   758
Elgin, Moray, Scotland.   327
Elland, Yorks.   21   3036
Ellesmere, Salop.   1685   2075
Elmley Castle, Worcs.   1899
Elverton, Hants.   241
Elvetham, Hants.   241
Embury, Wilts.   363
Emser, Hants.   147

Emsworth, Hants.   147   2968
Ensham, Oxon.   1040
Epping, Essex.   741
Epsom, Surrey   1401
Erpingham, Norfolk.   1984
Erwin, Ayreshire, Scotland.
    2762
Esscott, Yorks.   246   246 p. xxvii
Essex.   567   2346
Etton.   2922 p. xxviii
Evesham, Worcs.   2148   2695
Ewell, Surrey.   2006
Exeter, Devon.   117   464   733
    9 95   1321   1738   2670
Exmouth, Devon.   1651
Exon.   2760
Eynsham, Ensham, Oxon.   1068

F

Falkirk, Stirlingshire, Scotland.
    2748   2966
Falmouth, Cornwall.   84   450
    2954
Fareham, Hants.   2970
Faringdon, Berks.   1231   1232
Faringhill, Essex.   2190
Farnham, South; Surrey.   1653
Farway, Devon.   1215
Faulkland, Fifeshire. Scotland.
    155
Faversham, Feaversham, Kent.
    1014   2326   2553   2687
Feering, Essex.   2190
Felton, Norfolk.   1755
Ferry-bridge, Yorks.   1757
Filey, Salop.   1548
Fintree, Stirlingshire.   1125
Flempton, Suffolk.   1055
Fletching, Sussex.   1248
Foley Hill, Worcs.   179

Folkestone, Foulston, Kent. 1074

Fordingbridge, Fodenbridge, Hants. 19 805 858

Fordwich, Fordige, Kent. 3099

Foredyce, Banff, Scotland. 2339

Forrest, Northants. 505

Fosdyke, Fusdack, Lincs. 1980

Fouldon, Norfolk. 1755

Fownhope, Foundhope, Herefordshire. 2915

Foxton, Cambs. 910

France. 510 841 942 1180 1592

France
Boulogne. 773
Calais. 1705
Marsales. 2150
Paris. 1092
Toulon. 2082

Freiston, Freeson, Lincs. 2867

Froddingham, North; Yorks. 2380

Frodsham, Cheshire. 1577

Frome, Froome, Somerset. 237 677 1300 1319 1413 2187 2810 2857

Fulham, Surrey. 1735

G

Gadlane, Leics. 214

Galloway, Scotland. 1620 1769 1785

Garboldisham, Norfolk. 380

Garstang, Church Town, Lancs. 1466 1467

Gateshead, Durham
St. Mary. 2443

Geddington, Northants. 2375

Genna. 2273

Germany
Leubeck. 191
Nemvigo. 2509
High. 1892

Gibralter. 1913

Gillingham, Norfolk. 397

Glamorgan, Wales. 1792

Glamorganshire, Wales. 1712

Glascwm, Glascome, Radnor, Wales. 3021

Glasgow, Scotland. 25 37 812 891 1990 3101

Glastonbury, Somerset. 848

Glenisla, Angus, Scotland. 678

Gloucester. 653 769 898 1274 1655 2144 3008

Gloucester
St. Catherines. 731
St. Michaels. 2311
St. Nicholas 1305

Gloucestershire. 138

Godalming, Godliman, Surrey 3081

Gordon, East; Berwickshire, Scotland. 1308

Gosport, Hants. 458 797 1512 2811

Gotham, Notts. 530

Grafton, Warwicks. 1875

Grantham, Lincs. 1062 1357

Gravesend, Kent. 1975

Green, Sussex. 395 1186

Greensnorton, Northants. 1794

Greenwich, Kent. 1454 1532 1561 2115 2518 2906

Groby, Growby, Leics. 3020

Guildford, Surrey. 1973 2195

Gunton, Gurton, Norfolk. 34

H

Hacklescourt, Leics. 336
Hadleigh, Hadley, Suffolk. 1031
Hadley, Worcs. 701
Hagget Broughton, Worcs. 959
Hailsham, Sussex. 1174
Hailwood, Lancs. 54
Haislemere, Surrey 2919
Haisted, Essex. 626
Halesowen, Warwicks. 1921
Halifax, Yorks. 2539
Halmer End, Staffs. 1221
    1222 1223
Halstead, Essex. 626 2500
Halton, Warwicks. 132
Hambleden, Bucks. 2693
Hamburg. 1029 2581
Hamilton, Nr. Portsmouth 53
Hampnett, Hamnet, Sussex.
    2935
Hampstead Marshall, Berks.
    2189
Hampton, Herefordshire. 307
Hanningfield, West. Essex.
    2146
Hanover. 2191 2421
Hanslope, Bucks. 1793 2444
Harbury, Herts. 948
Harding, Herts. 2529
Harpendon, Herts. 2529
Harpingham, Norfolk. 1984
Harptree, West. Somerset.
    2597
Harrigate, Yorks. 1389
Harrow on the Hill, Mddx. 670
Harting South. Sussex. 817
Hartley Row, Herts. 886
Harton, Staffs. 2625
Harwich, Essex. 1255
Haslemere, Surrey. 1247 2919

Hassall, Derbyshire 1292
Hatfield, Herts. 547 2933
Haughland, East. Lanark,
    Scotland. 2110
Haughton. Staffs. 2625
Haver, Cambs. 2522
Hayes, Mddx. 1960
Heavitree, Hevetree, Devon.
    1058
Heckington, Lincs. 2513
Helmsley, Yorks. 1049
Helpringham, Lancs. 546
Hembruff. 958 958 p. xxvii
Hemingbrough. 958 p. xxvii
Hemingford, Hunts. 2228
Henbury, Hembury, Glos.
    2726
Henfield, Sussex. 99 100
Henly Upon Thames. 2472
    2865
Hensom, Oxon. 1040
Henthan, Denby, Wales. 1736
Henvill, Sussex. 99 100
Hereford. 115 609 732
    1718
Hertford. 905 993 1407
    1846 2293 2446
Hewish, Somerset. 1885
Hexham, Northumberland.
    537 698
Higham, Hyam, Kent. 2324
High Cross, Warwicks. 1614
Highlands of Scotland. 439
Hill Wootton, Warwicks. 2426
Hingham, Hinginham, Norfolk.
    2256
Hints, Hins, Staffs. 187
Histon, Hisson, Cambs. 58
Hitchin, Herts. 425 1192
    2885

Hodnett, Salop. 2048
Holbeach, Lincs. 649 1114
Holland. 2820
Holland
  Naarden 2244
Holmerry, Herts. 929
Holt, Worcs. 1884
Holywell, Hollywell. 1581
  2565 2565 p. xxviii 2223
Honington. 2335 p. xxviii
Hoo, How, Kent.
  St. Mary. 2602
Horndon, Berwicks. N. Britain.
  2087
Horndon, West. Essex. 3074
Horsham, Sussex. 538
Horsington, Lincs. 1342
Horton, Staffs. 2625
Hugglescote, Leics. 336
Hull, Yorks. 234 842 940
  2114
Hunnington. 2335 2335 p. xxviii
Hunslett, Yorks. 2763
Huntingdon. 2640
Hurley, Berks. 2442

I
Ilminster, Somerset. 1557
Inch, Galloway. 1866
Ingatestone, Essex. 262 1516
  2042
Ingham, Norfolk. 1821
Ingleby, Lincs. 793
Inverness, Scotland. 715 1128
  1776 1823 1867 2332
  2363 2366
Ipswich, Suffolk. 85 362 713
  1226 2169
Ireland. 1946
Irvine, Ayrshire. 668 2762

Isham, Notts. 1920
Isle of Ely, Cambs. 834
Italy. 102 2024

J
Jamaica. 578
James Deeping, Lincs. 941
Jedburgh, Teviotdale,
  Scotland. 15
Jena. 2273

K
Kaisher, Northants. 2005
  2005 p. xxviii
Kelminston, Somerset. 1220
Kemble, Wilts. Glos. 3093
Kemnay, Aberdeenshire,
  Scotland. 796
Kemton, Devon. 1076
Kenchurch, Herefordshire.
  3027
Kendal, Westmorland. 1878
Kenilworth, Warwicks. 489
Kenn, Somerset. 442
Kennett, Wilts. 791
Kenningham, Yorks. 2717
Kennington, Surrey. 2086
  2261
Kent, Herefordshire. 3027
Kettering, Northants. 528
  2663
Kettlethorp, Lincs. 1101
Keyingham, Yorks. 2717
Kibworth Beauchamp, Leics.
  2601
Kibworth Harcourt, Leics.
  2601
Kidderminster, Worcs. 2096
  2643
Kidwelly, Carmarthen. Wales.
  721

Kildrocker, Ireland. 311
Kildrought, Ireland. 311
Kilham, Killam, Yorks. 2541
Killingworth, Warwicks. 489
Kilmington, Kelweston, Kel-
  minston. 1220 p. xxvii
Kilrush, Kilriss, Co. Clare, Ire-
  land. 1729
Kiltormer, Gallaway. 1219
Kinharvie. 1784 p. xxvii
Kings Clere Hants. 2479
Kingsdale, Ireland. 2864
Kings Lynn, Norfolk. 814
  1479 1854
Kings North, Kent. 1853
Kingston, Notts. 1615
Kingston or Kingston upon Thames,
  Surrey. 849 1440 2913
  3053
Kingussie, Kengusey, Inverness.
  1871
Kinsdale, Co. Cork, Ireland.
  2864
Kirby Moorside, Yorks. 2478
Kirby, South. Yorks. 2037
Kirkawdey, Fifeshire. 2365
  p. xxviii
Kirkbean, Galloway, N. Britain.
  351
Kirkby, Yorks. 1681
Kirkcaldy. 2365 p. xxviii
Kircawdey, Fifeshire, Scotland.
  2365
Kirk Hammerton, Yorks. 4
Kirk of Shotts, Lanark, Scotland.
  558
Kirkoven, Galway, N. Britain.
  1784
Kirkudbright, Galloway, Scot-
  land. 316 1612

Kirkwell, Kirkwall, Orkney,
  Scotland. 261
Kirton, Lincs. 2306
Knaresborough, Yorks. 913
  1241 1389
Knebworth, Herts. 541
Knighton, Leics. 2174
Knowle St. Giles, Somerset.
  2654
Knowstone, Devon. 2090
Kyre, Worcs. 708

L

Ladykirk, Lydkirk, Berwickshire,
  N. Britain. 2087
Laindon, Essex. 1437
Lambeth, Surrey. 370 579
  621 743 928 1033 1278
  1551 1716 1936 2569
  2575 2619 2912 See also
  London and Mddx.
Lambeth, Surrey
  St. Saviours. 264
  St. Mary. 1057
Lample, Somerset. 1636
Langer, Notts. 2747
  2747 p. xxviii
Langham, Suffolk. 857 2550
Langholm, Roxbrough, Scot-
  land. 1650
Langport, Somerset. 298
Lanham, Suffolk. 857 2550
Lanrig, Lanrick, Scotland.
  2973
Lanton, Essex. 1437
Largo, Fifeshire, Scotland. 7
Laughton-en-le-Morthen,
  Lafton la Morthen, Yorks.
  3064
Lavington, West. Wilts. 2669

Leam, Cambs. 1077

Leatherhead, Surrey. 2802

Ledbury, Herefordshire. 1041
1082

Lee, Essex. 1958

Leeds, Yorks. 165 744 881
1276 1282 1850 2485
2804 2843

Leicester. 337 1093 1876
2712 2799 3032 2940

Leicester
St. Martins. 2285
St. Marys. 135 507

Leigh on Sea, Lee. 1958 p. xxviii

Leith, N. Britain. 1225

Lemington. 1011

Leominster, Limster, Lemster,
Herefordshire. 661, 2237
2560 2731

Letcomb, Low, Basset Regis.
Berks. 1325

Lewes, Sussex. 2744

Lewisham, Kent. 2030

Leyton, Low. Essex. 764 2092

Lichfield, Litchfield. 222
296 392 1159 1839

Lichfield, Staffs.
St. Mailes, Michaels. 280

Liddington, Leddington, Rutland.
1811

Lidlington, Beds. 920

Lilley, Herts. 50

Limehouse. 1230 1302

Limerick, Ireland. 1693

Limington, Hants. 317

Lin, Norfolk. 1854

Lincoln. 1303 2230 2231
2359 2847

Lincolns Inn Chappell 1498

Linlithgow, Lithgow, Scotland.
1067 1706

Linton, Cambs. 1283

Linton, Teviotdale, Scotland.
801

Lisburn, Co. Antrim, N. Ireland. 1974

Lisle, Flanders. 2875

Litchborough, Northants. 2497

Litleton, Worcs. 1331

Littlethorp, Leics. 2690

Liverpool, Lancs. 658 899
1116 1278 1411 1787
1788 2229 3024

Liverpool
St. Peters. 2390

Llanam Mouthwy. Merionethshire, Wales. 1543

Llanbadarnfawr, Cardigan,
Wales. 730

Llanboidy, Carmarthenshire.
Wales. 1586

Llandefeilog, Carmarthenshire,
Wales. 2999

Llanferring, Mon. 3013

Llangardock, Carmarthenshire,
Wales. 723

Llannon. Carmarthenshire.
Wales. 1554 1583

Llanrwst, Lanroost. Denbighshire,
Wales. 3005

Llansantfraid, Radnorshire,
Wales. 1570 2224

Llantilio Pertholey, Mon. Wales.
1845

Llanyre, Radnorshire, Wales.
720

LONDON AND MIDDLESEX.
Aldgate 103 420 513

LONDON AND MIDDLESEX

Aldgate contd. 592 705 952
 1138 1153 1262 2149
 2240 2270 2361 2791
 2851 2938 2985
 1680 p. xxvii 3121 p. xxviii
Aldersgate.
 St. Anns. 2834 3095
Allhallows, Barking. 1085
 1366 1856
Allhallows Lombard St. 643
 933 1695 1890
Allhallows London Wall, or
 in the Wall. 229 386
 459 460 1260 1379
Allhallows the Great, Thames
 St. 388 747 1723
Basingshaw 2977
Bednall Green. 676
Bethnall Green. 676
Billiter Lane. 1981
Bishopsgate. 1102 1146
 2120 3102
Bishopsgate St. 746 1915
Blackfryers 1673
Blackfriars
 St. Anns. 922 1430
 1472 1513 1908 2116
2504
Bloomsbury
 St. Georges. 887 1496
 1911
Brandford, Brentford 31 131
 2488 2516 2631
Brentford, Old. 142
Brentford, New. 382 1494
Bromley, Nr. Bow. 2837
Canon St. 1825
Charing Cross. 3082

LONDON AND MIDDLESEX

Chelsea. 120 342 596
 1382 1443 1540 1803
 1824 1835 2697 2964
Chiswick. 1034 1660 1859
Christ Church, London. 36
 763 1415 1648 1744
 2536 3035
Christ Church, Mddx. 1704
Christ Church, Spittlefields
 1 108 462 487 557 638
 892 893 978 1243 1004
 1727 1767 1934 2198
 2503
Clare Market 331
Clerkenwell, Mddx. 78 1943
Covent Garden 868
Covent Garden
 St. Paul. 6 51 926
 1194 1205 1916 1941
 2106 2434 2462 2592
 2673 2972
Cree Church, Leadenhall St.
 1394
Criplegate 1762 2427
Crutched Friars 1266
Drayton, Mddx. 2806
Ealing, Mddx. 38 142
Edmonton, Mddx. 1381
 1679 2620
Eling, Mddx. 142
Enfield, Endfield, Mddx. Herts.
 509 1872 2071 2102
Fulham, Mddx. 1086 1112
 1999 2050 2101 2179
Goodmansfield. 461
Goswell St. 2012
Great St. Helens, Bishopsgate.
 1183 2498 3075

LONDON AND MIDDLESEX

Hackney, Mddx. 525 830
2151 2618 2852 3043

Hampstead, Mddx. 44 990
2320

Hammersmith, Mddx. 1582
2898

Hampton, Mddx. 1148 2057

Harrow on the Hill, Mddx. 670

Hendon, Mddx. 795

Highgate, Mddx. 400 742

Holbourn. 1675

Holbourn, Holborn, etc.

St. Andrews. 71 101 139
153 188 232 244 271
299 313 321 322 324
328 330 335 364 401
404 431 503 632 727
808 837 846 870 873
879 908 960 1016 1059
1060 1066 1080 1196
1294 1480 1520 1617
1645 1764 1827 1914
2158 2160 2314 2436
2496 2534 2562 2604
2644 2710 2733 2784
2836 2901 2982 3034
3096

Holborn

St. Annes. 2861

St. Georges by Queen Squ.
2961

Horsleydown. 1535

Isleworth, Mddx. 1599 2299
2589

Islington, Mddx.

St. Mary. 912 1408 2709

Kensington, Mddx. 158 634
1375 3012 2297

Kingsbury, Mddx. 2626

LONDON AND MIDDLESEX.

Lambeth, Mddx. 2626

Limehouse. 1230 1302

Lincolns Inn Chappell. 1498

London 68 907 1806 2384
2681 2883 3056 971
1376 1412

London Wall 3076

Lothbury. 2239

Ludgate. 1030

Maddermarket. St. John
2035

Mark Lane. 2822

Marylebone. Mddx. 11 118
1089

Middle Temple 2492

New Church in the Strand. 1214

Newington, Mddx. 932

Old Bailey. 3098

Old Fish St. 1686

Poplar, Mddx. 339

Queenhithe. 2665

St. Albans, Wood St. 1081
2465

St. Alphage. 523

St. Andrew Undershaft. 3092

St. Andrews, Wardrobe. 635
1928

St. Bartholomews by the Exchange. 566

St. Bartholomews the Gt. 665
1013

St. Bartholomews, Little. 877

St. Benedict Broad St. 682

St. Bennets at Pauls Wharf.
422 813

St. Benets Gracechurch St.
903 2447

St. Botolphs Aldersgate. 26
410 543 1359 1372

LONDON AND MIDDLESEX

St. Botolphs Aldersgate contd.

1410   1492   1564   1912
1955   1982   2406   3115

St. Botolphs Aldgate. 289   438
441 486 637 726 863 1432
1700 1709 1754 1840 2052
2182 2271 2367 2458 2543
2658 2765 3006 3110

St. Botolphs, Bishopsgate.   39
239   247   314   451   466
652   669   1151   1371   1575
1741   1864   2107   2112
2142   2234   2317   2343
2719   2739   2967   3103

St. Botolph by Billingsgate.
28

St. Brides, Fleet St.   895 1047
1390   1924   2322   2460
2538   2675   2795   2877
2993   1887 p. xxviii

St. Catherine by the Tower
1901   1985   2028   2208
2761

St. Catherine Coleman. 1277

St. Catherine Cree Church.
968   1025   1501   1538

St. Clements in the Strand
824

St. Clement Danes.   43   73
69   430   580   581   587
603   642   654   774   780
949   986   1140   1228 1229
1237   1505   1541   1547
1765   1814   1841   1903
1925   2020   2137   2260
2438   2780   2790   2904
2942

St. Christophers. Threadneedle
St.   2133

LONDON AND MIDDLESEX

St. Dunstans.   1791

St. Dunstans, Fleet St. 1544

St. Dunstans in the East 2118

St. Dunstans in the West.   304
542   663   1714   2210   2419
2433

St. Dunstans in the Wall   2043

St. Edmund the King, Lombard
St.   483

St. Ethelburgs, Bishopsgate St.
1521

St. Faiths.   1270   2093

St. Georges, Hanover Square.
195   272   303   325   423
627   1224   1234   1558
1663   2319   2648   2920

St. Georges in the East, Mddx.
1208   2295   2368

St. Georges in the East, Ratclife, Mddx.   2242

St. George the Martyr, Mddx.
2711

St. Giles, Mddx.   1731

St. Giles Cripplegate.   17   290
300   377   429   591   628
785   897   934   974   1054
1056   1176   1210   1298
1309   1322   1335   1336
1435   1471   1473   1483
1488   1511   1607   1632
1640   1647   1728   1804
1882   1930   1998   2077
2088   2091   2119   2185
2257   2519   2590   2728
2737   2745   2759   2888
2937   3058   3069

St. Giles in the Fields.   20
42   79   89   97   112   143

LONDON AND MIDDLESEX

St. Giles in the Fields contd.

145 230 285 295 403
456 476 560 586 712
735 869 1042 1043 1078
1131 1162 1244 1267
1284 1304 1312 1316
1323 1362 1380 1426
1446 1484 1576 1596
1654 1691 1815 1849
1935 1978 1994 2001
2054 2058 2085 2159
2218 2238 2316 2389
2425 2429 2484 2524
2542 2566 2593 2727
2750 2886 2988 3025
3068 3084 3087 3113
1578 p. xxvii

St. Gregorys. 1622 1643
St. Gregorys by St. Pauls. 3072
St. James Dukes Place 517 888
St. James Clerkenwell. 467
532 753 938 1252 1465
1482 1503 1624 1747
1771 1843 2072 2833
3030 3047

St. Lawrence. 2605
St. Lawrence Jewry. 209 914
1950

St. Leonards, Foster Lane.
2839 2889

St. Leonards, Shoreditch, Mddx.
94 156 428 571 639
724 1018 1154 1200
1324 1373 1378 1493
1574 1641 1703 1742
1753 1842 2134 2163
2172 2200 2452 2561
2808 2814 3077

St. Lukes. 2741 574 606
1006 1233

LONDON AND MIDDLESEX

St. Lukes Old St. 434 783
2819 2824 2845

St. Magnus the Martyr by London
Bridge. 1847 1983 2800
2981

St. Martins in the Fields.
3 22 41 65 141 144
178 228 278 318 531
559 573 610 616 623
714 719 738 775 840
909 931 972 992 1000
1075 1111 1197 1227
1361 1419 1427 1429
1442 1456 1567 1627
1629 1766 1798 1808
1810 1813 1836 1909
1948 2007 2055 2080
2105 2123 2180 2204
2219 2222 2226 2246
2268 2287 2315 2351
2373 2381 2391 2392
2454 2564 2586 2684
2756 2838 2870 2893
2987 3016 3037 3097
3118 p. xxviii

St. Martins Ludgate. 59 804
1391

St. Martins in the Strand.
1254 2161

St. Martins le Grand. 1744

St. Mary Aldermary. 593
2595

St. Mary at Hill. 1099 2892

St. Mary Ax 1931

St. Mary le Bone 601 1328
1497

St. Mary le Bow Cheapside.
984 2068

St. Mary le Savoy in the Strand
2235 1657

LONDON AND MIDDLESEX

St. Mary le Strand, Mddx.
855 1606
St. Mary Magdalene. 504
St. Mary Magdalene, Old Fish
St. 2016 2194
St. Mary Woolnorth. 945
St. Matthews, Friday St. 1416
St. Mildred Poultry. 477
St. Michael Bassishaw. 2977
St. Michael Cornhill. 561
925 1134 1670
St. Michael Crooked Lane
699
St. Michael Queenhithe. 2312
St. Michael Wood St. 900
St. Nicholas Cole Abbey. 916
St. Olaves, Hart St. 686
1265
St. Olave, Oliver, Silver St.
220
St. Pauls Churchyard. 2186
St. Peters Cornhill. 383 630
2661 3078
St. Sepulchers. 235 259 761
957 1293 1642 1851
1954 2121 2212 2292
2327 2440 2515 2734
2735 2757 2786 2809
2829 2874 2887 2948
3051
St. Stephen Coleman St. 500
2420
St. Swithin by London Stone,
Cannon St. 2743
St. Thomas the Apostle. 2614
St. Vedast Foster Lane 9
2636 3107
Shadwell, Mddx. 286 2385

LONDON AND MIDDLESEX

Shadwell, Mddx.
St. Pauls. 589 991 1355
1689 2153 2305 2548
2676 2910
Shoreditch, Mddx. 748 2955
Smithfield, East. 851
Soho. 88 122 211
Soho.
St. Ann. 1708 2318
Spittlefields, Mddx. 225 964
1048 1180 1195 1397
1891 2377 2723 2817
3028
Spittlefields, Stepney. 284
2164
Staines, Mddx. 406 585
Stanmore. 915
Stepney. 16 140 150 177
212 263 305 339 341
465 521 570 582 594
671 697 707 759 872
923 976 1021 1035 1135
1259 1370 1688 1743
1751 1869 1910 2003
2017 2033 2061 2176
2184 2358 2371 2372
2416 2464 2466 2494
2571 2667 2668 2813
2816 2872 2895 2943
3002 3022 3060 3061
3066 3067
Stepney
St. Dunstans. 378 427
1977 2422
Stoke Newington. 2125
Suffolk St. Mddx. 2820
Sunbury, Mddx. 2089
Temple, The. 2060

LONDON AND MIDDLESEX

Tottenham High Cross, Mddx. 552

Tower Hamlets, Mddx. 2031

Tower Hill. 1961

Tower Liberty. 2817 p. xxviii

Trinity in the Minories. 2450

Wapping, Mddx. 1469 2640 2754

Wapping
St. Johns. 488 572 728 1937 2344 2736 2902 3054

Westminster. 2827
St. Annes. 86 96 217 360 367 545 617 853 1017 1024 1121 1168 1666 1817 2004 2132 2207 2259 2263 2508 2530 2815 2821 2958 3111

St. James. 33 105 154 162 197 293 376 412 415 417 419 449 473 480 498 550 614 647 662 667 683 691 750 772 803 818 845 859 871 917 989 1012 1037 1045 1201 1299 1351 1422 1518 1545 1546 1569 1587 1639 1720 1746 1752 1816 1907 1940 1942 2008 2047 2111 2171 2225 2247 2286 2303 2309 2356 2404 2501 2554 2594 2596 2645 2647 2651 2652 2720 2732 2742 2773 2781 2782 2823 2853 2890 2974 3010 3100

LONDON AND MIDDLESEX

Westminster
St. John. 1409 1598 2905

St. John the Evangelist. 1962

St. Margarets. 23 27 64 189 219 252 253 254 266 283 356 482 613 787 896 954 979 1053 1179 1395 1438 1445 1453 1459 1560 1584 1662 1726 1783 1829 1964 1970 1997 2045 2300 2329 2333 2379 2424 2432 2481 2483 2544 2577 2587 2638 2714 2840

Whetston, Mddx. 2181

Whitechapel. 134 136 306 350 352 490 983 998 1046 1207 1414 1690 1699 2013 2486 2608 2642 2691 2778 2826

Whitechapel
St. Mary. 8 18 98 185 711 807 890 944 1377 1470 2463 2580 2794 2818 2947 3090 3094

Whitefryers. 1838

Willesden, Wilsden, Mddx. 970 1799

Longberry. 2963 2963 p. xxviii

Long Bredy, Dorset. 2963 p. xxviii

Longhope, Glos. 1809

Longner, Salop. 1452

Looe, East. Cornwall. 1010

Loughborough, Leics 180 2576

Loughton, Essex. 24

Luddenden, Luddington, Yorks. 1611

Ludlow, Salop. 722 2805

Luton, Beds. 361
Lydlinch, Lidlidge, Dorset. 1759
Lymington, Hants. 317
Lyneham, Lineham, Wilts. 2704
Lynn, Norfolk. 249 416 768 937 981 1450
Lynn Regis, Norfolk. 814 1479

M

Macclesfield, Cheshire. 1399
Madeley, Salop. 1676
Maer, Staffs. 359
Maidstone, Kent. 385 492 725 1256 1929
Makerfield. 2044 p. xxviii
Malden, Essex. 1873
Malden, Malling, Surrey. 1449
Malling, West. Kent. 1420
Malpas, Cheshire. 146 2401
Manchester, Lancs. 208 334 437 767 1235 1239 1417 2014
Mangotsfield, Glos. 693 1495
Mansfield, Notts. 1393 1510 2467
Mansfield Woodhouse, Notts. 1601 2455
Mansorell, Leics. 288
Marbeth. 1956 1956 p. xxviii
March, Isle of Ely, Cambs. 210 1986
Marden, Kent. 2272
Margate, Kent. 226 679
Margrove, Queens Co. Ireland. 444
Market Deeping, Lincs. 674
Market Drayton, Salop. 2495
Market Harborough, Leics. 874
Market Overton, Leics. 2167

Market Weighton, Yorks. 1515
Markfield, Leics. 533
Marlborough, Wilts. 182 511 1275 2621
Marlington, Devon. 2262
Marlow, Bucks. 2612
Marport, Nr. Frankfort. 2155
Marther, Brecknock, Wales. 157
Marton, Yorks. 2403
Marsfield. 2044 2044 p. xxviii
Marston, Lincs. 2848
Marsworth, Bucks. 2199
Maryland. 371
Mauchline, Ayreshire. 1967
Maxfield, Glos. 693
Maxfield, Cheshire. 1399
Melford, Suffolk. 2233
Melton Mowbray. 2081
Mendim, Suffolk. 308
Menham, Suffolk. 308
Mere, Meer, Wilts. 969
Merionethshire, Wales. 1566
Merthyr Tydfil, Brecknock, Wales. 157
Michaelstow, Cornwall. 729
Mickhills, Lancs. 83
Middletown, Somerset. 1117
Milden, Suffolk. 2507
Milford, Derbyshire. 1144
Milner, Suffolk. 2507
Milton, Somerset. 1367
Milton, Little, Oxon. 57
Milton next or near Sitting-bourne, Kent. 56 2521 3059
Modesfont, Hants. 172
Moly Swanton. 1295
Monkland, Herefordshire. 1694
Monmouth, Wales. 270 3011

Monmouthshire. 1181

Monson, Annandale (Dumfriesshire)
Scotland. 3070

Montrose, Scotland. 443

Montrose, Meirns, Scotland.
2701

Moore Green, Notts. 3040

Moppus, Cheshire. 146

Moreton in Marsh, Glos. 1461

Morland, Westmorland. 645

Morpeth, Northumberland. 2410

Morton, Lincs. 1597

Mottisfont, Hants. 172

Moulton, Northants. 1761

Mountsorrel, Leics. 288

Mousley, Worcs. 977

Mouthey, Merionethshire, Wales.
1543

Much Hadham, Herts. 1805

Mugland, East. Lenrick, Scotland. 2110

Munster. 1933

Munster, Ireland. 565

Murren, Cornwall. 506

Muskham, Muscom, Notts. 2908

Muthill, Muthell, Perthshire.
1862

N

Nantwich, Cheshire. 329 2617
3062 3112

Narberth. 1956 p. xxviii

Narborough, Leics. 2690

Nebworth, Herts. 541

Netherdeen, Beds. 1169

Newberry, Berks. 62 1269
2066

Newbiggin, Cumberland. 1971

Newcastel Upon Tyne, Northumberland. 269 348 399

contd.   577 875 951 1424
1652 1732 1748 1938
1972 2411 2738 2998

New Church, Argyll, Scotland.
2646

Newington, Surrey. 3109

Newington, Surrey
St. Mary. 1464 2009

Newington Buts, Surrey. 201

Newington Butts. Surrey.
St. Mary. 204

Newnham, Oxon. 1384

Newport, Salop. 597 1330
2975

Newport Pagnell, Bucks. 281
1123 2323 2921

Newton Toney, Wilts. 2702

Newtown, Montgomeryshire,
Wales. 1457

New Windsor, Berks. 762

Norrill, Beds. 373

Northallerton, Yorks. 2849
2894

Northampton. 113 381
474 479 688 955 1147
2615 2871

North Bradley, Wilts. 124

North Britain. 2480

North Curry, Somerset. 687

Northill, Beds. 373

North Petherton, Somerset.
224

Norwich. 149 369 806
1157 1677 1923 2879
3080

Norwich, Norfolk.
Bear St. 702 1209
Best St. 2296
Conisford. 2456
Laurance. 1178

Norwich, Norfolk contd.

St. Andrews. 338

St. Augustine. 291 1451
2349

St. Edmunds. 1339

St. Georges. 2623

St. Georges, Colegate. 967
2696

St. Giles. 752 843

St. Gregorys. 3120 p. xxviii

St. James. 104 109 1602

St. John Timberhill. 1286
1425

St. Margarets. 2313

St. Martins. 1190

St. Martin at Pallace. 696

St. Martins in the Oak. 1051

St. Marys. 1253

St. Michaels at Coslany.
358 1156

St. Michaels at Thorne. 2439

St. Pauls. 3015 3086

St. Peters. 2177

St. Peters a Mancroft. 310
2108

St. Peters Mountergate. 469

St. Saviours. 1888

St. Stephen. 885 1280

St. Swithins, 2459

Nottingham. 205 258 347
555 595 1087a p. xxvii
1486 1818 1883 1969
2493 2775

Nottingham

St. Marys. 1485 2557

St. Peters. 1158 1527

Nun Eaton, Warwicks. 1348

Nutfield, Surrey. 2996

O

Oakham, Rutland. 1365

Oakingham, Berks. 2769

Oakley, Essex. 3046

Oakley, Great, Much. Essex.
1329

Ockendon, South. Essex.
274

Ockham, Surrey. 493

Oler, Somerset. 46

Olive St. 1711

Ollerton, Notts. 344

Ollesham, Norfolk. 2457

Onehouse, Suffolk. 2613

Orkney, Scotland. 40
800

Ormskirk, Lancs. 2216

Osbournby, Osbornby, Lincs.
2758

Ospringe, Kent. 1476

Oswestry, Salop. 1556
3018

Oundle, Oundell, Northants.
12 447 1988 2713

Ousburn, Ouseburn, Osborn,
Little. Yorks. 408

Over, Cambs. 2522

Overbury, Glos. 255

Over Kibworth, Leics.
2601

Over Norton, Oxon. 1100

Oxford. 130 137 1026.
1065 1202 1421 2076
2130 2157 2227 2278
2526 2662 2939

Oxford.

Maudlin. 2127

St. Clements. 2694

St. Peters 1044 2129

St. Peters in the East. 2128

St. Peters le Bailey. 651

P

Painswick, Glos. 1552
Panborough, Somerset. 1881
Panton, Little. Lincs. 1216
Parkgate, Cheshire. 87
Partibor, Montgomeryshire, Wales 2724
Partnal, Beds. 375
Paulerspury, Northants. 455
Paulton, Somerset. 1926
Pausher, Worcs. 186
Peckham, Surrey. 1007
Peebles, Scotland. 1491
Penistone, Penniston, Yorks. 3089
Penrith, Cumberland. 766 1106 1668 1991
Penryn, Penrin, Cornwall. 2532
Pensutt Nr. Bristol. 660
Penzance. Cornwall. 681
Pershore, Worcs. 186
Pertenhall, Beds. 375
Perth, Scotland. 717
Peterborough, Northants. 413 494 757 1523 2680
Petersfield, Hants. 1175
Petherton. 539 p. xxvii
Petherton, South, Somerset. 1332
Pluckley, Kent. 2386
Plymouth, Plimouth, Devon. 625 1130 1263
Pocklington, Yorks. 789 1976 2842
Pontefract, Yorks. 1027
Porbury, Somerset. 1881
Portessie, Portsey, Scotland. 1770
Portsmouth, Hants. 13 32 175 276 343 387 454 478 515 569 1631 1707 1852 1987 1993 1996 2070 2178 2279 2409 2527
Portugal. 1337
Posset, Somerset. 648
Prachin, Northants. 260
Preston, Pressen, Herefordshire. 1388 1898
Preston, Lancs. 1439
Preston Gubbals, Salop. 1542
Preston Pans, Midlothian, Scotland. 2255 2282
Prestwich, Lancs. 1831
Prittlewell, Essex. 1658
Puckeridge , Herts. 694
Pucklechurch, Glos. 2383
Purfleet, Great. Essex. 536
Putney, Surrey. 607 799 1563
Pwllheli, Portalley, Caernarvon-shire, Wales. 1166

Q

Queens County, Ireland. 444 1038

R

Radnor, Old. Wales. 394
Rainham, Essex. 452
Raisby, Lincs. 1281
Raise of Huntly, Aberdeenshire. 1107
Raithby, Lincs. 1281
Ramsbury, Wilts. 93
Ratcliff, Notts. 1392
Ratley, Warwicks. 1238
Rawcliffe, Yorks. 2342
Rayner. 1889 1889 p. xxviii

Raynham. 1889 p. xxviii

Reading, Berks. 424 496 499
 576 1217 1400 1514 1855
 1945 2205 2214 2502
 2653 2862 3065

Redbourn, Herts. 2254

Redmile, Leics. 1489

Reigate, Rygate, Surrey. 484
 2489

Ren, Somerset. 442

Richmond, Surrey. 243 312
 472 1088 1326 1957
 2812 2917

Rickmansworth, Herts. 2011
 2376

Ridgley, Staffs. 918
 918 p. xxvii 3117
 3117 p. xxviii

Ringhouses, Nr. York. 148

Ringwood, Hants. 323 568

Ripon, Yorks. 345

Risely, Beds. 1358 1499

Roade, Northants. 999

Roadley, Glos. 251

Roadley, Rodley, Leics. 251
 256

Roby, Lancs. 1333

Rochdale, Lancs. 2706

Rochester, Kent. 786 2277

Rockcliffe, Cumberland. 1524

Roddell, Yorks. 66

Rokeley, Cumberland. 1524

Romford, Rumford, Essex. 911
 1522 1684 2649

Romsey, Rumsey, Hants. 1745

Ross, Herefordshire. 736 1171

Ross, Old. Wexford, Ireland.
 2525

Rostherne, Roston, Cheshire.
 1428

Rotherham, Yorks. 876

Rotherhithe, Surrey. 393
 664 1296 2029 2232
 2288 2487 2591

Rothley, Leics. 256

Rothwell. 2573 p. xxviii

Rowell, Glos. 1715

Rowell, Northants. 2573
 2573 p. xxviii

Rowley, Warwicks. 551

Ruabon, Denbigh. Wales.
 1165

Rugeley, Staffs. 918 p. xxvii
 3117 p. xxviii

Ruston, Norfolk. 129

Ruthin. Denbigh. Wales.
 1455 1539 1733

Rye, Sussex. 166

S

St. Albans, Herts. 77 1760
 1932 2074

St. Austell, Cornwall. 265
 2882

St. Catherine, Precinct of.
 516

St. Clements, Cornwall.
 1619

St. Edmonsbury, Suffolk.
 320 575 788 1669
 2511 2584 2793 3073

St. Erme, Cornwall. 2301

St. Giles Chayfont, Herts.
 1001

St. Ives, Hunts. 2022
 2664 2131

St. Margarets, Herefordshire
 2217

St. Mary Cray, Kent. 445

St. Merryn, Cornwall. 506
St. Michaels, Lancs. 83
St. Neots, Hunts. 883 1630
St. Thomas Without the Gates,
  Exon. 2760
St. Winnow, Cornwall. 2382
Salisbury. 709 1635 1826
  2523 2570 2774 2873
Sampford Peverell, Devon.
  1285
Sapcote, Leics. 206
Sapsud, Herts. 755
Sawbridgeworth, Herts. 828
Sawley, Saul, Derbyshire. 2520
Saxelby, Saklesby, Leics. 1096
Saxmundham, Suffolk. 2990
Scarborough, Yorks. 2476
  2863
Scotland. 1773
Scoulton, Norfolk. 751
Seamer, Seamore, Yorks. 2139
Seaton, Rutland. 1193
Sedgefield, Durham. 1347
Selby, Yorks. 2397 2445
Selkirk, Scotland. 514 1672
  2415
Shaftsbury, Dorset
  St. Peters. 3114
Sheerness, Kent. 519 622
Sheffield, Yorks. 1213 1444
  2956 2957
Shelford, Great. Cambs. 2796
Shenstone, Staffs. 689
Shepton Mallet, Somerset. 640
Sherborn, Dorset. 1354 2408
Sherborne, Hants. 1064
Sherfield, Hants. 2065
Shields, Sheilds. Northumberland.
  127 826 1108 1318
Shilburnhaugh, Northumberland
  1206

Shirley, Derbyshire. 2630
Shrewsbury, Salop. 384 411
  865 1504 1772a 1820
  2378 2628 2729 2866
  1772a p. xxvii
Shrewsbury, Salop
  St. Chads. 1079
  St. Gillians. 1572
Shropshire. 754
Sible Hedingham, Sibil Ingin-
  ham, Essex. 61
Silesbey, Leics. 1687
Silverton, Devon. 2252 2253
Singleton, Sussex. 656
Siron Cester, Glos. 861
Sittingbourne, Kent. 553
Skipton, Yorks. 470
Slapton, Northants. 1953
Slawston, Leics. 1822
Sneed. 883 883 p. xxvii
Snelston, Derbyshire. 1944
Sodbury, Glos. 426 827
Soham, Soam. Cambs. 2685
Somercotes, Summer Coats,
  North. Lincs. 2692
Southampton, Hants. 161
  2461 2718 1795 2641
  2965 1826 2683 2027
  2707
Southerland. 435
Southmolton, Devon. 2431
Southwark, Surrey 169 2010
Southwark, Surrey
  St. Georges. 55 74 223
  391 468 673 1431 1509
  2170 2249 2250 2336
  2437 2716 2740 2830
  2835 2927 2994 3044
  St. Johns. 502 1008
  2797 2979

Southwark, Surrey, contd.
St. Mary Overs. 982 2124 2856
St. Olaves. 207 250 522 554 672 973 994 1120 1334 1352 1644 1796 1834 2000 2069 2073 2136 2145 2606 2610 2715
St. Saviours. 95 267 446 548 825 1087 1191 1423 1896 1897 2015 2041 2166 2537 2666 2705 2855 2980 3029 3039
St. Thomas. 524 1633 2025 2026
Southwell, Notts. 2402
Southwick, Wilts. 124
Sowe, Warwicks. 1600
Spain. 2008
Spalding, Spalden, Lincs. 418 2350 2352 3048 3050 1204
Spennithrone, Yorks. 2165
Spilsby, Lincs. 2746
Spithead. 810
Stafford. 1713 2021 2807 2880
Stainland, Yorks. 3036
Stainton, Great. Durham. 2109
Stalbridge, Dorset. 3004
Stamford, Lincs. 287 379 2331
Stanborough, Herts. 948
Standon, Herts. 694 2624
Stanehive, Aberdeenshire. 2844
Stansfield, Yorks. 2677

Stansted. 2345
Stanton, Suffolk. 2362
Stanway. Glos. 151
Stewkley. Stutley. Bucks. 1877 2609 2611
Stillingrave. Northants. 174
Stockerston, Leics. 3026
Stockholm Sweden. 1403
Stockwell, Surrey. 1020 2950
Stoke d'Abernon, Surrey. 2435
Stoke sub Hamden, Somerset. 1434
Stoke Underham, Somerset. 1434
Stolmerry, Herts. 929
Stondon, Essex. 1589
Stone, Staffs. 1301 1487
Stonehaven, Kincardineshire. 2844
Stoney Stratford Bucks. 611 1009
Stortford, Herts. 2491
Stoughton, Leics. 1638
Stour, East. Dorset. 1739
Stourbridge. Stowerbridge, Worcs. 92 605 963 2251
Stow, Glos. 2616 2616 p. xxviii
Stowe on the Wold. 2616 p. xxviii
Stowmarket. Stow Markit, Suffolk. 1095 2588
Stranraer, Strinrow. Galloway, Scotland. 2671
Stratford. Essex. 1211
Stratford Upon Avon. 1022 2932

Stretton, Herefordshire. 2241
Stroud, Glos. 1900 2040 2310 2558
Stroudwater, Glos. 3088
Strowan, Perthshire. 1865
Stukeley, Stutley, Hunts. 2788
Sturminster, Dorset. 1182
Sturry, Kent. 1604
Stuston, Suffolk. 2126
Sudbury, Sidbury, Derbyshire. 1091
Sudbury, Glos. 426
Sudbury, Suffolk. 355
Suddick, Wilts. 124
Sunbury, 501
Sunderland, Durham. 854 1529
Sutton, Cheshire. 1595
Sutton, Staffs. 183
Sutton, Warwicks. 1257
Sutton, Wilts. 1297
Swalwin. 2046 p. xxviii
Swalwin, Northumberland. 2046
Swansea, Swansey, Glam. Wales. 82 1667 1667 p. xxvii 3019
Swanton Morley. Norfolk. 1295
Swarland. 2046 p. xxviii
Sweden. 2525
Swell, Lower. Glos. 2884
Switzerland. 1803
Swords, Co. Dublin, Ireladd. 919

T

Tadcaster, Yorks. 1015
Tadnam, Glos. 1011
Tamworth, Staffs. 233
Tamworth, Warwicks. 2355

Taplow, Bucks. 2147
Tarporley, Tarperley, Cheshire. 2703
Tashell, Staffs. 2777
Taunton. Somerset. 199 583 1385 1857 1992
Taunton dean, Somerset. 734 1258 1345 1740 2143 2248 2995
Tenbury, Worcs. 2971
Tenterden, Kent. 562
Tew, Great, Oxon. 2924
Tewksbury. Glos. 901 1649 1721 2953
Ticehurst, Tilehurst, Sussex. 2056
Tickhill, Yorks. 2764
Tickleburg, Norfolk. 2755
Ticknell, Derbyshire. 357
Tilbury, East. Essex. 2549
Tilley, Salop. 1548
Tingary. Beds. 1634
Tiverton, Devon. 1122 3014
Todenham. 1011
Toft. Cambs. 2307
Torsely, Kent. 240
Tottham, Great. Essex. 2854
Towcester Northants. 1628
Tower Liberty. 3119 p. xxviii
Town Malling Kent. 1264 1420
Town Sutton, Kent. 125
Thame, Oxon. 657 1702 2175
Thelwall. Cheshire. 2722
Thorncombe. Devon. 1506
Thorndon, Little. Essex. 3074
Thorne, Yorks. 2451
Thorney, Isle of Ely, Cambs. 309

Thornholm, Yorks. 2911
Thornton, Cheshire. 534 1528
Thurnham, Lancs. 2911
Trentham, Staffs. 1338
Trevathan , Mon. Wales.
1710
Tring, Herts. 2931
Trosley, Kent. 240
Trottiscliffe, Kent. 240
Trotton, Sussex. 2083
Trowbridge, Wilts. 641 655
659 1608
Tunbridge Wells. 2113
Turoe, Galloway, Ireland. 1605
Tynemouth, Northumberland.
1475

U
Upminster, Essex. 2034
Uppingham. 1341
Upton, Bucks. 414

W
Waddington, Lincs. 2002
Wadhurst, Sussex. 508
Waisley, Hunts. 242
Wakefield, Yorks. 396 2269
2686
Waldingfield, Waringfield, Little.
Suffolk. 2555
Walesby, Whalesby, Lincs. 1812
Wall Wotton, Warwicks. 2426
Walsall, Walsal. Warsal, Staffs.
629 1310 1320 2952
2986
Walsham, Norfolk. 598
Waltham, Walton, Hants. 2559
Waltham, Lincs. 1621 p. xxvii
Waltham Abbey, Essex. 80
636 2969

Walthamstow, Essex. 1433
2803
Walton-on-the-Naze, Essex.
1519
Wandsworth, Wandser, etc.
Surrey. 366 1097 2099
2290 2348 2473 2655
Wanstead, Essex. 1405
2428
Wanstrow, Somerset. 398
Wardington, Oxon. 2860
Ware, Herts. 292 650
1340 1526
Wareham, Norfolk. 432
Waresley, Hunts. 242
Warmfield, Yorks. 396
Warren, Yorks. 2183
Warrington, Lancs. 850
Warsop, Notts. 2357
Warwick. 2243
Warwick
St. Mary. 1002
St. Nicholas. 685
Waterford, Ireland. 1314
Watford, Herts. 5 924 3104
Watham, Lincs. 1621
1621 p. xxvii
Wellingborough, Northants.
1070 2051 2828 2992
Wellington, Herefordshire. 47
Wellington, Salop. 1360
3106
Wellington, Salop.
1502 p. xxvii
Wells. 152 1368
Wells, Norfolk. 1023 2678
Wells, Somerset. 844
Welsh Pool, Montgomery,
Wales. 718 1719
Wem, Salop. 2302

Wereham, Norfolk. 432
Westbie, Withbey, Lancs.
 2531
Westborough, Warwicks. 1127
 1127 p. xxvii
Westborough, Wilts. 2325
 2325 p. xxviii
Westbury, Glos. 1458
Westbury Under the Plain, Wilts.
 2989
Westbury, Wilts. 2325 xxviii
West Compton, Somerset. 2925
Westerleigh, Glos. 776
West Ham, Essex. 192 p. xxvii
 192 2418 2546
Westleigh, Lancs. 2095
Westleton, Westilton, Suffolk.
 1052
Wethersfield, Essex. 2475
Weybridge, Waybridge, Surrey.
 2876
Whaddon, Bucks. 1291
Wharram le Street, Yorks.
 2183
Whetstone, Herts. 2038
 2038 p. xxviii
Whickham, Wickham, Durham.
 2907
Whitchurch, Hants. 1819
 2453
Whitchurch, Salop. 1565
Whitehaven. 690
White Roding, Ruden, Essex.
 340
Whitham, Essex. 128
Whittington, Salop. 864 2328
Whittlebury, Northants. 505
Whittlesey, Isle of Ely, Cambs.
 838 2688

Wick, Scotland. 631
Wigan, Wiggan, Lancs. 615
 2321 2398
Wilersey, Warwicks. 704
Willington, Derbyshire. 1696
Willington, Salop. 1502
 1502 p. xxvii
Wilton, Wilts. 2122
Wimblington, Isle of Ely,
 Cambs. 1346
Wincanton, Somerset. 2997
Winchester, Hants. 29
 1507
Winchcomb, Winscombe, Glos.
 2490
Windlesham, Surrey. 2298
Windham, Norfolk. 1725
Windom, Norfolk. 1189
Windsor, Berks. 618 739
 975 1242 1402
Windsor, New. Berks. 353
 1396
Winnell, Willenhall, Yorks.
 76
Winton, Westmorland. 1947
Wircompton, Somerset.
 2925
Wirksworth, Derbyshire.
 1150 2960
Wisbech, Wisbitch, Wisbidges,
 Isle of Ely, Cambs. 332
 778 1922 2567 2632
Wisborough Green, Sussex.
 395 1186
Witham. 181 181 p. xxvii
 128 p. xxvii
Witney, Oxon. 1356
Wiveliscombe, Somerset.
 1172
Woburn, Beds. 1591

Wokingham, Berks. 2769
Wolverhampton, Staffs. 962
  1966 2140 2535 2752
  2825
Wombridge, Salop. 1005
Wonhouse, Suffolk. 2613
Woodbridge, Suffolk. 556
  1918 1919
Woodford, Essex. 811 1398
Woodford, Northants. 30
Woodstock. 2334
Woodstone, Northants. 526
Woolcombe, Woolscome, Som-
  erset. 193
Woolwich, Kent. 781 2869
Wootton, Lincs. 2308
Wootton, Warwicks. 1279
Wootton Bassett, Wilts. 248
  2374
Wootton Wawen, Warwicks.
  2426
Worcester. 35 75 194 485
  856 904 1246 1383
  1462 2283 2396 3083
Worcester.
  St. Johns. 2049
  St. Nicholas. 1737
Worksop, Worsup, Notts. 1028
  1588
Wormsley, Worcs. 977
Worsell, Staffs. 1289
Wotton Under Edge, Wotton
  Hundrigge, Wooton, Glos.
  72 608 1418
Wrexham, Denbyshire Wales.
  943 2291 2578
Wuesley, Westmorland. 1949
Wybunbury, Cheshire. 2471
  2789

Wymondham, Norfolk. 1189

Y

Yalding, Kent. 81
Yarcombe, Devon. 3023
Yardley, Warwicks. 3007
Yarmouth, Norfolk. 1590
  1860 2417 2983
Yarnton, Oxon. 2097
Yaxley, Hunts. 1530
York. 123 878 1344 1481
  1701 2574 3091
York.
  Castlegate. 2510
Yorkham, Devon. 3023

Additional Servants' Indentures found at the Guildhall,
London, among the Court of Alderman's papers.

3118   ASHTON, John. Plumstead, Kent. Brickmaker. J. T.
4 yrs. Jam. 29. M. 2 March, 1730.   96D

3119   ATKINSON, Richard. St. Sampson, York. Barber and
Peruke-maker. P. Si. 4 yrs. Barb. 20. S.   32C

3120   BARNS, Francis. Dunstable, Beds. Sawyer. J. T.
4 yrs. Jam. 19. S. 16 March, 1730.   96R

3121   BASKARVILL, Thomas. Kington, Herefords. Taylor.
P. Si. 4 yrs. St. C. 22. S. 29 Jan., 1730.   32A

3122   BIGSBY, Robert. St. Dunstans-in-the-West, London.
Cordwainer. P. Si. 4 yrs. Va. 25. S. 7 Jan.,
1730.   17A

3123   BULLEY, Mathew. Casehorton, Surrey. Baker. J. T.
J. T. 4 yrs. Md. 20. S. 27 March, 1727.   42A

3124   CARTLIDGE, Ann. Chesterfield, Derbys. Spinster.
P. Si. 4 yrs. Jam. 22. M. 1 March, 1730.   96A

3125   CLARK, George. St. Andrew, Holborn. Wine Cooper.
P. Si. 4 yrs. Jam. 22. S. 27 Jan. 1730.   31H

3126   COULTHRED, Mathew. All Hallows, Barking, London.
Labourer. P. Si. 4 yrs. St. C. 26. S. 29 Jan. 1730.
    32B

3127   CULBERSON, William. St. Clement Danes. Coachman.
P. Si. 4 yrs. Jam. 35. S. 22 Jan. 1730.   31C

3128   DEALL, Peter. Walthamstow, Essex. Gardener. W. Bu.
4 yrs. Jam. 22. S. 16 Jan., 1730.   25B

3129   DELANY, Cavan. Paris, France and late of St. James,
Westminster. Clerk. W. Bu. 4 yrs. Md. 22. S.
2 March, 1730.   96J

3130   DIXON, Henry. St. Ann's, Westminster. Carver. P. Si.
4 yrs. Jam. 48. S. 2 March, 1730   96C

3131   DRIVER, John. St. Mary Whitechapel. Labourer. P. Si.
4 yrs. 38. M. 7 Jan., 1730.   17B

3132   FLAGDIN, Henry. Nessen, Cheshire. Husbandman. P. Si.
4 yrs. Jam. 19. M. 6 Jan., 1730.   11A

3133   HARPER, Henry. St. Botolph, Aldgate, London. Basket-
maker. P. Si. 4 yrs. Jam. 23. S. 25 Jan., 1730.   31F

3134   HEALEY, Joseph. Spitalfields. Weaver. P. Si. 4 yrs.
Md. 22. 7 Jan., 1730.   17C

3135   HOGG, Mary. St. Botolph, Aldgate. Spinster. P. Si.
5 yrs. Jam. 18. M. 27 March, 1727.   42B

3136   JACKSON, Mary. Westminster. Spinster. P. Si. 4 yrs.
Jam. 16. M. 20 Jan. 1730.   29A

3137   JAMES, Henry. Willian, Herts. Gardiner. P. Si. 4 yrs.
Jam. 23. S. 18 Jan., 1730.   26A

3138   JONES, Richard. All Hallows, Barking, London. Coachman. J. T. 4 yrs. Jam. 22. S. 15 March, 1730.   96Q

3139   JORDAN, John. Southshields, Durham. Labourer. J. T.
4 yrs. Jam. 36. S. 2 March, 1730.   96E

3140   KENDALL. Thomas. Polesworth, Leics. Husbandman.
W. Bu. 5 yrs. Va. or Md. 20. M. 18 March, 1730.
                                         97A

3141   LODGE, Adam. St. Mary Whitechapel. Labourer. W. Bu.
5 yrs. Pa. 20. S. 5 Sept., 1730.   89A

3142   MACMILLAN, Martin. Galloway, Scotland. Husbandman. J. T. 4 yrs. Jam. 31. S. 2 March, 1730.   96G

3143   MAYNE, Robert. Dunstable, Beds. Barber and Peruke-
maker. J. T. 4 yrs. Jam. 24. S. 15 March, 1730. 96P

3144   MOLISON, Thomas. Brechene, Forfar. Clerk or Writer.
W. Bu. 4 yrs. Md. 21. S. 6 March, 1730.   96N

3145   PERCY, Robert. St. Botolph, Aldersgate. P. Si. 4 yrs.
Jam. 16. S. 2 March, 1730.   96H

3146   PRESTON, Samuel. Banbury, Oxon. Smith and Farrier.
P. Si. 4 yrs. Va. 24. S. 26 Jan., 1730.   31G

3147   RICHARDSON, James. St. Andrew, Holborn. Tailor.
P. Si. 4 yrs. Jam. 34. S. 22 Jan., 1730.   31B

3148   SHAW, Richard. Yarmouth, Norfolk. Labourer. P. Si.
4 yrs. St. C. 22. S. 27 Jan., 1730.   31J

3149   SIMMONS, John. Fulham, Middx. Labourer. J. T.
4 yrs. Jam. 25. S. 2 March, 1730.   96F

3150   SMITH, Charles. St. James, Westminster. Baker. N. M.
4 yrs. Pa. 24. S. 7 Sept.. 1730.   90A

3151   SMITH, James. St. Giles, Cripplegate, London. Book-
keeper. W. Bu. 4 yrs. Md. 21. S. 3 March, 1730.
    96K

3152   STAIN, Richard. Boslam, Staffordshire. P. Si. 7 yrs.
Jam. 15. M. 11 Jan., 1730.   22A

3153   TAYLER, Andrew. Kelrenny, Fife. Husbandman. J. T.
4 yrs. Jam. 18. S. 6 March, 1730.   96M

3154   TAYLER, William. St. Leonard, Shoreditch, Mddx. Cordwainer. W. Bu. 4 yrs. Md. 23. S. 3 March, 1730. 96L

3155 THOMPSON, Robert. St. Giles in the Fields. P. Si.
7 yrs. Jam. 15. S. 7 Jan. 1730. 17D

3156 TOOP(E), Johanna. St. Katherine Coleman, London.
Mantua maker. P. Si. 4 yrs. Jam. 21. S.
5 Jan., 1730. 8A

3157 VINNELL, George. Stepney, Mddx. Weaver. W. Bu.
4 yrs. Md. 29. S. 1 March, 1730. 96B

3158 WALKER, William. Bingley, Yorks. Clerk. P. Si.
4 yrs. Jam. 26. S. 22 Jan. 1730. 31E

3159 WATSON, William. St. Giles in the Fields. P. Si.
7 yrs. Md. 16. M. 11 Jan. 1730. 22B

3160 WEBB, William. Aldgate, London. Weaver. P. Si.
4 yrs. Jam. 21. S. 22 Jan., 1730. 31D

3161 WILLIAMS, Henry. St. George, Southwark, Surrey. Tailor.
P. Si. 6 yrs. Md. 18. S. 8 March, 1730. 96O

3162 WILLIAMSON, John. St. Martin-in-the-Fields. Calender.
P. Si. 4 yrs. Md. 22. M. 21 Jan. 1730. 31A

3163 WINCHESTER, William. St. Martin-in-the-Fields. P. Si.
5 yrs. Md. 19. S. 16 Jan., 1730. 25A

These 46 additional items are not included in the index
on p. 259 - 288 and have not been added to the analysis
of the emigrants' destinations on p. 257.